W9-CRK-831

60° N—

Sitka (Novo-Arkhangel'sk)

NORTH AMERICA

40° N—

20° N—

0°

SOUTH AMERICA

Marquesas Is.

20° S—

Easter I.

VOYAGE OF KRUZENSHTERN AND
LISIANSKI ON THE NADEZHDA
AND NEVA (1803-1806)

Valparaiso

40° S—

- - - - - Track of Neva

———— Track of Nadezhda

Cape Horn

60° S—

160° W   150° W   140° W

THE
RUSSIAN DISCOVERY
OF HAWAI'I

THE
RUSSIAN DISCOVERY
OF HAWAI'I

The Ethnographic and Historic Record

Glynn Barratt

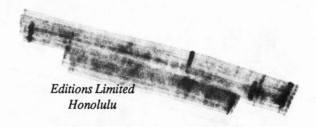

Editions Limited
Honolulu

Published by Editions Limited
1123 Kapahulu Avenue
Honolulu, Hawaii 96816

Library of Congress Cataloging in Publication Data

Barratt, Glynn.   The Russian discovery of Hawai'i

Includes bibliographical references and index.
1. Hawaii — Discovery and exploration — Russian.
2. Hawaiians.   I. Title.
DU627.1.B37 1987   996.9'02   87-29750
ISBN 0-915013-08-8

Printed in the United States of America

December 1987

The Neva by Lisianskii

Dedicated to Pat Polansky and the memory of
Hyatt R. Alamoana (1928-1983)

Table of Contents

Introduction and Acknowledgements

It was fitting that the first of many Russian voyages around the world, that of *Nadézhda* (Captain I.F. Kruzenshtern) and *Nevá* (Captain Iu. Lisianskii), should bring Russian seamen to Hawai'i and, indeed, to the precise boulder where Cook had fallen twenty-five years earlier. Cook's influence and name had permeated Kruzenshtern's and Lisianskii's early lives, during the course of which versions of Cook's *Voyages* repeatedly appeared, in English, German, French or Russian. Kruzenshtern himself had talked to veterans of Cook's last voyage--James Trevenen, for example--who were serving in the Russian Baltic Fleet. Even a quarter-century after his death, the very emphases of Cook's Pacific ventures were not only borne in mind by the ambitious Lisianskii at Kronstadt, but were seen as *proper* to such distant undertakings. Among these emphases were certain scientific ones.

Cook had no orders to concern himself particularly or at length with 'curiosities', as ethnographica continued to be termed, on setting out on any of his voyages. Nevertheless both he and Joseph Banks had shown a lively interest in native artifacts, and in the languages, beliefs, and social life of distant peoples met. Such an example was not lost on Kruzenshtern or on his virtually independent second-in-command, Lisianskii, when *Nevá* entered Kealakekua Bay and he was literally able to retrace Cook's steps to Ka'awaloa, to Kamehameha's 'palace', up to Hikiau *heiau*. This book presents the ethnographic and related evidence--of artifact, drawing, or narrative--that Kruzenshtern, Lisianskii and their people left us. Russian eyewitness accounts of the position on Hawai'i Island--which was at that time governed, in Kamehameha's absence, by an English 'viceregent', ex-sailor John Young--are self-correcting: half-a-dozen careful pictures of essentially the same events, places and time (June 1804) not only deepen perspective but also sharpen focus, bringing us, the modern students of the Islands scene, far closer to the likely truth. And as the narrative accounts translated here are inevitably complementary, so are the physical and illustrative evidence of artifacts which were in use in 1804, *i.e.* the objects still in Leningrad today and those sketched by Lisianskii or by Fourth Lieutenant E.E. Levenshtern of the *Nadezhda*. For ethnographers, the Russian evidence in question is of major value. Ethnohistory and local history are also richer for it.

Brief comments on the Kruzenshtern-Lisianskii expedition and on Russian ethnological activities while in or near Hawai'i, may be useful here. *Nadézhda* and *Nevá* (formerly the British ships *Leander* and *Thames*), of 452 and 380 tons respectively, left the Baltic seaport of Kronstadt in August 1803, bound for the East by way of Cape Horn and the Hawaiian Islands. The expedition was to take supplies to Petropavlovsk-in-Kamchatka and to Russian North America (modern Alaska), pick up furs belonging to the Russian American Company, attempt to trade this peltry at Canton, conduct research and make discoveries at sea. For good measure, it was also to convey an envoy to Japan, where trade and commerce were to be discussed. Taking passage in *Nadézhda*, to the growing irritation of her captain, Kruzenshtern, were both that (most unwanted) envoy, Nikolai Petrovich Rezanov, and his entire suite. Rezanov was an acquaintance of the tsar himself and the most influential person in the Company, to which the captain was now seconded, and it was unclear to what extent the Envoy had authority over the naval officers or vice versa. Tension was inherent in this blurring of the limits of authority and, more than once before *Nadézhda* and *Nevá* stood off the south shore of Hawai'i, it had led to bitter arguments.

Kruzenshtern's orders were to make for the Hawaiian Islands from Brazil, to water and revictual, and thence to make directly for Japan, leaving *Nevá* to make her own way north to Kodiak. In fact, the Russians visited two Polynesian archipelagoes, the Washington-Marquesas and the Hawaiian, in their search for food, water and rest. During a ten-day stay at Nuku Hiva in the Marquesas, many artifacts were purchased from the natives, sketched and stowed, and many journals filled with ethnographic data. For the people of *Nevá*, especially, it was a dry run for the coming visit to Hawai'i. Bartering procedures were refined, the eye attuned, and questions better phrased.

The Russians reached Hawai'i on 8 June 1804 and drifted hopefully southwest along the Puna-Ka'ū coast toward Ka Lae. They were seriously short of meat; the Nukuhivans had proved loath to part with hogs of any size. The Hawaiians also disappointed their Russian visitors. Craft came out to sea as was expected, but in ones and twos, not swarms; nor did the natives offer much other than sweet potatoes, coconuts, and 'trifles'. Russian ironware did not impress them. It was cloth that they demanded--unsuccessfully. A pattern had been set, at least for Kruzenshtern who, two days later and despite the probability that (for a price in cloth) Kealakekua would supply his needs, made the decision to proceed immediately to Kamchatka with a view to getting down to Nagasaki and avoiding seasonal monsoons. *Nadézhda* and *Nevá* thus parted company on 11 June, *Nevá* moving north and rounding Palemano Point into Kealakekua Bay.

During their six-day stay, the Russians bought all the provisions they desired, hogs included; made as detailed a study of their hosts as time allowed, using an English beachcomber named Lewis Johnson as interpreter; examined sites connected with 'the celebrated Cook'; and bartered Russian goods for artifacts that are on permanent display in Leningrad today. Thanks partly to the Russians' civil attitude toward their hosts, partly to the friendliness displayed by the now powerful royal advisor Young and by the chief responsible for the Kamehameha properties at Ka'awaloa, all went very smoothly. Husbandry and agriculture, diet, social mores, arts and crafts, religious practices, political conditions: all were scrutinized by the intelligent and, in the main, objective visitors. Sketches

ix

were made and notebooks filled with observations, as at Nuku Hiva earlier and Sitka later. Of the records kept, none was more balanced than Lisianskii's own, though both Lieutenant Vasilii N. Berkh and the Company clerk aboard *Nevá*, Nikolai Korobitsyn, made points about Hawaiians on the Kona coast that he did not.

Lisianskii had been hoping for a meeting with King Kamehameha and was not quite content to hear the details of the king's life and victories from Young, the temple priests at Hikiau, the local chief, their own English interpreter, and a Hawaiian named George Kernick who allegedly had spent some seven years in England. However, news of an epidemic raging on O'ahu where the king was readying his forces for a long-delayed advance on Kaua'i--then an independent island under Kaumuali'i--changed Lisianskii's plans to visit Kamehameha. *Nevá* sailed with her holds crammed with supplies and passed close by Kaua'i, keeping well clear of O'ahu. Winds were fickle and the ship's progress was slow. King Kaumuali'i took advantage of this situation to pay Lisianskii an impromptu visit during which he bluntly sought the Russians' armed assistance in the fight against Kamehameha. Though they sympathized with him, the passing Russians gave him nothing of political or military value. They themselves, conversely, saw the value of his islands, Kaua'i and Ni'ihau, as a food source for the settlements of Russian North America, Kamchatka, even Northeastern Siberia. The seeds of later Russian colonizing impulses were sown.

This volume is itself the fruit of my awareness, which has been growing steadily over the past few years, of the genuine significance of the neglected first, seminal visit of the Russians to Hawai'i in June of 1804 and of the value of an ethnographic source too long ignored by Western scholars. Our ethnologists, generally speaking, have no mastery of Russian while historians and Slavists in Hawai'i and indeed in the Americas at large have shown no interest whatever in the artifacts which, in the early contact period, went to St Petersburg. In this brief study of the first and ethnographically most fruitful of the many Russian visits to Hawai'i in the early nineteenth century, I try to fill the gap, that is, to stand between the Slavist and ethnologist as intermediary.

A modified form of the Library of Congress system for transliterating the Cyrillic alphabet has been used in this survey, thus: Andrei, Fedor and Lisianskii. However, recognized anglicized forms are used for Russian proper names, such as Alexander and Moscow. Rouble values are expressed as silver units. Russian and Hawaiian words used in the text are translated in glossaries at the back of the book, along with a list of Russian transliterations of Hawaiian place and proper names and their modern forms.

There are a few problems inherent in the rendering into English of those Hawaiian proper names that the Russians transcribed in Cyrillic characters, and in providing modern forms of those names. As Russian lacks certain letters-- notably 'h' and 'w'--*Gavaii* would be the standard rendering of Hawai'i. Hawaiian (or English) aspirates may be rendered in Russian by 'g' or by 'kh', hence Oʻahu may appear as *Oagu,* or *Oakhu,* or even--and more usually in early nineteenth century texts--as *Ovagu.* Here, historical considerations join linguistic ones, for Russian *Ovagu* reflects the *O-Wahoo* preferred over *Owahoo* or *Wahoo* by certain of Captain Cook's people. Similarly with Hawaiʻi, the forms *O'why'he, Ou-why-hee* and *Ouwaihee* (preferred, respectively, by the editor of Cook's final journal Dr John Douglas, Surgeon Samwell, and Midshipman Edward Riou of *Discovery*) are reflected in early nineteenth-century Russian *Ovagi* or *Ovaigi.* Matters are further complicated by a general lack of consistency in the Russian, as in the earlier British, manuscripts and printed texts, and by various conventions adopted by particular Russian memoirists. Broadly speaking, all the Russians whose texts are here translated follow eighteenth-century British precedent where the rendition of Hawaiian terms and place names is concerned. This is plain in, for example, Russian attempts to list Hawaiian names for days, months and *kapu*; and in the ever-present tendency to incorporate Hawaiian nominative and other prefixes into a given Russian variant. As Samwell renders the geographical districts of Kaʻû, Puna, and Kona as Acaw, Apoona, and Ocona, so does Lisianskii render the days Hilo, ʻOlepau and Kâne as ohiro, orepau, okané.

By considering the Russians' sources, which were mostly but not exclusively British in 1804-09 when most of these texts were being prepared for printing, one can readily gloss such names as Atuvai (Kauaʻi: from Cook's and King's Atoui), Origoa (Lehua: from Cook's Orre'houa), or Gammamea (Kamehameha: from King's Ka Mea Mea). Nor are the origins of Russian forms like King Tomari (Kaumualiʻi of Kauaʻi) or Karakekua Bay (Kealakekua) hard to find within the English-language literature of the 1780s. That David Samwell wrote *Atowai* is indeed significant, reflecting as it does both the nominative prefix and the old Hawaiian use of 't' rather than 'k' (E Tauaʻi), but the imitative Russian renderings add nothing to knowledge of ancient usage and simply corroborate earlier English observations. They have been retained here, along with Russian spellings of other Polynesian placenames, to preserve some sense of the original; the modern forms of the Hawaiian words are contained in brackets beside the first appearance or two and are subsequently omitted to avoid the distraction of a constant repetition.

Among those to whom I am indebted for assistance or advice are: Dr N.A. Butinov of the N.N. Miklukho-Macklay Institute of Anthropology and Ethnography of the Academy of Sciences of the USSR (Australasian and Oceanic Division); Dr L.G. Rozina-Bernstam, formerly of Leningrad, now of Ann Arbor, Michigan; V.V. Kuznetsova and Dr A.A. Senchura, both of the All-Union Geographical Society of the USSR, Leningrad; N.A. Smirnova of the Museum of Anthropology of Moscow State University; D.D. Tumarkin of the Institute of Ethnography of the Academy of Sciences of the USSR, Moscow; I. Novozhilova, Director of the State Russian Museum; V.I. Aleksandrova of the Leningrad Division of the Archives of the Academy of Sciences of the USSR;

I.G. Grigor'eva, Director of the International Exchanges Division, Saltykov-Shchedrin Public Library, Leningrad; Dr L.A. Shur of the Hebrew University of Jerusalem; Patricia Polansky, Russian Bibliographer at the Hamilton Research Library of the University of Hawai'i at Manoa; Dr Alex Spoehr of Honolulu; and Ms Cynthia Timberlake, Librarian at the Bernice Pauahi Bishop Museum, Honolulu. Thanks are also due to the following, all of whom have shown me marked kindness in different ways and places: Mrs Ella Wiswell of Honolulu; Mrs Sirje Annist of the Estonian State Museum of History in Tallin, ESSR; Dr Richard Pierce of Kingston, Ontario and Berkeley, California; Dr Roger Rose, Senior Ethnologist at the Bernice Pauahi Bishop Museum, Honolulu; and Ross Cordy of Honolulu and Kosrae. In addition, I record my indebtedness to the Academic Secretaries of the State Historical Museum, Moscow; the Library of the Central State Archive of the Navy of the USSR (TsGAVMF); and the Central State Historical Archive (TsGIAL), in Leningrad. Finally, I am grateful to the Social Sciences and Humanities Research Council of Canada for a grant enabling me to collect material for this study outside Canada, and to my own university, Carleton, for humane dealings.

Plates A-T here are reproduced from Iu.F. Lisianskii's *Sobranie kart i risunkov*... (St Petersburg, 1812)--that is, from the 'atlas' accompanying the original Russian edition of *Puteshestvie vokrug sveta v 1803, 1804, 1805 i 1806 godakh, na korable "Nevá"*..., by courtesy of Renée Heyum and the staff of the Pacific Room, Hamilton Library, University of Hawai'i at Manoa. Plates U and V are reproduced from the holograph of Emelian E. Levenshtern's (Loewenstern's) journal for June 1804, now held at the Central State Historical Archive of the Estonian SSR in Tartu, under reference: *fond* 1414, *op.* 3, *delo* 3. They are presented here through the collaboration of M.Ia. Kapran and the staff of the Main Archival Administration of the Council of Ministers of the USSR (Glavnoe Arkhivnoe Upravlenie pri Sovete Ministrov USSR).

All translations and all opinions in this work are those of the author alone.

Glynn Barratt
Carleton University

Ottawa, 1986

This book has been published with the help of a grant from the Social Science Federation of Canada, using funds provided by the Social Sciences and Humanities Research Council of Canada.

Captain Iurii F. Lisianskii

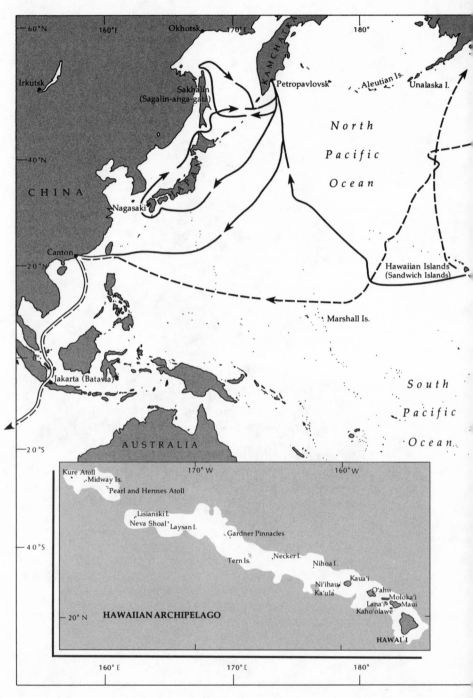

60°N   160°E   Okhotsk   170°E   180°
Irkutsk   Aleutian Is.   Unalaska I.
                                        Sakhalin   Petropavlovsk
                                   (Sagalin-anga-gata)   North
40°N
                                                                                        Pacific
CHINA
                                              JAPAN   Ocean
                          Nagasaki
Canton
20°N   Hawaiian Islands
                                                                                  (Sandwich Islands)

                                                      Marshall Is.
        Jakarta (Batavia)   South

                                                                            Pacific
20°S
                AUSTRALIA   Ocean

40°S

        Kure Atoll   170° W   160°W
         Midway Is.
          Pearl and Hermes Atoll

             Lisianski I.
        Neva Shoal Laysan I.
                                   Gardner Pinnacles

                           Tern Is.   Necker I.
                                            Nihoa I.
                                        Ni'ihau   Kaua'i
                                        Ka'ula   O'ahu
                                                    Moloka'i
        20° N   HAWAIIAN ARCHIPELAGO   Lana'i Maui
                                        Kaho'olawe

                                                       HAWAI'I

        160° E   170° E   180°

xiv

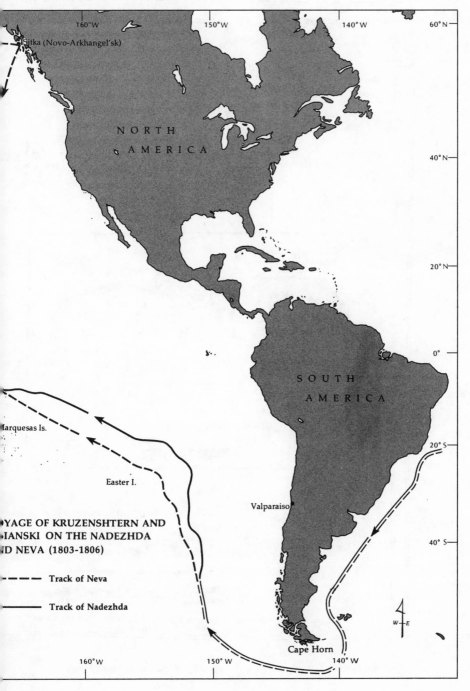

160°W · 150°W · 140°W · 60°N

Sitka (Novo-Arkhangel'sk)

N O R T H
A M E R I C A

40°N

20°N

S O U T H
A M E R I C A

0°

Marquesas Is.

20°S

Easter I.

Valparaiso

**VOYAGE OF KRUZENSHTERN AND
LIANSKI ON THE NADEZHDA
AND NEVA (1803-1806)**

40°S

– – – Track of Neva

——— Track of Nadezhda

Cape Horn

W–E

160°W · 150°W · 140°W

xv

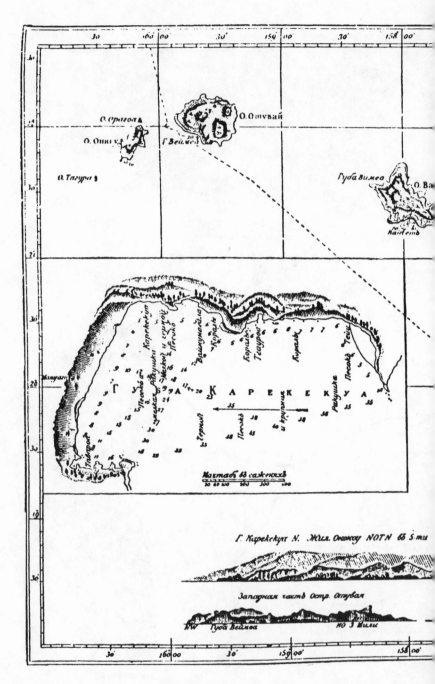

Lisianskii's map of Hawai'i showing *Neva's* route and an inset

Остро́ва Сандви́чевы.
Губы Карекекуи

Долгота .... 156. 4. 00. W.
Широта .... 19. 28. 22. N.
Склоненïе компаса . 8. 22. 00. O.

Примѣчанïе.

(Translation of circle above)
Sandwich Islands
Kealakekua Bay

Longitude ...   156° 4' 00" W.
Latitude ...   19° 28' 22" N.
Compass Variation ... 8° 22' 00" E.

Note: The Southern Cape of Hawaiʻi Island and
Kealekekua Bay were fixed by the ship *Neva*
in the year 1804. Other places determined
in conformity with description
by Captain Vancouver.

of Kealakekua with remarks ("Black sand and large shells").

xvii

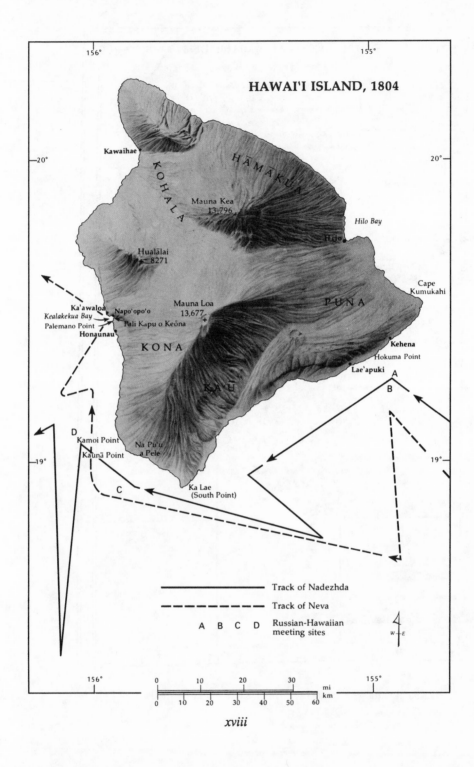

HAWAI'I ISLAND, 1804

Kawaihae

KOHALA

HAMĀKUA

Mauna Kea
13,796

Hilo Bay

Hilo

Hualālai
8271

Ka'awaloa
Kealakekua Bay
Palemano Point
Honaunau

Napo'opo'o
Pali Kapu o Keōna

Mauna Loa
13,677

PUNA

Cape
Kumukahi

KONA

Kehena
Hokuma Point
Lae'apuki

A
B

KA'U

Kamoi Point
Kauna Point

D

Na Pu'u
a Pele

C

Ka Lae
(South Point)

—————————— Track of Nadezhda

– – – – – – – – Track of Neva

A B C D   Russian-Hawaiian
            meeting sites

W —— E

0	10	20	30	mi
0	10 20 30	40 50	60	km

xviii

Captain Ivan F. Kruzenshtern

Nikolai Petrovich Rezanov

Georg Heinrich Langsdorf

PART ONE

Preparations

Cook, the Russian Navy, and the Sandwich Isles

Russian knowledge of the harbors, climate, products and conditions of the Sandwich islands rested, largely and inevitably until the last months of the eighteenth century, on British naval sources. More specifically, it stemmed from information gained first through British publications, then from French and German versions of those publications and so, finally, at first hand from participants in Captain Cook's last voyage, that of 1776-1780. As awareness grew in high government circles in St Petersburg of the enormous implications of that voyage--of the wonderful potential of the North Pacific fur trade, and of threats already posed to Russian interests in the Aleutians and along the Northwest Coast of North America by foreign mariners[1]--so, in the early 1780s, did the Russian Naval Staff and Russian Admiralty College cease to view the Sandwich Islands in a purely academic light.

For fifteen years at least, when Captain Cook anchored off Unalaska Island with *Discovery* and *Resolution* (mid-October 1778), Catherine II had deliberately not supported the expanding Russian enterprise in the Aleutian Islands in an os-tentatious way. At most, she had ennobled individuals and given gold medallions to energetic and successful merchants based in the remote Northeast, Kamchatka, and Okhotsk.[2] As a result, the Russians' maritime and military weakness in an area so large and rich in sea otter and other peltry, or 'soft gold', was self-per-petuating: for the empress was not willing to provoke either the Spanish or, especially, the British government by an assertiveness in North Pacific waters that could lead to confrontation and retreat. As well they might, given the value and extent of cossack fur-based interests and weakness in those most distant regions of the empire, officials in St Petersburg and in Siberia alike had, in the '70s, evinced anxiety on learning of advances on the Northwest Coast of North America planned in Madrid, New Spain, or London.[3] Evident even by 1774, when Catherine had promised a hospitable reception to the ships of friendly powers if they called at a Kamchatkan or Aleutian settlement, for instance Petropavlovsk, unofficial and official Russian apprehension of the foreigners' advances up the Coast of North America toward the Russian zone of influence had leapt in 1776. It was then that Russian agents sent the news that Spanish naval captain Juan Perez, who had two years previously reached a northern latitude of 55°, was being followed on his northern route by other able Spanish captains, namely Heceta and Bodega y Quadra.[4] News of *Resolution*'s and *Discovery*'s arrival in the lee of Unalaska, and of Cook's and his associates' activities and objects to the north of the Aleutians as reported by the cossack hunter Gerasim Izmailov through von Behm or Bem, Kamchatka's Governor,[5] caused the authorities distinct concern. Reports that both those ships had called at Petropavlovsk twice, in May and August 1779, and of persistent British probing in an area claimed tacitly by Russia, sent by other and more xenophobic officers like Captain V.I. Shmalev, led to action.[6] More artillery was painfully transported overland to Petropavlovsk from Irkutsk and other centers in Siberia; and both the empress and her courtiers paid heed, as they had not done hitherto, both to available accounts of the *Adventure-Resolution* expedition (1772-1775) and, especially, to prospects for obtaining solid data on the captain's latest voyage, in the course of which the Sandwich or Hawaiian Islands had been sighted and examined. Suddenly, because of Cook, the Russian Government and Admiralty College were receptive to accounts of any voyages into the North Pacific Ocean from the South. Suddenly, Russian knowledge of the Sandwich Islands, among other distant places, grew apace--as Captain Cook's and his subordinates' activities and writings made it possible and necessary that it grow, within a North Pacific context.

The availability in European Russia of such published narratives as those of Cook himself and of Heinrich Zimmermann, late of *Discovery*--the 'jack-of-all-trades from the Palatinate who liked to wander'[7]--had acquainted Russian readers with Hawai'i, in connection with the far North and the fur trade, quite some time before the great potential of the Canton market for Aleutian and American sea otter skins had been appreciated in St Petersburg. From the beginning, the Hawaiian Islands had enjoyed a favorable press in Russia, notwithstanding Cook's own death at the Hawaiians' hands in 1779.[8] As for the Empress Catherine herself, she hid whatever doubts she had--doubts fanned by various intensely xenophobic small officials in Kamchatka and Irkutsk[9]--about the purity of scientific motive of the last Cook expedition, and at once took steps to find out all she could about its movements and results. "The Empress," wrote the British ambassador in Russia, Sir James Harris, to Sandwich at the Admiralty Board (January 7/18 1780), "has exprest a very earnest desire of having Copys of such Charts as may tend to ascertain more precisely the extent & position of those... parts of her Empire."[10] And no less useful in their way, of course, were eyewitness descriptions of 'remote and unexplored parts' of that empire. Work was accelerated on translation into Russian of the English (1777) text of the *Ad-*

venture-Resolution expedition;[11] nor thereafter did the empress or officials of the Admiralty College or the new Commerce Commission ever cease to seek, and welcome, firsthand data on the physical conditions, sailing routes, and commerce of the North Pacific Ocean, or the workings of the seaborne, *i.e.*, Coast-to-China, fur trade. Incidentally but surely, in such circumstances, information about South (and mid-) Pacific archipelagoes was gathered by the Russian government. It was a government increasingly annoyed by news of profits being made by British merchantmen in China from the otter skins so easily collected on the Northwest Coast,[12] and understandably concerned to win a share of the new oceanic fur trade and to safeguard the existing trade with Chinese pelt dealers still conducted far inland at Kiakhta-Mai-mai-cheng.[13]

In short, the Russians had no choice but to act swiftly to defend their own resources from the British and New England merchantmen and stake a claim in the new Canton market. Hardly, however, did they recognize this fact before a welcome and unlooked-for extra source of information about North Pacific waters and the fur trade of the East made an appearance in the shape of former members of Cook's final expedition. Yet again new incidental information about places visited by *Discovery* and *Resolution*, on their passages both to and from the Arctic, was available to Russians with a need to learn.

Even in 1779, some of the better educated men in those two ships had thought of entering the North Pacific fur trade on their own account or, failing that, of getting British, American, or even Russian backing for the venture. (The less educated dreamers simply fled, stealing a boat.[14]) On their return to Europe, these imaginative individuals were led by economic pressures to develop and attempt to sell their North Pacific schemes.[15] Two members of Cook's final expedition in particular, Lieutenant James Trevenen (1760-1790) and John Ledyard (1751-1789), the Connecticut marine who while on Unalaska Island had established the first contact between Russian and American in the Pacific,[16] clung to memories of the enormous profit made in China. There, a single good sea otter skin, bought for a hatchet, could be sold for $50.[17] In due course, driven by fear of unemployment and a vision of prosperity, both Ledyard and Trevenen went to Russia with their North Pacific projects. The American, alas for his extraordinary schemes, did not manage to attach himself to Captain Joseph Billings, also late of *Resolution*, like himself, and now successfully exploiting his connection with the celebrated Cook in a venture which was to proceed in a politically sensitive area--the remote Northeast and beyond Chukotka.[18] Nor was he allowed to walk in peace across Siberia toward Bering Strait, the Northwest Coast, and home. Ledyard was arrested at Irkutsk, just to the north of central Mongolia, in February 1788 and deported in March. Nevertheless, he spent some time whilst in St Petersburg with Peter Simon Pallas, the distinguished German botanist, and so passed on to the Imperial Academy of Sciences much information about natural resources and conditions on the Coast--and on Pacific Islands. For James Trevenen, the decision to proceed to Russia brought professional advancement but an early and heroic death in battle. First, however, he would play his part in reinforcing an official Russian consciousness of the Hawaiian archipelago and of its probable utility to Russians in the East.

Lieutenant James Trevenen, RN, found himself on half-pay by 1784. Bored and anxious for variety, he set off for the Continent with Captain King, late of *Discovery*. The Continent soon palled. Back in England, he examined his position. Unsuccessful at the Admiralty Board, he thought of venturing his capital in a commercial undertaking on the Northwest Coast of North America, or in New Holland [Australia]; but again he was frustrated.[19] It was then, as his biographer and fellow-Cornishman, Charles Vinicombe Penrose, informs us, that his "ardent mind embraced the world as his country, and he formed a plan."[20] That plan was offered to the minister plenipotentiary for Russia to Great Britain, Semeon R. Vorontsov (1744-1832). Vorontsov, who was an anglophile, "saw its merits and transmitted it to his mistress (*i.e.* his employer, Catherine), then on her journey to Cheronese" (the newly-conquered Crimea). It was, in essence, a commercial plan; but it was very versatile and, perhaps by chance, it faintly echoed the assertive note struck by the empress in a recent edict, of 22 December 1786.[21] Vexed by the "poaching and encroachments" in the "Eastern Sea" of English shipmaster James Hanna and his countrymen, and urged by Vorontsov's own brother, then directing at the Commerce College, to adopt a firmer policy toward that nuisance, Catherine had only weeks before concurred with her advisers that "to Russia must belong the American coast from 55°21'N.L., extending northward,... all islands situated near the mainland and extending west in a chain, as well as... the Kuril Islands of Japan."[22] She was pleased by the Trevenen plan's allusions both to warships and to growing trade, and she agreed to take another English officer into her fleet.[23] James Trevenen left for Russia, via Holland and the Baltic States, in June 1787. With his papers went two copies of his North Pacific plan, of which short extracts may be cited:

North Pacific Project

February 1787

The plan has for its immediate objects: 1) the augmenting the consequence of Kamtschatka and its value to Russia by increasing its commerce to America for furs. 2) A consequence of the first--the increase of trade with China. The accomplishment of these will open the prospect for others, secondary indeed, but no less important and by no means chimerical: 1. The opening of a trade with Japan...; 2. The creating an excellent nursery for Russian seamen by means of navigation, which will make them acquainted with the varieties of climate and manoeuvre. 3. The augmenting the Imperial revenue...

We will begin with the first article. In order to carry this prospect into execu-
tion with effect, it will be necessary to equip three stout ships in Europe and send
them round Cape Horn to Kamtschatka. These vessels must be loaded with
those articles which are best adapted to commerce with the inhabitants of
America and which are not to be procured in Kamtschatka... The ships, which
ought to sail from Europe in the month of September, will touch at some Spanish
or Portuguese part of South America and after having doubled Cape Horn will
proceed to some of the islands in the South Sea. From thence they will steer for
that part of the coast of North America which is situated north of California and
employ the summer in collecting furs...
The second object, viz., the augmenting trade from Kamtschatka to China,
naturally follows from the first: for it appears to us beyond a doubt that the con-
sumption of China will be equal to any quantity of furs that America can supply...
Russia will be supplied with all the produce of the East Indies in her own ships, it
will afford considerable exportation of her own manufacture, and create an
equally considerable nursery of seamen... It will become as necessary as ad-
vantageous to keep always a respectable force at Kamtschatka...
The Empress of Russia will have the glory of putting the finishing stroke to the
so-much celebrated discoveries of the maritime nations, and of rendering the
geography of the globe perfect... Of the three ships that go out from Europe, one
ought to be of 500 tons, the others of 300 tons each.[24]

Trevenen's plan prefigured in important ways that adopted when eventually, in
the fall of 1803, the Russian government did send two vessels, *Nadezhda* and
Neva, from Kronstadt to the North Pacific. Those two vessels did, in fact, as
urged some sixteen years before their sailing, touch at South America (Brazil)
before "proceeding to the islands of the South Sea" (the Marquesas and Hawaiian
Islands), and return by way of China and South Africa. They did in fact carry a
cargo of the sort envisaged by Trevenen, (plus 300,000 roubles' worth of gifts for
the Mikado [emperor] of Japan,where *Nadezhda* would attempt to open trade).
The venture, lastly, did indeed become "a nursery of seamen", while its officers
did, for their part, grow deeply conscious of the value of discoveries of islands in
the currency of international maritime prestige. Of only one large aspect of that
venture, the deliberately scientific, had Trevenen not already given notice to the
world. But, then, he was himself no *savant* in the mold of Joseph Banks, and he
was right in thinking at the time that it was power, not philosophy, that interested
Catherine in such a plan as he proposed. He could not have foreseen the crucial
role that Baltic Germans were to play in Russia's North Pacific enterprise.[25]
Political events in Europe--Russia's war first with the Ottomans, then with
Sweden--scotched Trevenen's hopes of seeing his Pacific project put into effect.
He did not even reach St Petersburg before discovering that these hostilities with
Turkey had made it thoroughly unlikely that his project could be realized. He
also learned that, nonetheless, four Russian warships had for weeks been fitting

out at Kronstadt for a North Pacific voyage. That voyage was to be made--if it had not already started (thus avoiding an imperial embargo on such distant ventures)--by a bastard son of Count Ivan G. Chernyshev, minister of the marine, and not by himself.[26] Even by then the concept of a watering-and-victualing call at the Hawaiian Islands, when at last a Russian squadron *did* proceed to the Pacific from the Baltic, had received the formal blessing of the Russian Naval Staff. So much is evident from an examination of the orders written for the bastard son (and well-trained naval officer) in question, Captain G. Mulovskii.[27] Those instructions plainly echoed the experience of Cook.

Grigorii Ivanovich Mulovskii's squadron, consisting of two larger vessels, *Kolmogor* (600 tons) and *Solovki* (530 tons), and two smaller ones, the *Sokol* and the *Turukhtan* (approximately 450 tons each),[28] had been commissioned in the White Sea not the Baltic, ostensibly for purposes of commerce and discovery. It was, in fact, to form an armed deterrent in an area where Russian interests were threatened both by growing Spanish consciousness of the activities of cossack hunter-traders[29] and, more formidably, by American and British traders. Catherine II's private secretary, P.A. Soimonov, had been troubled by the ease with which Cook's vessels had been able to pass at will through, if not Provinces [*gubernii*], at least extremities of Russia's empire. The news of Captain Hanna's pioneering North Pacific cruise, during the course of which 500 skins were gathered in a mere six weeks, to be disposed of for a $20,000 profit, shook both him and Vorontsov.[30] Soimonov quickly drafted 'Notes on Trade and Hunting Ventures in the Eastern Ocean', urging that at least two Russian frigates be dispatched to the Aleutians or Kamchatka to protect the national interest where it was obviously threatened. Thus originated the *ukase* [edict], already mentioned, of 22 December 1786: "The Admiralty College... will send from the Baltic Sea, with no delay, vessels armed as were those employed by Captain Cook..., together with two small armed sloops. The latter shall be naval craft or otherwise, as the aforementioned College may think best..."[31] The College acted promptly under pressure. A committee was established to decide on routes for vessels, suitable revictualing, watering and resting points on the Pacific crossing, and a rendezvous in case of separation on the way. Among the works consulted by committee members was a recent French translation of Cook's final *Voyage, Troisième Voyage de Cook, ou, Voyage à l'Océan Pacifique... en 1776, 1777, 1778, 1779 et 1780* (Paris, Hôtel de Thou, 1785), by Jean-Nicolas Demeunier (1751-1814). Of the essential suitability of the Hawaiian archipelago as a revictualing point for any vessel on her way from South America toward the northern rim of the Pacific, there could be no doubt. British descriptions of the productivity, luxuriance, sweet springs and pleasant climate of Hawai'i were persuasive. The committee recommended that the squadron make the longer eastward passage to the South Pacific, round South Africa not South America, proceeding through the Sunda Strait or round New Holland as conditions might suggest, then stop or rendezvous at the Hawaiian Islands. In its view, there was no better region for a Russian company to gird its loins in preparation for the subsequent, more crucial tasks before it. Final touches could be put to ships and, while seamen gained in strength from fresh provisions, to the several commanders' sailing orders for the North. At length, when all was ready in Mulovskii's view, two vessels would move northwest to make a necessary survey of the Kuril Islands, 'Sagalin-anga-gata' or Sakhalin, and of the Amur River mouth, while the remainder made direct for Nootka Sound.[32] All shores of North America north of the 55th degree of northern latitude would be annexed to Russia ceremoniously, iron crests marked with the proper year being left at certain spots.[33]

Despite Catherine's last-minute cancellation of Mulovskii's expedition,[34] on the grounds that all available and solid vessels such as his were needed in hostilities then imminent around the Black Sea, the instructions issued to him are replete with interest for the Hawaiian and American historian. They remind us of the growing strength and meaning of the Anglo-Russian fleet naval link--a link already old by 1680 and the infancy of Peter Alekseevich, creator of a modern Russian fleet,[35] and venerable by the time Mulovskii himself served aboard British warships as a Russian Volunteer (1769-71).[36]

Since the early years of Catherine II's reign (1762-1796), the hiring of able and (in some cases) disgruntled British officers and seamen had been paralleled by the dispatch of Russian officers to England for a period of training with the Royal Navy which, effectively, did rule the waves for Britain. From the first, the brothers Semeon and Aleksandr Vorontsov had played a large role in encouraging the empress to send such volunteers and, in general, the policy had proved successful. Catherine's approach for British help in the development of a completely modern navy had, predictably, been warmly welcomed by a British government that saw a chance to strengthen ties with an important Power. Sixteen Russians were in England by 1763 for naval training and experience and, though the flow became a trickle in the mid-1770s, the sending of such youthful Volunteers abroad--for periods of two to four years--continued till the early 1800s.

Satisfied with the performances in naval conflicts with the Swedes of British officers like James Trevenen (who was killed in action in this conflict in 1790) and of British-trained young Russians like Grigorii Seniavin, Semeon Vorontsov urged Catherine to send young Russians of distinction and/or promise to Great Britain on a fixed, annual basis. For awhile, he was thwarted by resentment of the British against Russia for the Armed Neutrality (1780); but he persisted and, in 1791, produced a scheme to regulate that policy. "It would," he wrote, "be useful...to select twelve young and disciplined lieutenants from our Fleet and send them...to serve four years without a break in English ships at sea. We should then dispatch a similar number of young officers, for the same period, to replace that initial group, and repeat this, so that within a twenty-year period Russia would acquire sixty men qualified to command warships..." (V.A. Bilbasov, ed. *Arkhiv grafov Morvinovykh*, StP, 1902, III:338). Fourteen officers in fact headed for England in October 1793, some of whom, as we shall see, later saw service in the South and mid-Pacific. Twelve more followed, in July 1797 and, once again, some served the Crown in Oceania.

Mulovskii's orders make apparent that the Admiralty College in St Petersburg was willing to draw lessons from the English service and experience, where ocean voyages and naval practice were concerned. What could be borrowed to advantage should be borrowed: maps, accounts of useful places on the voyage to the North Pacific Ocean from the South--for example, the Sandwich Islands-- even new-fangled equipment like "a stove for the distilling of sea-water into pure".[37] The Mulovskii orders also offer early evidence that an essential difficulty in the effort to maintain a naval squadron in Kamchatka, at Okhotsk, or by a Russian settlement in the Aleutians, had been understood: that, lacking dockyards and a suitably located source of grains and other foodstuffs in the far Northeast or East, the Russian government must keep on sending ships around the globe at huge expense.[38] Either the Navy must obtain proper facilities for the construction and repair of naval vessels of some size, and find a way of feeding men on inhospitable Pacific shores and islands, or the Crown must bear the burden of dispatching vessels to maintain its own authority and dignity so far away. In either case, it was important to have friendly ports of call, in case of need, along the routes to Petropavlovsk and the settlements. There is no need to labor the connection, made already in the minds of men responsible for Russia's embryonic naval venture in the East, between Hawai'i and hunger, scurvy and provisionment. For even if the scientific emphases of Cook's last expedition had not yet been fully recognized at Kronstadt as essential, his success in getting fruit, water, and viands at Hawai'i had already made its mark; nor would the Russians ever cease to view that place as a potential farm-cum-depot of political significance and economic moment for the Russian undertaking in the North Pacific basin as a whole. Mulovskii's orders and Trevenen's thwarted plans were themselves indicative of the extent to which the interested branches of the Russian government *had* grown aware of Cook's discovery in two or three short years, and to what extent that consciousness continued to expand during the '80s thanks to prospects of a Russian expedition to the North Pacific Ocean being actually launched.

Also indicative of that awareness of Cook was, of course, the availability of Cook's and his subordinates' accounts of their impressions of, and dealings in, the Sandwich Islands. In an age when English was not usually learned by the Russian nobility, a significant proportion of the younger Russian naval officers did read it passably. This was a consequence as much of their professional connections with the British[39] as of knowledge of the Royal Navy's primacy among the navies of the world. But a command of English was not absolutely necessary to read of Captain Cook's achievements: they were readily accessible in French, *langue de la politesse* in Russia, and the empress had instructed that Cook's final *Voyage*, like the second, be translated into Russian with dispatch, under the aegis of the Admiralty College. Her intention was less to acquaint the Russian Navy with the work of Cook than to acquaint a wider public and the government at large with a dramatically developing new Eastern and Pacific situation.[40] The effect of the accessibility of Cook's two narratives[41] to the whole fleet by 1810 was, nonetheless, to cause his star to rise still higher in the naval firmament when it would otherwise almost inevitably have declined.[42] Not until 1825 or thereabouts did the most promising of youthful Russian officers cease to revere the name of Cook;[43] nor even later did such influential admirals as I.F. Kruzenshtern and F.F. Bellinsgauzen [Bellingshausen] cease to think of Cook's aides and professional descendants--George Vancouver and Matthew Flinders--with a measure of the same respect.[44]

To Loggin Golenishchev-Kutuzov (1769-1845) fell the task of translating into Russian first the second (1777), then the last of Cook's three *Voyages*. Through his endeavors Russian officers and others gained a great deal of such information as they had about the Sandwich Islands in the last years of the eighteenth century and first years of the nineteenth. Loggin Golenishchev-Kutuzov was the son of Admiral Ivan Logginovich (1729-1802), head of the Admiralty College in the reign of Paul I. He had inherited from a distinguished father mingled maritime and literary interests. Ivan Logginovich wrote sentimental letters *à la* François Fenelon and made translations from Voltaire (*Zadig*, 1765).[45] The father's literary attitudes toward translation were, unfortunately from the modern standpoint, visited upon the son. Neither thought literal precision in translating texts a "worthy altar for the sacrifice of elegance".[46] Loggin Ivanovich, indeed, did not elect to work with Cook's own prose, turning instead to Suard's 1778 version of the *Adventure-Resolution* expedition.[47] The decision to translate at second hand was not a happy one; nor, having settled on the French text, did the intermediary between Russia and the Great South Sea press on at speed. Not until May 1796 did he complete even the first of six parts of Cook's second *Voyage*, that *dans l'hémisphère australe...* As for the long anticipated final *Voyage*, he had hardly started it by 1801, such were the pressures of professional success.

This gentle pace, which so contrasted with the urgency of Catherine's instructions, was itself a telling commentary on the kaleidoscopic international (military and naval) situations of the day and of the period preceding it. Those situations had obliged the Russian government to turn its back on the Pacific, for the moment, and to concentrate on Europe. The French took up the slack in the translation area, as though unwilling to concede that *their* involvement in the crises of the age hampered attention to their interests in the Pacific. Thus were Russians temporarily indebted to the French, the very nation then distracting them from Eastern and Pacific enterprise of the variety envisaged by Trevenen, and postponing their immediate acquaintance with the people and resources of Hawai'i. By 1802, impatient even with Demeunier's more literal reflections of the narratives of Cook, King, and Vancouver, Russians cast aside French mirrors, going straight to the originals at last.

In sum, the overall significance of the Kutuzov versions of Cook's *Voyages,*[48] and of his seminal descriptions of the Sandwich Islanders, was lessened by the work of French translators of the same time and, less markedly, by their belated publication. Nonetheless, they did spread knowledge of discoveries in the Pacific, and of Cook, among a wider Russian readership; and, like accounts of recent voyages by other leading European seamen of the age, they did spread knowledge of Hawai'i in particular among the Russian officers and high officials most aware-- or becoming most aware--of the economic promise of the East. Among those government officials were Counts S.R. Vorontsov and N.P. Rumiantsev, later Chancellor of Russia and a powerful supporter of the Russian North Pacific enterprise in all its forms. Among the officers were two who had already traveled far with a view to studying that promise for themselves-- Lieutenants I.F. Kruzenshtern (von Krusenstern), who had been to China, and Iurii Lisianskii, who had been to India. It was a laudable initiative, which was to bring them both, at length, to the Hawaiian Archipelago of which, in Russian, French or English, they and many of their officers had read since James Trevenen and Mulovskii had been serving in their midst.

The Mounting of the
Kruzenshtern-Lisianskii Expedition

The Kruzenshtern-Lisianskii expedition (1803-1806)--during the course of which a large and on the whole very perceptive Russian company had dealings with the natives of Hawai'i and, more fleetingly, Kaua'i Island--owed its origin to Kruzenshtern's own journey to, and subsequent reports on the expanding commerce of, Canton (1798-1800). That grueling yet voluntary journey stemmed in turn from his preceding service with a wartime British navy, as a Volunteer. It had been an active period, in which he traveled almost ceaselessly--from Halifax to Surinam, Barbados and Bermuda to the West Mediterranean approaches--and which stimulated earlier awareness of the political significance of Eastern trade, Pacific exploration and, as Russians termed it, 'ocean voyaging' in general. So much is evident from Kruzenshtern's own introduction to the 1809 St Petersburg edition of his *Voyage Round the World...[Puteshestvie vokrug sveta...]*, from which short passages may well be cited here:

While serving with the English fleet during the revolutionary war of 1793-99, my attention was both caught and held by the significance of the English trade with the East Indies and China. It seemed to me quite possible that Russia too could take some part in the seaborne trade with China and the Indies... And there was little doubt that she would benefit from doing so despite her lack of all establishments in those parts. The problem was that... few but Englishmen, and even few of those, had any real knowledge of the Eastern Seas. So I resolved to go to India myself. Count Vorontsov, then Russian ambassador in London, soon arranged the necessary passage for me and, early in 1797, I proceeded on an English warship to the Cape of Good Hope, and from there, in a frigate, to India.[49]

For students of important expeditions--and the Kruzenshtern-Lisianskii expedition *was* important, from the naval, scientific, and strategic points of view, for all its failure as a diplomatic venture[50]--there is always the temptation to regard them, in an almost Marxist fashion, as predictable, even historically inevitable. Having said as much, however, one must recognize that underlying Kruzenshtern's whole earlier career like a current was a chain of circumstances, contacts, meetings, bearing him and others with him to the East. Hardly, for instance, had he started his career in professionally happy days (the outset of the Russo-Swedish War, 1788-90), than he met Captain Mulovskii and was introduced to members of a veritable North Pacific club, headed by Grevens of the ship *Podrazhislav*.[51] A few months passed, and he established friendly contact with Pacific-conscious officers like V.Ia. Chichagov and A.S. Greig, spending a furlough in the company of Vitus Bering's grandson.[52]

Then came England and secondment to the Royal Navy. Nothing altered save the power of a current drawing Kruzenshtern and his immediate associates, Lieutenant Iurii Lisianskii chief among them, to a just appreciation of the promise of the East and the Pacific for themselves, and for their country. Barely settled in the wardroom of the frigate *Thetis* (Captain Robert Murray), bound for North America and action,[53] Kruzenshtern was growing friendly with a Captain Vinicombe Penrose whose wife was sister to the late Trevenen's widow; and, as if on cue, a half-dozen other British officers with Russian or Pacific links and interests, or both, now crossed his path.[54] For the best part of his early service life, Lieutenant Kruzenshtern was readying himself, and being readied, for eventual appointment to an Eastern and Pacific expedition.

But how, specifically, did wartime service in the Baltic or the North Atlantic, or this wide experience abroad, prepare him for service of the sort required on a long, multi-purpose expedition to the far side of the globe? And how, specifically, since we are here focusing on the Hawaiian Islands, was Lisianskii's time abroad, replete with violence and action as it was, either reflected in or relevant to dealings with a Polynesian people?[55] After all, the European forms of warfare, in which they had been engaged for months on end,[56] were hardly fitting preparation for ambassadors to Polynesia. To consider either question, one must recognize that war can never wholly engross a man's activity or movements. In reality, both Kruzenshtern and other Russian Volunteers with the Royal Navy's Halifax-based squadron[57] spent a third of all their time in British service on secondment simply traveling, observing, and incubating new impressions. As was natural if not inevitable, given their position and limited finances,[58] they inclined to travel cheaply, making a sally from a British port when possible and remaining, by and large, in friendly, English-speaking territory. Surinam, Barbados and Antigua, Maryland, Virginia, the Carolinas, the Bahamas and Bermuda--such were the places on which Russian naval visitors, of Kruzenshtern's era and later, largely focused their attention.[59]

In Antigua Lisianskii and in prosperous Barbados Kruzenshtern made careful studies of the late eighteenth-century colonial administrations that they saw. Both reflected on the workings of the local slave-based commerce. If that commerce struck them forcibly as savage ("never," wrote Lisianskii from Antigua on 24 March 1795, "would I have credited that Englishmen could be so cruel to their fellow men, if I had not myself observed the truth"),[60] the administration seemed to them at least efficient. It could certainly not be denied that British planters of the Caribbean colonies were wealthy; and the value to England of the *West* Indies, they had learned, was fairly modest in comparison with that of the East Indies, Malacca and beyond. Such thoughts reminded them that Russia, too, had island colonies, on the Pacific rim. Regrettably, those colonies could not support themselves, still less export some useful crop. Perhaps administrative practices and lessons might be borrowed from the British to advantage. What is here to be noted is the sober and objective way in which the Russians made their studies of colonial administration, trade and commerce. They not only paid attention to the Negro slave, but also held to principles of scientific objectivity when describing what they had seen.[61] It augured well for any scientific aspect of a voyage with which either was professionally linked. So also did Lisianskii's growing competence in botany and, more especially, in zoology--twin sciences which he pursued when he was able in the Caribbean islands and America and, like ethnology, would doubtless have developed on Antigua had a bout of yellow fever not forced him to return to Halifax.[62] By happy irony, a violent recurrence of that fever while at Cape Town two years later forced him to remain several months in southern Africa where he not only gathered shells and bones enthusiastically, but also broadened his acceptance of the need for what, if either he or Cook had known the term, they might have called ethnography.[63]

Three years had passed since their departure from St Petersburg for England[64] when Lisianskii, Kruzenshtern, and their compatriot Baskakov took their passage back to London from America aboard the frigate *Cleopatra* with a view to travels in the East.[65] As seen, they did not waste a day before approaching Vorontsov and, after rapid preparations and discussions with at least one trader, Pierce, who had visited the Russian Northwest Coast and the Aleutians, departing for Cape Town.[66] Thence they pressed on eastward to India, and sickness. In November 1798, Kruzenshtern at last entered Canton, weakened by illness and the strain of staying solvent in the company of shipowners and merchants from Bengal. As soon as possible, he launched himself into a comprehensive study of the China trade in general, and of its North Pacific seaborne branch in particular. That was the branch from which his countrymen were totally excluded thanks to maritime incompetence;[67] the lack of ships, seamen, charts and pilots in the far Northeast (Kamchatka and Okhotsk); and, above all, want of knowledge of a great and growing market.[68]

Kruzenshtern himself relates the story of his progress toward ultimate professional success and, on the way, to the Hawaiian archipelago:

During my sojourn at Canton in 1798-99, a small craft of about 100 tons, commanded by an Englishman,[69] arrived there from the Northwest Coast of North America. She had been fitted out in Macao, the venture had not taken more than five months, and the cargo, which consisted entirely of furs, was sold for 60,000 piastres. My countrymen, I knew, conducted a considerable trade in furs with China... but were first obliged to take the peltry to Okhotsk, and thence to Kiakhta overland. Two years or more were thereby lost, and (as I also knew) several vessels and their rich cargoes were lost even crossing from the islands of the Eastern Sea. It seemed to me that profits would decidedly be greater if we Russians took our goods straight to Canton from the Aleutians or the Coast... And, on my passage home from China, I composed a memoir to that effect which I intended to present to Soimonov, then the minister of commerce.[70]

Kruzenshtern's return to Russia coincided, by ill luck, with the climax of a set of power struggles in St Petersburg. As a result, far from welcoming his plan, the

fractured government dismissed it without consideration. It was a galling interlude, symbolic of that time of petty tyranny that was the reign of Paul I, and led
the ardent planner close to premature retirement. Political developments,
however, soon outran that notion: Paul was murdered, and an able officer of
liberal persuasions, Admiral N.S. Mordvinov, was appointed minister of the
marine.[71] Kruzenshtern's Pacific-Eastern project was approved with only slight
alteration.[72] His spirits rose.

The central element in Kruzenshtern's design, as in Trevenen's, was that vessels should be sent from Kronstadt to the Northwest Coast, barter for otter skins
with Indians,[73] proceed to China, sell some skins and purchase Chinese mer-
chandise before returning to the Baltic. Other parts of the design were that whole
companies of Russian seamen and their officers should gain in sea experience,
and that their efforts should produce certain political as well as economic gains.
In short, his plan owed much to earlier ambitions and designs, with which the
names of James Trevenen and Mulovskii had been linked. And it was altogether
right, since the Hawaiian interlude of 1804 could have occurred only within the
broader framework of the Kruzenshtern-Lisianskii expedition or another very
like it--led by other, no less able officers--that its objectives and its origins
should have been thus considered. What are here to be emphasized, however, are
two aspects of the 1802[74] design for a Pacific-Oriental undertaking with which
few writers have dealt: its latent scientific factor and the probability of contact
with Pacific Islanders inherent in the very route and schedule envisaged for a
squadron with a double (West and Northeastern) Pacific destination.[75]

It was not until 7 August 1802 that Kruzenshtern was formally appointed to
command an expedition which, he learned to his dismay, was quite expected by
its co-sponsors, the Crown and the Directors of the Russian-American (fur trading) Company, to leave the Baltic Sea that season.[76] After crossing the Atlantic
and revictualing quickly in Brazil, it seemed, his squadron was to round Cape
Horn in early January, and in case of separation to re-form at Valparaiso in Chile.
As a sailing schedule, it was quixotic. Preparation for a large and highly complex expedition had as yet barely begun. Not even ships had been produced; and
in the best of circumstances they could not have left the Baltic till the last days of
September. Any untoward delay, any misfortune in Brazil or on the mid-Atlantic
crossing, and the schedule could not be kept. And if the Horn were even
rounded, say, in March, it would be necessary to revictual and rest in, as
Trevenen said, "some of the islands in the South Sea", before pressing on for late
summer and autumn in the North. Mordvinov backed up Kruzenshtern's firm
protests against rushing an expensive and important undertaking, and so lessening its chances of complete success. Departure was delayed, by one full year;
thus the squadron faced the same exacting schedule for the Atlantic crossing,
rounding of Cape Horn, and passage north.[77] Neither willing to object again, nor
greatly troubled by the need to make a swift Atlantic crossing and to ready ships
and people in Brazil without one setback, Kruzenshtern addressed himself to

other matters: the selection of his officers, for instance, and the choosing and equipping of his ships. Without exception, his lieutenants had already given evidence of high ability and, in their fields, scientific bent.[78] From the perspective of the modern anthropologist, ethnographer of the Pacific, and historian of the Marquesas and Hawai'i, the situation was already far more promising than even Kruzenshtern himself might have believed at the time.

As seen, he had already shown himself at least as sensitive to cultural and ethnic differences between peoples as a Baltic German officer, brought up between the Slavs and Germans, Ests and Baltic *Herrenvolk*, might well have been expected to be. Within a month of his appointment as commander he was arguing, within the limits of his new authority, for the appointment to the coming expedition of the excellent zoologist and botanist, Wilhelm-Gottlieb Tilesius von Tilenau (1769-1857), recommended by the celebrated naturalist Freiherr Hans von Manteufel of Prussia.[79] If the scientific aspect of the enterprise *was* latent, in the plan approved in 1802, it was the consequence of Kruzenshtern's own policy. That policy was, first and foremost, to ensure that the Crown and the directors of a powerful, monopolistic company would back a North Pacific venture. That assured, he could carefully develop other, scientific aspects of his project: those specifically suggested by the voyages of Cook.

Lisianskii and a shipwright named Razumov, meanwhile, were looking out for vessels suitable for a protracted multipurpose expedition of the sort intended. They eventually found them, not in any Russian port or on the waterfront of Hamburg where the Company directors had supposed they might be found and duly loaded with supplies bought locally or taken down from Russia overland, but by the River Thames.[80] *Leander,* built in London in the spring of 1800, was a 431-ton sloop. *Thames* was a lately finished ship of 370 tons, only a trifle heavier, therefore, than Cook's *Endeavour* of 368 tons, but without the reinforcement and the massive, blunt construction of the Whitby collier. Lisianskii, whose arrangements with the embassy in London and its bankers left him free for rapid action, bought the two vessels for cash and had them modified internally in preparation for a long Pacific voyage. The purchase price, £17,000, was high, as were the costs of alteration,[81] but both vessels served the Russians quite as well as was expected by Lisianskii and Razumov--and considerably better than the Company's own critics would allow.[82] *Nadezhda* and *Neva,* as they were now respectively renamed, left England for the Baltic in May 1803, docking at Kronstadt on 5 June. Both made eleven knots or better on the crossing, in steady winds.

Kruzenshtern, meanwhile, was digesting another piece of news, delivered by Rumiantsev, now Minister of Commerce. *Nadezhda,* he was told, would face a wider range of tasks than had originally been envisaged for her: she would undertake both scientific and commercial missions and, additionally, would take a personal acquaintance of the tsar, Nikolai Petrovich Rezanov, as envoy to Japan.[83] *Nadezhda* and *Neva* would part in mid-Pacific, and Lisianskii would enjoy his own command for many months. He too, however, would remain under the Company's surveillance, inasmuch as a *prikazchik* [clerk] in Company employ and well regarded by the Company directors would be taking passage to the Northwest Coast. Fedor Ivanovich Shemelin and Nikolai Ivanovich Korobitsyn would voyage with *Nadezhda* and *Neva* respectively. It was an augury of future complications: both the clerks were shrewd and able men, by no means admirers of the Navy.

Kruzenshtern discovered what he could about Rezanov and his diplomatic mission while the ships were fitting out. One year earlier, he learned, the tsar had asked Rezanov to reorganize the Senate's First Department on less oligarchic lines; but even while he did that job, Rezanov had been fostering the plans of other men for the Pacific and the East, including Kruzenshtern's own project. There had been no thought, however, of his traveling himself. As an important State official, as the virtual controller of the Company, and as a man in frequent contact with the tsar, he had enough to keep him busy in St Petersburg. Then, in November 1802, his wife died of puerperal fever and he entered a decline. Daughter of the wealthiest and most successful of Kamchatka-based fur merchants, Grigorii Ivanovich Shelikhov, Rezanov's wife had long sustained his active interest in the Aleutian and American possessions of the Company in which, because of her, he had a handsome block of shares. Now, her death led to his personally visiting the settlements that he had read about for years in the Company reports.[84] With kindly motives, Alexander sent him to Japan as Russian envoy, with *Nadezhda* and *Neva*.

Rezanov's very presence in the Kruzenshtern-Lisianskii expedition, in the joint capacity of envoy to Japan and influential Company official, was symbolic of a coming confrontation between Company and Navy in the North Pacific Ocean. We may see it in F.I. Shemelin's text, presented here. Fundamentally, it was a question of confused authority. Upon *arrival* in Japan, or in the settlements, Rezanov the grandee would command; but meanwhile the officers and men of *Nadezhda* and *Neva* regarded Kruzenshtern alone as their commander, and Rezanov as an arrogant and interfering passenger.[85] To reinforce the likelihood of trouble on the voyage out, the captain and the envoy had their own sets of instructions, and while Kruzenshtern's had been composed by Admiral Mordvinov's naval staff in consultation with Rumiantsev's own, Rezanov's, which were not (yet) shown to Kruzenshtern, had been drafted at the ministry of commerce by Count A.R. Vorontsov on behalf of Alexander, who had signed a formal document addressed to the Mikado of Japan.[86]

At first, these blurrings of the limits of authority seemed actually to assist the preparation of the expedition; for they made it almost certain that whatever was regarded by the Company or Navy as conducive to the expedition's ultimate success would be provided, by one government department or another. The phenomenon was reinforced by the participation in the venture of a trading enterprise and the Academies of Sciences and Arts. The former sent to Kronstadt splendid maps and monographs, including Cook's, Vancouver's, and assorted other *Voyages*. The Admiralty yard at Galley-Port, St Petersburg, sent brand new rigging. Goods arrived from Germany and Switzerland, and scientific instruments were checked at the Academy of Sciences. The tsar himself evinced a certain interest, traveling out to Kronstadt in his carriage to inspect the preparations for departure. Kruzenshtern indeed had reason, as he put it, to "conceive himself particularly fortunate" for, on this visit, Alexander gave instructions that the revenues of an estate "amounting to the yearly sum of 1,500 roubles" should be paid to his wife for twelve years.[87] Lisianskii, meanwhile, supervised the stowing of a quantity of foodstuffs, instruments, Company stores and, for good measure, trinkets to appeal to the native peoples to be met in the Pacific.

Kruzenshtern had named Lisianskii as his second-in-command because he knew him to be "zealous in the service" and a thoroughly accomplished officer.[88] Similarly in 'inferior commissioned officers', he looked for steadiness of temper and a first-class service record. Makar' Ivanovich Ratmanov, whom he took as first lieutenant in *Nadezhda,* had commanded ships of war for fourteen years. Second lieutenant Romberg had achieved success while with the frigate *Narva.* Golovachev, third lieutenant, was based at Kronstadt. Fourth lieutenant Levenshtern (von Loewenstern) had served with Nelson's bugbear, F.I. Ushakov, in the Mediterranean Sea.[89] Like Romberg and Ratmanov, he was better read and far more widely traveled than were most of his contemporaries in the Russian naval service. Insofar as he could do so, Kruzenshtern excluded men of narrow outlook, malcontents, and idlers. His ordinary seamen were, with few exceptions, literate; his officers and specialists, with few exceptions, men of subtle mind. It was with thoughts of Captain Bligh in mind, as well as of the need to run a calm and ordered ship which could for months or even years serve as maritime laboratory and office for the expedition's scientists--Wilhelm Gottfried Tilesius von Tilenau, naturalist; Johann Caspar Horner, astronomer; and Karl Espenberg, *Nadezhda's* surgeon – that he emphasized the virtues of 'attachment and obedience'.[90] On his instructions, clothes and mattresses were issued to each member of both crews. It was his object to establish an *esprit de corps* by handsome pay, good food, consideration, and by lofty expectations, not by isolated acts of generosity. The Navy and the Company alike, in short, were willing that the new Pacific service should be special, as it were a special section of the Navy, with an enviable promise of advancement for the few.

But what of personal relations between Kruzenshtern himself and the ambassador, who now delayed his embarkation and whose books and paintings, trunks, mirrors, and models, wine and gifts for the Mikado were continuing to mount up on the quay at Kronstadt? ("I was in the roadstead and effects were still arriving, which I was not a little puzzled how to stow...")[91] In truth, the captain had been very vexed by the ambassador's appointment, not as such, but as the leader of the mission as a whole, in a peculiarly ill-defined and cloudy sense. Rezanov's coming had deprived him and Lisianskii of a certain sum of money and, potentially at least, of fame. When *Nadezhda* and *Neva* finally weighed anchor, on 4 August 1803, the wind swung to the west, further delaying their departure. Nerves were strained.

The Ethnographic Impulse

It was Kruzenshtern's particular achievement to develop what had started as an economic scheme into a scientific venture of importance to the educated world. The point becomes apparent as one weighs the text of the Russian-American Company Directors' statement of intention and appeal for imperial assistance of 29 July 1802, that is, immediately after the extraordinary meeting of the Company's own stockholders and board at which the pros and cons of Kruzenshtern's new Coast-to-China project were assessed.[92] "First," observed the Company Directors led by Nikolai Petrovich Rezanov, "the provisioning of the American colonies for many years at once would decrease the volume of goods passing through Okhotsk port; and this in itself would lower the very great cost of overland transport while still protecting the whole of Iakutsk Province from want... Second, our Company may well succeed in establishing a lucrative trade in furs at Canton..., gaining the upper hand over foreign nations. On the return voyage, we might even attempt trade in the settlements of foreign East Indies companies, *e.g.*, Calcutta, Bengal, and Batavia..., in due course bringing sugar, coffee, indigo, and other goods straight to St Petersburg."[93] No word here of academic challenges or scientific work at sea; no mention of hydrography or any other branch of naval science, let alone of any study of the living world of animals and men. And yet, as seen, less than a month after his naming as commander of the expedition, Kruzenshtern had sought and won permission for an eminent zoologist and botanist to join his company. The speed and energy with which he pressed Rumiantsev and (through him only) the board for the appointment of Tilesius von Tilenau, were symbolic of his own determination--which Rumiantsev smiled on--that scientific opportunities should not be lost.[94]

It was, in large measure, Rumiantsev's and the Court's involvement in the coming expedition that enabled Kruzenshtern successfully to challenge the Directors' massive emphasis on the commercial aspect of his mission in another, more decisive way. Originally, the Directors had proposed to send two graduates of the St Petersburg Commercial Institution on the expedition.[95] They had solid grounds for doing so. Experience suggested that such graduates could, on the basis of a few days' observation in a foreign port, write factually accurate and well-balanced reports that went some way toward removing the essential disadvantage of the Russians in the East and the Pacific--that of ignorance of true market conditions. Such reports had been prepared about Western European trading centers; and the graduates selected would be likely to remain in Company employ. Pragmatically insisting on the dangers of an overcrowded vessel and the modest size of his *Nadezhda*, Kruzenshtern used all his leverage with Count Rumiantsev, a supporter of the sciences at large, to have these graduates replaced by an astronomer. Johann-Caspar Horner, a Swiss, was nominated to the post, at once accepted it and, to avoid unnecessary travel, signed a contract with the Company in Dresden.[96]

By delaying the departure of the expedition, the Directors of the Company, Rumiantsev, and the Court itself contributed, to varying degrees, to the enhancement of its academic aspect and potential. By the same token, they reinforced a tendency that, in the present writer's view, was plain even in August 1802: to take the voyages of Cook as patterns for the first grand seaborne venture to be launched by Russian subjects in the Great South Sea. It was, as Soviet historians might say, 'no accident' that the Hawaiian Islands, Cook's last resting place in the Pacific, had been thought of from the first, in that connection, by the planners of the Kruzenshtern-Lisianskii expedition.

For a quarter century after his death, James Cook remained the great exemplar for the Russians of the leader of a voyage of discovery.[97] For Kruzenshtern, he was "the great Cook", whose determinations of position were in general so accurate that other men's chronometers could be adjusted to them,[98] whose relations with his officers and men had been exemplary. Cook's influence had permeated Kruzenshtern's early career, in the course of which, as seen, a stream of versions of English hero's *Voyages* appeared in a range of languages. Never was France's influence to equal England's in St Petersburg and Kronstadt where the scientific voyage and the seaborne exploration were concerned: for thirty years after his death, the form and emphases of Cook's Pacific ventures were not only borne in mind by the ambitious Russian officer of scientific bent, but were perceived as proper to such ventures. And among those emphases were certain scientific ones. Banks and the Forsters had been botanists, zoologists. Astronomy had been regarded, in the spirit of enlightenment that M.V. Lomonosov had refracted onto Russia, as deserving of pursuit *per se*. Cook had himself taken an active interest in native 'curiosities' or artifacts and in the languages, beliefs, and social life of other peoples, such as the Hawaiians, though indeed he had no orders to concern himself particularly or at length with ethnographica. It was to gaze on Venus in Tahiti and to complete a grand botanical design, while on his way to a conjectured southern continent, that he had sailed in *Endeavour*. Nonetheless, both he and Banks *had* shown a lively and objective interest in native peoples they encountered; and the pattern was repeated on the second and the final voyages despite the dryness and immutability of his instructions on the subject.[99] Stress fell first, officially at least, upon discovery and the attendant naval sciences (hydrography, marine astronomy), then on the twin natural sciences: zoology and botany. In fact, Cook and his people made as full and close a study of the natives whom they saw as time allowed, collecting representative (pre-contact) artifacts, a few of which found their way to St Petersburg and remain there today.[100] It was an attitude conducive to the welfare of an infant science, soon to be baptized 'ethnology'.[101] No such example could be lost on Kruzenshtern whom, in a gesture well designed to stress the fact, the Academy of Sciences elected as a corresponding member, at the decisive moment (25 April 1803).[102] His election was, on one level, no doubt, an act of faith in an important individual who had not yet published a single learned work, but on another it was simply an expression of a bond between his enterprise itself and the Academy. That bond was realized by Academic readiness to lend or check equipment, to advise on any scientific point, even to draft complex instructions for the benefit of expedition members, in zoology and botany and mineralogy.[103] For the Directors and the Company at large, there was no choice but to accept the situation gracefully, acknowledging that what had been initially envisaged as a grandiose commercial venture had acquired academic and political significance beyond their own control. This was accepted, unofficially and tacitly, in April 1803, and officially a few weeks later. Here are the crucial lines in Kruzenshtern's instructions from the Company, to which he and Lisianskii were seconded by the Navy, dated 29 May 1803:

All that you learn on the basis of your observations or acquire during the voyage that has significance for natural history, geography, navigation or other sciences, together with any maps or descriptions made, you will of course present without fail to the Company. We think it superfluous to go into detail in these matters, having learned of your zeal in this regard.[104]

Essentially, then, Kruzenshtern was given liberty not only to insist upon but also to construe the broadly scientific aspects of his own instructions. As had Cook, he chose to read them in a way that favored study of all native peoples met along the way, though not indeed at the expense of naval sciences. It was perhaps predictable that he should do so: he was, after all, a Baltic German officer, alive since childhood to ethnic, cultural, and temperamental differences.[105] On his orders, broken iron hoops, beads, nails, mirrors, knives and other objects readily and cheaply found, were stowed aboard *Nadezhda* and *Neva* for use in barter in the North and South Pacific. He was not to blame if, lacking recent information, he misjudged the wants and tastes of the Hawaiians (whom he reckoned in any case to be meeting only briefly) and did not take on sufficient broadcloth, red material, or extra canvas.

Kruzenshtern chose as lieutenants men whose service records showed those qualities that he himself embodied: loyalty, intelligence, and diligence. If fellow Baltic German officers loomed large--even disproportionately--on the list of the appointees,[106] that itself was some reflection of the socially prestigious, academic, and exclusive character of what was, basically, an infant 'special branch' of naval service. Romberg, Loewenstern, and Berg: the very names suggested influence, political and academic acumen to the contemporary Russian ear. True, some senior lieutenants were of ancient Russian stock: Ratmanov and Golovachev in *Nadezhda*, Povalishin and Arbuzov in *Neva*. But these were more than counter-balanced, both numerically and in terms of influence ashore, by the Germans in Ambassador Rezanov's suite, or serving as cadets with mighty patronage, or on secondment to the Company like Kruzenshtern himself.[107] Nor, broadly speaking, would contemporaries have been wrong to think the two ships' companies distinguished ones by any naval standards. Writing four years later, Kruzenshtern himself had this to say of them: "I wished to fill the spare room in my ship with such men as might contribute to the advancement of the sciences. For it seemed to me that our long awaited sojourn in the Southern Hemisphere, and the tasks of philosophy itself, must surely offer useful employment for them all..."[108]

Kruzenshtern did not actively look out for men more likely than the mass of their contemporaries in the Navy to support him in an ethnographic effort. Nevertheless it was just such men--thanks to the application of his own criteria for choosing his subordinates, the nature of the latter's training in the arts of observation and description, and his lofty expectations of them--who accompanied him out to the Pacific and Hawai'i. Long accustomed to be accurate in measurement and reckoning, conservative in guesswork, and above all thorough when surveying the unusual or unfamiliar, such men *were* likely to make useful contributions to Pacific and American ethnography. The point bears emphasis.

So too with the astronomer, the surgeons, and the other men of science on the expedition, led by Brykin and Laband: while not especially prepared for ethnography (no university taught the subject at the time), they were accustomed to the scientific discipline of careful scrutiny of what was new, and they were able to apply it to descriptions of Pacific Islanders. So much is evident both from their published and unpublished journals and, more eloquently yet, from such a paper as Tilesius von Tilenau's 'On the Natural and the Political Condition of Inhabitants of Nukuhiva Island'(1806).[109] The historian of the Hawaiian Islands must regret that Kruzenshtern revictualed and rested first in the Marquesas, there pouring forth much of his ethnographic energy.[110] Tilesius von Tilenau would no doubt have done Hawai'i proud. We may be grateful, on the other hand, that he and other well-trained European scientists were even *in* a Russian naval expedition to the North and South Pacific at that time.

Already matters augured well for would-be students of Pacific ethnographica aboard *Nadezhda* and *Neva*. Developments in 1803 improved them even further. The Academy of Arts placed two experienced and able draughtsmen at the Company's disposal. One of them, Stepan Kurliandtsev, joined *Nadezhda* as the Expeditionary Artist. Space proved to be lacking for the other man, Prichotnikov, to his distress. Then, in the final days of August as the two ships victualed in Copenhagen roads, occurred the greatest stroke of fortune from the standpoint of contemporary science: the arrival of the young but versatile German *savant*, Georg Heinrich Langsdorf (1774-1852). Langsdorf was hoping that, despite the known appointments of Tilesius von Tilenau and of Horner to the expedition and the lateness of the hour, he might also be allowed to join the venture. Kruzenshtern and, more especially, Rezanov were impressed most favorably by his energy and readiness to go without a salary. That he was admirably qualified to join the expedition, there could be no question: Langsdorf was a protégé of Johann Friedrich Blumenbach the anthropologist and physiologist, whose student he had been at Göttingen while Kruzenshtern had been in action as a Russian Volunteer. Subsequently, he had lived and worked in Lisbon, moving always in the highest medical and social circles.[111] His request to join the expedition as a naturalist, comments Kruzenshtern, "could not have been approved in St Petersburg, Tilesius von Tilenau having already been engaged. Such however were his ardor and his anxiety to be part of our expedition that he had gone to Copenhagen, undeterred, there making another and successful attempt to gain his end."[112] Of the significance for Pacific anthropology of Langsdorf's very presence in *Nadezhda* (as Rezanov's private secretary-physician), suffice to note that his mentor Blumenbach, the father and most eminent practitioner of craniology, was well acquainted with Sir Joseph Banks and perfectly familiar with Cook's achievements. Had he not been, he would hardly have discussed them, publicly and often, at the University of Göttingen.[113] In sum, all smiled on the ethnographic impulse that was only one of Cook's several legacies to Russia and her navy.

The Voyage and
Arrival off Hawai'i

After stops at Copenhagen and at Falmouth on the southwest tip of England, where fresh viands were purchased while the ships' hulls were examined by their carpenters and instruments were brought by road from London, *Nadezhda* and *Neva* set sail for Brazil in company. One further stop was made, at Teneriffe in the Canary Islands. During the winter months of 1803-04, the Russians made their way from Santa Cruz in the Canaries to the Washington-Marquesas Islands via Santa Catarina Island near Rio de Janeiro and Cape Horn. Almost immediately after their departure from the port of Santa Cruz, where more supplies were purchased, Kruzenshtern imposed a strict routine on both ships' companies. Henceforward, nothing but disaster was to halt the clockwork rounds of testing, sampling, reckoning and measurement which now engrossed the time of J.C. Horner and the German naturalists. Reckonings of latitude and longitude, checkings of compasses and other instruments, testings of air and water temperatures, humidity, ships' headway, water content, botanizing, all proceeded under many watchful eyes--but not Rezanov's. The ambassador remained below, alarmed by the abuse with which his first and clumsy effort to exert his own authority over the naval officers had been received.[114]

Nadezhda and *Neva* entered the South Pacific on 3 March. Winds were calm and friendly on the crucial day, but not long afterward the two vessels were parted by a sudden and tremendous storm. They rendezvoused only at Nuku Hiva in the Washington-Marquesas group, some nine weeks later. Meaning to provision there if possible, Lisianskii brought *Neva* up toward Easter Island on 17-20 April. He approached it closely enough to see the surf and understand that any landing would be perilous, but put a boat off with a view to hurried bartering outside the reefs. Lieutenant Povalishin had a measure of success, under the circumstances. Russian mirrors, knives, and baubles were exchanged for badly needed fresh provisions, and Lt Povalishin gave descriptions of the local dwellings, cultivated plots, and huge stone figures. Lisianskii vainly scanned the island's coasts for any serviceable harbor.[115] Kruzenshtern, meanwhile, was approaching the Marquesas. *Nadezhda* came to anchor inside Taio-hae Bay (named 'Port Anna Maria' by Vancouver's colleague Hergest of the *Daedalus* when he had visited it thirteen years before), by the looming wooded shores of Nuku Hiva, at approximately 5 p.m. on 7 May 1804. The Russians refer to 'Anna Maria', showing their familiarity with Vancouver's *Voyage*.

The Russians spent ten days at the Marquesas. Their arrival was politically and scientifically significant. It set a pattern for Lisianskii's later dealings with the people of Hawai'i whom, inevitably, he compared and contrasted with *enata*, the people of Nuku Hiva.[116] For the first time an entire Russian company, indeed two companies, had dealings with a group of South Sea Islanders and vice versa. The event had understandably been troubling the cautious Kruzenshtern, to whom it was apparent that such visits called for careful management if errors that had clouded relations between other Europeans and such peoples were to be averted. For a guide, he turned to Cook, modeling orders for the people of *Nadezhda* as they closed in thankfully on Nuku Hiva, on the Englishman's of forty years before. His 'Marquesan Orders' merit our attention--in themselves and as reminders of the dangers facing European captains in the South Pacific: petty theft, overfamiliarity, and lethal retribution by the gun. They were the touchstone for all subsequent official Russian dealings with the natives of the South and mid-Pacific:

The principal object of our calling at the Marquesas Islands is to water and take on fresh provisions. Though we might well accomplish all this even without the natives' goodwill, risks both to them and to us prevent our having recourse to any such approach; and I am certain that we Russians will depart from the shores of a tranquil people not having left behind a bad name for ourselves... Accordingly, I have judged it to be necessary, to avoid unpleasantness, to lay down a code of behavior. It will be very natural if, on our arrival, unfamiliar objects provoke in many the desire to have them. You, for your parts, would gladly barter European goods for the various curios of these people. But lack of caution might have undesirable results: the natives, anxious to acquire objects of ours and getting them in plenty in exchange for things of little value to them, would no doubt end by wanting objects that we could not surrender before they would satisfy our genuine needs... When we have furnished ourselves with all provisions necessary for the continuation of our voyage, and only then, will I give sufficient notice to permit every man to barter with his own possessions, in accordance with his means and inclination...

It is emphatically reaffirmed that no member of the lower deck is to use a firearm, either on board or ashore, without special orders to that effect from the officers.

        Kruzenshtern[117]

Nadezhda had not anchored before islanders surrounded her and Kruzenshtern was coping with the problems that he had foreseen. The Nukuhivans were accommodating. Some proposed to barter fruit for iron--cracked or broken iron hoops from barrels had been brought out from the Baltic and were speedily produced. Others clambered up the vessel's sides, onto the bowsprit and the decks. Among the visitors were women, some of whom had more than fruit to give the Russians.[118] In the latter's view, their gestures were lascivious and lewd. And yet, to a remarkable extent judging by subsequent accounts of the Marquesan visit,[119] Kruzenshtern succeeded in preserving Russian seamen from temptation as embodied in these nymphs, and in averting other troubles. There were thefts, but they were calmly viewed. As to liaisons, it is claimed that not one Russian fell from grace.[120] Russian descriptions of the physical conditions and political and social institutions that obtained at Taio-hae are objective and, as such, retain significance today for the historian of Oceania in the immediate post-contact period. Various Russian manufactured goods were bartered for a range of local artifacts, many of which are on display now in the Peter-the-Great Museum of Ethnography of the Academy of Sciences, in Leningrad.[121]

Once again the influence of Cook and Joseph Banks had proved significant in ways that bore directly on the Russians' June encounters with Hawaiians.[122] Of similarities between the Russians' conduct while at Nuku Hiva and in Kona on Hawai'i Island, more especially in their recording and collecting practices, three merit mention here. At both islands, they first traded for foodstuffs, then deliberately set about acquiring a representative collection of the local artifacts. At both stops, they relied for information and for practical assistance on the local chiefs and, with some proper reservations, on the local European castaways. And at Hawai'i, as at Nuku Hiva, they made swift but sober studies of the agriculture, dress, religious practices, canoes, and social mores of their hosts. The modern student of Hawaiian history may regret that Nuku Hiva, not Hawai'i, drew the greatest single ethnographic effort from the Russians as they crossed the South Pacific, yet appreciate that Taio-hae Bay prepared them all, as no amount of studying in Europe could have done, for coming meetings with Kamehameha's subjects. For Lisianskii in particular, the stay at Taio-hae Bay was *sui generis* a dry run for Hawai'i. It is pertinent that it was he, not Kruzenshtern, who on 12 May took the initiative and organized a visit to the 'palace' of the 'king' or local chief.[123] He was an officer of ceaseless curiosity and was not burdened, like the careful Kruzenshtern, with all the tribulations of an overall command.

One of these tribulations, which ensured that there would be a Russian visit to Hawai'i as had always been envisaged, was the almost total unavailability (to them) of animal stock on Nuku Hiva. Kruzenshtern had hoped to make a few discoveries of islands on the passage north from the Marquesas group to Petropavlovsk-in-Kamchatka. Now, the lack of meat ("we had managed to obtain no more than seven hogs for both ships' companies"), concern about his people's health, and a desire to avoid the annual monsoons of late September off Japan, led him to change his plans. The meat shortage particularly (he asserted some time later), made it his "duty" to proceed to the Hawaiian Islands, "where plentiful supplies of fresh provisions might be had--or so we anticipated, with good reason." Supposing that Hawaiians would put out to sea "15 or 18 miles", as in other times, to barter with a European vessel, he proposed simply to "bring to for a day or two".[124] If native traders and provisioners of southeastern Hawai'i Island did not satisfy his needs, he could continue round the island in a clockwise direction.

All these factors doubtless did bear, to some extent, on Kruzenshtern's decisions of mid-May and on his brittle mood; but, we may think, all such decisions had been influenced--far more immediately--by developments aboard *Nadezhda*. There was open confrontation between Kruzenshtern and his annoy-

ing passenger, Rezanov. The two had a dramatic argument, indeed, before assorted witnesses.[125] Rezanov read his orders out, aloud and with a flourish, on
the quarter-deck; but his performance did not end, as he supposed it must, in his
triumphant vindication. The lieutenants were not cowed by his assertion of complete authority over themselves. The envoy took the setback--or, more accurately,
the humiliation--very badly, falling ill. Thereafter Kruzenshtern was recognized
by all and sundry as commander of the North Pacific venture. Even so, he had
been shaken by the crisis and the strain was soon to tell on his behavior.

From the first, Kruzenshtern's expectations of the Hawaiians, as purveyors of
Having coasted WNW for one full day from Nuku Hiva with the object of
confirming a supposed sighting of land by Etienne Marchand (nothing was seen),
Nadezhda and *Neva* headed northwest. *Nadezhda* crossed the equator on 25 May
and met the northeast tradewind four or five days later. *Neva* dropped steadily
astern of her. Then, on 4 June, *Nadezhda* sprung a leak.[126] It was not serious
because the ship was riding high and the extent of oakum rotting was quite
limited, below the waterline. Nevertheless, it troubled Kruzenshtern, made frequent pumping necessary, and later limited all his lieutenants to a rapid barter
session with the natives of Hawai'i.

From the first, Kruzenshtern's expectations of the Hawaiians, as purveyors of
provisions on the high sea, were too high. Lisianskii, less preoccupied and tense,
arrived off Puna on 8 June in, for the purposes of practical ethnology, a more
receptive frame of mind than his superior. He was already benefitting from the
knowledge that whereas *Nadezhda* was to hasten to Kamchatka and proceed to
Nagasaki with Rezanov in a hectic three-month period, *Neva* was merely to sail
up to the Northwest Coast of North America within a reasonable time, untroubled
by Rezanov or the prospect of monsoons. He stood at an advantage over
Kruzenshtern as an observer of the mid-Pacific scene, despite the absence of an
artist or a scientist of note aboard *Neva*.[127]

PART TWO

The Texts

Annotated translations follow of the eyewitness accounts of their experiences on or near Hawai'i Island of Iurii Fedorovich Lisianskii and Nikolai Ivanovich Korobitsyn, of *Neva*, and Ivan Fedorovich Kruzenshtern, Nikolai Petrovich Rezanov, Fedor Ivanovich Shemelin, Georg Heinrich Langsdorf, Emelian Levenshtern, and Vasilii Nikolaevich Berkh, of *Nadezhda*. Because the 1812 (St Petersburg) text of Lisianskii's *Puteshestvie vokrug sveta...* [*Voyage Round the World...*] differs in numerous, by no means insignificant, ways from the 1814 (London) text, both are included here in English, for the purposes of collation and completeness. Rezanov's 1825 and 1806 accounts of his Hawaiian dealings are presented here in that order, as both content and internal references make appropriate. The Berkh text is placed last for the same reason. Detailed information on the provenance of sources given here, and on publication histories, is given separately (see Part 5).

Iu F. Lisianskii (1812)

On the eighth of the month [June 1804], at nine in the morning, we caught sight of the island of Ovigi [Hawai'i] away to the northwest. At noon, its eastern extremity* bore 3°NW of us at a distance of some twenty miles. We were now in latitude 19°18'N, longitude 153°51' according to chronometer no. 136 or 15°45' according to no. 50, from which it would follow that the former instrument was 1° in error, the latter 46' in error, while the ship's reckoning gave 5°39' too much to eastward.

By 2 p.m. or so we were close enough in shore to be able to make out with ease the native dwellings of which there are, in fact, quite a number on the eastern tip of the island. And now we were approached by six craft, each holding two or three men. Coming up onto the deck, the first islander grasped the hand of everyone he met with the words "How do you do?"[1] He had picked the phrase up from some Englishman or other living on the island, of course. I had at first entertained pleasant hopes of obtaining fresh provisions of some sort from these natives, but was soon completely disabused of that expectation. For the islanders, it turned out, had brought out to us only a few pieces of material and other trifles of little significance in our sight. We continued to lie to until five o'clock, then spread sails in order to stand off shore during the night, which promised to be misty and rainy.

At three o'clock on the morning of the 9th we bore west. Toward eleven o'clock, the southwestern extremity of the island became visible.** We weathered it, then brought to opposite a native dwelling in order to wait for two native craft that had set out in our direction. Both, however, made for *Nadezhda*. The first had brought out a hog weighing some two and a half *pood*.[+] Broadcloth was requested in exchange for it. There being none aboard, the natives carried it back to the shore. We remained in more or less the same position until four o'clock when, not seeing a single native craft about, we again put out from shore for the night. We fixed the southern cape of the island at 18°35'N.

The weather proved pleasant on the 10th. The moderate east-northeasterly wind, however, eventually veered north and so dropped that we were quite unable to move in shore. At noon, when Ovigi's southern cape bore 79°NW of us, we reckoned our latitude again, by observations, and found it to be 18°58'N. Captain Kruzenshtern took his leave of me on this day, having come to a firm decision to proceed to Kamchatka that very night.[2] I would fain have persuaded him to delay another three days or so in order to obtain fresh provisions. Such was his want of them that even his officers had been eating only salt meat for up-

---

*Cape Kumukahi
**Ka Lae, not Kauna or Kamoi Points
[+] about 90 pounds

ward of two months. However, his zeal and his determination to see his mission
through in the best possible style were unshakable. To my representations, he
answered simply that all *Nadezhda*'s men (according to the physician's statement) were in sound health. An easterly wind sprang up at eight o'clock that
evening and *Nadezhda* set a southwesterly course while we continued to lie to.

At dawn on the 11th the wind swung round to the west again and, with its aid,
we moved up to Karekekua [Kealakekua] Bay.*   It was our intention to enter
this bay, for we knew from the experience of the previous three days that it
would not be possible to get fresh supplies along the island's coasts. The southwestern cape of Ovigi bore WSW at this time, and the northwestern was N by E.

At about eight o'clock, a craft came out to us from a little place called Peri-
Rua,** which lay not far from the island's southwest extremity. In it sat an
Englishman named Lewis Johnson and a boy named George Kernick, a native of
Ovigi, who had sailed with Captain Puget and lived seven years in England.+ In
reply to my queries as to conditions generally on the island of Ovigi and whether
we could get provisions without difficulty and without exposing ourselves to
danger, Johnson said that the local king had resolved to wage war against the island of Otuvai [Kaua'i]† and was presently living on Vagu [O'ahu] with all his
senior chiefs, but that--though we should find only the common people at
Karekekua--we should certainly be received with all possible civility. He added
that in the king's absence authority lay with an Englishman called Young, who
would no doubt come out to us shortly after learning of our presence despite the
fact that he resided several miles from the bay in question. Notwithstanding this
assurance, I gave orders for the ship to stand prepared against every eventuality.
This first native craft was followed out by three more, one of which brought us
two small hogs. We exchanged them against nine *arshin*‡ of thick cloth, also acquiring native cloth for a piece of particolored ticking material.

Bearing north while we closed in on the shore again, we took the opposite tack
when the wind veered northwest. At noon, when Karekekua Bay lay 15°NE of
us ten miles distant, we fixed our position as being 19°17'08"N. Moving a little
west, we again followed the shore. The wind now permitted us to set a course
NW by N: were it not for a strong current also helping us north, however (a current that hereabouts nearly always prevails in that direction, and right by the
shore, as it is asserted), we should hardly have cleared the bay's southern cape.
When still a mile from the shore, I sent the yawl and cutter ahead to tow us, so
steering as to gain maximal possible advantage from the sea-current. Clearing
the southern point of the bay++ at five o'clock, we dropped anchor in 17 *sazhen*

---

* Cook's and King's 'Karakakooa'
** Pelelua, if it existed, has been lost as a place name.
+ circa 1796-1802, if he indeed sailed in the armed tender *Chatham*
† The Russians often followed Cook's and King's nomenclature.
‡ 21 feet; width not given but probably 3 feet
++ Palemanô Point

[fathoms] of water, sandy bottom with mussels. The south end of the bay lay due south of us, the north--80°W.* Evening approached, so we then moored on a NNE-SSW axis with three-quarters of a cable each way, in 20 *sazhen* of water...

On approaching this bay, I had feared that we should be met by a large number of little craft, and that these might hamper us in our operations. In the event, we did not see a single one--a result, as I discovered, of a *tapu* [*kapu*] that had been placed preventing any individual from entering the water.** At sunset however, when the ban ended, about one hundred women swam out to us. As I would not permit a single one of them to board the ship, they in due course went back to the shore whence they had come, lamenting their setback.

At dawn on the 12th, native craft came out to us with articles of local manufacture and supplies of various kinds. We first of all bought such fresh foodstuffs as they had, later taking material and other rarities as well. On learning that Young had prohibited the sale of swine to Europeans without his knowledge and consent, I immediately sent Johnson to tell the local chief that if he did not send me fresh meat at once, *Neva* would put out to sea that very same evening. The announcement quickly produced an effect. The local chief himself came out to us, bringing with him two hogs and a fair quantity of tubers.+ We received him with great attention, presenting him with three bottles of rum, two axes, and an adze. Expressing his pleasure with all this, the chief undertook to continue to supply us with fresh provisions. Our purchasing of native rarities had been progressing so satisfactorily, meanwhile, that both officers and men had soon acquired a quantity of articles of various sorts. Though the islanders were exchanging their goods for knives or small mirrors readily enough, it was our printed cloth† and striped ticking that they really prized. For a single four-and-a-half *arshin*‡ length of either material--a length that they called *pau*++ in their own tongue--they would surrender as much as twenty *arshin* of their own best material. And they put a high value even on plain canvas. On the other hand, they would hardly deign to look at the iron hoops with which we were, it seemed, too abundantly supplied.

I invited the chief to dine with us. He accepted, and declined nothing offered, not even spirits and wine. Everything brought to the table, indeed, he ate with a keen appetite. In the end, he became quite drunk.

That evening, a numerous troop of Venus's handmaidens again surrounded the ship, but I gave instructions to my interpreter to inform them that not one single female would ever be allowed aboard. At the same time, I asked the local chief

---

*Neva was thus anchored in *Discovery*'s position of February 1779.[3]

**kapu hua. Vancouver also witnessed the *kapu* on the 12th of the month.[4]

+Russian *koren'ev*. The word is used elsewhere to mean sweet potatoes, and probably is here.

† The Russian term, *naboika*, suggests a finer material than broadcloth (*.r.kholst*).

‡ about 10 1/2 feet

++*pâ'û*--literally a woman's skirt, thus referring to a piece of cloth about 3 feet wide and 7-10 feet long

to order all craft to stand off. The sun, I observed, was already about to set and after that time I should not allow a single islander to remain on ship. He at once did as I requested, and as a result we found ourselves alone when our ensign was lowered. Very pleasant the change was to us all, it must be confessed, after the excessive racket that had gone on all day.[5] Despite Young's ban, we had this day acquired two large hogs, two smaller ones, and ten fowl, as well as a cask-full of sweet-potato and a good number of coconuts, taro roots, and sugar-canes.

At about eight o'clock next morning, the 13th, the ship was once again surrounded by little craft;* and toward noon the chief himself arrived, bringing us four large hogs. One he gave me as a gift. For the others, he took one and a half iron bars. I offered him other articles in exchange for them, but the chief declared that the hogs belonged to the king, and the king had ordered that they should be sold only for bar-iron. Besides these hogs, we also obtained about a dozen fowl and twelve small pigs that morning.

After our noon meal, I told the chief that I wished to go ashore. He accordingly went on ahead. Toward evening we set out. All twelve oarsmen in the launch were armed. The surf by the village of Karekekua itself proved so great that we were obliged to make our landing at Vainu-Nagala [Waipunaula], where the chief duly met us and informed us that he had placed a *tapu* on all the inhabitants. Sure enough, not a single person followed us on our stroll: all remained in their houses.

Passing by a number of poor huts,[6] we came into an alley of coconut trees, on the trunks of which the chief pointed out to us many slits and holes. They had been produced by cannon-balls at the time of Captain Cook's death.[7] The chief assured me that many people had been killed by the English, on that occasion. From the alley, we continued on our way along the beach by ourselves:[8] the chief had excused himself from accompanying us, as a temple lay on the way and he could not pass by it.

On entering the settlement of Karekekua, the first structure to catch our gaze was a very large shed or barn-like building. Here, prior to the present war, the king had kept a schooner built by Captain Vancouver.[9] From this building we went into a second, where a double canoe was in the process of being built for the chief, who, rejoining us, then took us to his own house. Having rested a little there, we went to look over the king's palace. It proved to differ only in its size from other native structures around. It is made up of six houses or, more accurately, huts built by a pond. There is nothing artificial or contrived about it: everything has been left in a natural state. The first hut we entered was called the royal dining-room; the second was where the king entertained his noblest subjects and visiting Europeans; the third and fourth were designated for his wives; the fifth and sixth served together as the kitchen. All six huts had been constructed in the same fashion from poles enclosed and covered by leaves. In some

---

* evidently single canoes [*kaukahi*]

of them, two small windows had been made at a corner; but others had only a
door, 2-1/2 or 3 feet wide. Every house here stands on a small, elevated stone
platform and is encircled by a low palisade. I cannot say in what state this palace
is kept when the king is resident. At the time of our inspection, however, there
was nothing but disgusting untidiness and uncleanliness to be seen. Even so, the
chief took off the hat, shoes and caftan given to him by my officers upon entering
the first hut, and assured me that no islander may enter the chambers of the ruler
of the Sandwich Islands with outer clothing on. He must wear the girdle or *maro*
[*malo*] alone, with which these people cover their private parts for the sake of
decency.

From the palace, the chief conducted us to the royal temple. It was surrounded by a palisade.* Before its entrance stood an idol representing a deity
worshipped by the islanders. Within the paling and to the left, right by the
entrance to the structure itself, stood six other large idols. We ourselves, said our
escort, could not go into the little building beyond. Even from the outside,
however, we could easily see that there was nothing in it. In front of the
aforementioned palisade was another enclosed spot. There, too, several idols had
been placed. Not knowing these islanders' language, I could get no information
about their beliefs or religious rites. Against my will, therefore, I was obliged to
let my curiosity on that subject rest. The chief accompanying us, not being one of
the noble grandees of the place, could not walk up close to this principal temple.
We, however, continued on our way up to it without him.

The temple lies on an elevation and is surrounded by a palisade of poles.** In
length, it is approximately 10 paces, in width approximately 30. It is rectangular
in shape. On the side nearer the hill adjacent, 15 idols have been erected.[11]
Before them stands an altar[+] built of unfinished poles and looking uncommonly
like a drying-rack for fish. It is to this spot that the islanders bear their sacrificial
offerings. In the course of our inspection of the place, we noted a quantity of
scattered coconuts, plantain, and a small roast pig which had evidently been
brought only recently. To the right of the altar we saw two more small statues
and, not far off, another small altar for another three idols. Facing these, on the
opposite side, were yet more statues, three in number, one of them propped up by
a pole because of its decayed state. And by the sea stood a little house almost
collapsing from neglect or age.

Even as we looked over this scene in its entirety, the chief priest of the place
came up to us.† I put many questions to him through my interpreter, but he by
no means satisfied my curiosity. All I could gather from him was that the 15

---

* *paehumu* [taboo enclosure]
** the *lananu'u* [high frame where *heiau* images were placed] partially or wholly replacing that
bought by Cook as firewood on 3 Feb.1779[10]
[+] *lele*
†The Russian implies that there were other *kâhuna* at Hikiau.

statues wrapped in material from the waist down* represented the gods of war;
that the idols standing to the right of the [main] altar represented the divinity of
spring or the beginning of growth, while those opposite were divinities of
autumn or guardians of the ripeness of crops; and that the small second altar,
which I mentioned above, was dedicated to the god of joy and that, in the appropriate season, the natives made merry and sang before it. It must be confessed that the temples of the Sandwich Islanders can inspire no feelings in the
traveler but regret at their blindness and ignorance. There is neither cleanliness
in them nor even the decent ornamentation proper in such places. Indeed, were it
not for the idols in them which, however, are carved out in the crudest manner,
the passing European might well mistake them for cattle pens.

On leaving this despicable place, we climbed over a low stone wall. The
priest, however, squeezed himself through its gate or, to describe it better, loop-
hole, assuring me that if he dared to follow our example, then, according to their
law, he would lose his life unfailingly. In these islands, there are a great many
such injunctions, all absurd and based on pure barbarism; and the helpless foreigner in his ignorance of them, may sometimes be liable to punishment, albeit
less cruel than that to which the native of the country is subject.

From this temple, we set off back to our ship's boats by a different path, one
that proved to be so thickly strewn with stones that, leaping from one to another,
we pretty nearly broke our legs. We met with and passed many huts, but noticed
only three or four of the so-called bread trees, and even they were in poor condition. The plant used here to dye material red**, conversely, was growing in relative abundance. Of the natives' dwellings, it may broadly be said that dirtiness
and slovenliness were everywhere apparent. Dogs, swine, and hens are more or
less inseparable companions of these islanders, and both sit and eat with them.

We left the shore at about six o'clock. Perhaps a thousand of the natives who,
on the chief's orders, had theretofore remained in their houses, now poured out to
take a look at us. On reaching the ship, I learned that in our absence but few
provisions had been bought.

Right from the early morning of the 14th, however, barter went on advantageously for us. It continued to do so till the local chief's arrival on the
scene, whereupon prices of foodstuffs promptly rose. Suspecting that a certain
islander was responsible for this, I ordered that he should be driven away. He
was; and trade then proceeded as it had earlier. The chief had this time brought
two large hogs with him. He sold them to us for two pieces of clothing that we
had specially prepared as gifts. Besides the hogs, we also bartered for twelve
small pigs and a few fowl; but these cost us quite a bit. Since daybreak a rumor
had been circulating that a large vessel had arrived in Tuvai-Gai [Kawaihae][+]

---

* that is, they were 'girded' [hume].[12]
** probably ama'u or ma'uma'u tree ferns; see p. 135
[+] Kawaihae Bay, 40 miles north

Bay and that, for that reason, Young would not be able to come to see us. I regarded this rumor as a false one, however, by means of which the natives hoped to alarm us and so sell their things to us for higher prices than usual.

On 15 June, trade continued as before, only everytything except birds became more expensive; and Young himself arrived after breakfast. He deeply regretted that, until the previous day, he had heard nothing about our arrival here. Supposing that this had resulted from the chief's indolence, I did not invite him to dinner on this day. The chief immediately felt this, promising not only to help us in our purchases of supplies in future, but also to bring us a very large pig as a gift--in order to make amends for his previous act. Young brought with him six swine, two of which he gave me and for the rest of which he requested one and a half pieces of fine canvas, assuring me that the animals were the king's. As I was un- willing to give him more than one piece of canvas, however, I was unable to pur- chase the extra swine.

After dinner, I set off for Tavaroa [Ka'awaloa] with my officers and with Young, wanting to see the place where Europe had lost her most celebrated mariner, Captain Cook. Right at the spot where we disembarked from the cutter, we saw the stone on which that immortal man had fallen; and shortly afterward, we also saw the hill where, according to the natives, they had burned his corpse. In the cliffs here were many caves, in which the bones of the dead were preserved. Also here was that spot where, since ancient times, the skeletons of the rulers of this island had been placed. The last king, Tairebu [Kalaniopu'u], had been buried there.

In Tavaroa there are nine small temples or, more accurately, enclosures full of idols. The priest attached to them had gone fishing at this particular time, so we could not go into these enclosures. There was no difference between them and the great temple at Karekekua however beyond the fact that they were far smaller. Each temple was dedicated to a particular deity, and belonged to one or other of the local chiefs.

After this, we called on the sister of the chief of Tavaroa [Ka'awaloa], who was himself with the king's army. She was said to be over 90 years old. Young said no more than that a ship's captain had arrived and she seized my hand and tried to kiss it, remarking that, as she had lost her sight, she could not see what I looked like. We found her seated beneath a tree and surrounded by people who, it seemed, were more inclined to mock her great age than to respect it. She said a good deal about her attachment to Europeans, then invited us to enter her house. It differed only in its size from all the other dwellings.

We walked right round the village. Nowhere, from the seashore right up to the hills, did we see any vegetation,[13] the whole area being covered with lava--lava used even to enclose houses in place of the usual stone palisade.[14] Returning to the ship, we found on board two Americans from the United States. One of the two had been on the Northwest Coast of America the previous year and told me of the destruction of our settlement situated in Sitkinskii or Sitka Bay by the natives there.* I regarded this information as probably true, the more so as something of the sort had been asserted even before our departure from Kronstadt, in the Hamburg newspapers.

The following morning, Mr Young returned and let us have the four hogs that he had carried off the day before, now accepting a single bale of sailcloth. For the same price, I bought another four from the local chief. By noon, we had taken on all the supplies that we required and so, after our meal, we began to unmoor. We set sail at about nine o'clock with the land breeze which blows invariably by Ovigi. (In hot climates, there is always a land-breeze at night, if not when the sun disappears beyond the horizon, and a sea-breeze during the day.) We were sorry to find that both anchor cables were somewhat chafed, the forward one particularly, even though we had dropped anchor on a sandy bottom. One must conclude that coral lies beneath the sand...

But we had hardly got under way before we were pretty well becalmed and obliged even to leave the bay under tow. Mr Young parted with us at this juncture, Johnson having gone off in the morning. I presented them both with many useful and necessary articles, also sending a gift to the young chief with whom Johnson lived, since he himself had earlier sent us gifts and had intended to visit the ship but was prevented from doing so by the death of his wife.

By daybreak on the 17th we were six miles from our previous anchorage, and at noon we reckoned ourselves in latitude 19°34'49". The northern cape of Karekekua then bore 67° SE of us, while the western tip of the island bore north 6° west. At six o'clock we were under way again, a light breeze having sprung up; and in due course the island of Move [Maui] appeared opposite the western cape** of Ovigi. So far as I could ascertain, the sea current outside the northern cape of Karekekua Bay prevails toward the northwest. Within the bay itself, however, it runs directly toward the cape in question, so that one must be very careful when near that spot. A sudden lull in the wind might set one on a sandbank. By 3 p.m. the wind had swung round to the northeast and by 7 p.m. it was so strong that we were covering 8 miles each hour. This pleased us considerably. It is not pleasant to battle against fickle airs and the danger of becalmment, especially when near shores where one cannot anchor because of the great depth of water.

On setting sail from Ovigi, I had originally intended to call at the island of Vagu [O'ahu], where the king of Ovigi then was with his whole fleet and army, and to take a look at the Sandwich Islanders' military preparation. A few days might well have been lost for the sake of a matter of slight import but considerable interest. Learning that a contagious disease had broken out on Vagu, however, I resolved to go straight to Otuvai [Kaua'i]. At noon, by our observa-

---

* Tlingit Indians
** Keahole Point

tions, we were in 20°20'N, and 157°42'W. Chronometers 136 and 50 concurred in this.

At five o'clock on the morning of the 19th we spotted the island of Otuvai away to the northwest, and at approximately eight o'clock we passed its southern extremity* and brought to by the shore. Near Veimea [Waimea] Bay, four craft put out to us. One contained five individuals, the others--one man. They brought with them only spears, which, however, my officers duly purchased from them, and a large fan made from the tail feathers of tropical birds.** This fell to my lot. I gave a small knife for it.

The wind continued fresh until we reached the western cape of the island, where we were completely becalmed. The current alone drew us between the islands of Onigu [Ni'ihau] and Otuvai+ till evening fell. By then, however,we had received a visit from the king of these islands, Tamuri [Kaumuali'i].† On boarding, the king at once spoke to us in English, presenting letters of recommendation from sea captains whom he had supplied with fresh provisions. Having read these papers through, I tried to explain to the king that Europeans, fearing to subject themselves to risk in his domain, now called there seldom and stopped unwillingly. On the same basis, I even advised him to earn Europeans' trust by good and honorable behavior as had the ruler of Ovigi, Gammamea [Kamehameha], on whom from ten to eighteen ships now called in the course of one year. In reply, the king assured me that he had truly attempted to win the trust and affection of the Europeans, but that he had had no success: no one visited him .

Learning that we had only recently left the island of Ovigi, the king asked about the general situation there. It was not hard to guess what he was driving at in his curiosity. I told him that Gammamea was on the island of Vagu, whence he would have proceeded to Otuvai even before my own arrival, had he not been prevented from doing so by a disease‡ that was even obliging him to return home++ and abandon all his martial preparations. I saw plainly that my words occasioned great joy in Tamuri who, nevertheless, gave me to understand that he was resolved to defend himself to the last drop of blood against his enemy. On the island of Otuvai, he further assured me, there were up to 30,000 persons, including five Europeans, as well as 40 falconets,+++ three six-pounders, and a considerable number of muskets.

---

*Pû'olo Point

** a *kâhili* [royal standard]; St Petersburg already boasted one such, in the Cook collection of Pacific artifacts (item 505-2 today), obtained at Petropavlovsk-in-Kamchatka in May 1779.[15]

+ north into Kaulakahi Channel

† elsewhere called by the Russians Tomari

‡ known to the Hawaiians as *'ôku'u* (probably cholera)

++ Kamehameha returned to Hawai'i island that month.

+++ swivel guns

With the king, as he boarded us, had come a man bearing a small wooden bowl, a feather fan, and a towel.* Seeing that many human teeth had been set into the bowl, I asked the meaning of it. I was told that the king spat into the bowl, and that the teeth were those of his former friends.** The vessel would seem, however, to have been kept for appearance's sake alone, for the king was meanwhile spitting almost constantly on the deck. I presented him with a woolen blanket and various trifles, but he then asked persistently for bar-iron and paint, observing to us that he was building a large vessel. I was obliged to refuse these requests. And so our guest went back to the shore, having drained two glasses of grog. The king did not differ in the least from the other islanders in the color of his skin, but was portlier than most of them.

While the king remained on the ship, a native craft overturned. The two paddlers responsible for it showed such agility that it was immediately righted. They also caught hold of every article that had been upset. Such occurrences are common here, even out at sea.

At two o'clock on the morning of the 20th, a wind sprang up from the northeast. By sunrise it was so high that Otuvai, bearing 65° SE of us, was already 20 miles distant. At about six o'clock we suddenly lost it from view... It was my intention now to steer a course for Unalashka [Unalaska] Island, then to make for Kad'iak [Kodiak].

The island of Otuvai is mountainous and in clear weather must be visible from far off. Its western shore, by which we passed close, is populated and has a pleasant appearance. Near the sea, the land is low-lying, but it rises steadily toward the interior. It seemed to me that the houses of this island were better than the Ovigian ones. Every structure was surrounded by trees, moreover. It is only to be regretted that there is no good harbor there, Veimea being open to all winds but easterlies.

Onigu Island lies to the west of Otuvai. Though it is not large, it is very high. It has two adjacent islets, one on its north side [Lehua], the other to its south [Ka'ula]. Various rootcrops, sweet potatoes and other sorts of vegetation grow there in intentional abundance: European ships may provision there more than adequately.

In conclusion, I must give their due to the inhabitants of the Sandwich Islands, and especially to those of Karekekua where we stood at anchor six days. Though constantly surrounded by native craft, we never had the least cause for dissatisfaction. Every islander who came to barter his goods with us might tend to remain from sunrise to sunset, but all was quietly and peacefully done. In a word, none of us found anything in them but integrity.[17]

---

* Kaumuali'i's *Kâhili* bearer (*pa'a kâhili*) also carried an *ipu 'aina* and a large piece of *kapa* [bark cloth][16]
** traditionally, those of enemies were supposedly used

A Description of the Sandwich Islands, and of Ovigi in Particular

The Sandwich Islands were discovered by Captain Cook in 1778. In the opinion of some, they were known to Spain as early as 1542; but the Spaniards [it is said], then concerned only to discover precious metals, thought it necessary to conceal their true position from the world. It is indisputable, at all events, that Europe had no information whatsoever about this important archipelago until the close of the eighteenth century...

At the time of its discovery by Captain Cook, the archipelago belonged to three separate rulers. Now, however, it is divided into two principal possessions, the first consisting of the islands of Otuvai,* Origoa [Lehua] and Tagura [Ka'ula],** the second of the other islands lying further south. Otuvai is now ruled by Tamuri, Ovigi by Gammamea. (Many call him Tomeomeo, Komeomeo, or Taamama, but all these are incorrect.)

According to all the information that I could gather, Gammamea is held to be a man of rare abilities and extremely brave. Since the very time of his acquisition of authority over the islands that belong to him, he has in every way tried to merit the trust of Europeans. For this reason ships call at his islands not only without the least danger but in full expectation of being kindly received and supplied with all necessary things for seafaring. His conduct has also brought great benefit to himself, for arriving European ships furnish him with many things, some useful, others essential for his society. As for his militia,+ it has been brought to such a state that it may be regarded as invincible by South Sea Islanders.

Up to ten years ago, iron was so rare on Ovigi that a small piece of it was held to be the best possible gift. Today, however, no one there will deign to look at it. In the interval, Gammamea has managed to build up a small arsenal. He has as many as fifty Europeans with him, who partly act as his Council, partly direct his forces. The United States of America supply him with cannon, falconets, firearms and other sorts of weaponry, so all such things have ceased to be wonderful for the islanders.

The Sandwich Island kings have autocratic power. Their possessions are considered hereditary, indeed; but it seldom happens that, on the death of a king, the most powerful islander does not pretend to the throne. Gammamea himself came into his authority in a violent fashion on the death of Tairebu [Kalani'opu'u]. Initially, he shared power on Ovigi with the king's son [Kiwala'o]. Later, he seized the entire island for himself. After the king, the largest authority in these islands is that of the chiefs, or *nui-nui-eiry* [*nuinui ali'i*],[20] some of whom are so powerful that they hardly yield place to their own sovereigns.

---

*probably a fairly accurate reflection of the local Hawaiian pronunciation[18]
**Cook's Orre'houa and Otaoora[19] Lisianskii omits Ni'ihau from this list.
+or, his forces (Russian: *voisko*)

The military force of the kingdom consists of all islanders able to bear arms. Every Sandwich Islander is trained for martial feats from his earliest youth on. On launching a campaign, the king may instruct all or only some of the *nui-nui-eiry* (grandees) to follow him with their subjects. But besides this militia, so to speak, the king also maintains a small guard [*papa kaua*]. Formed of the most skillful warriors, it is always by his person.[21] With the aid of Europeans, Gammamea has also built himself several schooners weighing between 10 and 30 tons, and has armed them with falconets.

Inasmuch as there are no established laws here and the natives have no conception of law, force has replaced it. At his merest caprice, the king may take the life of every islander subject to him; and the same degree of power is enjoyed by every chief in the district governed by him. If these princelings argue among themselves, they either settle the dispute without reference to anyone else or, on occasion, complain to the king of insults offered them. The latter's usual decree is, "let the argument be ended by arms." Should any *nui-nui-eiry* affront the king, however, the latter sends his guard either to kill the offender or to bring him to the royal presence. In the event of disobedience, and supposing the offender to be strong and with many adherents, civil war is inevitable.

To give some indication of the morals of the natives of these islands, it will suffice to adduce two events that occurred while Mr Young was on Ovigi. A certain islander ate a coconut at a forbidden or *tapu* time, for which the penalty was death. On hearing of so strange a way of managing things and wishing to save the unfortunate's life, one of the Europeans asked the king to pardon him. The king heard the European's representation out with great attention, but replied that, since Ovigi is not Europe, there are naturally also differences in punishments. The guilty party was killed. A second example: the king gave Young some land, with a certain number of people on it. In one of the families was a boy everyone liked. The boy's father argued with the mother and decided to divorce her. There was then contention as to who would keep the boy. The father absolutely insisted that he remain with him, and the mother wanted to take him away with her. In the end, the father grabbed the boy by the neck and by a leg and broke his back across his knee. The unfortunate child died in consequence. Hearing of this barbarous deed, Young complained to the king and sought punishment for the murderer. The king asked Young whose son the boy was. Hearing that he had belonged to his murderer, the king said that "as the father harmed nobody else, on killing his own son, he was not liable to punishment." He added to Young, however, that the latter had complete dominion over his own subjects and, if he wished, might take the life of the man of whom he complained. From these two instances one may judge of the Sandwich Islanders' morals in general. What would be considered the slightest transgression anywhere in Europe is punished by death on the island of Ovigi. On the other hand, a cruel and barbaric act is left unnoticed, or is sometimes even considered just.

All civil and religious decrees here are subsumed by *tapu* [*kapu*]. The word itself has various meanings, but properly speaking it signifies a prohibition. The king is free to place a *tapu* on anything he pleases; there are, however, instances of *tapu* that he himself is absolutely bound to observe. These were established in ancient times and are observed with respect and with the greatest punctiliousness. The principal *tapu* is that called *makagiti* [*makahiki*], which is also the twelfth month of the year. Besides this, there are four *tapus* in every month except *oitua* [*'Ikuwâ*], the eleventh.* The first, which falls on the first day, is called *ogiro* [*Hilo*]; the second, on the twelfth of the month, is *mugaru* [*Môhalu*]; the third, on the 23rd, *orepau* [*'Olepau*]; and the fourth, on the 27th, *okane* [*Kâne*].** *Ogiro* lasts two days and three nights, the others last one day and two nights. These periods of *tapu* might be considered as religious. All others are civil or temporal, and depend on the will of the king, who announces them to the people through priests.

The *tapu* called *makagiti* resembles our yuletide.+ The people spend a whole month in various amusements such as singing, games, and mock battles. The king must open this festival, wherever he may be. Before sunrise he puts on a rich cloak--a garment or shawl decorated with red and yellow feathers, a precise description of which has already appeared in a number of voyagers' accounts. With several craft or, sometimes, in a single craft he then sets out from the shore and is so steered as to touch the shore again as the sun rises.† One of the strongest and most skillful warriors is appointed to meet the king as he lands. This warrior follows the king's craft, moving along the shore then, as soon as the craft touches and the king has thrown off his cloak, hurls a spear at his sovereign from a distance not more than thirty paces. The king must either catch the spear or be killed--for in all this, they say, there is no jesting. Seizing the spear, the king turns it around so that the blunt end is uppermost and, holding it under his arm, continues on his way into the *geiava*‡ or principal temple of the gods. This serves as a sign to the people for the festivities to commence. Sham battle breaks out suddenly and everywhere, and the air is instantly filled with flying spears made with blunt ends [*kânekupua*] expressly for the occasion. All punishments cease for as long as *makagiti* lasts. So strictly are these customs observed that, even should a person decide to attack some outlying district of the kingdom or a territory belonging to one or other of the grandees, none of the latter would be able to leave the place where he was passing the festival. Some have advised the present king to abolish this festival, observing that he is at present obliged to ex-

---

*Lisianskii's sources were unreliable. Observance of makahiki began on Hawai'i Island in the month of 'Ikuwâ--the 12th.

**Lisianskii was given the names of days (*Hilo, Môhalu, 'Olepau, Kâne*) not the corresponding *kapu*.[22]

+ Makahiki was, in fact, a long series of ceremonies involving *kapu*.

† *kâli'i* ceremony[23]

‡ This appears to be an attempt at *heiau*.

pose his life to danger annually without the least benefit. Gammamea has replied with haughtiness that he is quite as able to catch a spear as the most skillful of his subjects is to cast one, and consequently he has nothing to fear.

Time is divided in the following manner in the Sandwich Islands. One year consists of twelve months, and each month of thirty days. The days are divided, in turn, not into hours but into parts: sunrise, noon, sunset; the time between sunrise and noon is split into two, as is the time between noon and sunset. The Ovigian year begins with our November. Their first month is called *Makagiti* [*Makali'i*], their second, *Kaero* [*Kā'elo*]; the third, *Okaurua* [*Kaulua*]; the fourth, *Onana [Nana]*; the fifth, *Oero* [*Welo*]; the sixth, *Oikiki* [*Ikiiki*]; the seventh, *Kaona* [*Ka'aôna*]; the eighth, *Goineery* [*Hinaia'ele'ele*]; the ninth, *Ogirinegu* [*Hilinaehu*]; the tenth, *Ogirinima* [*Hilinamâ*]; the eleventh, *Oitua* [*'Ikuwâ*]; and the twelfth, *Makagiti* again.* The names of the days of each month are these. The first, *Ogiro* [*Hilo*]; 2nd, *Goaka* [*Hoaka*]; 3rd, *Kugagi* [*Kukâhi*]; 4th, *Turua* [*Kulua*]; 5th, *Tukoru* [*Kukolu*]; 6th, *Kupau*; 7th, *Orikukage* [*'Olekukâhi*]; 8th, *Orikuruga* [*'Olekulua*]; 9th, *Orikukoru* [*'Olekukolu*]; 10th, *Oripau* [*'Olepau*]; 11th, *Guna* [*Huna*]; 12th, *Mugaru* [*Môhalu*]; 13th, *Gua* [*Hua*]; 14th, *Oatua* [*Akua*]; 15th, *Gotu* [*Hoku*]; 16th, *Magearona* [*Mahealani*]; 17th, *Turu* [*Kulua*]; 18th, *Rao-kukage* [*La'au Kukâhi*]; 19th, *Raa-kuruga* [*La'au Kulua*]; 20th, *Raa-opau* [*La'aupau*]; 21st, *Ore-kukage* [*'Olekukâhi*]; 22nd, *Ore-kuruga* [*'Olekulua*]; 23rd, *Ore-pau* [*'Olepau* or *'Olekupau*]; 24th, *Karo-kukage* [*Kâloakukâhi*]; 25th, *Karo-kuruga* [*Kâloakulua*]; 26th, *Karo-pau* [*Kâloapau*]; 27th, *Okane* [*Kâne*], 28th, *Ronu* [*Lono*]; 29th, *Mouru* [*Mauli*]; 30th, *Omuku* [*Muku*].

Natives of the Sandwich Islands recognize the existence of good and evil. They believe that after death they will have a better life. Their temples are full of idols as were those of pagans in antiquity. Some of these idols represent the deity of war, others the deity of peace, others again the spirits of gaiety and merriment, etc. Fruits, swine and dogs are brought as sacrifice; the natives slaughter their own kind in honor of the gods only when they are prisoners or disturbers of the general peace and opponents of the government.[24] Human sacrifice has thus more of a political than a religious nature. The local priests are prepared for their calling right from infancy and, in times of *tapu*, give directions to the people. There is also a special sect here whose adherents claim that, through prayer, they can obtain from the gods the power to kill whomsoever they choose. This absurd sect is called *kogunaanana* [*kâhuna 'anâ'anâ*] and, it would seem, its members too are trained from their earliest years in numerous ruses and deceptions. When one of them takes it into his head to make such a godless prayer, he lets the object of his evil wish know of it, by hearsay. And this poor fellow, because of his

---

*actually *Welehu*. The preceding list tallies quite well with those of W.D. Alexander and other, native, authorities, if one removes the initial 'o' and replaces 'r' with 'l'. Only *Goineery* is barely recognizable as an attempt at *Hinaia'ele'ele*.

blind superstition (which is almost without limits among the Sandwich Islanders), comes to hear of the prayer for his ruin and loses his mind, wastes away, or kills himself. It is true that relations of the unhappy man who has been driven to suicide have the right to hire a member of the aforementioned fraternity so that, through his prayer, the evil act may be avenged. It has never yet happened, however, that a single one of the associates in question has lost his life because of this, or has even gone mad.

The *geiava* [*heiau*] or temple of the Sandwich Islanders is nothing more than an open rectangular space fenced in by paling or spears, with a semicircle of statues by a little raised platform [*kîpapa nu'u*]²⁵ at one end. Before the cluster of idols stands an altar, also made of poles. And there are idols along the sides of the palisade, also representing various gods. A large statue usually stands at the temple entrance. In general, it may be said of Sandwich Island places of worship that there is nothing to be seen in them but extreme disorder and filth. The idols are fashioned in the crudest way, with no sense of proportion: many show a head three times as big as the torso, which is left like a pillar. Some have no tongue, others have tongues--many more than is natural. Yet others have carved blocks set on their heads,²⁶ or mouths extended beyond the ears.²⁷ In brief, the Sandwich Island deities look like bogeys and can inspire only loathing in an enlightened person.

As was mentioned above, these islanders bring disturbers of the peace and prisoners to their idols as sacrifices. This barbarous offering of sacrifices takes the following form: if the victim is of high birth, between six and twenty of his confederates are killed with him, depending on his rank. A special altar is prepared for the occasion in the large temple, and is covered with coconuts, plantains, and tubers. The corpses are first scorched, then placed on the foodstuffs, the principal victim in the center and his comrades and assistants on both sides of him, feet toward the chief god of war, a little distance apart from each other. Swine and dogs are then placed in the gaps. So they remain until such time as the flesh has rotted away. Then their heads are put on the temple palisade* and their bones put in a specially prepared spot. It was the chief priest of the great temple at Karekekua who told me all this, through our interpreter. Mr Young, however, assured me that the account was not accurate. According to him, special altars were never prepared everywhere for such occasions: the bodies, he said, are simply placed face down on the ground, heads facing the idols and with arms across each other's backs. The corpses are not scorched,** he added, nor are dogs sacrificed except when the prayers being offered to the idols concern women: for in the Sandwich Islands, dogs belong rather to members of the female sex than to men. Young also informed me that when this rite of sacrifice

---

*to become *po'o kea* [ash colored]
**as *môhai kuni* [burnt offering]

is over, a *tapu* is placed [on the temple]. It is apparently called *gaikanaka** and lasts ten days,[28] at the end of which period the heads of the victims are cut off and stuck on the temple fencing and the arm- and leg-bones and ribs are placed in their special spot, the rest being burned. I cannot say which of the two accounts is the more accurate. One would suppose that Young, having lived a long time amongst the islanders, would be able to get a clear idea of their procedures of sacrificial offering.

As for funerals on the island of Ovigi, they are conducted as among us, in general with less pomp but depending on the rank or position of the parties. The poor are wrapped in simple material and buried by the shore or in the hills. The legs of the corpse are bent in such a way that the heels and the spine touch.[29] The wealthy and noble, on the other hand, are dressed in rich apparel and put in a coffin or tomb, stretched out with the arms on the belly. The corpse is then left in a little house, which is expressly built for the purpose, until it has wasted entirely. The bones are only then collected and placed in a special spot.** In honor of a deceased grandee, as many as six of his most beloved subjects may be killed. The most savage and inhuman rites of all, however, take place on the death of a king. On the first two days after the death, two men are killed per day. Then a little house is built to hold the king's corpse, dressed in the most magnificent way possible on the island; and while this house is being constructed, two more men are slaughtered. Once the royal corpse has rotted away, another structure is prepared, and another two men lose their lives. The king's bones are carried to this second resting-place and dressed anew. The first apparel is allowed to rot with the flesh. After some time has elapsed, a temple[+] is built in the late king's honor, and four more men are sacrificed. When brought to this last place, the king's bones are arranged as though he were sitting, or else put in the fetal position. Lastly, the bones are dressed for a third time--and left forever. On the death of a king, all his subjects go naked and give themselves up to debauchery for a whole month. For so long as this period lasts, a man may demand whatever he wishes from any woman, nor does any woman, not even the queen herself, dare to refuse his demands. Similar absurdity prevails on the death of a local grandee in these islands, only not so long and only within the territory of the deceased. I learned the above details from the aforementioned priest, but, again, Young found much to be incorrect. Young asserted: 1) that there are no tombs whatsoever on the Sandwich Islands[†] and that, bones having been removed from the arms, legs and belly, the rest are generally burned with a corpse's flesh; 2)

---

* actually, the word *haikanaka* means the offering of human sacrifice: (*hai*=offering, sacrifice; *kanaka*=person, human)
** *i.e.*, secret, the corpse becoming *hûnâkele* [hidden in secret]
[+] a shrine [*hale poki*]
†Young and Lisianskii may have had a failure of communication here: there were indeed no *coffins* [*grobov nikakikh net*] and Young may well have meant coffins, not graves.[30]

that the consorting of men with women lasts a few days only, although young
people sometimes enjoy themselves longer; and 3) that, on the death of a king or
grandee, suicide is voluntary and is committed by those who have sworn to die
with the deceased while he was still living. These persons, said Young, live better than other subjects. Which of these views is the more correct, I cannot say,
not having myself witnessed the rites in question. I did, however, note a certain
inconsistency in the priest's account of the royal funeral. According to the priest,
the bones of every deceased ruler must be left forever in a *geiava* or other temple
specially built for the purpose; but I was shown a cave in a rockface where rested
the bones of the local kings up to and including the late Tairebu.* Possibly, the
bones are transported there after a certain time has elapsed. Possibly, a special
place is prepared for each deceased ruler inside the cave itself and called a
geiava. Grief is expressed, at all events, by the knocking out of front-teeth, the
cutting of hair, and the scratching of the body in various parts until blood is
drawn. On the death of a grandee, each of his subjects knocks out one of his
front teeth. Should a man outlive many masters, he would ultimately lose all his
teeth! Strange though it is, and introduced to Ovigi not so long ago, this custom
is observed with great faithfulness.[31]

The Sandwich Islanders are of medium height and are light chestnut in color.
Their countenances are various, but many of the men look like Europeans. The
women generally have round faces. The nose is nearly always flattish and the
eyes very dark. What is more remarkable, though, is the extent to which they
resemble each other. The hair is black, coarse and straight in both sexes. Men
cut their hair in various ways, but the commonest look is that of the Roman helmet.[32] Women, on the other hand, cut their hair quite close, leaving a ridge
about an inch and a half long sticking up in front. They smear this ridge every
day, after dinner, with a sort of lime obtained from coral: it produces a light yellow coloring. The men sometimes do almost exactly the same thing with the hair
that forms the crest, as it were, of their helmet. On seeing the effect, one might
almost think that these islanders have two-toned hair from birth. Unlike nearly
all the other islanders of this ocean, the Sandwich Islanders do not smear anything onto their body and do not pierce their ears. I noted earrings only on the
king of Otuvai. However, they do wear arm bracelets made from sea elephant or
some other kind of bone; and the women sometimes decorate their heads with
wreaths made of flowers or multicolored threads unravelled from the cloth that
they get from Europeans. As regards other clothing, it consists of a piece of
material some 4 1/2 *arshin* long and half an *arshin* wide or a little more.** Men
use it as a girdle, while women wrap themselves in it or, in cold weather, put a
rectangular piece of thick stuff, folded several times, round their shoulders. This
serves them in place of our fur coat. In normal times the rich and the poor dress

* the Pali Kapu o Keôua, at Ka'awaloa
** 10'6" by 15"

alike, but at feasts or on other special occasions the former don the feather cloaks which, taken together with helmet and fan, would certainly make a splendid spectacle even in a European theatre. At the same time, though, these people are very fond of European clothes. Worn shirts, jerseys or jackets may very advantageously be bartered for their fresh provisions and other goods. We let them have clothing that was so threadbare as to be of no further use to us and they were delighted with it, many of them coming out to the ship wearing our cast-off garments. Many of the navigators who preceded us have asserted that the Sandwich Islanders are too prone to thievery. If they were, they seem now to have abandoned that tendency. I, certainly, observed nothing of the sort alleged, and, though we only allowed them onto *Neva* a few at a time, they could no doubt have stolen something or other. Every day, as many as a thousand individuals came to trade with us,* but we experienced nothing but honesty.

It must be said, however, that the absence of one vice was replaced by another: the natives were the worst of profiteers. By general agreement, they would firmly maintain the price of any ware that one of them had sold us. And should one man happen to make a good sale, it was known in all the craft around. At once, all demanded the same price for a similar article. Iron, which was once held in great esteem here, is now worth almost nothing,[34] though the islanders will still take it quite willingly in the form of bars. During our own stay, the most wanted goods were simple canvas,** printed cloth, scissors, little knives with pretty handles, and mirrors. For the pieces of iron hoop that secured us six or ten coconuts or two bunches of bananas on the island of Nuku Giva, we could get only the most insignificant objects at Karekekua. Ovigi has indeed changed greatly over the past ten years, everything now being far more expensive than earlier, as the appended price list shows. The prevalence of these high prices must certainly be attributed to the United States vessels, as many as eighteen of which sometimes call in a single summer to take on all the provisions needed for the remainder of their voyages.

Price List of Purchases

4 large hogs cost	1 bale of fine canvas
3 ditto	1 1/2 iron-bars
1 medium-sized hog	2 axes
1 small pig	1 axe
1 suckling-pig	1 piece of printed linen, 4 1/2 arshin in length
6 to 8 bunches, sweet potato	the same, cut into strips
1 hen	1 penknife or pair of scissors

* Kealakekua Bay's population had dropped since 1778-79.[33]
** or broadcloth

I found the Sandwich Island houses displeasing in comparison with those of the Markizskie [Marquesas] Islands. They seemed to me unsuited to the climate and, indeed, rather resemble our peasant barns, with the difference that the roofs are higher and the sides much lower. Rarely do they have windows, and if they do, they are tiny. Most are built with a single door only, with a frame as round our dormer windows, through which one can barely crawl. The ground is strewn with dry grass; bast [woody fiber] matting is placed on the grass. The rich have up to six huts or shanties built one beside the other, each with its own name, such as sleeping quarters, dining room, women's quarters, quarters for manservants or maidservants, kitchen. They are built on stone foundations and surrounded by a low palisade. The latter has usually been broken in many places by swine or dogs.

The Sandwich Islanders' diet consists of swine and dog meat, fish, fowl, coconuts, sweet potato, bananas, taro, and yams. Sometimes they eat fish raw; but everything else they bake. The women are forbidden pork, coconuts, and bananas. The men may eat anything. They do not kill swine with a knife but stifle them by tying a rope round the snout. The animal is prepared for eating as follows. A hole is dug. One or two rows of stones are placed in it and a fire is lit on them (fire is obtained by friction). More stones are so positioned that the air can freely circulate around them. When the stones are very hot, they are spread out evenly and covered with a thin layer of leaves or reeds. The beast is placed on it and turned over until all the bristles have disappeared. If any hairs still remain, they are scraped off with knives or shells. Having thus cleaned the carcass, the natives next open up the belly and remove the viscera while the fire is laid again. As soon as the stones are hot in the pit again, they take them out, leaving one layer only, on which they duly spread leaves and then the hog. Hot stones wrapped in leaves are put into the disembowelled beast, which is covered over with leaves and more hot stones. Sand or earth is finally scattered on top. The animal is thus left until baked. Tubers are prepared in the same manner, with the difference, however, that water is poured over them before they are covered with hot stones.

Nobles or *eiry* [*ali'i*] may not make use of fire that has been produced by the common people, but must make their own. They may not only take fire from others of their own rank, however, but may also prepare their own food on other nobles' fire. I do not know if the commonalty are permitted to borrow fire from their master. I was told that it sometimes happens.

With regard to the eating of food by women, a most odd custom is observed here. Not only are women forbidden to eat in a house where a man is eating; they may not even enter that house. A man may be in a female dining place, but may not touch food. Outdoors, in the fields or on a craft for example, the sexes may eat together unless the food be a pudding made from taro roots.*

---

* the doughlike *pa'i 'ai*

The Sandwich Islanders use salt and are very fond of salted fish and meat. They also prepare little balls of taro-root flour,* for consumption on long journeys. By soaking these in fresh or salt water, they produce something rather like meal dough.

On these islands there are no marriage rites whatever. If a man and woman like each other, they live together until they fall out. In the event of dissatisfaction of any sort, they simply separate without the slightest reference to the government. Each islander may have as many wives as he can maintain, but it is usual for the king to have three, nobles two, and ordinary natives one.** Priests have the same right with regard to wives. All the same, the Sandwich Islanders are extremely jealous unless they are dealing with Europeans.

So far as we could tell, the natives of the Sandwich Islands are pretty intelligent and respect European ways. Many of them speak English quite passably. All, without exception, know a few English words and pronounce them in their own fashion, that is, incorrectly. They would seem to be very fond of travel: many asked me to take them with me, and not only demanded no pay but would have surrendered all their movable property. Young assured me that United States vessels quite frequently carry islanders away, and that the latter in time become good sailors. All in all, it seems likely that the Sandwich Islanders will be completely changed within a little time, especially if the reign of their present king continues a few years more.   One of the king's sons[+] has rare gifts. Nominated to the succession and receiving a European education, it will not be hard for that son to accelerate the civilizing of his own fatherland. He will need to strengthen his position through the common people, who are very attached to their rulers, and so eliminate opposition on the part of local grandees or the *nui-nui-eiry* and other important chiefs. For they alone, with their own advantage in mind, may decide to stand against the new order.

The Sandwich Islanders occupy a country that, given a little industry, could bring them huge profits. They have wood enough, and some of it is suitable for the construction of small vessels. Sugar cane alone, which grows in great abundance and without the slightest supervision, might give them huge wealth if they saw fit to turn it into sugar or rum. Both products, after all, are now sold on the coasts of America in great quantity. The Islands' main disadvantage is simply the fact that not one of them has a harbor sheltered from all winds. There are, however, bays in which ships might anchor more securely than Teneriffe or Madeira.[†] The people themselves appear to have considerable taste and ability, and their skill in the making of cloth exceeds what may be readily imagined. On

---

* *'ai pa'a.* Dried baked taro or sweet potato, known as '*ao*, was also used thus.
** In fact, these practices were not regularized, as is suggested here.
[+] the future Kamehameha II
† Some time after writing this, I learned from the skipper of the Boston ship *O'Cain* that the island of Vagu has an excellent harbor, sheltered from all winds. – Lisiansikii

first seeing them, I could not believe that savages could be possessed of such elegant taste. The color combinations and artistry of design, taken in conjunction with the strictest observance of proportion, would bring fame to a maker even in Europe. And all is the more remarkable when one bears in mind these rare and wonderful things are produced with the simplest of implements.

The Islanders make their cloth from the tree known to European botanists as *Morus papyrifera,* and in the following manner. When bark is stripped from the tree, the bast is separated, split up into little pieces like shavings,* and soaked in water until they start to rot. In that state they are beaten on a rectangular board [*kua*].** As a result, the stringy pieces combine to form a flat, fine material which may later be dyed with coloring substances obtained from roots and berries.[35] Stripes and other patterns are painted on by a narrow bamboo stick, one end of which has been split. It falls to the female sex to prepare these cloths and to paint designs on them, which they do with the aid of various round and rectangular blocks [*i'e kuku*].[+] Each face of these blocks is carved in a particular way. For example, there might be narrow stripes on one side, thicker stripes on the other. A third might have checks, a fourth snaking lines, and so forth.

The Reign of Gammamea

On the death of King Tairebu, there was a time of troubles on the island of Ovigi. The consequence was that the late king's dominions were divided between his son, Kiauva [Kiwala'o], and a relation, Gammamea. As war had long subsisted between Ovigi and the islands lying to its north, Gammamea, having first brought his domestic affairs into proper order, set out in 1791 against King Gaikeri [Kahekili], who then ruled Vagu [O'ahu], Morekai [Moloka'i], Renai [Lâna'i], and Move [Maui]. He went with 2,000 canoes and 8,000 warriors. He first attacked Move, as the principal dwelling place of his enemy; and the latter, after several bloody engagements, was forced to submit to the stronger man. On the surrender of Move, the Ovigian horde moved against Morekai and Renai, which were similarly subdued after stubborn opposition. At the beginning of the year 1792, just as he was preparing to put his further martial objects into effect, Gammamea had news that Kiauva had fallen on his own possessions. That very moment, he knocked out several of his own front teeth and set off for Ovigi with all his forces. The defeated Gaikeri, who had gone to Vagu, took advantage of his recent conqueror's absence and moved back to Move, regaining what he had lost.

---

* This is incorrect.
** *kapa* anvil
[+] Some confusion is implicit here as beaters ('blocks') were not used for painting; rather, they produced an imprinted 'watermark' design. Lisianskii took at least one such second-stage beater back to St Petersburg. It is item 750-2 in the '1804 Hawaiian Collection' in Leningrad: see Part 4 below.

On landing at Tovai-Gai [Kawaihae] Bay, Gammamea found his opponent alarmed by so sudden and unexpected a return. That opponent, indeed, withdrew into his possessions; but Gammamea chased after him and, after a few minor engagements, triumphed by means of a stratagem. He spread a rumor that he wished to end the war and return to his own possessions in order to build a temple to the gods. Kiauva's troops believed it and relaxed all vigilance. Gammamea naturally took full advantage of such negligence, falling on his enemy with tremendous energy and completely routing him. Kiauva himself barely escaped with his life, and the conqueror ordered a number of the dead or captured nobles to be sacrificed to the gods. Military operations ceased shortly after this because of the start of the *tapu makagiti,* but as soon as it ended Gammamea split his forces into two divisions, giving command of one of them to the brave Taiana [Kaiana]* and setting out on campaign himself with the other. Kiauva had not been idle, meanwhile, but had gathered all his forces together and resolved to defend that part of his patrimony which remained his. But nothing could counteract the valor of his opponent. An unhappy and sanguinary campaign lasted until the beginning of 1794 when, seeing himself perfectly impotent, Kiauva was forced to give himself up. He did not live long thereafter. Gammamea ordered that he should be brought to Tovai-Gai, where he was then residing, apparently with the intention of reaching some reconciliation; but the unhappy prince no sooner approached the shore than the victor's furious troops suddenly set upon him. He and all those with him were killed, and Gammamea thus became sole ruler of the whole of Ovigi.

Such was the position in the Islands when Captain Vancouver arrived there. Hearing that the natives lived in a constant state of enmity, the captain tried all means to bring about a reconciliation. He flattered himself, indeed, with having succeeded in so laudable a matter; but his ships had hardly disappeared from view before the enemies of quiet and of harmony were once again committing their pernicious acts. The natives of Move, it is said, stole some Ovigians and, having sacrificed them to their gods, angered Gammamea. It seems more likely to me, however, that the latter had simply become far more powerful than earlier and now reached the firm decision to possess himself of his neighbors' dominions. The news came, at all events, that Haikeri had died and that his son Traitshepur [Kalanikupule] had quarreled with his uncle, the ruler of Otuvai.** At once Gammamea ordered his army together.[36] It now included eight Europeans. Having mounted swivel guns on the schooner built by Captain Vancouver and taken aboard three bronze three-pounders, he set out on campaign. (The cannon in question had belonged to the schooner "Fair American", which the islanders had seized in 1791; everyone aboard her had been killed except one

---

* whom Meares had taken to Canton in 1789
** Ka'eokulani, Kaumuali'i's father

Devis [Davis],* who is still living on the Islands today. He and Young won Gammamea's full confidence, and one or other of them is always with him.)

War again began on the island of Move; but this time neither Move itself nor the other islands showed the same stiff resistance as before, and all but Vagu were soon taken. And Vagu too fell, in 1795 and on the death of Taiana, of whom a good deal has been written in accounts of voyages preceding ours. In the end, this brave man had turned traitor against his king. On setting out against Vagu, Gammamea ordered Taiana to follow him with his division of troops, but instead of doing so, Taiana landed his forces in another spot and joined up with Traitshepur. Gammamea reached the arranged shore and awaited his captain, supposing him still at sea. Suddenly, he saw him armed and standing against him. Such an occurrence would have shaken most, but the valiant Gammamea quickly decided to attack the rebel. After a bloody battle, he defeated him. Young told me that he himself had been only a few paces away from Taiana and witnessed the fall of that Ovigian Hercules. The whole point of the spear that had pierced him protruded from his back. After the conflict, this unhappy man and many of his comrades too were sacrificed and their heads stuck on the paling of a temple.

In 1796, Gammamea was obliged to go to Ovigi to quell a rising fomented by a brother of the late Taiana, Chief Namatagi [Namakeha]. He remained on that island about a year, before returning to Vagu in order to make ready for a campaign against Otuvai.

According to Mr Young, Gammamea has approximately 7,000 troops and 50 armed Europeans with him. He also has seven four-pound cannon, five three-pounders, and one six-pounder, forty falconets, six small mortars, and as many as 600 hand guns; nor does he lack powder or other military supplies. As for his naval forces, they consist of the usual native craft plus twenty-one** schooners, of ten to thirty tons burthen, which are commanded by Europeans and armed with swivel guns in case of need.

It had been Gammamea's intention to move against his foe with all these forces the spring previous to our arrival, but a disease then raging deprived him of many of his Ovigian warriors on the island of Vagu, and prevented him from doing so. While we were at Ovigi, many of the islanders were of the opinion that, postponing his expedition against Otuvai, he would soon be returning to Ovigi, where his presence was seriously needed. (Left without supervision in the absence of their king and all his principal chiefs, the people there had become so idle that the land was producing nothing like what it previously had.) It had evidently been part of Gammamea's policy to take all the *nui-nui-eiry* with him, leaving Young alone to govern the island. Since the latter is an important per-

---

* Isaac Davis
** The Russian texts differ over the number of Kamehameha's schooners. This is the highest estimate, but dates from 1807 or later, not 1804.

sonage on Ovigi, the reader will not object to my saying a few words about him.[37]

Young was formerly boatswain in a United States vessel which, in 1791, called at Ovigi for fresh provisions. The captain gave him permission to spend a night ashore, observing that he would be weighing anchor in the night and that Young should be by the harbor in the morning. Young heard a cannon-shot at dawn and accordingly went to the shore; but on reaching it, he discovered that a *tapu* had been placed on all native craft. He wished to put out in one craft notwithstanding the ban; but the king told him that such insolence would cost him his life. The following day, he might take whatever craft he liked. Young was forced to accept the situation. But the next day the king heard that the schooner "Fair American", commanded by the son of Young's captain, had been captured on the north shore of the island and all aboard her save Davis killed. The news obliged the islanders to keep Young among themselves, but the king gave his word that Young might depart whither he wished on the first European vessel that put in. Young's own ship had meanwhile departed without waiting for her boatswain. Each of the native noblemen, wishing to console him, gave him a plot of land. As a result, he was suddenly rich; and he soon won the respect of king and people alike by his conduct. Since then, he has taken part in many battles. He has now been left on Ovigi and fulfills the duties of a viceroy.

Ovigi is the largest of all the Sandwich Islands, stretching 80 miles from north to south and almost as many from east to west. Its shores are precipitous in many places. At other points, however, they slope up gently. Rising little by little toward the interior of the island, the land culminates in mountains: Roa [Loa], Kau [Kea], and Vororai [Hualâlai], the first being 18,000 feet high; such, at least, is the measurement mentioned in Captain Cook's third *Voyage*. Judging by the lava and other inflammable substances that are everywhere on the shores of Ovigi, the island at one time contained great subterranean fires. Even now, the natives say, there is between the island's eastern cape and Mount Roa [Mauna Loa] an aperture which belches fire, known locally as Taura-Peri [Ka'ula Pele?]. And Young told me that three years previously [1801], Mount Makaura [Makahuna], lying on the west side of the island near Tovai-Gai Bay, threw up sufficient lava to fill in a small bay at its base, destroying a number of settlements. Since then, however, it had quietened down again. Only the aperture remained.

Though the shores of Ovigi promise nothing special and are populated solely with a view to fishing and trade with ships that may arrive, the interior is extremely fertile. It is peopled with farmers who provision foreign ships with the surplus of their labors. The island produces coconuts, bananas, plantain, taro, yams, sweet potato, onions, cabbages, radishes, melons, watermelons, pumpkins, and other things besides. But most important of all for the mariner in need of fresh meat is the fact that many swine are raised on Ovigi. During his stay there, Vancouver left a few horned cattle.[38] They are now numerous, and arriving

Europeans will soon be able to eat both beef and mutton. Nanny-goats, too, have been bred in great numbers: we bought two for a trifle and their meat was tasty. The only pity is that all these animals have grown wild and live in the hills. This fact itself, however, is the true explanation of their propagation, for nature herself looks after such animals far better here than do the islanders. Not long ago, a herd of bulls came down into a valley and damaged numerous small plantations. The king ordered that the beasts should be caught, and a thousand men were detailed for the operation; but the wild bulls, seeing themselves encircled, became furious and themselves began the battle. They killed four men before losing themselves in the hills again. It may indeed happen that Ovigi will pretty soon be full of wild stock. Only on the king's property did I see a cow and calf which were to be domesticated.

Originally, there were only hogs and dark-haired rats a little larger than the average mouse here. There are still so many of these rats on Ovigi that the islanders are forced to hang everything up as high as possible from the ground. An American vessel recently brought two horses: the present king has so won the affection of foreigners that each one of them who returns brings something novel and useful for the islanders.

As for birds, there are few species on Ovigi. The fowl is the only domestic one, and even the fowl is not numerous. Wild birds are represented by the grey goose, the snipe, hawks, crows,* and a small bird with a hooked beak, red belly and plumage, and dark grey head and tail (the Sandwich Islanders make their cloaks and helmets from its red belly feathers).** Lastly, there are two species of grey bird rather like our linnet to be mentioned, and a tiny yellow bird, extremely rare, the feathers of which are used as ornamentation.[+]

Fish are quite abundant by the island's shores. I saw the islanders with various kinds of salted fish, including flying-fish [*mâlolo*] about a foot long. There are almost no creeping creatures except lizards, hairy ones being held sacred by the natives. It generally lives in their houses and is extremely ugly in appearance.

Ovigi is divided into six parts, named as follows: Kona, Kogola [Kohala], Gamakua [Hâmâkua], Gidus [Hilo], Puna, and Kau [Ka'û]. These are the possessions of the *Nui-Nui-Eiry* or grandees of the island. Each of them is divided into *Gopuas* [*ahupua'a*] or districts, which are run by the *Pekinery-Eiry* [*pekepeke ali'i*];[†] and districts are split up in their turn into parcels of land and distributed among the farmers. Each island farmer is free to leave the land of one master and transfer to another's or, indeed, to take up any unsettled spot, but that

---

* *i.e.*, ravens, including the *.h.'alalâ* [Hawaiian crow *Corvus tropicus*]. "Snipe" perhaps does duty for *kioea* [Bristle-thighed curlew *Numenius tahitiensis*] and *'auku'u* [Black-crowned night heron *Nyctictorax n. hoactli*].
** perhaps *i'iwi* [Scarlet Hawaiian honeycreeper *Vestiaria coccinea*]
[+] *mamo* [Black Hawaiian honeycreeper *Drepanis pacifica*, endemic to the island of Hawai'i and not seen since the 1880s]
† lesser chiefs [*lit.* dwarf chiefs], as compared with the *nuinui ali'i* or important chiefs

very rarely happens. A large *gopua* might contain as many as thirty such small parcels. Every islander pays a double tax, one to the king, the other to the *Nui-Nui-Eiry* of the part he lives in. The taxes consist of swine, dogs, cloth [*kapa*], the red and yellow feathers used in decorating cloaks, and other things.

Iu.F. Lisianskii (1814)

At nine o'clock in the morning of the 8th [of June], we descried the island of Owyhee to the north-west; and at noon the east end of it bore from us, by the compass, north 3 west, twenty miles distant. By observation, we were in latitude 19°10' north, and in longitude, by the chronometer No. 136, 153°51', and by No. 50, 154°5' west; by which it appeared, that the first was sixty, and the last forty-six miles to the eastward of the true longitude. This, however, was but a trifle in comparison of our ship's reckoning, which was found to be 5°39' to the eastward.

At two o'clock in the afternoon we were so near the shore, that we could distinguish the habitations, which were numerous, and some of them charmingly situated.* We were visited here by six canoes, containing two or three men each. These persons accosted us with much familiarity, as if we had been acquainted with them for years. On coming on deck, they shook hands with every one they saw, repeating the word, *how-lo-lo,* meaning, as I conceived, *how do you do.* They brought us, however, no fresh provisions; and it seemed as if the sole object of their visit was to inquire who we were. Having satisfied their curiosity, they left us, and we proceeded in our course; but the weather becoming thick and rainy about sun-set, we determined to keep in good offings for the night.

At day-light we approached the shore; and at eleven o'clock saw the south-west point of the island, which appeared like two eminences rising beyond the south point, which is low compared with the adjacent land.** We passed the south point about noon, and brought-to, to wait for some canoes that were paddling towards us. Two of these came alongside of the *Nadejda,* and proposed exchanging a large hog, they had brought with them, for some woollen cloth; but finding their wish could not be complied with, they carried the hog back, refusing every other article that was offered for it. At four in the afternoon we sailed along the shore, to induce other canoes to come out with fresh provisions, of which both ships were much in want, but especially the *Nadejda,* whose officers had subsisted on salt meat alone for some time:[+] but, unfortunately, not a soul appeared till late in the evening, when we were obliged to steer off shore. From observation of this day, the south point of the island was 18°35'north.

The light breezes, which prevailed during the whole of the next day, would not permit us to get near the shore. At noon we brought the south point of the island to bear north 79 east, and by observation we were in latitude 18°58' north. Towards evening, captain Krusenstern took leave of me, intending to sail for Camchatca [Kamchatka] in the night. I urged him to stop a few days longer to refresh himself, but I could not prevail; and a favourable wind from the east

---

*on the southern shores of Puna between long. 154°50' and 155°07'
**Ka Lae is, in fact, a low grassy spit.
[+]in fact, as Dr Espenberg records, they had also been eating essence of yeast and a salep made of orchidaceous tubers picked at Taio-hae Bay[39]

springing up about eight o'clock, he shaped his course accordingly and departed. Having found, by experience, that nothing could be obtained by cruizing round the coast, I determined, on the 11th, to come to anchor, and for that purpose steered for the bay of Caracacoa [Kealakekua].

On drawing near the shore, a canoe came along-side from a village called Pereerooa, not far from the south-west point. In this canoe were an Englishman, of the name of Johns,* and a native, who called himself George Kernick. This native spoke the English language remarkably well, having been seven years in England, whither, he said, he had been carried by captain Paget.** My first questions related to the present state of Owyhee [Hawai'i], as to provisions; and I was glad to find that, though the king and all the nobles were then on the island of Wahoo [O'ahu], in consequence of a war with the inhabitants of Ottoway [Kaua'i], I might be sure of procuring all sorts of refreshments, and on reasonable terms. He added that, during the king's absence, the island was governed by an Englishman of the name of Young, who would no doubt come on board to pay his respects, the moment our arrival should be known to him. Soon after the first canoe left us, three others of a similar description came off, and brought with them three small pigs, which I purchased for eight yards of common Russian cloth.[+]

In the mean time the wind shifted a-head, and obliged us to tack. At noon, having the bay of Caracacoa north 15 east, about ten miles distant, we found ourselves by observation in 19°17'8" north. Soon after the wind, inclining again a little to the westward, allowed me to steer for the anchorage; which, however, I could not have fetched, but for a strong current to the northward that, it is said, always prevails here.[†] Sailing close in shore, we had two boats towing a-head, and we kept the ship by the wind till five o'clock when, having passed the south point of the bay, we dropped anchor in seventeen fathoms; the south point bearing south, and the north point 80 west. Before night the ship was moored north-north-east and south-south-west, with three quarters of a cable each way. The decreasing depth of water as we entered the bay, was forty, thirty-five, twenty-eight, twenty-two, and seventeen fathoms, over a bottom of sand and shells.[‡]

From the accounts of former navigators, I expected to have been surrounded by the natives as soon as the ship had dropped anchor; but to our good fortune, not an individual was seen till after sun-set; which, I found, was owing to the taboo. I call it good fortune, because we were enabled to secure the ship without molestation. Just before dark, a company of about a hundred young women made their appearance in the water, swimming towards our vessel, and exhibiting, as they approached us, the most unequivocal tokens of pleasure, not doubt-

---

*In other texts, 'Johns' is called Johnson.
**_i.e.,_ Peter Puget, Vancouver's companion
[+]In the 1812 Russian text, it is only 7 yards: see p. 30.
[†]between Ka' Loa and Palemano Points
[‡]with coral outcrops, as Lisianskii later discovered

ing of admittance. It was with a degree of regret that I felt myself obliged to give a damp to their joy: but I was too firm in the resolution I had formed, not to permit licentious intercourse on board, to be won from it by any allurements or entreaties, by any expression of joy or of sorrow; and this troop of nymphs were compelled to return with an affront offered to their charms, which they had never experienced before, perhaps, from any European ship.

The next morning, believing the taboo to be still in force, I was preparing to go on shore; when I found the vessel surrounded by canoes, furnished with different articles for sale. In consequence, I altered my intention, and commenced the necessary and important business of traffic. As none of the canoes brought any live stock, I was induced to ask the reason; and was given to understand, that Mr. Young had forbidden any pigs to be sold to ships that might arrive, without his express permission. As I was uncertain when this important personage might be at the bay, I dispatched Mr. Johns, an Englishman, who had engaged to remain with me as interpreter, to the chief* of the bay, to inform him that if I could not be supplied with fresh provision here, I should put to sea in the night to seek this commodity in some more hospitable place. My message had the desired effect. The chief came shortly after on board, and presented me with two middling-sized hogs, and a considerable quantity of different sorts of vegetables. I paid him great attention, and presented him in return with three bottles of rum, two axes, and an adz; which pleased him so much that he promised to supply me daily with such necessaries as I might want during my stay. In the mean time the general trade had been carried on so briskly, that by noon, not only the officers, but the men, were possessed of a variety of articles, many of which, though pleased with them for the moment, they afterwards threw away as useless and cumbersome. Though the islanders took knives and small looking-glasses in exchange for their goods, they always gave the preference to our printed and common coarse linens, while pieces of iron hoop, of which we had a great number, were held by them in no estimation. As a compliment, I invited the chief of the bay to dine with us; and I had the satisfaction of observing the keen appetite with which he honoured our repast, and the handsome manner in which he afterwards paid his respects to the bottle, filling his glass alternately with Port wine and brandy** till he became so inebriated, that it was with difficulty we could get him out of the ship.

As night approached, the vessel was again surrounded by the female troop, who had so kindly offered us their company the preceding evening, and who now seemed resolved upon intrusion, if not admitted freely to our society. But I made known to them the impossibility of their succeeding in their attempt; and I requested also the interference of the chief, who gave orders that all his people, male and female, should in future leave the ship at sun-set. In consequence of

---

*more precisely, the *konohiki* responsible for Kamehameha's *ahupua'a* at Kealakekua
**Compare p. 31 ("spirits and wine"): Lisianskii makes numerous such minor changes for the benefit of his English readership.

this injunction, we found ourselves generally alone, as soon as our ensign was lowered; and it must be confessed that, after the noise and bustle of the day, which were hardly supportable, this change of scene was very agreeable to us. The cause of my peremptoriness as to these female visitors, was the fear of their introducing among my crew a certain disease, which, I had been given to understand, was very prevalent in the Sandwich Islands; and certainly the persons of several of the inhabitants, of both sexes, bore evident marks of its ravages.* In spite of Mr. Young's prohibition, we purchased during the day two large hogs, two smaller ones, two goats, ten fowls, and cocoa-nuts, sweet potatoes, taro-root and sugar-cane, in abundance.

In the morning of the 13th, we were again surrounded by canoes. About noon the chief brought us four large hogs, one of which he gave me as a present, while for the others I was obliged to pay a bar and a half of iron. I offered him several other articles by way of exchange; but he refused them all, signifying that these animals belonged to the king, who had given directions that they should be sold for bar-iron only. Besides these, we purchased, in the course of the morning, twelve more small ones, and as many fowls.

In the afternoon, I informed the chief of my intention of paying him a visit on shore, with some of my officers. He seemed much pleased, and immediately left us, to prepare for our reception.** In the mean time our long-boat was armed, and towards evening we left the ship. The surf was so heavy at the village of Caracacoa, that we were obliged to land at a place called Vainoonohala [Waipunaula],[+] where we were met by the chief, who informed me, that he had enjoined taboo on the people every where around. The consequence of this was that, during our stay on shore, no one dared to quit his house; and our walk, which would otherwise have been rendered disagreeable by the crowd, proved to be extremely pleasant.

After passing some poor cottages, we came to a grove of cocoa-nut trees, many of which we observed had marks of shot; and we afterwards learned, that these trees had been struck by the guns from the English ships, after the unfortunate affray in which captain Cook lost his life.[†]

On quitting this grove, we proceeded along the beach; but the surf was so great, that we were completely wet before we reached Caracacoa. The chief had gone by another road, alleging, that he could not with propriety pass in front of a temple,[‡] which we should see on our way. The first object we met with, deserving of notice, was a large building, in which a schooner that had belonged to cap-

---

*The Russian edition contains no such explicit reference to venereal disease--the Hawaiians'*kaokao* and Cook's "Clap" or "fowl distemper"; but Lisianskii had lately reread Cook, and was obviously on the lookout for precisely such "marks" of "ravages".
**by placing a daylight *kapu* on the localities to be visited
[+]a pull of some 300 yards from *Neva*
[†]14 February 1779
[‡]Hikiau *heiau*, on the beachfront

tain Vancouver, was kept. Here the chief joined us and, after showing us his double canoe, that was on the stocks, but not yet finished, conducted us first to his own house, and afterwards to the palace of the king. This palace differed from the common habitations of the island in size only. It consisted of six distinct huts, erected near a tolerably large pond of stagnant water. The first hut we entered constituted the king's dining-room, the second his drawing-room, the third and fourth the apartments of his women, while the last two served for kitchens. These huts, which were all alike, were constructed of poles, and covered with leaves. In some of them, the door was the only means of admitting light, while others had two small windows for the purpose; one near the corner, in front, and the other near the same corner, in the side of the hut. They are all erected upon a sort of pavement of stone, and are enclosed. I know not in what state the palace is kept during the king's residence in it, but when we saw it, it was uncommonly filthy: it is, however, held by the natives in such high veneration, that no one presumes to enter it, with any covering on his body, except the *maro* [*malo*], which is merely a piece of cloth tied round the waist. Our chief, on entering it, took off his hat, his shoes, and the great coat we had given him, though none of the natives were present.

From the palace we went to the royal temple, which is a small hut, fenced round with paling. Before the entrance stands a statue of middling size, and further on to the left six large idols are seen. We were not permitted to enter this holy place, in which, we were told, his majesty takes his meals during the taboo days. Near to this was another enclosed spot, containing different idols: but the chief, who was our guide, spoke English so indifferently that we could scarcely understand a word of what he said respecting it. On approaching the great temple, called by the natives *Heavoo*, not *Morai*, as some navigators have said, the chief refused to follow us, signifying that, as he was not of the first nobility of the land, he could not with propriety enter it. This was rather mortifying to us, as we might stand in need of his assistance; he was not, however, to be persuaded, and we were obliged to proceed alone. This temple is merely a piece of ground, enclosed chiefly with wooden rails, but here and there with stones, and of the form of an oblong square, the extent of which is about fifty yards by thirty. On the side towards the mountains* is a group of fifteen idols, which were wrapped in cloth from the waist downwards; and before them a platform, made of poles, is erected, called the place of sacrifice, on which we saw a roasted pig, and some plantains and cocoa-nuts. On the side to the right of the group of fifteen, are two other statues; further on, on the same side, is an altar with three more; and on the opposite side another group of three, one of which is in a state of great decay.** On the side towards the sea stands a small cottage, which is also in a ruinous state. The several groups of figures were arranged so as to form

---

*the east side
**This vignette is very like David Samwell's of 1779. [40]

within the enclosure a sort of semicircle. During our research we were joined by the chief priest of the temple, who informed us that the fifteen statues wrapped in cloth represented the gods of war; the two to the right of the place of sacrifice, the gods of spring; those on the opposite side, the guardians of autumn; and that the altar was dedicated to the god of joy, before which the islanders dance and sing on festivals appointed by their religion.

These temples were by no means calculated to excite in the mind of a stranger religious veneration. They are suffered to remain in so neglected and filthy a condition, that, were it not for the statues, they might be taken rather for hogsties than places of worship. The statues, meanwhile, are carved in the rudest manner: the heads of some of them are a great deal larger than the body. Some are without tongues, while others have tongues of a frightful size. Some again bear huge blocks of wood on their heads, and have mouths reaching from ear to ear.*

In coming out of this place, we leaped over a low stone fence; while the priest came out by a narrow opening; observing, that to do as we did, would be a crime in him punishable with death. There are many laws of this nature, which strangers should be careful of observing; though transgressions are not so strictly punished in them as in the natives.

From the temple we returned to the place where we had landed, by another road, so strewed with loose and rugged stones, that we were every moment in danger of falling. As I passed the different habitations, I could not help observing that hogs and dogs were the constant companions of their masters, with whom they fed, and lived; which occasioned a general filthiness, disgusting to more senses than one. I was surprised at not meeting, during this excursion, with more than three or four bread-fruit trees: the best grounds were covered with a plant from which, I was told, a good red dye is extracted.

As soon as we had embarked in our boats, the people, who had kept within their houses in consequence of the taboo, ran out in crowds, loudly wishing us a good night. On getting on board, I was sorry to find that scarcely anything had been purchased in our absence.

In the morning of the 14th the barter for provisions commenced briskly; but on the arrival of the chief of the bay on board it almost instantly ceased. Suspecting this personage to be the cause of the change, I ordered him out of the ship; and I had the satisfaction to find that I was right in my conjecture, for immediately upon his departure the traffic was renewed, and I obtained a considerable quantity of live stock. To enhance the price, a report was spread that a large ship had arrived in the bay of Toovyhy [Kawaihae], and that Mr. Young was gone to visit her, which was the reason we had not yet seen this gentleman. I however doubted the truth of the report, and it failed of its end.

---

*the Hawaiian 'ole 'ole style[41]

The next morning Mr. Young arrived. He expressed much sorrow at not having waited upon us sooner; declaring, at the same time, that he had not been informed till yesterday of our arrival. Concluding that this arose from the intriguing disposition of our chief, I determined to punish his knavery by not inviting him to our dinner of to-day; which he felt so keenly that, to make amends, he gave me a large hog, at the same time owning his fault, and promising never to conduct himself towards me in any under-hand manner again. On the promise I forgave him, and we were once more friends.

Mr.Young had brought with him six hogs, two of which he made me a present of, but asked me for the other four a piece and a half of canvass, assuring me they belonged to the king, who had set this price upon them. I however declined purchasing them at so exorbitant a rate, and they were sent on shore.

In the afternoon we made a party to go to the villiage of Tavaroa [Ka'awaloa], to see the memorable spot where Europe had been deprived of her most celebrated navigator, captain Cook. We landed at the very rock where this truly great man lost his life; and were afterwards shown the part of a mountain where his body had been burned. This mountain has several excavations, in which the bones of the dead are deposited: and one in particular is said to contain the precious remains of the kings of the island, down to the last deceased Tyreboo [Kalani'opu'u].

Tavaroa bears much resemblance to the other villages which I saw in the island: it has a mean appearance, and contains nine heavoos, which we could not enter on account of the absence of priests [*kahuna*]: they differed, however,from the great heavoo in no respect but size. They were dedicated to different deities, and belonged to the different chiefs of the country,* who were then in the army with the king.

After walking about for a while, we stopped to pay our respects to an old lady, the sister of the great chief of Tavaroa. She was about ninety years of age, and perfectly blind. On Mr. Young's introducing me, she took my hand, and would have kissed it, if I would have permitted the condescension. She was sitting under a large tree, surrounded by a crowd of young people, who seemed to amuse themselves with the oddity of her appearance. She talked chiefly of her attachment to Europeans, and greatly lamented the death of captain Cook.

The environs of this village exhibit scarcely any signs of verdure. The ground is covered with pieces of lava, which are used here for a fence to the houses. On our return to the ship, we found on board some sailors belonging to the United States; one of whom, during the preceding year, had been on the north-west coast of America. He informed us that the Russian settlement of Archangel, in Sitca, or Norfolk Sound, had been destroyed by the natives; to which I was the more in-

---

*who had had them built[42]

clined to give credit, from its corresponding with what had appeared in the Hamburgh papers previous to our departure from Europe.*

Having provisioned myself with what provisions I wanted, I determined to put to sea; and on the 16th, the ship being unmoored, we set sail at nine in the evening with a land-breeze, which blows pretty regularly in this bay.... On clearing the bay, we had a few light breezes, but they soon died away, which obliged us to tow hard, with all the boats a-head, to keep out of danger. In the morning I dismissed Mr. Johns, my interpreter, after having recompensed him for the services he had rendered us, and given him a few trifling presents for his chief, who had sent me a pig a few days before and had further intended me the honour of a visit, but had been prevented by the sudden death of his wife. For Mr. Young's civilities, when he left us the preceding evening, I filled his canoe with biscuits, porter, brandy, and wine.

At day-break on the 17th, we found ourselves about six miles from the bay, and at noon had an observation in latitude 19°34'49" north. The north end of Caracacoa bore south 67° east ,and the west point of the island was north west. At six in the afternoon a breeze sprung up, with which we reached the western point of Owyhee. We should not have distinctly seen the island of Move [Maui], but the weather was so thick and cloudy, that its summits alone were visible. In the morning of the 18th, the wind blew so strong at north-east that the ship went at the rate of eight miles and a half an hour. This was a very agreeable change, after the tiresome calm of the two preceding days.

On leaving Carracacoa, I purposed making for the island of Wahoo, to see the king of Owyhee, who was there with his army. So great indeed was my curiosity on this subject, that to gratify it, I would have sacrificed a few days to the business nearest my heart, that of arriving at Cadiack [Kodiak]. Learning,** however, that a species of epidemic was raging in that island, I relinquished my intention, and took my course for Otooway. By observation at noon, we found ourselves in latitude 20°20' north, and longitude by the chronometers, No. 136 and 50, by which I shall reckon for the future, 157°42' west.

On the 19th, at five o'clock in the morning, the island of Otooway appeared to the north-west,and at eight we passed the south end of it. On reaching the bay of Weymea [Waimea], I brought-to, to wait for four canoes that were paddling towards us. In one of them were five men; the others had only a man in each. They had nothing to sell but a few spears,+ and a fant of exquisite beauty, made of the feathers of the tropic birds, which I obtained for a small knife.

---

*In fact, several items about the impending Russian expedition had appeared in the Hamburg press; and a few had been reprinted in Karamzin's *Vestnik Evropy*.[43]
**presumably at Kealakekua Bay; both here and in the Russian text, however, the phrasing is vague and leaves one in doubt
+see Part 4 here on the '1804 Hawaiian' spears in Leningrad
†obviously a *kahili*, but this item is not in Leningrad today

The wind blew fresh till we came up with the west end of the island, where we were perfectly becalmed; the currents, however, dragging us till night and forcing us between the islands of Otooway and Onihoo [Ni'ihau]. Meanwhile the king of these islands, whose name was Tamoory [Kaumuali'i], paid us a visit. On entering the ship, he accosted me in English, and presented at the same time several certificates of recommendation, as he supposed, that had been given him by the commanders of the different vessels which had touched at Otooway: but, on inspecting these papers, I found that some of them were by no means in his favour; and I gave him a hint on the subject and advised him for the future to be more obliging to those of whom he wished to receive testimonials of his honourable conduct, and to treat better European navigators, who prefer at present touching at the island of Owyhee.

On hearing that we had just left that island, he was anxious to know what was doing there. I informed him that the king was at present on the island of Wahoo; and that he would have been at Otooway long ago, but for an epidemic disease, which had spread among his troops, and would perhaps oblige him to relinquish his conquests, and return home. This intelligence was extremely gratifying to our royal visitor; who, however, assured me that, happen what would, he was determined to defend himself to the last; adding that he had thirty thousand warriors on the island, meaning, probably, all the inhabitants, amongst whom were five Europeans; that he had besides, three six-pounders, forty swivels, a number of muskets, and plenty of powder and ball.

The king was waited on in the vessel by one of his subjects, who carried a small wooden bason,* a feather fan, and a towel. The bason was set round with human teeth,** which, I was told afterwards, had belonged to his majesty's deceased friends. It was intended for the king to spit in;[+] but he did not appear to make much use of it, for he was continually spitting about the deck without ceremony.

On quitting us, he expressed some displeasure at my not being willing to spare him either bar iron or paint, the last of which he very much wanted, to finish a vessel, he said, he was building. He did not, however, refuse to accept a blanket, and other more trifling articles, of which I made him a present.

During his stay with us, by some accident one of his canoes overset; but it was soon righted again. Things of this kind very frequently happen; but the islanders are so expert in swimming that no misfortune ensues.

The island of Otooway is high and, in clear weather, may be seen at a great distance. The shore, on the western side, rises gradually from the water; and, from its numberless habitations, which appear better built than those of the island

---

*a basin or bowl
**Traditionally, those of enemies were used, probably as an insult to their previous owners.
[+]actually, to deposit scraps of unwanted food in.[44] Bowls used by Hawaiians as spittoons were called *ipu kuha*.

of Owyhee, presents every where a most beautiful landscape. I am sorry to say that there is not a single good anchorage round the whole island, except in Weymea Bay, which is also exposed to westerly winds.

The island of Onihoo, with its two small islets or rocks, is situated to the west of Ottoway. It produces such an abundance of sweet potatoes, and other esculent* roots, that ships may be supplied with them in any quantity.

From the increasing importance of the Sandwich Islands, I shall devote a chapter to a further account of them; in which, I trust, will be found some particulars curious and interesting.

Account of the Sandwich Islands

The Sandwich Islands serve at present as a resort for all ships going to the north-west coast of America, as they can refit there and take in provisions. The islands are divided in two dominions, of which one, consisting of the islands of Otooway [Kaua'i], Origoa [Lehua], and Tagoora[45] [Ka'ula], is governed by Tamoory [Kaumuali'i];** and the other, including all the islands to the southward, by Hamamea. (By some navigators he has been called Tomeomeo, Comeomeo, and Toamama, but incorrectly.) Hamamea is said to be a prince of ability and courage. He is so much attached to Europeans, that their ships enter his ports not only without the least fear, but with a certainty of obtaining, on the best terms, every thing the place they may anchor at is capable of furnishing. By this conduct, he has not only obtained various articles of necessity for his subjects, but has even formed an army that may be styled, compared with others among the South-Sea islands, invincible. Add to this,that he has upwards of fifty Europeans in his service; and so great a quantity of small guns, swivels, muskets, and ammunition, supplied by the ships of the United States, that these articles in the island of Owyhee have greatly sunk in value.[46]

The power of the kings is unlimited. The succession to the throne is hereditary, though it is often disputed by the most opulent grandees of the island. Hamamea himself obtained his elevation by violence. On the death of the late king Tyreboo, he contrived first to divide the dominions with the son of the deceased, and afterwards to seize upon the whole himself. Next to the king, the greatest power on the island vests in the chiefs, or grandees, who are called Nooy Nooy Eiry.

The military force of the country consists of all who are capable of bearing arms. Every man is brought up to war from his infancy, and is obliged, if called upon, to follow his chief wherever he may go. Besides the general army, Hamamea has a body-guard, composed of the best warriors on the island, which is always near his person.+ He has also several schooners, from ten to twenty

---

*edible
**By oversight, Lisianskii omitted Ni'ihau from this list.
+This clearly refers to a Hawaiian king's guard.[47]

tons, built by Europeans, after the plan of captain Vancouver's, and armed with swivels. We saw, however, none of these vessels, as they were all in the expedition with the king.

Here, as in the Marquesas, force reigns instead of laws.* The king may take the life of his subjects at his pleasure, and the chiefs may do the same with those who are subordinate to them. The grandees generally decide their own quarrels by the strength of their respective adherents; but if one of them should disobey the king, the body-guards are immediately dispatched to put him to death, or to bring him alive to the royal presence. Should it happen that the chief or grandee on this occasion conceives himself sufficiently powerful, he disputes this despotic mandate, and a war generally ensues between the sovereign and his rebellious subject.

To give the reader some idea of the jurisprudence of this people, I shall furnish him with two incidents that were related to me by Mr. Young, and which had taken place on the island of Owyhee since the period of his arrival there. An islander was condemned to death for eating a cocoa-nut during the taboo. One of the Europeans on the island, hearing this, went to the king, and interceded for the life of this man, representing that the crime was of too insignificant a nature to deserve so severe a punishment. The king heard the representation of the stranger without interrupting him; and when he had done, replied, with all imaginable coolness, that, as there was a great difference between the inhabitants of the two countries of Owyhee and Europe, there must of necessity be a difference also as to crimes and punishments: and without further delay, the poor culprit was deprived of his life.[48] The other anecdote is of a still more sanguinary nature. The king had given to Mr. Young a piece of land, with several people on it. Of these, one happened to have a quarrel with his wife; and, on their separating, rather than resign to her his child, a beautiful boy, he put him to death. Mr. Young, hearing of this cruelty, immediately went to the king to demand justice on the offender. But how great was his astonishment, when told by his majesty, that the man was not an offender liable to punishment, since by killing his child, he had injured no one but himself. The king however added that Mr. Young, as master of his own people, might act respecting them in what manner he pleased. From these two instances we may form some judgement of the morals of a country, where the most trivial fault is often punished with death, while the blackest crime is left unnoticed.

The word taboo signifies here, as in the Marquesas, a sacred prohibition. The king may lay a taboo on any thing he pleases; and there are instances in which he is obliged to observe it himself: these are established by religion, and are held by him in the highest veneration. The principal taboo is that called Macahity [*makahiki*], which answers to the twelfth month of the year. Besides this, there

---

*The laws were, of course, explicit in the *kapu*. This comment reveals the Russians' ignorance of the true complexity of the society.

are four taboos in every month, the eleventh excepted, which has no established taboo. Of these four, the first is called Ohiro [*Hilo*], and takes place on the 1st day of the month; the second, Mooharoo [*Mohalu*], on the 12th; the third, Orepaoo ['*Olepau*], on the 23rd; and the fourth, Ocane [*Kane*], on the 27th. Taboo Ohiro continues three nights and two days, and the other three only two nights and a day. The taboo Macahity is not unlike to our festival of Christmas. It continues a whole month,[49] during which the people amuse themselves with dances, plays, and sham-fights of every kind. The king must open this festival wherever he is. On this occasion, his majesty dresses himself in his richest cloak and helmet, and is paddled in a canoe along the shore, followed sometimes by many of his subjects. He embarks early, and must finish his excursion at sunrise. The strongest and most expert of the warriors is chosen to receive him on his landing. The warrior watches the royal canoe along the beach; and as soon as the king lands, and has thrown off his cloak, he darts his spear at him, from a distance of about thirty paces, and the king must either catch the spear in his hand, or suffer from it: there is no jesting in the business. Having caught it, he carries it under his arm, with the sharp end downwards, into the temple or heavoo. On his entrance, the assembled multitude begin their sham fights, and immediately the air is obscured by clouds of spears, made for the occasion with blunted ends. Hamamea has been frequently advised to abolish this ridiculous ceremony, in which he risks his life every year; but to no effect. His answer always is, that he is as able to catch a spear, as any one on the island is to throw it at him. During the Macahity, all punishments are remitted throughout the country; and no person can leave the place in which he commences these holidays, let the affair requiring his absence be ever so important.

The division of time on the Sandwich Islands is this. A year is divided into twelve months, a month into thirty days, and a day into five parts, sun-rise, noon, sun-set, the time between sun-rise and noon, and the time between noon and sun-set. The year begins with our November. The first month of it is called* Macaree; the second, Caero; the third, Ocaoorooa; the fourth, Onana; the fifth, Oero; the sixth, Oykeekee; the seventh, Caona; the eighth, Hoynere; the ninth, Oherenahoo; the tenth, Oherenima; the eleventh, Oytooa; the twelfth, Macahity.** The days of the month have all different names, which are these: the first, Oheero; the second, Hoaca; the third, Coohahi; the fourth, Toorooa; the fifth, Toocoroo; the sixth, Coopaoo; the seventh, Oricoocahe; the eighth, Oricoorooha; the ninth, Oricoocoroo; the tenth, Oripaoo; the eleventh, Hoona; the twelfth, Mooharoo; the thirteenth, Hooa; the fourteenth, Oatooa; the fifteenth, Hotoo; the sixteenth, Mahearona; the seventeenth, Tooroo; the eighteenth, Roacoocahe; the nineteenth, Roacoorooha; the twentieth, Roaopaoo; the twenty-first, Orecoocahe; the twenty-second, Orecoorooha; the twenty-third, Orepaoo;

---

*See the 1812 text or the glossary for the Hawaiian equivalents of these names.
**really *Welehu*

the twenty-fourth, Carocoocahe; the twenty-fifth, Carocoorooha; the twenty-sixth, Caropaoo; the twenty-seventh, Ocane; the twenty-eighth, Ronoo; the twenty-ninth, Mowry; the thirtieth, Omoocoo.*

The people of the Sandwich Islands believe in good and in evil spirits, in the resurrection of the dead, and a better life in another world. Their heavoos are crowded with idols, representing, as I have described, the gods of war, peace, joy, etc., to some of whom sacrifices are offered of fruits, pigs, and dogs. The human sacrifice is only practised on prisoners and rebellious subjects, and is therefore more a political than a religious institution. The priests are brought up to the offices of religion from their infancy, and early learn by heart what they have to speak on the days of taboo. A particular sect of these priests pretend to have the power of killing, by means of prayer, any person they choose. They call themselves Coohana-anana [*kahuna 'ana'ana*], and are the greatest scoundrels imaginable.** As soon as their vile praying against any individual is in agitation, the unfortunate being is sure to hear of it, in some way or other; and so great is the superstition that reigns here, that, believing himself the sure victim of malice, he puts an end to his existence, or loses his senses, or withers away till he dies. It is true, the religion of the country permits the relations of the chosen victim to hire some one belonging to this wicked fraternity, to pray against the murderer; but it never happened that these counter prayers had the effect of depriving any individual of the sect of either his senses or his life.

The ceremony of sacrifice to the gods, of prisoners of war and rebels, was differently related to me by different persons; but in the main points of this horrid business, there was but little variation in the accounts. The mode of death is strangling. If the victim to be sacrificed is a person of note, a certain number of his adherents, from six to twenty, according to his rank, must be strangled with him. On such occasion, a particular platform or place of sacrifice is erected in the great heavoo, and is almost entirely covered with cocoa-nuts, plantains, and yams. When prisoners are sacrificed, after being strangled, they are singed, and then laid on the platform, parallel to each other, with spaces between, their feet directed towards the idols representing the gods of war, before whom these sacrifices are performed. The chief victim is always placed in the middle, and the vacancies between him and his fellow-victims are filled up with dogs and pigs, well roasted or baked. In this state, everything is left till time shall have wasted away the flesh, when the heads of the sacrificed are stuck upon the rails that enclose the heavoos, and the bones deposited in a place constructed for the purpose.

This account I had from the chief priest of Caracacoa Bay. Mr. Young, however, to whom I communicated it, assured me, that no particular platform

---

*Like their British predecessors, the Russians almost invariably incorporated prefixed articles into Hawaiian names, and into many other words as well.[50]
**The opinion is second-hand, probably Young's.

was erected for the sacrifice; that the victims were simply laid on the ground, with the face downward, their heads towards the idols, and their arms stretched out on the back of one another.[51] He told me also, that no singeing took place, nor were there any dogs in the ceremony. He confirmed the circumstance of the heads of the sacrificed being cut off, and fixed on the wooden rails enclosing the heavoo; but said that it commenced immediately after the expiration of ten days, during which the taboo called *Canaca* prevailed.* He added, that only the bones of the arms and legs were taken away, to be deposited in a place appointed for the purpose, and that the other parts of the body were reduced to ashes. The reader must judge for himself respecting the contrarieties in these two accounts. I can only surmise, that they might be in some degree owing to the imperfect knowledge my interpreter had of the language of the natives; and it was by him that my conversation with the priest was carried on.

The funerals here vary according to the rank and wealth of the parties. The poor are buried any where along the beach, after being wrapt in a piece of coarse cloth, manufactured in the islands. The rich are dressed in their best apparel, and put into coffins,[52] which are placed in small buildings or cemeteries, where they are permitted to rot in state. When the flesh is gone, the bones are taken away, and deposited elsewhere. If the deceased be a person of great consequence, six of his favourite servants must be put to death, and buried with him. On the death of the king, a scene of horror takes place that is hardly credible. Twelve men are sacrificed; and shortly after the whole island abandons itself for a month to the utmost disorder and licentiousness. During this period, both sexes go entirely naked, and men cohabit with women without any distinction: the woman who should dare to make resistance, would be considered as violating the laws of the country. The same licentiousness is observed on the death of a noble: but it does not extend beyond the domains of the deceased, and is of a much shorter duration, not continuing, as Mr. Young informed me, more than a few days, though attempts are made by the youth of the party to prolong the period. Those who are put to death on the demise of the king, or any great personage, are such as have offered themselves for the purpose during the life of their master; and they are in consequence considered and treated by him as his best friends, since they have sworn to live and die with him. When I reflect upon the horrid nature of this ceremony, I hardly know how to credit its existence amongst a race of men so mild and good as these islanders in general appear to be; but Mr. Young, whose veracity I had no reason to doubt, assured me of the fact.

Their modes of expressing mourning are by scratching the body, cutting of the hair, and pulling out the teeth. On the death of the king, every one in his dominions must pull out a tooth; and if a great man dies, those who were subject to him must do the same; so that, if an individual should have lost many masters,

---

*The priest was referring to the ten-day period [*anahulu*] of a traditional *luakini kapu*; 'Canaca' is presumably, therefore, a mangled allusion to the human sacrifice itself. See note on p. 44.

he may at last not have a tooth left in his head. (Mr. Langsdorff, who saw among the islanders that came aboard the *Nadejda* many who had lost their front teeth, supposes, erroneously in my opinion, the defect to have arisen from the teeth having been knocked out in battle by the slings.)[53]

The inhabitants of the Sandwich Islands are of a middle stature and of a dark complexion. In the men, the form of the countenance varies; some have even a perfect European face. The women, on the contrary, nearly resemble each other; the face in all being round, the nose small and flattish, and the eyes black. The hair of both sexes is black and strong. The men cut theirs in different forms; but the prevailing fashion at present is that of a Roman helmet.[54] The women crop theirs close, leaving a ridge, about an inch-and-a-half long, sticking up, and extending from side to side on the forehead. This ridge of hair they daub over every afternoon with a sort of pomatum (if I may use the word), made of shells and corals, to give it a yellowish appearance. The men do the same with theirs, colouring only the hair which forms the crest of the helmet. From this practice, we were at first led to believe the hair of the head to be of two natural colours, for the ridge and the crest retain a portion of the hue they acquire by the frequent daubings. Contrary to the usage of their neighbours (the other islanders of the South Sea), these people neither paint the body nor wear ornaments in the ears. They have, however, bracelets on their arms, made of bone.

The women ornament their heads with wreaths of flowers, or worsted threads, of different colours, raveled out of European stuffs. They commonly wrap themselves in a long piece of cloth, of the manufacture of the country; and in cold weather cover the body with broader pieces of it, several times doubled. The rich and poor are in common dressed alike; but, on particular occasions, the rich put on their feather cloaks, which, with their helmets and fans, form a dress that must be admired every where.

These people are extremely fond of the European dress, and receive with pleasure, old shirts, jackets, and trowsers. We parted here with all our rags, in exchange for provisions, and other articles, of which we were in want.

They have been described by former navigators as thieves and swindlers; I have, however, nothing of the kind to allege against them. During our stay in Caracacoa Bay, we were surrounded by them every day, and did not lose a single thing. They are certainly very difficult in bargaining, and know how to keep up the price of whatever they have to sell; and, if it happened that we purchased anything at a dear rate, it was immediately known to the whole throng, and the article could not be obtained afterwards cheaper. They would even let a day or two pass, in hopes of bringing us to their terms: but aware of this, and unbending as themselves, we generally obtained what was wanted reasonably. Iron, which was considered formerly as of the greatest value here, is now little regarded, unless in bars. Our rusty hoops, which were deemed so precious on the island of Noocahiva [Nuku Hiva, Marquesas], availed us nothing.

The island of Owyhee has undergone, within the last ten years, a very considerable change. Every thing at present is dear, on account of the many American ships which, in navigating these seas, always touch at the Sandwich Islands for refreshments. In the course of a twelvemonth, the bay of Caracacoa has been visited by no less than eighteen different vessels.*

The provisions I obtained for my ship were at the following rates: For four large hogs, I gave a piece of thin canvass; for three others, a bar and a half of iron; for a middling-sized one, two iron axes; for a small one, a single iron axe; for a sucking-pig, a piece of printed linen, measuring nearly three yards, but cut in two, lengthwise. The same for six or eight bunches of sweet potatoes, or a hundredweight of yams; and, lastly, a small knife for a fowl.

I cannot say that the houses of Owyhee pleased me so much as those of Noocahiva. They resemble our wooden barns with this difference, that the sides are lower, and the roofs higher, in proportion. The furniture of these dwellings consists of mats,** which are spread on the floor, and some domestic utensils, made of the calabash [gourd], or of wood, which are hung up out of the reach of the different animals, which are here the constant companions of their masters. The rich have separate huts, for the several purposes of sleeping, cooking, eating, etc., as I have mentioned before. They are rather larger than the huts of the poor, and have stone foundations: they are also railed round; but the railing is so bad, that dogs and swine can get in with ease.

The food of the islanders consists of pork, dog's flesh, fish, fowls, cocoa-nuts, sweet potatoes, bananas, taro-roots, yams, etc. They sometimes eat their fish raw; but they bake almost every thing else, their fruits excepted. I was told that the women were forbidden to eat pork, cocoa-nuts, and bananas. Animals are not slaughtered here, but stifled, by tying a strong cord tight over the muzzle. The flesh is afterwards barbecued or baked, in holes made in the earth. This method of cooking is too well known to require explanation.[+] I must observe, however, that the meat so dressed was excellent, even preferable, I thought, to ours by roasting.

The nobility here are not permitted to borrow, or take any fire from one of the commonalty, but must provide it themselves, or obtain it from their equals. I am not sure, whether commoners may make use of the fire of the nobles; but I was given to understand that this sometimes happened. I was puzzling myself to discover the cause of this curious custom, when an old priest told me that the nobility were considered as too great to use any thing not belonging particularly to themselves; which, if true, is surely ridiculous enough.

The women are forbidden, when in their houses, to eat in company with men, and even to enter the eating-room during meals. The men, on the contrary, may

---

*presumably, in 1803-04[55]
**The Russians acquired some, and one specimen remains in Leningrad: see Part 4 below.
[+]Shemelin 'explains' it nonetheless: p. 102.

enter the rooms in which the women dine, but must not partake of any thing. When in the fields, or at sea, the two sexes may eat together and may use the same vessels, the calabash [gourd] excepted, in which each sex has its own tarro dainty.

The inhabitants of the Sandwich Islands take salt with their food, and are excessively fond of salted meat. Among their articles of provision, is one made of tarro-flour into small balls, which, by being put into fresh or salt water, is converted into a pudding. It is very nourishing, and will keep for a long time.*

The marriage tie is here, as in other islands of the Pacific Ocean, very lax; a man and woman live together as long as they please, and may at any time separate, and make choice of other partners. A man may, in reality, have as many wives as he is able to maintain. In general, however, the king has three and the nobles two, while the common people content themselves with one.[56] It might be supposed that jealousy would be a feeling scarcely known to these islanders; whereas, in fact, it is extremely prevalent; though with regard to their wives they allow to Europeans great freedom, which, as I have before stated, proceeds from interest.**

The Sandwich Islands are inhabited by a race of men who are not deficient in talents. They are extremely attached to European customs. Some speak English tolerably well, and almost all attempt to pronounce a few words of the language, however indifferently they may succeed; as, for instance, *nypo* for a knife, *how lo lo* for, how do you do, and *cabeca* for a cabbage. They are fond of travelling; many offered me their services, and would have given me all they had to have been taken on board as sailors. Ships of the United States often take them to sea, and find them in a short time very useful.

I am of opinion, that these islands will not long remain in their present barbarous state. They have made great advances towards civilization since the period of their discovery, and especially during the reign of the present king. They are so situated, that with a little systematic industry they might soon enrich themselves. They produce an abundance of timber,[+] some of which is fit for the construction of small vessels. The sugar-cane also thrives here, the cultivation of which alone would yield a tolerable revenue, if sugar and rum were made of it; and the more so, as the use of these articles is already known to the savages of the north-west coast of America, and becomes daily of more importance there. The principal inconvenience is the want of a good harbour.† There are, however, a number of bays, which are in no respect worse than the bay of Teneriffe, or that of the island of Madeira.

†Mr. Okeen, whom I shall mention hereafter, has informed me that the island of Wahoo has a very fine harbour. (Lisianskii's original footnote)

---

*normally wrapped in ti leaves; see notes on p. 48
**hope of gain
[+]Lisianskii nowhere mentions sandalwood.[57]

The inhabitants are very ingenious in fabricating their cloth, as well as in colouring it. I was astonished at their skill, when I saw the instruments by which it was effected. Their cloth greatly surpasses that made by the inhabitants of Noocahiva; who, I am persuaded, would part with their most costly things in exchange for this, as it would be deemed by them, excellent article.*

I shall here introduce a brief history of the reign of the present king, Hamamea.

On the death of the late king, Tyreboo [Kalani'opu'u], great troubles ensued in the island of Owyhee, the consequence of which was, that his dominions were divided between Kiauva [Kiwala'o], his son, and an ambitious relation of the name of Hamamea. As war still raged between Owyhee and the islands to the northward of it, Vahoo, Moreky, Renay, and Move,** which had Haykery [Kahekili] for their king, Hamamea, after settling affairs at home, proceeded, in the year 1791, against these islands. Having an army of eight thousand men, and two thousand canoes, he soon subdued his enemy, so far as to take from him all his possessions except Vahoo. In the year following, when this conqueror was about to terminate, as he supposed, a war so successfully begun, he received information that his own dominions were in danger from Kiauva. This unexpected news enraged him so much that, in his fury, he knocked out several of his own teeth. He returned immediately to Owyhee; while Haykery, who had retained only the island of Vahoo, on hearing that Move was abandoned by his enemy, took possession again of that, and all the other islands he had lost.

Hamamea, landing in the bay of Towyhy [Kawaihae], found Kiauva there, who, not expecting this encounter, retired into the interior. Hamamea followed him. Many battles were fought, with various success; when, at last, the conqueror of Move completely defeated his adversary by stratagem. He gave out that he was going to construct a new heavoo, or temple, to his gods; and, on that account, ordered hostilities to be suspended. The enemy, believing him sincere, relaxed operations, which Hamamea observing, attacked him suddenly with all his forces, and completely routed him. Kiauva, however, saved himself by flight; but many of his chiefs were taken prisoner and sacrificed.

During the taboo of Macahity, no war could be carried on; but as soon as it ceased, Hamamea, forming his army into two divisions, gave the command of one to his chief captain, Tyana [Kaiana], and put himself at the head of the other. Kiauva, in the meantime, had been by no means dilatory. He collected what forces he could, and was determined to defend himself to the last. Nothing, however, could withstand the courage and resolution of his adversary. Tyana on one side, and Hamamea on the other, carried death and destruction every where. This unfortunate war continued till the year 1795, when Kiauva, dejected by his frequent misfortunes, and deserted by almost all his chiefs, delivered himself up

---

*The *i'e kuku* [*kapa* beater] Lisianskii bought is still in Leningrad: see Part 4
**O'ahu, Moloka'i, Lana'i and Maui

to the mercy of his enemy. His life, after that, was of short duration. Hamamea ordered him to be brought to Towyhy, where he was massacred, with nearly all his principal followers. On the death of this last branch of the Tyreboo family, Hamamea became master and sovereign of the whole island of Owyhee.

Such was the situation of affairs when captain Vancouver arrived. Hearing of the implacability of the islanders, he did all he could to soften their ferocity and render them less savage; and he thought he had, in some degree, succeeded; but, on his departure, as soon as his ships were out of sight, the monster Discord began again to rear her head. A report was spread, that the inhabitants of the island of Move had stolen some people from Owyhee, and had sacrificed them on a certain occasion; and the wrath of Hamamea was again kindled and he resolved on vengeance. It is probable that, finding himself strong and in condition for war, he was himself the author of this report, meaning to take advantage of it to conquer his neighbors.

Haykery was, it seems, now dead, and his son and successor, Tryshepoor [Kalanikupule], was quarreling with the king of Ottoway,* his uncle, who had advanced pretensions to the dominions of his deceased brother. Hamamea, hearing of these dissensions, ordered his warriors to get ready, and, with a reinforcement of three brass cannon, and eight Europeans with muskets, he set out against his enemy, in the schooner presented to him by captain Vancouver, which was armed with swivels.

The three cannon belonged formerly to a schooner of the United States, called the *Fair American,* which had been seized upon, in the year 1791, by the islanders, and all her crew murdered except one, a Mr. Davis, who still resides here,[58] and shares the king's favour with Mr. Young. The war, thus renewed, was first directed against Move; but, as neither that island nor the others had the same means of defending themselves, they were in a short time all taken, as before, except Vahoo where king Tryshepoor himself resided. In the next year, 1795, Vahoo was also taken; and in this affair Hamamea's chief captain, Tyana, ignominiously lost his life, fighting against his sovereign. The circumstances were these. When Hamamea set out on his expedition against Vahoo, Tyana was to proceed by sea, to join him with the rest of the army; instead however of joining the king, he went over to the enemy. Hamamea had waited a long time for the forces under Tyana, believing them to be still afloat; when he received information of the treachery of his favourite. An unexpected circumstance like this, might have overwhelmed a common mind, but it produced upon Hamamea a very different effect. This brave warrior attacked both his enemies without delay, and, by his courage and the rapidity of his motions, vanquished them both. Mr. Young told me, that he himself was in this expedition, and saw Tyana fall, pierced by a spear. The body of this rebel, and those of many of his associates,

---

*Kaumuali‘i's father, Ka‘eokulani

were sacrificed in the usual manner, and their heads stuck on the palings of the heavoo.

In 1796, Hamamea was called home by the rebellion of Tyana's brother, Namotahy [Namakeha], and he remained a whole year at Owyhee; but his ambition would not let him rest, and he again returned to Vahoo, where he is at present, to forward the necessary preparations for a war he had planned against the island of Otooway.

By Mr. Young's account, the forces of Hamamea consist now of about seven thousand natives and fifty Europeans. He has six hundred muskets, eight guns, carrying a ball of four pounds, one carrying a ball of six pounds; forty swivels, and six small mortars, with a sufficiency of powder, shot, and ball.*

His navy is as formidable as his army. Exclusive of a great number of war-canoes, it consists of twenty-one schooners, from ten to twenty tons,[59] some of which are armed with swivels, and commanded by Europeans.**

With such an armament, he certainly would have reduced Otooway last spring,[+] if a disease, as I have mentioned in my narrative, had not spread amongst his troops, and destroyed the flower of his army. When we left the bay at Caracacoa, it was the general opinion there, that he would postpone the expedition against the island of Otooway, and return home; where his presence was very much required, as his long absence, with the whole of the chiefs, had occasioned such languor and inactivity amongst the common people, that the produce of Owyhee was not half what it used to be when the king and his nobles resided in it. I am confident, that in taking his chiefs with him to the war, and leaving Mr. Young to preside over the island in his absence, Hamamea was governed more by policy than necessity.

This Mr. Young was formerly boatswain of a merchant-vessel belonging to the United States. He says of himself, that happening to be on shore when his ship sailed out of the bay, he was detained on some false pretext by the inhabitants, and that he has continued with them from that time, which was in the year 1791. He had recommended himself successfully both to the people and the king. The latter he has accompanied in several of his wars, and appears to enjoy his full confidence. He has also acquired a handsome landed property, and some hundreds of Spanish dollars, the value of which is very well known in this island.[+]

---

*Berkh elaborates on this slightly: see p. 105.
**We were told on our arrival at Canton, by an American captain, that he afterwards obtained, in exchange for a schooner, an American ship of twenty guns called Lilly Bird (Lelia Byrd), which had been run ashore, and could not be got off by the crew; and that in this ship, which the natives contrived to set afloat, the king sailed to Otooway, and conquered the island.
[+]1804
†Korobitsyn and Langsdorf confirm this: see pp. 80, 114.

Owyhee is the largest of the Sandwich Islands, and is remarkable for containing one of the highest mountains in the world, Mount Roa.* Considering the quantity of lava, and other volcanic substances, that are found every where in this island, it would seem as if it had formerly been subject to eruptions in more places than one; though there is only one mountain at present, called Tavoorapery [Ka'ula Pele], where they occasionally happen. I was told, indeed, that three years ago Mount Macaoora [Makahuna], by a sudden burst, did much mischief,** but had since that time been perfectly quiet.

Though the coast of Owyhee does not give to the eye much promise of abundance, except in some few scattered spots, and is inhabited chiefly on account of its fishery and the trade with European ships, the interior is very fertile, and furnishes a variety of excellent fruits and vegetables. What is of still greater importance, the island abounds also with swine, the flesh of which is delicious, and with goats and fowls, which are both delicate and cheap.

Some cattle, which captain Vancouver left in this island, have very much multiplied. It is a pity they have been permitted to run wild; though this has probably been the cause of their increasing so fast. It is said, that some time ago a herd came down from the mountains, and committed great ravages in the plantations of the valleys. A body of armed men was sent to drive them away; and in effecting it, four lives were lost. This determined the king to breed some of these animals in a domesticated state; and I saw a very handsome cow and calf, in an enclosure set apart for the purpose.

Before the introduction of different animals by Europeans, there were swine only on this island, and a small species of rat. This last animal is so numerous, that the inhabitants are obliged to hang up every thing, that it might not be destroyed by them. The king has lately received a couple of horses, that were brought out to him by a ship of the United States, and I understand that he has been promised a stallion and a mare from Spanish America.[+]

There are but few species of birds in the island, and of those the fowl is the only domestic one. The wild tribe consists of a small gray goose; woodcocks; hawks; little gray birds, with a bill like that of our parrot, and red feathers under the belly, of which the most beautiful cloaks and helmets are made; two other species that resemble our linnet, and some small birds, of no rarity.[61]

The coast of Owyhee abounds in fish, many of which are proper for salting. Amongst the rest is a flying-fish [*malolo*], which is caught in considerable quantities, and is sometimes more than a foot long.

I am told, that the island is perfectly free from all sorts of venomous reptiles. There is but one species of lizard, which is the hairy one [*makaula*]; it lives about the houses, and, though very ugly, is highly revered by the natives.

---

*Mauna Loa
**Makahuna had erupted in 1801 and caused damage in Kohala.
[+]*Lelia Byrd* had in fact brought four horses to Hawai'i from Spanish California in 1803.[60]

Owyhee is divided into six provinces, the first of which is called Cona [Kona]; the second, Cohola [Kohala]; the third, Hamacooa [Hamakua]; the fourth, Hidoos [Hilo]; the fifth, Poona [Puna]; and the sixth, Kau [Ka'u]. They are governed by the Nooy Nooy Eire [*nuinui ali'i*], or grandees, of the island. These provinces are again divided into Hopooas [*ahupua'a*], or districts, which are in the disposition of the second sort of nobility, called Pekynery Eiry [*pekepeke ali'i*].* The hopooas, or districts, are subdivided into farms, which are let to different families of the commonalty. These divisions are very useful, in collecting the revenues, which are paid by the farmers to the king and the nobility, in animals of different sorts, in cloth, and in red and yellow feathers.

Though in the account I have given of the Sandwich Islands, many things may strike the reader as extraordinary, I can assure him, that I have recorded no circumstance but what came under my own observation, or was related to me by persons whom I believed to be entitled to credit. For the truth, however, of what I derived from others, I can only thus far answer to the public, that I took all the care I could not to be misled.

In the Appendix, No. II, will be found a small but, I trust, not ill-chosen vocabulary of the language of these islands.** It is given more for curiosity than use, as there are several Europeans there, who may serve as interpreters; and, from the increasing civilization of the natives, the English language becomes better known to them every day.

I cannot take a final leave of these islands, without acknowledging, that the inhabitants behaved in the most friendly manner to us, during the whole of our intercourse with them. Surrounded by hundreds every day, we never experienced the smallest injustices or injury: on the contrary, we had many proofs of their honesty and hospitality; which shows, at least, how much they have improved since the time of captain Cook.

NOTE: *Neva*'s sailing from Kaua'i, on 20 June 1804, did not mark the end of Lisianskii's contributions to Hawaiian studies; nor had he "taken a final leave" of the Islands. Having wintered on Kodiak Island off southeastern Alaska, where much ethnography was once again undertaken, the Russians proceeded, on 20 August 1805, from Novo-Arkhangel'sk to Canton with a cargo of Company wares. Lisianskii had no intention of returning to the Hawaiian Islands; he meant merely to sail south to latitude 36°30'N, moving westward from approximately longitude 166°, examining an area where Nathaniel Portlock had supposedly seen signs of land in 1786. No islands were observed where they were more or less expected. On 3-15 October, however, vast clouds of birds

---

*lesser (*lit.* dwarf, midget, tiny) chiefs, as compared with the *nuinui* (great, grand, important) chiefs
**The list of words is given as Appendix C, on pp. 209-213.

surrounded *Neva* in latitude 26°40' N, longitude 173°23' W, by the Russians' reckoning; and at 10 p.m. that night, after the special watch had been dimissed with lowered spirits, "the vessel received a violent shock".[62] *Neva* ran aground on the low island that had been discovered. Heavy articles, including guns, were jettisoned in such a way that they might later be reclaimed, the ship was delicately floated off the shoal, and a disaster was averted. A sudden squall at 5 a.m. once again flung *Neva* shoreward but, once again, Lisianskii's luck held good. At 9 a.m. on 18 October 1805, a Russian party landed on 'Lisiansky's Island', which was occupied only by giant seals and aggressive, pecking birds. They left behind a message buried in a bottle, to record the visit for posterity, and hastened back aboard. From *Neva* Lisianskii then surveyed his desert island (not a single stream nor living tree was seen). It lay in latitude 26°2'48"N, longitude 173°42'30"W, and was a mile and a quarter across on its NW-SE axis. Neva Shoal, on which they had earlier almost come to grief, lay a mile to its ESE. On Lisiansky Island, the Russians spotted several large tree trunks like redwood, which had evidently drifted from America, countless raucous pigeons, and a small calabash with a round hole cut in it--perhaps a lost Hawaiian gourd. Lisianskii's own chart of his find was printed in St Petersburg in 1812,[63] then reprinted by John Booth after an engraving supervised by Aaron Arrowsmith in the English edition of Lisianskii's *Voyage Round the World*.[64] Lisiansky Island (as it is now spelled) has, during this century, been under the control and jurisdiction of the US Navy.

N. I. Korobitsyn

Twenty-one days out from the Markeskie [Marquesas] Islands, we came in sight of Ovigii [Hawai'i], one of the Sandwich Islands. On 29 May, at five o'clock in the afternoon, *Nadezhda* took her leave of us and went on her way to Kamchatka and thence, with the embassy aboard her, to Japan. She signaled to us. We went up to her and wished her a successful voyage. An 11-gun salute was then exchanged, as the proper flags were raised aloft on both ships. Having thus taken leave of our companion, we made for the island of Ovigii. *Nadezhda* had already set a course for the SW and by seven o'clock she was no longer visible on the horizon.

We drew up to Ovigii and entered Karakakoa [Kealakekua] Bay at 4 o'clock on 30 May. We let go anchors and came to a stop as swarms of islanders came out to us in their native craft,* bringing with them produce of various sorts and other art objects ** peculiar to their nation. Compared with the Markeskie Islanders, these people did not seem particularly wild in their behavior. Their way of life, though, is very like that of the Markeskiens. Most of them, too, go always naked. However, in point of physique, stature, and countenance, the Ovigiians are quite different from the Markeskiens; and among those who boarded our ship, not a few were strangely attired, not in shirt, breeches and shoes indeed, but in frock-coat or caftan or seaman's jacket, with hats on their heads. Such dress struck us as particularly extraordinary at the very start of our visit only. All such clothing, of course, is picked up from the English and the Americans from the United States that call at these Islands annually to get necessary provisions for their vessels and, particularly, to get fresh water, which the islanders furnish from springs in the mountains of Ovigii. Because of the inconvenience of bringing the water down in barrels, they lug it from the hills on their shoulders, using calabashes a bit like pumpkins to look at.† Each one holds from two to three buckets full of water. Then they get the water from shore to ship in their own craft. For all this, they receive from the Europeans mostly articles of clothing which, when donned, give them a very strange and wonderful appearance.

Observations on the Island of Ovigii

By reason of its large population and size, the island called Ovigii is generally considered the most important of the Sandwich Islands. It lies in latitude 19°28'N, longitude 155°56'W, extending from south to north. It has a fairly high elevation, a pleasant appearance, and boasts a sufficiency of well situated planta-

---

* Korobitsyn's memory is at fault, to judge by the evidence of Gedeon and Lisianskii: see p. 31.
** *natsional'nye i khudozhestvennye predmety* (literally 'national and artistic objects')
† *hue wai* [water gourd]

tions and extensive plains. There are on Ovigii two large mountains, Mouna-Roa [Mauna Loa] and Mounika [Mauna Kea], the former being hardly shorter than the peak of Teneriffe [Canary Islands], if indeed it is not taller. It looks almost flat, however, because of the enormous area it occupies, and the summit is usually lost in clouds because of the thickness of the atmosphere. We could not examine the second mountain, it being too far distant from the coast.* On the west coast of the island there is a bay called Karikakoe [Kealakekua]. It was there that we had anchored, the water being between 17 and 40 *sazhen* [fathoms], sandy bottom with coral and mussels. The bay offers shelter from winds from the north, east,and south.

Around this bay and indeed all along the west coast of the island there are numerous native dwellings made of coconut palm and reed leaves. In arrangement, these dwellings are something like the straw-roofed sheds** that one sees in Russian villages, or the brickyards with the lofty, two-pitched roofs but low walls: they too sometimes have doors only three feet high and one or two windows of proportionate dimensions.[66] There are no floors in the native huts, only grass mats[67] thrown over the earth and serving as beds for the inhabitants. Nor did we see any such indispensible household articles as dishes and crockery. There were only calabashes. As regards cleanliness, these people cannot be compared with Markeskiens.

The Ovigiians, men and women alike, wear hardly any clothing but pieces of bark-cloth† which they [men] put on as one would a girdle [*malo*], passing them between the legs and so covering the private parts.‡ From the same bark-cloth, the women make what they term a *pau* [*pâ'û*], between 1/2 and 3/4 of an *arshin* wide.+ They wear it like a skirt, though in its brevity it does not reach down to the knees. This is the national dress. As for tattooing or incising the body itself, it is not a general custom among the Ovigiians as among the Markeskie.

The Ovaigians are of middling height and not especially strong in their physique. They have a light brown complexion. Many bear scars on their body that result from some venereal or scorbutic disease or other. They consider aienia ['*aieana*] root an effective preventative against the disease in question, and for the same reason will drink sea water which, they suppose in their ignorance, is also quite efficacious.++ In their incontinence, however, they infect one another; nor do they exercise any control over themselves where food is concerned.

Among the edible fruits and other products that flourish on the island are significant quantities of bananas and coconuts, as well as breadfruit, sweet potato, taro, watermelons, cabbage and radishes, and a fair amount of sugar cane. A

---

* from Kona. Mauna Kea is actually 3 miles nearer to salt water than is Mauna Loa.
** Cook's "oblong corn stacks"[65]
† literally 'papyrus'
‡ literally 'the body's shame' (Russian: *sramotu tela*)
+ between 14" and 21"
++ but see p. 96 on the supposedly harmful effects of immersion in it

quite adequate number of swine and goats are raised by the natives, as well as fowls. On occasion, a native may also have horned cattle: the English navigator Cook left bulls and cows behind on the island for breeding purposes.* Since the Ovigiians are inexperienced in the art of cattle-raising, though, they have allowed the stock to roam and multiply in the woods away from all villages, with the result that the animals have grown so wild as to run at human beings just like wild beasts. But the king alone, it should be noted, may eat these cattle. Another prohibition affects the consumption of the first two varieties of animal that I mentioned, swine and goats. Only males may eat their flesh; women are prevented from doing so by the native laws and *tapus*. Women are likewise prevented from eating a type of plant--the banana. The Ovigiian women are not adequately nourished, because of this local custom of imposing *tapus* on certain kinds of food. One may add, in this connection of prohibitions, that they are also forbidden to eat food in the presence of their husbands, and are even deprived of the right to enter their husbands' quarters freely. Special yurts** are allotted for their use, and their husbands visit them in them at night. The Ovigiians regard all these customs as inviolate law. In general, they live in the same fashion on all the inhabited islands of the chain. All but one island, Atuvai [Kaua'i], are now in the possession of the King of Ovigii, Tomi-Omi [Kamehameha], whose sway over all those in his realm is very great. The people of Ovigii Island itself especially regard him as their absolute sovereign, with power of life and death over his subjects both on that island and elsewhere within the compass of his domains. Those subjects may number as many as 30,000 men, women,and children.

The better to govern his people, the king has appointed elders or officials to every village and throughout the islands. Among the officials are two Englishmen, named Young and Devis [Davis], who enjoy the king's confidence. The former stands in for the king at the helm of government during his absence from Ovigii Island, while the latter acts as his military chief of staff when it is a question of conquering new islands. Some fifty British sailors have also made their homes there. They are employed in necessary tasks, for instance, in building ships, and in other useful arts. The king already has perhaps twenty small schooners, built for him by the English; as for the things needed to fit those schooners out, such as anchors, heavy canvas, cannon and cannon-balls, the Ovigiians have no trouble in getting them from the United States of America each year. The Ovigiians, and their king especially, may be said to engage in substantial trading for supplies with the Americans.

While we were at the island, at Karikakopskaia† Bay, the king and all his warriors, embarked on eight schooners and a great many native canoes, were gathered at other islands under his jurisdiction to prepare an attack against the

---

* an error: Vancouver left the breeding stock, in 1794
** little huts; no skin-over-frame structure (literal translation) ever existed in Hawai'i
† Korobitsyn makes various attempts at Kealakekua.

ruler of the island of Atuvai. The royal residence, which is on the Bay, consists of six dwellings or yurts, but is no different in construction from the dwellings of the people. Not far away is a small lake or pond with a few coconut-palms and banana trees planted about it.* On its banks stand two heathen temples, called Ogio and Kaira,[69] where sacrifices are offered and which contain respectively three and nine wooden images resembling neither man nor beast. In front of them are strewn great quantities of coconuts and other produce, which the natives bring as offerings. Entrance to these temples is forbidden to the common people, only the king and his officials and the priests having that privilege. They are not large structures** and are in no way distinguished from the native dwellings or yurts.

A short distance from these temples, on a stone elevation, stands another large temple.† It contains fifteen idols of the same workmanship. In front of these idols is a sacrificial altar built on four stakes, man-high, where the natives bring as offerings the corpses of criminals and captives, whose heads they impale around the temple, side by side, as on a prison stockade. The idols in this larger temple are regarded as the gods of war and vengeance or of the beginning and culmination of growth. All such services to the many native deities are performed only by the king, his officials, or the priests: the rest of the people have no knowledge of ritual or of the offerings, and have not the least conception of any form of divinity.

Should one native commit an offense against another, the case is brought before the elders. Important cases may be submitted by the latter to the king himself, and it is he who imposes punishment, according to the gravity of the transgression, after judgment has been made. On occasion, an offended party may, without duly observing all the rules, pay priests to pray to the gods for the death of the offender, or for avengement of the offense. If his antagonist finds out about this, he may well not wait for the gods' vengeance to strike him down, but grow pained with anxiety or even lose his mind. These are circumstances in which many natives will, for one specific reason or another, take their own lives. There are customs, moreover, that make it obligatory on everyone but the young to pull out a tooth on the death of a king. Similarly when the elder of a village dies, all the inhabitants will extract one tooth. Even today, this custom is strictly observed on Ovigii, as if it were an established law.

While at anchor by the island, we replenished our ship's provisions by obtaining, through barter with the natives, eleven hogs. For those animals, we gave two *pood* and 20 pounds‡ of bar-iron and sail-cloth more than 40 *arshin* in length.⁺ We also acquired edible roots and garden produce, in exchange for axes,

---

* Korobitsyn retraces Samwell's steps of February 1779.[68]
** or, 'they are not of massive structure'
† 'an even larger place of idols'
‡ 94 pounds
⁺ 93 feet

adzes, and Tiumen'* carpets. We were not in need of water, having stowed an adequate amount of it at the Markeskie Islands.

Of natural products, so to speak, only seashells and corals are to be found on Ovigii in some quantity; of artistic products made by the natives, mention may be made of objects from bark-cloth, grass mats, and plaited straw helmets. All may be had in exchange for items of worn-out clothing or for any one of a number of iron articles, such as axes, adzes, knives, scissors, and the like, but not for mere pretty bagatelles as at the Markeskikh [Marquesas] Islands or for 4" pieces of hoop-iron. In consequence of the annual visits to their shores of English and American vessels, the Ovigiians have some notion of the true value of things they need. In this respect, they differ from the Markiziane [Marquesas Islanders].

With regard to the Ovigiians' character, I would say that it is necessary to deal with them very carefully under all circumstances, avoiding any cause for dissatisfaction on their part. It is that people's custom, one must remember, to avenge themselves in any way feasible for the smallest offense given. As conclusive proof of this, one may cite the death of the world-famous English mariner Cook, who lost his life prematurely at the Ovigiians' hands because of his severe treatment of some of them.

We left Ovigii on 4 June. Sailing from Karekakoiskaia Bay at 10 p.m., under a gentle NE breeze, we laid a course to the northwest, making all speed toward our destination within Russian possessions, Kadiak [Kodiak]. On the 7th, we passed by Atuvai Island which, as seen, is separate from the other Sandwich Islands, being ruled by its own king. That monarch, whose name is Tamurii [Kaumuali'i], came out in his canoe to visit us and proved able to express himself, after a fashion, in English. Knowing that preparations for an attack against him were even then being made by the King of Ovigii, Tamurii wanted us to bring our ship up to Atuvai and so protect him from that other ruler. In return for this, he would willingly have agreed to place himself and his island under Russian domination. In view of the absence of our ambassador, Rezanov, however, who was already on his way to Kamchatka aboard *Nadezhda*, we did not think ourselves in a position to concur with the king's plans. Nor would we have been acting prudently in failing to take advantage of a wind that now chanced to be very favorable to us. For both these reasons we went round the island without putting in. Lying in latitude 22°N and longitude 159°55'W, I will just say here, Atuvai is pleasantly situated, boasts an abundance of fresh produce and sugar cane, and is suitable for the growing of rice and wheat alike. It has more than one bay appropriate for use as an anchorage...

* coarse rugs of a sort made and sold in that Russian town

N.P. Rezanov (1825)

The number of our sick was increasing and we impatiently awaited our arrival at the Sandwich Islands in order to refresh ourselves somewhat. On the 27th,* to our no small delight, we finally caught sight of Ovaigi at eight o'clock in the morning. Holding our course toward its southeastern extremity, we hoped to be able to tack around it** and take on fresh provisions in abundance. On this day we had highly favorable weather, the winds so hastening our progress that we arrived earlier than we could have expected to.

As Dixon and La Pérouse relate in their *Voyages*, the Sandwich Islands were discovered by the Spaniards in the 16th century.+ Gaetan found them in 1542, while on his way from Mexico, and called them King's Islands. Another chain, twenty miles to the west, he called Garden Island. Sailing from the Society Islands, to North America in 1778, Captain Cook spotted Woa [Oʻahu], Atuai [Kauaʻi], and Onigio [Niʻihau] on 18 January, Origau [Lehua] on the 24th, and Tagura [Kaʻula] on the 28th. He put in at Atuai and Onigio. On his passage back from North America, in the same year, he found Move [Maui] and other adjacent islets on 26 November, and Ovaigi [Hawaiʻi] on the 30th. The whole chain consists of 11 islands, lying between 18°53' and 22°15'N, and between 154°54' and 160°24'W..... All but Marotogi [Molokini] and Tagura, the sixth and eleventh islands [from the east] are inhabited. Cook gave them the general name of the Sandwich Islands in honor of Count Sandwich,† under whose patronage he had performed that voyage.

Ovaigi is the largest and most southerly of the islands. At four o'clock in the afternoon we were some 5 nautical miles distant from its southwestern shores. We already saw from afar the flatness of the great Mount Roa [Mauna Loa], which is given in Cook's *Voyage* as 724 feet higher than the Peak of Teneriffe [Canary Islands]; and the closer we drew to the island, the more pleasant it seemed. Mountains whose summits were lost in clouds inclined insensibly toward the watery horizon, forming an amphitheatre beautified yet further by coconut palms and other trees whose variegated greens made a lovely spectacle.‡

Shortly after this, we saw canoes approaching us, one with a sail. There were two islanders in the first canoe and they were bringing a woman out. They were not allowed aboard but were ordered to come with provisions. Many natives then came out with coconuts, sugar cane, and a piglet and a few *batates*++ were

---

* Old Style; 7 June 1804 New Style. See comments on calendar use in the Introduction.
** This is puzzling. Rezanov possibly means 'about near' it.
+ This is, today, not accepted as fact by most historians.
† *i.e.*, John Montague, 4th Earl of Sandwich (1718-1792), at that time First Lord of the Admiralty (1771-1782)
‡ The present Hawaiʻi Volcanoes National Park and southwestern limit of Puna.
++ sweet potatoes

also brought. The natives wanted to barter skillfully made barkcloths, ropes and the like against our goods, but we demanded supplies. Their craft were like those of the Markezskikh [Marquesas] Islanders, but they themselves were far worse looking than the Nukugivans [Nukuhivans]. They were naked, the hair on their head being cut in various ways but usually along the sides so as to leave a crest running, as it were, like a casque-like helmet across the whole length of the head. They were lean, and their bodies were covered with scabs. Many had front teeth missing and had tattoos on their bodies representing animals: wild beasts, lizards, fish. One individual had a tattooed musket-and-bayonet on him. They spoke a few words of English, but so few and so incorrectly that their knowledge did not make it any easier for us to explain our needs. A high wind brought our barter to an end. We moved further off shore and the islanders returned home, having promised to bring us out supplies on the following morning.

By 4 a.m. on the 28th, we were about thirty miles from shore. Standing in for it again, we neared the island's southern point at 10a.m.: at a distance of three or four miles we could see a number of native dwellings* and, at that juncture, several canoes came out to us with supplies. We traded three *arshin* of particolored material for a suckling pig. The natives had brought out a large hog, too, but we failed to come to terms over it: we offered an axe, a piece of particolored material, knives, shirts, and a blanket, but nothing sufficiently tempted the islander in question and he carried the hog back to shore.

The Sandwich Islands had been fixed as our point of separation from *Neva*, which was to proceed thence to the Northwest of America. Though all instructions for that country had been issued by me even while we had been in Brazil, and sent across to *Neva* in case of an unexpected parting of the ways, still I busied myself with additional directions. I also, at this time, sent off to Kodiak a carpenter and some hunters** who had been in *Nadezhda*.

Toward nightfall we stood away from the coast. Around 3 a.m. on the 29th, however, we again moved in to the island: for want of fresh provisions, we intended to call in at Karakontsa [Kealakekua] Bay, where the celebrated Cook ended his life in an unhappy manner, but a headwind hindered us. The wind was followed by a perfect calm which kept us some distance off shore. We could see the island, with its famous Mount Roa, in the mists.

At six o'clock that evening we did part company with *Neva*. Flags were hoisted on both vessels and sailors on *Neva*'s shrouds shouted, "Hurrah!" We responded in the same way. *Neva* then went on to the [Hawaiian] Islands for supplies while we, wasting no time, set our new course. A leak in *Nadezhda* had grown to such a point that water now needed to be pumped out twice or three times a day. The fact had deprived us of our opportunities of making the ac-

---

* These were necessarily, in view of *Nadezhda*'s course, along the shores NE of Ka Lae, toward (modern) Nâ'âlehu.
** *promyshlenniki*

quaintance of the Sandwich Islands themselves and of the natives' customs; but failure to obtain supplies obliged us, exhausted though our strength already was, to subject ourselves to new trials.

Joseph the Marquesan* is coming with us further. He did not care for the natives of the Sandwich Islands: he feared they might eat him, nor could he even understand their language. His pronunciation and theirs sounded similar to us, but they could not make each other out.

---

*Jean le Cabri, a French castaway whom Kruzenshtern had carried from Nuku Hiva to Hawai'i, then on to Kamchatka.[70]

I.F. Kruzenshtern

At six o'clock on Thursday morning, 7 June, we reckoned ourselves to be at no great distance from the eastern side of the island of Ovagi [Hawai'i]. I therefore altered course from NNW to NW by W. At half past eight we in fact caught sight of the eastern extremity of the island: it lay NW of us at a distance of 36 miles.* We could not make out the mountain Mouna-Ro [Mauna Loa], however. By noon we were in latitude 19°10', and the eastern extremity of Ovagi, in latitude 19°34', lay due north of us. Inasmuch as the longitude of this point had been fixed by Captain Cook with great precision,[71] and found to be correct by his disciple and follower Vancouver, we found it a suitable opportunity to check our chronometers for error. The longitude of the point was given as 154°22' 30"W by chronometer no. 128, 154°45'00"W by chronometer no. 1856, 154°29'30"W by the Pennington, and had been determined by Captain Cook as being 154°56'00"W.[72] The observations of Captains Cook and Vancouver left no room for doubt, so far as the true longitude was concerned, and our own lunar observations on 4 and 11 June, the day after our departure from Ovagi, completely confirmed the fact. Our readings of 4 June made the error of no. 128 to be 39', and of 11 June 35', too much to east. We had thus only to correct the longitude of our watches by this newly ascertained difference, and to rate them as best we could while still at sea....**

Whilst in Port Anna Maria [Taio-hae] we had managed to procure from the Nukugivans, on both ships, only seven hogs, not one of which weighed more than two *pood*.⁺ It was the acute want of viands that had imposed on me the obligation of calling at the Sandwich Islands, where I supposed, with some degree of certainty, that I should be able to supply myself with a sufficiency of them. My people were all healthy,† indeed, but bearing in mind that salt-beef had been their diet on the protracted voyage from Brazil, save only during the first weeks after our sailing thence, I was naturally apprehensive lest scurvy appear among them despite all precautions. Since we would be bound to spend at least a month at Kamchatka if we were to be in a condition to reach Nagasaki by mid-September (when the change in the monsoon occurs by the shores of Japan), it was important to hasten there. Nothing, however, could be of more importance than the preservation of my people's health; and I accordingly abandoned my hope of following a different route from the Washington [Marquesas] Islands from those taken by all my predecessors in those seas--a route along which I might reasonably have hoped to make discoveries. In short, I felt obliged to

---

* According to notes inserted in Table VI of vol. 3 of Kruzenshtern's *Puteshestvie* (p. 45), however, Hawai'i had first been glimpsed 39 miles off to the NW, at 8 a.m.
** Hydrographic data have been omitted here.
⁺ 74 lbs
† Rezanov demurs: see p. 83.

touch at the Sandwich Islands without fail. To lose as little time as possible in doing so, however, I decided to drop anchor nowhere and merely to coast by the shores of Ovagi for a couple of days; for according to the accounts of all mariners who had visited these islands, the natives would come out to ships 15 or even 18 miles from shore to barter foodstuffs for European goods.[73] Having already reached this decision, then, I first stood in for the southeast coast of Ovagi, reasoning that if we sailed right round the island we should certainly acquire quite sufficient provisions. Events showed how greatly we were deceived in such expectations.

After approaching the shore to within six miles, we went about and kept on a course parallel to it under nothing but topsails. Spotting a few native craft coming out to us, we hove to. Nothing that the islanders brought out with them corresponded in the least to our expectations. A small amount of sweet potato, a few dozen coconuts, and one small suckling-pig were all we could get from them by barter, and even those trifles we did not get without difficulty or without paying a high price, for the islanders would take nothing for their wares but broadcloth, of which there was not an *arshin* aboard at my disposal.* Cloth of their own manufacture they offered us in quantity, but our acute need of provisions obliged me to prohibit our accepting anything else in payment. On this same occasion, one elderly native had brought a quite young girl out, presumably his daughter, and from pure venality was offering her to us as a victim to lust. To judge by the girl's bashfulness and modesty, she was still entirely innocent. The native was unsuccessful in his efforts and left highly vexed that he had brought his goods in vain. Poor weather accompanied by rain and squalls prevented our seeing any craft that might have come out from the shore after this, so we moved away from the island, steering SSE under a fresh easterly wind.

The scarcity of provisions that we had met with surprised me not a little, for the coast of Ovagi that we were moving past seemed quite heavily populated and looked well cultivated too. The part of the island that we saw had, in truth, a delightful appearance. To judge by it, not one of the Washington Islands can be compared with Ovagi. The whole shore was dotted with dwellings and covered with coconut palms and plantations of various kinds. Even the number of craft that were plainly visible on the shore left us in no doubt about the size of the local population.[74]

From its low eastern extremity, the coast of the island rises gradually to the foot of the mountain called Mouna-Ro, the summit of which, by the reckoning of our astronomer Horner, is 2,254 *sazhen* high and hence 350 *toises* higher than the peak of Teneriffe [Canary Islands].** It is a remarkable mountain, both in height

---

* Kruzenshtern bends the facts here. None, perhaps, was immediately accessible, but a good deal had been stowed at Kronstadt: see p. 94.
** The mountain's true height is 13,677 feet above sea level. Horner was accurate to within 153 feet.

and in general appearance, and is justly known as Table Mountain, for its top, which at this time of year was free of snow, is perfectly level save for an almost imperceptible rise on the eastern side. On our first day here, it had been clear of clouds only for a few moments--it is nearly always, in fact, enveloped by cloud cover; but on the following two days we were several times able to admire its awesome mass, the summit of the mountain alone covering an area of 13,000 square feet. Even then though we did not gaze on it in its entirety; nor can one often do this, for when the upper part is free from mist, the center is lost in almost perpetual clouds which seem somehow suspended from the majestic peak above them. Mouna-Ro is most plainly visible in the morning, when the air is not yet full of vapor.

Judging by those of them who boarded us, the Sandwich Islanders cannot be compared with the Nukugivans in point of looks. By the standards of the latter, indeed, they are an ugly people. They are shorter than the Nukugivans,* of anything but stately build, and far darker in color. Their bodies lack the heavy tattooing and body ornamentation that covers so many of the Nukugivans. Of the Ovagians that we saw, however, there was hardly a single one whose body was not marked by patches caused either by the disease of lasciviousness or by immoderate drinking of kava ['awa]. Such marks, one must add, could hardly have been produced by the latter cause among the poorer part of the natives. Decided though the advantage appeared to be in the Nukugivans' favor from the physical point of view, however, the Ovagians seemed equally superior to their southern neighbors in point of intellectual capability. Their constant dealings with Europeans, particularly Englishmen, of whom there were several living in the Islands, had no doubt contributed more than a little to produce that effect; and we noted cheerfulness, agility, and animation in the eye of all Ovagians with whom we had occasion to deal, to greater or lesser extent.

The Ovagians build sea-going craft and sail them with far greater skill than do the Nukugivans, to whom the sea does not seem a natural element. From the few specimens given in Captain Cook's *Voyages* of words of the languages spoken by natives of the Sandwich and Mendoza [southern Marquesas] Islands,[76] it should seem that the natives in question ought perfectly to understand each other. For certainly the words given by Cook indicate the greatest similarities. Our wild Frenchman,** however, could not in the least comprehend the Ovagians and was quite unable to serve us as interpreter among them. It was only the few English words that these islanders pronounced fairly plainly that enabled us to understand them to some extent and after a fashion. But our wild Frenchman possibly failed to understand them because of a significant difference in pronunciation. At all events, he formed so poor an opinion of the Ovagian Islanders that he repented of his earlier decision to settle down among them, and asked me to take him along

*King had found them similarly "not tall"[75]
** the Frenchman le Cabri

with me. Though I had good enough reason to punish him for his unsatisfactory conduct toward us at Nuku Giva, I could not refuse his request, plainly foreseeing that, given his character, he would be even more despised and unfortunate among the Ovagian Islanders than he had been among those of Nuku Giva.

At dawn on the morning following, we made for the southern point of Ovagi where, by Cook's account, we expected to find that large village from which an abundance of provisions had been brought to him.[77] I was hoping to acquire fresh provisions, with equal facility, both at this place and along the southwestern side of the island. We weathered the point [Ka Lae] at eleven o'clock: it was conspicuous because of a low broken rock, and because surrounded, at a distance of several hundred *sazhen*, by a stony reef over which waves broke with a great roar. By Cook's reckonings, this point lies in latitude 18°53', and longitude 155°45'. At midday it bore 78°SE of us, at a distance of no more than three miles. Astronomer Horner and Lt Levenshtern fixed the latitude, and found it to be 18°54'45" N, that is, almost what Cook had determined. With regard to longitude, we found the error of our chronometers to be one minute less than on the day before.

Just as soon as we spotted the village mentioned above, we lay by, perhaps two miles out. After two hours or even longer had passed, three native craft came out toward us. In the first was a large hog weighing some two and a half *pood*.* The sight cheered us considerably, indeed, I was already destining the animal as Sunday dinner for my people on the morrow. My mortification was therefore the greater when I realized that it would not be possible to purchase even that, the only beast brought out to us. I offered everything I had at my disposal for the hog; but the vendor refused the best axes, knives and scissors as well as whole pieces of material and complete suits of clothes, demanding only a piece of broadcloth large enough to envelop him, like a mantle, from head to toe. And we were not in a position to give him one.** From another canoe we bought a small suckling-pig:[+] it was the only other victual to be had from all three craft. On this occasion there had also come out to us a very smartly got up

---

* 2 1/2 *pood* = 90lbs[78]

** The "pieces of material" offered by Kruzenshtern (Russian: *kuski tkani*) were plain textile fabrics; the "broadcloth" in question (Russian: *sukonnoi plashch'*) was relatively fine woolen cloth, referred to by Lisianskii as "plain cloth" (*prostoi kholst*). The Hawaiians were very willing to take this woolen cloth but, so we learn from three informants, they preferred striped ticking cloth (*polosatyi tik*) or, better yet, printed calico or linen (*naboika*).[79] The broad distinction between coarse woolen fabric and printed linen is correctly suggested by the "common Russian cloth" and "printed coarse linens" in the (1814) English version of that Voyage.[80] A separate trade was conducted in sailcloth (*ravenduk* or *parusina*), of which both Young and the Hawaiians themselves had a high opinion and some need.[81] One piece of fine canvas secured four hogs for *Neva*. See also p. 92 below. Further discussion of Russian-Hawaiian trade and 'materials' and 'cloth' occurs in Part 3: 'Barter' and 'Clothing and Body Ornamentation', below.

[+] for 7' of cloth, according to Rezanov

and shameless young woman who spoke a few words of English. Her fate was no different from that of her sister the previous day.

This day's unsuccessful barter with the islanders convinced me that without broadcloth, which they wanted even for trifles, we should not manage to get anything even in Karakakoa [Kealakekua] where, as it was the residence of the Ovagian king, the celebrated Tamagama [Kamehameha], the natives certainly lived more luxuriously and where, in consequence, all foodstuffs might be supposed to cost more. Such, it seemed, was the enormous change that had taken place in the circumstances of these natives, in the space of only ten or twelve years! Tianna [Kaiana], a chief of the island of Ottu-Vai [Kaua'i], whom Mers [Meares] had taken to China with him in 1789, had invariably asked in Canton, when he had wanted to know the price of some article, "How much iron for this?"[82] A whole year was this Tianna constantly in the company of Europeans, yet he did not lose the ingrained habit of valuing iron highly. Today, though, the Ovagians almost despise the metal, nor have they much time even for the most necessary objects made from it. Nothing would satisfy them when we were there that did not serve to gratify their vanity.

Seeing not a single craft more coming out to us, we moved under small canvas along the southwest side of the island* then, at six o'clock, steered south to keep clear of land during the night. Though I had now but little hope of acquiring fresh provisions, still I did not mean to give up altogether until I had tried my luck on the west coast and in the vicinity of Karakakoa. So about one o'clock next morning I put the ship about to the northward and by five o'clock Mauna-Roa lay NNE of us, the southern tip of Ovagi, NE by E. A thick mist covered the entire island. Then, at eight o'clock, the wind veered to the northward and grew so faint that, even had it been blowing favorably for us, we should have had little hope of getting up to Karakakoa. I resolved to leave Ovagi without wasting any time and to make for Kamchatka, where we were due to arrive by mid-July. Before announcing my new intention, though, I had Dr Espenberg examine all our people most minutely. Happily, not the slightest signs of scurvy were detected on any man. Had Espenberg detected even one or two indications of the disease, I need hardly add, I should unfailingly have gone to Karakakoa even if it had cost us a precious week. (A change of my original plan, as I said, now obliged me to reach Nagasaki that same summer; and that would certainly be done with the greatest difficulty only if the NE monsoon set in.) I then announced my decision to proceed immediately to Kamchatka to my officers, explaining the reasons for it. For three months already, they and I had shared our common seamen's diet. They had been rejoicing in the prospect of soon reaching Karakakoa and nurturing hopes of getting fresh provisions. Yet, despite that, no one seemed displeased by the change of plan. Captain Lisianskoi, whose time was not of equal consequence to him, decided that he would stay a few days at Karakakoa before proceeding on this way to Kad'iak [Kodiak] Island....

---

* by Kauna Point

F.I. Shemélin

At 9 o'clock on the morning of 27 May,* we caught sight of the shore of the
large island in the Sandwich group, Ovagii [Hawai'i]. Its eastern extremity lay to
the NW of us, at a distance of thirty miles or a little more. The largest mountain,
which lies lengthways across the island and is called Mauna-ro [Mauna Loa] in
the native language, was hidden by clouds at this time. (Of all the great mountains on earth, Mouna-ro is a colossus with which only a few lying in the Cordil-
lera in Peru can be compared. Our astronomer, Mr Horner, reckoned it to have a
perpendicular height of 2,254 *sazhen*, that is, 4 1/2 *versta*, and so to exceed the
height of the peak of Teneriffe by 300 *toises*.)** Mouna-ro does not often, in
fact, reveal its majestic summit, for it is almost always enveloped in fumes of its
own production.+

As mentioned earlier, the Captain intended to touch at these islands only to get
the fresh provisions which, in his opinion, were most necessary if the ship's company was to be fortified. He feared that his sailors, who had long been on a salt
provisions diet, might suffer from scurvy and other diseases. But, in order to
waste no time, he had decided not to enter Karakakoa Harbor [Kealakekua Bay],
where stood the capital and the permanent residence of King Tomio-omio
[Kamehameha], and had judged it best merely to coast along Ovagii in the hope
that the islanders, seeing our ships, would at once bring poultry and fruit out to
us. With this in view, a shot was fired from our cannon when we had approached
the shore to within four or five miles.† Shortly after, three craft did in fact row
out from the island toward our ships. There were four natives in each of them.
The first craft headed straight for *Neva*, and was followed by the other two. At
first, though, they did not go right up to the ship's side but stood a little way off.
When various signs were made inviting them to approach *Neva*, they consented
to do so. We expected such visitors to call on us also with provisions, but were
forced to wait a long time, and a longing to get some fresh supplies rendered all
of us, and the seamen especially, impatient to the point of faint-heartedness. At
length, one of the craft that had visited *Neva* did come over to us, and so did
another. In the first there was only a young girl of 13 or 14, whom a native
presented by signs and wished to offer to the ship. When his proposal was
rejected, this native took his girl back to the shore with evident dissatisfaction at
his setback.[83] Inasmuch as the caresses of the beautiful Nukugivan maidens only
lately left by our sailors had not yet vanished from their hearts and memories,

---

*Old Style, see note p. 83
** 1 toise=6 feet, 1 verst=3500 feet, so Horner's estimate of the mountain's height above sea
level was 13,524 feet or, by the rougher *versty* measure, 13,750 feet.
+ mists, not volcanic gases
† off Hokuma Point: see Part 3,'Barter: The Coastal Encounters'

this dull-colored beauty had no worth to them in any case.* We then carefully examined the second craft, in the hope that it had better and more useful goods for us than the first had; and some men spotted a little suckling pig--a pig that, at this moment, no one would have exchanged even for the most beautiful woman, let alone for a savage girl. So much was evident from the satisfaction that suddenly flowed around the ship in her entirety. Everyone uttered the word 'piglet' with the keenest expression of voice. "They've brought a piglet," said one to another with delight. "There it is, in that craft under the leaves! What a sweet and plump little piggy!" Mistrusting the situation and afraid lest the native prove stubborn and decline to sell it, and take it off to *Neva* or to the shore, individuals spoke to the Captain about it, asking him to make the purchase as swiftly as possible. The piglet was duly purchased, for three *arshin* of red material. Included in that price were six coconuts and twelve *batates*, or sweet potatoes. Besides, we acquired one skein of fine and skillfully twined and very strong rope, which could serve to replace our best log-line, the price paid being 1 1/2 *arshin* of the same motley red stuff. Such was the extent of our trade that day. Toward evening we left the coast and stood out to sea ready to return to it in the morning.

On 28 May[84] we made for the southern point of the island, where we trusted to find the large village near which the celebrated Cook had acquired swine and other provisions in abundance.[85] By noon, we had rounded the cape, known to our Captain from Cook's description of it, had spotted the village, and were lying to. We were no more than two miles from the shore. After two hours or even longer, we spotted a craft heading straight for us. In it were three men and a young woman or girl of about 18, quite attractive to look at. It was she who, with amazing agility, leapt first onto the ship by way of the side-ropes and, at the first step on deck, said in English, "Good morning!" Looking at all with merry eyes full of animation, she held out her hand to everyone approaching her, or else went up to individuals and did the same. I watched her with particular attention, for her boldness and the freedom with which she was behaving with us were decidedly unusual for a native. Her vivacity was matchless. As for her nakedness, it was covered by nothing but an end of *khiabu* [*he pâ'û]** that is, a sash covering her in front. Her ornaments were not products of the island itself, such as the Nukugivans boasted, for on her arms, at her neck, and by her ankle-bones she wore beads of various hues, blue, green, red, white and cherry,+ though only in single strings. Cropped around, her hair had been cut off in front in the old French *à la verger* [straight-fringed] style, and was a light yellow color. The female islanders produce this coloration by a technique that merits note. They

---

* Shemelin and Levenshtern are far more explicit than the other informants on the matter of physical contact between Russian seamen and native women at Taio-hae.
** '*He*' is the Hawaiian indefinite article. The extreme brevity of one *pâ'û* let Clerke to mistake it for a (female-style) *malo*[86]
+ All these hues *could* have occurred in a natural seed necklace,[87] but Shemelin probably noted glass.

make an ointment from a certain light white stone thrown up by the sea,* then repeatedly smear their black hair with it. As a result, the hair turns the color of a light bay horse. They comb this spot upward, leaving the rest of their hair in its natural state.

Besides the commonplace complimentary expressions, this woman knew quite a few other English words, with the help of which she was able to assist her fellow-islanders in their trade with us. She served, indeed, as a spontaneous interpreter. There were no foodstuffs in the craft in which she had come out; nor was there anything else save material like that on Nuku Giva, threads, cords, mussel shells** and other trifles, at which no one even wanted to look. Besides, these things belonged to others and not to her. From her words and motions, however, it was obvious that she had come out to us with quite another sort of commerce in mind. She had no more success than had the girl the evening before.

Soon after this first craft, as I said, came a second; and in that one, there was a large fat pig. It may easily be imagined how the morsel struck men emaciated by a three-month fast, and what joy was occasioned by the prospect, promised us by this animal, of the most delicate and dainty meal. The Captain himself was among those anxious for such a feast and, though he had not yet bought the pig, he was already mentally arranging for it to be divided into suppers, on the morrow, for two tables: the gentry's and the seamen's. All awaited the conclusion of the purchase with impatience. But what misfortune! In exchange for the pig, the Captain offered his owner axes, whole pieces of red cloth and various small objects of metal, that is, iron-mongery; but the islander did not care for any of the goods shown him and would accept none of them for his livestock. He seemed calculating to us, of course; and in truth the axes shown to him were small and of slight value, as too were the caftans that we offered--though these might cost ten times as much as the axes. But the native was ignorant of the use of caftans. He wanted broadcloth, and he asked for it. The Captain did not see fit to satisfy him in that way.+ The native, in consequence, supposed that we had nothing whatever aboard and to hand that he would be prepared to accept for his pig and, not wanting to swap idle words with us, quickly went off home with it. Naturally, we were all vexed over this incident. But at whom were we to direct our dissatisfaction? At the Ovagiian or ourselves? The former was hardly to blame for not having chosen to exchange his beast, which weighed no less than three *pood*†, for eighty-kopek axes or clothing for which he had no call. And as for knives, scissors and other small ironware, his people had been supplied with

---

*powdered seashells or coral, in reality, often later mixed with grey clay[88]
** possibly *Nerita* or *Cypraea* shells, as used in *lei pipipi* and *lei leho*. Shemelin was a landsman, inclined to see 'mussels' by the seashore.
+ Elsewhere, Shemelin says that the captain was unaware of these unhappy developments in an important pig deal.
† 108 lbs--1 pood=36 lbs

them in such quantity by the Bostonians and Englishmen who called at their ports that they regarded such things as bagatelles. We ourselves had made an error in having other, better goods, yet not showing them to the vendor: for the Company had stowed aboard the ship large axes, which had not been shown to the Ovagiian, as much as 6,000 *pood* of bar iron,* and not a little sailcloth, which these islanders gladly purchased. The Ovagiian had seen none of these things. Finally, we had a sufficient store of broadcloths, of various prices and qualities, including some of cheap varieties, so that for one 30-rouble roll, measuring 22 *arshin*,** we could have bought a half-a-dozen pigs no matter how expensive. Having parted company with us, and being bound for the Russian-American Company settlements, the ship *Neva* put in at Karakaroa [Kealakekua] harbor, and there Captain-Lieutenant and *Chevalier* Lisianskii exchanged bar iron and sailcloth for such a quantity of swine as not only satisfied all the needs of his people, but also allowed him, because of a surplus, to land some on Kodiak alive,+ to breed. The leader of our expedition was no less concerned about preserving the health of his people and, as agent of the Company, I would certainly not have raised objections based on cost, observing that in such extreme circumstances price could hardly be a factor. And when refreshment of the crew was necessary in the Captain's own view,and when he (rightly) feared lest scurvy attack them, how could any expense be considered anything but trifling by the Company? Sadly, the Captain could do nothing whatever to help matters, not having been kept posted of developments. He learned the truth late, and when he did, he expressed the most profound and heartfelt regret, saying that he would not have regretted a whole bale of broadcloth, let alone a few pieces, if the purchase could thus have been sealed. And indeed a bale, if it had gone on fresh provisions, would have cost the Company no more than 400 roubles, given the low prices of those days, and would have provided 294 *arshin*† of cloth.

Having failed to purchase anything by the village on this day, as the day before, we put out from the shore and coasted up the southwest of the island. The Captain wished to try his luck on the morrow on its west coast near Karakakoa, and so gave orders at 1 a.m. to turn north, but a small and slightly contrary wind led him to despair of reaching that place. This was later offered as a pretext‡ for our not having sojourned in the harbor of Karakakoa, with its abundance of provisions. The Captain's own reasoning on this score, as may be seen from his own account, was as follows: from the day's unsuccessful trade with the is-

---

* This would be some 96 tons, a surprisingly large amount of ballast in bar-iron form, even though the Company settlements were in need of it.
** 51 feet 4 inches
+ Lisianskii speaks, in his own *Puteshestvie*, of landing a ram and ewe (brought from Brazil), but no hogs, on Kodiak. The question of Shemelin's reliability is again raised.
† 229 yards
‡ Company clerk Shemelin's less-than-friendly feelings toward Captain-Lt Kruzenshtern of the Navy become evident at this point of his text.

landers, it could be seen that, without broadcloth, nothing would be had at Karakakoa itself where--since it was the residence of the Ovagiian King Tamagama [Kamehameha]--the natives lived more luxuriously, and where consequently foodstuffs cost far more. To this, the Captain adds the consideration that he was bound to reach Nangasaki [Nagasaki] that same summer and that he anticipated meeting the NE monsoons by the Japanese coast if he delayed. These circumstances and his ignorance of what he might manage to get even at Karakakoa (he says), led him to alter his plans and so he decided to make straight for Kamchatka, wasting no more time. These reasons were at once communicated to the ship's company....

Right from the time when we left Brazil, I have had no occasion to speak of the leader of our expedition.* This, however, I think an appropriate place to explain the position he found himself in during the passage from the Washington [Marquesas] to the Sandwich Islands. Events that had occurred at Tatio-gae Bay (over which I may be allowed to pass in silence,)** the torrid clime, and the coarse food aboard had lowered his spirits. In consequence, he was imagining only the horrors of death and the constant dangers that could lead to it, though there were not the slightest reasons for such fear. At the slightest sound, knocking on the quarterdeck, or other sound in the Captain's quarters, his expression would change. He trembled and shook. For quite some time he could not bring himself to take up his pen and write something on paper with a shaky hand. In short, on the way to the Sandwich Islands and for want of fresh provisions and more particularly in consequence of spiritual agitation and unease of some other kind, his health so weakened and failed that we feared we should lose him forever. Here was a true object for pity. The restoration of his health alone, or even some alleviating of his suffering, would have merited and justified the sacrifice of a few days at Karakakoa, in which he might have rested and recouped his strength.

The Sandwich Islands having been fixed as our final rendezvous, it was here that *Nadezhda* and *Neva* were to part: *Neva* was to proceed to the island of Kodiak on the Coast of America, *Nadezhda* to Kamchatka. The present day was accordingly appointed the day when each ship would proceed on her way. A farewell ceremony began at 6 p.m. On *Neva*, all the seamen stood on the shrouds and three times shouted, "Urá!"+ We, on *Nadezhda*, responded in the same manner. Each ship then set course.

---

* He obviously saw Rezanov in this role.
** another in the series of open confrontations between Rezanov and Kruzenshtern which marked the whole voyage to Kamchatka: see Introduction
+ Hurrah![89]

A Brief Description of the Inhabitants of Ovagii

For two whole days we had had up to ten natives of the island of Ovagii on board with us. In their ugliness, they seemed repulsive to us, for their bodies were covered with some kind of sore which excreted morbid matter of a reddish-white color.[89] There were few parts of their body not covered in these sores, indeed; and where there were none, weals and cicatrices took their place. Certain travelers have ascribed this skin disease of the Ovagiians to excessive consumption of the drink called *kava* [*'awa*], made from a plant called pepper-plant.* This drink is known in all the islands of the Southern Hemisphere, but is drunk only by old men. The young do not touch it. The disease has also been ascribed to the licentiousness which, over a period of many years, has so intensified and spread that the disease is in the blood of every native, so that he is, as it were, born with it. Others again believe that the torrid clime in which these islanders live has some effect on their blood, the inflammation of which produces such sores. I reject all these opinions as incorrect and rest on statements made by Vasilii Moller,** a native of the Sandwich Islands, of whom I shall speak further. Moller declares that not all islanders are in fact subject to the disease, but only those who need on various occasions to be long in sea water and those who frequently bathe in it. The salinity of the water corrodes their dirty bodies. As proof, Moller adduces the fact that those of his countrymen who live at a little distance from the sea and, having less occasion to wash in sea water, bathe in fresh water, are quite free of the sores and have cleaner and whiter bodies even than those who are in good condition but now and then bathe in salt water. All this seems quite in accord with probability, for on the bodies of the islanders we did see there was filth and a disgusting lack of cleanliness. The natives could not be troubled to wash all this off in streams of pure water. A result was that their skin had grown so hard that wrinkles had formed even on the young: and these wrinkles had cracked, giving rise to sores of another kind. All the uncleanliness described here apart, the islanders' bodies looked as though they had had poured over them a whitish liquid[91] of some sort, which had dried to their back. But this

---

* *Piper methysticum*[90]

** a Hawaiian youth, Kanehoe (?)--in Russian Kenokhoia--whom Rezanov had in 1806 arranged to have sent from the Northwest Coast of North America to St Petersburg. Rezanov died at Krasnoiarsk, Eastern Siberia, in 1807, but Kanehoe did eventually reach St Petersburg and found another patron and protector, Vasilii Fedorovich Moller, a high State dignitary with an interest in naval matters. Christian baptism was followed by traditional Hawaiian name exchange, as least as far as Kanehoe was concerned, and he thereafter answered to the name Vasilii Moller. The Hawaiian remained in European Russia for eight years, taking passage from St Petersburg to Sitka in the Company vessel *Kutuzov* (Captain-Lieutenant L.A. Gagemeister [Hagemeister]) in September 1816, and reaching the Russian Northwest Coast fourteen months later. He apparently went on to Honolulu by the Company transport *Otkrytie* (Sitka to California) and some other craft. At least, Gagemeister's orders to Lieutenant Ia.A. Podushkin to that effect are extant. Of his subsequent fate in the Islands, nothing is known.

was, in all probability, nothing more than dried sea salt. The Nukugivans, living in a far hotter climate, not only suffer from no such sores (though they too frequently bathe in salt water,) but also have clean, soft, and--in the case of youngsters and women--even delicate skin. This is perhaps because of their greater cleanliness and habit of bathing many times every day in the deep streams of fresh water that flow in abundance from the granite hills surrounding their settlements. Besides,the Nukugivans smear their cleansed bodies with coconut oil, thereby again protecting themselves against the disease to which the Ovagiians are subject, and which, according to mariners, holds away in many islands of the Southern Hemisphere.

The Ovagiians whom we saw were not of large stature, lean, not especially well-knit in the body. Their facial features were not pleasant. Their glance was quick and stern, their behavior with us, though bold, lacking that liveliness and attractiveness that nature has bestowed on the Hercules of Nuku Giva. The Ovagiians did not have the custom of drawing designs on their body by way of ornamentation: though a few patterns were in evidence on some individuals, they struck me as irregular and showing no symmetry. The Ovagiians shave their head from the brow to the occiput, leaving a band two or three inches wide untouched, however. This narrow band alone is cut, being never more than one *vershók** in length, with the result that the native head looks strikingly like the helmet of the ancients, complete with plumage. The weals and cicatrices that we observed on their bodies had been left by wounds, voluntarily inflicted on themselves with a knife,** in order to honor or express grief at the passing of a father, relative, or friend. Front teeth knocked out had the same significance as bodily wounds: all the men who came aboard us had three or four front teeth missing.[93] This was done in accordance with the ancient customs of their forefathers.

Given that the inhabitants of islands scattered over the great expanse of the South Sea, the Mendoza [southern Marquesas], Washington [northern Marquesas] and Society Islands, Otagiti [Tahiti], and the Sandwich Islands themselves, had a similar language, we were supposing that the Frenchman Joseph Cabrit[+] who was sailing with us and who knew completely the tongue of the Nukugivans, among whom he had spent many years, would prove useful to us in our converse and dealings with the Sandwich Islanders. He wished to stay and live on these islands, or rather *had* wished, until the opportunity to return to the island of Nuku Giva might arise. It turned out, however, that he could not make out a word of what the Sandwich Islanders said, nor could the latter understand him. For this reason, he lost all inclination to remain among them and asked Captain Kruzenshtern to take him on to Kamchatka.

---

*1.75 inches
** no longer with the traditional shark's tooth[92]
+ Jean le Cabri; see p. 85, p. 88

The reigning king of these islands, Tomio-omio [Kamehameha], had made himself autocratic ruler of all of them, except for one or two, by dint of military victories and intellectual activity. (The island of Atuu or Otavai, the king of which is Tamura, or Tamu-Aru as Moller says it [Kaumuali'i], remains yet unconquered.) It is Tomio-omio's concern that his subjects, abandoning their natural propensities, beastliness, coarseness and sloth, should exercise themselves for the common good, tilling the land, raising domestic livestock, birds, etc. To this end, chiefs appointed by him vigilantly supervise the working people, and while thus engaging them in useful occupation, the king himself is not ashamed to pursue knowledge appropriate to his rank.

On Cattle Breeding and the Cultivation of Vegetables on Ovagii

For the spread of horned cattle, swine, and kitchen vegetables amongst them, the inhabitants of the island are indebted to a certain English captain whom they call, in their own language, Kankono.* The islander Kenokhoia, now Vasilii Fedorovich Moller, does not know at what date this captain delivered, apparently all together, ten cows and several bulls.** Not realizing how this livestock could be useful to them, the natives left the animals in complete independence and they, to find food for themselves, went off into the woods and hills where they bred. The islanders do not shoot these animals and do not consume them. Only foreigners, with the king's consent, sometimes kill a few head for their own requirements. At the same time, the captain in question also brought the Ovagiians billy-goats and rams, which today comprise their domestic livestock. The same Kankono also gave them seeds of various plants and taught them to lay out seed beds and to sow. Now, certain diligent proprietors can provide at any time of the year such greenstuffs as watermelons, melons, cucumbers, cabbage, potatoes and turnips. I think it proper to include here the names of these vegetables in the Sandwich Islanders' own language: watermelon, *ipu-khave* [ipu haole]; melon, *ipu-ara* [ipu 'ai];[+] cucumbers, *ipu-maia* [ka'ukama]; potato, *uvara* ['uala kahiki]. The islanders also call their own sweet-potato, *uvara* ['uala]. Moller has forgotten the words for cabbage and turnip in his own language.

Lieutenant of the Navy and *Chevalier* Gagemeister, once in the service of the Russian-American Company and a man who has wintered in these islands, has the following to say amongst other things† about the natives' principal crops.

The islanders' main foods are taro root and the sweet potato or *uvara*. Taro is cultivated in pools dug six feet deep. The earth excavated from the center,

---

* Vancouver
** February 1794
[+] *ipu* literally means 'cup' or 'container'
† in letters and reports of 1809-10 to the Company Main Office, and perhaps to Shemelin in person in 1815-16

placed round the edges, forms slopes up to the sides of the pools. When the latter are quite dug out, fresh water is introduced into them by way of narrow ditches; and when the bottom is flooded, the islanders stamp on it with their feet to soften it further,* thereby making it the more suitable for planting. Well-established grassy stems cut from a taro root are then planted out in the pool at a distance of one foot from each other. The taro ripens [matures] in six months unless prevented from doing so by prolonged drought. For the complete ripening of the root, the plant above it should stand in two feet or more of water. Sweet potatoes are similarly cultivated by means of transplant. They are placed at a shallow depth in the earth. Around the ponds in which taro grows the natives grow bananas, burying the young cut stems [shoots]** in the ground up to half their height. There are quantities of wild bananas in the woods and hills, indeed, as also of native taro; and the latter is very good. But it is yet better and firmer when cultivated in the pools. In other parts of the island there are many coconut palms and breadfruit trees. Rope⁺ is made from the former, albeit in small quantity. The king, who has taken possession of all coconut palms, gives the islanders one kernel apiece with which to make some.

Breadfruit, or [mountain] apples,† are placed in pits for two months when not quite ripe. After that time has elapsed, they are ready for use. Quite an amount of sugar cane is cultivated, though it serves mainly as pig food.‡ Moreover, much sugar cane grows wild in the hills, especially on the island of Atuai; and though the cane is fairly thick and tall, it seems juicy in comparison with West Indian sugar cane. There is also a root growing wild in the hills here called *Ti* [*kî*], from which the natives distill a good deal of rum.⁺⁺ Ti leaves are used instead of plates and to wrap up fish or meat†† when being cooked. The dry root may weight up to 10 pounds. When cooked, the taste suggests treacle. New ti rum does not have a very pleasant smell, but if left awhile it becomes very good. The king has several casks of it that have stood four years and hardly yield to good Brazilian rum--if they do not excel it, indeed: but the price is high. Mr Gagemeister had intended to buy himself some of it, but since the king wanted three piastres [$US3] in specie‡‡ per gallon he thought better of it, the more especially as he did not want to drive up the price prematurely: he was thinking of the future requirements of (Russian) America.

---

* Actually, the earth is stamped *before* flooding to compact the soil and slow drainage.
**suckers [*pôhuli*]
⁺ *'ahaniu* [sennit][94]
† *'ôhi'a 'ai* (*Eugenia malaccensis*)
‡ In fact, Hawaiians ate it and used it in medicine.
⁺⁺ This term was at that time used generically to means spirituous liquor of any sort.
†† as *pî'ao*
‡‡ Even by 1796-1798, Spanish, British and New England coins were being imported and exchanged in a confused and confusing manner, though Spanish piastres seem to have been the usual units of tender.

A fair amount of tobacco grows wild, and some is planted. Our sailors bought some at the rate of 10 pounds a piastre. It was not fumed, but the leaf was quite large and thick. There is a huge amount of wild ginger* in the mountains. It is strong but has a certain bitterness which, perhaps, might be lost if the ginger were transplanted. Kurkuma** or Indian saffron, with its yellow root, which is well known to commerce and medicine, does grow, but the islanders cultivate but little of it, having no great need of it. They use it only to color their *maro-pau* [*malo* and *pâ'û*] a bright yellow hue. (The *maro* is a belt or sash worn by men, the *pau*--one worn by women and reaching to the knee.)

The land, and the surrounding sea for fishing purposes, have been divided up among the native court grandees and other deserving persons. The king personally has large tracts of cultivated land,⁺ and frequently takes land even from those to whom he has given it, or does so through his minister. Sometimes he takes only part of the land, at times all of it. He thus rules through a nobility who obey him not so much out of attachment as through fear. The grandees have the right to farm out their land, and a tax-farmer then works it; the latter may himself give up some of his profits to another man, and live easily. Land taxes, which are paid to the king as well as the grandees, take the forms of swine,[95] dogs, fish, *maro, pau,* and *karra* [*kapa*], that is, shawls [*kîheî*] or cloaks made from bark and used by men and women alike in times of cold or rain. In truth, the position of the ordinary farmer on the island is a wretched and onerous one, for the king will sometimes, regardless of all circumstances, take as much as two thirds of the taro and potatoes he has grown.[96] Natives now deliberately cultivate both crops on various small plots so that the king will take produce from one or two of them, but not all. There are also many who, though they possess a sufficiency of their own swine and dogs, have never had the opportunity to eat their meat, or even to try it. And besides the oppressive and heavy tax by which his subjects are already too burdened, the present king has placed another load upon them, viz: he often assembles cultivators even from remote corners of the island,† some to work his lands, others to assist with the construction of sea-going rowed craft or buildings, barns [storage sheds], etc. And not only does he pay them nothing for their labor, he even declines to feed them. Much evil springs from such unskillful government and extreme burdening of subjects: insufficiencies in food supply result, and even in recent times hunger has destroyed many people. There were formerly as many as 150,000 people on the island of Ovagii alone. Now, there are barely 100,000 on all the Sandwich Islands.[97] Settlements of the poor are situated right by the sea, where the people can nourish themselves on fish as well as taro.

'awapuhi (*Zingiber domestica*)
** '*ôlena* or turmeric [*Curcuma domestica*]
⁺ *kô'ele*
† *kua'âina*

Dried and pounded taro is hardly inferior in any way to flour and is important in the islanders' diet in itself. Diligent hands, as seen, can obtain sugar and rum from sugar cane. Saracen millet was once sown on the island as an experiment, and it produced an excellent yield. In fact, all moderate and hot climate plants can be grown.

In Ovagii, King Tomio-omio draws advantages from trade. He himself owns the best of the island's productions and ships calling in can provision themselves with everything they need in a very short time. Thanks to the trade that he personally has conducted with foreigners for many years now, he has accumulated such quantities of various sorts of European goods that many such wares lie unused. Nor has he need of anything more, save objects necessary for his fleet. Since his products are necessary if not indispensible to his visitors, however, he values them and will not sell them cheap. Frequently, indeed, he will part with swine only for Spanish piastres.

Still, it is possible to bring these islanders broadcloths of lesser quality, also walrus-tusks, from which they make themselves an ornament like a hook, to be worn at the neck.* And from them, for use in America or Kamchatka, one can take good salt, dried taro, and new ti-root rum which improves in quality on the voyage and on being left for a time. As for their bast cord,** it is not as good as hempen cord perhaps but it can still be used in case of need, when hempen cord is wanting. The islanders will purchase broadcloth whether it be heavy or fine, just so long as it is dense and closely woven; nor do they prefer one shade to another, all are equally acceptable. However, they do not cut the cloth out, do not sew it, and make no clothing from it: the men wear it in their maro sashes, but for that they need no more than a quarter-*arshin*[+] length, while the women wrap a piece of cloth round themselves then fix it just beneath the breast, so covering themselves down to the knee.[98] The cloth thus makes a sort of attractive skirt.

When putting in at Karakakoa Bay, Americans from Boston take a certain number of the islanders aboard as seamen. The latter serve them well and cost the shipowners very little in upkeep and pay. Ovagiians are to be found in Canton and in Boston itself. Though some return home when opportunity arises, not all do so. The islanders make these voyages of their own free will. Not only does the king not prevent their making them; he does not want to know about it. As for the Bostonians, they either render an account to the islanders for their return home or do not return them at all, not infrequently even selling them to other native peoples who purchase them as sacrifices for the deity they themselves worship. Captain Wolf† of Boston, when at the port of Novo-Arkhangel'sk

---

* *lei niho palaoa*
** probably *olonâ* cordage
[+] 7-inch
† John D'Wolf, a Rhode Island trader and shipmaster, sold his vessel *Juno* and her cargo to the Russian-American Company in October 1805.

on Baranov Island which belongs to the Russian-American Company, had as many as six Sandwich Islanders among his men on the *Iunona*. Among them was a youth of perhaps sixteen whose native name was Kenokhoia and who, at the invitation of Kammerherr and *Chevalier* Rezanov, who was on the island at that time, agreed to travel to Russia with him. The youth had already been in both Canton and Boston. He is at present in St Petersburg in the care of the Government, as desired by His Majesty the Emperor. He has accepted the Christian faith and is known, after his godfather, as Vasilii Fedorovich Moller. Moller has been taught to read and write Russian and is now studying shipbuilding and other sciences, including grammar, law, sacred history, arithmetic, geography, history, English, marine draftsmanship, civil architecture, and sketching.

On the Method by which the Drink Ava* or Rum is Produced from the Ti Root on the Sandwich Islands

As I have already said, the islanders consume the sweet root of the *ti* plant as a food. Besides that, however, they cook the root and so make a drink called *ava* in their own language, or rum in English. The process is as follows. A deep square pit is dug in preparation for the cooking or steaming, of a size appropriate to the roots to be cooked. Two or three rows of stones are then placed on the bottom of the pit, and a fire is laid on them. The fire burns until the stones are red-hot. Damp grasses are next laid on these hot stones, and the roots are placed onto the grass, then covered over with more green stuff. The entire pit is then filled in with earth and sand, and so the roots are left for twenty-four hours in the course of which they become soft and juicy. The drink-maker next chops these steamed roots up fine, puts them in a cask, adds the right proportion of pure water, and leaves them to turn sour. When the liquid has finished fermenting, the brew is distilled in a boiler. The king alone, and a few of the Bostonians and Englishmen living on the islands, are in a position to make this drink, because only they possess boilers.** For want of such vessels, the ordinary islanders cannot engage in the activity.

The natives cook taro on hot stones in just the same way as ti roots, then, when it is soft, push or spread it onto flat stones[+] and add a little water, consuming the resultant soft food [*'ai pa'a* or *poi*] or else, dividing it up into pieces, allowing it to dry in the sun. When scraped with a knife or shaken, dried taro is quickly reduced to a flour not unlike rye-flour in flavor. The moist root is not

---

*actually, *'ôkolehao*. *'Awa* is made from the root of the pepper plant [*Piper methysticum*] and is narcotic rather than alcoholic.
** Obviously, this drink was invented after the introduction of iron pots. It is called *'ôkolehao* after the cauldron: *'ôkole* = buttocks, *hao* = iron. The Hawaiians noted the resemblance between the shape of these vessels and the human *derrière*.
[+] *Papa kui 'ai* were usually boards, a fact suggesting that Shemélin's informant, Gagemeister, was generalizing from experience on Kaua'i.

used as a food as such, and quickly goes off. In order to preserve stores of the root from spoiling, one must cook it as soon as possible and, drying it, produce rusks which keep their goodness for a very long time. Tomio-omio packs casks with such rusks, or with flour made from them, and so preserves that provision for considerable periods.

When the taro is ripe, the islanders pluck it from the ground and put it in their storerooms. The stalk [is] cut off by the root, [which] they place back in the earth; and the graft takes, producing more such stalks in due season. *Ukhi* [*uhi*] roots too, or iniam* in English, are by no means despised by the islanders as a food. The roots are nutritious and tasty and are similarly prepared for consumption by cooking.

There is much salt on Ovagii. It is not obtained from sea water by boiling but is broken from a salt lake, and is of the best quality and may be had there in great quantity. The *orona* [*olonâ*] tree,** from which bast is stripped, is also known there under that name. *Akhu*⁺ rope is made from it, and the bast is also used to make fishing-nets. *Orona* bast is in fact more like hemp than bast, so it is hardly surprising that it can be made into rope so stout and serviceable that it can sometimes replace the running tackle on a ship.†

The eastern tip of the island of Ovagii lies in 19°34'N.L. The longitude, as reckoned by Captain Cook and confirmed by Vancouver, is 154°56'00"[W]. The island's southern extremity, where Cook found a large village and where we had hoped to find abundance of victuals, lies--according to the reckonings of the celebrated Cook--in 18°54' N.L., 155°45"W. Our point of separation from *Neva* and of departure from the Sandwich Islands was 18°58' N, 156°20'W....

---

* yam. Shemelin's knowledge of English was minimal.
** a shrub, *Touchardia latifolia*
⁺ The Russians commonly convey the Hawaiian aspirate 'h' by Cyrillic'kh': *aho* thus becomes *akhu*, and *he pâ'û--khiabu*.
† *Nadezhda* apparently acquired a skein of (thinner) bast cord: see p. 92.

V.N. Berkh

The entire group of the Sandwich Islands is now in the possession of two rulers. One of them, named Tomi-Omio [Kamehameha], controls seven islands: Ovagi [Hawai'i], Movi [Maui], Kagulave [Kaho'olawe], Renai [Lâna'i], Torou,* Morotai [Moloka'i], and Vagu [O'ahu]. He has a number of vessels and more than eighty seamen, who deserted English ships over the years. These men surround the king, forming a guard to protect him against his own people, who abhor him in consequence of his vicious temper: in tyrannical fashion, he had all the former rulers of the islands just named put to death. By now, he has effectively suppressed the power of the native higher nobility, too. Even so, the latter would have found a way to bring him down, had he not been surrounded by the foreign guard.

The other king, Tomari [Kaumuali'i] by name, is by contrast a civil and pleasant as well as very able man; but he rules four islands only: Atuvai [Kaua'i], Nikhau [Ni'ihau], Legua [Lehua] and Kaula [Ka'ula]. King Tomari would long ago have fallen victim to the insatiable greed of King Tomi-Omio, had his possessions chanced to be nearer to the island of Ovagi than they are. (Ovagi is his enemy's residence.)

I myself had the pleasure of meeting King Tomari in 1805,** and had some conversations with him in English, which he knows tolerably well. The arrival of our ship, *Neva,* had elated the unhappy king who tearfully gave us to understand that he expected an attack from Tomi-Omio from hour to hour. Since his own forces were not so strong, he said, he feared that he would fall victim. "Should that savage Tomi-Omio seize my islands," he added, "he will assuredly put me and my entire family to death in a horrible manner." And indeed, Tomi-Omio plans into the future: when he possessed himself of Vagu, Morotai, Renai and Movi, he did in fact have their former rulers put to death in his presence, together with their relatives and adherents. Tomari tried quite persistently to persuade us to stay by his islands for a time, in order to defend him, and at the same time asked us for guns and powder; but we were obliged to refuse his request, notwithstanding our very friendly feelings toward him. So tearfully did he repeat his request for a final time, as we were taking our leave of him, that Lieutenant Arbuzov and I gave him our swords. King Tomari accepted them with deep appreciation and gratitude. We left, not a little troubled about his situation and prospects.

Unbounded ambition is checked by a wise Providence, and the further schemes of the rapacious Tomi-Omio were accordingly broken. Except for those belonging to Tomari, as I said, all the Sandwich Islands had already fallen to

---

* Torou does not, and did not, exist.
** Berkh is mistaken; it was 1804.

him; and again and again he sent messengers to Tomari demanding the surrender of his domains. But no satisfactory reply was received to all these demands, so Tomi-Omio collected a mighty army. He himself and that army were on the island of Vagu at the very time when we were on Ovagi, having parted with our respected leader, Captain-Lieutenant I.F. Kruzenshtern. We subsequently* heard that Tomi-Omio had about 7,000 warriors with him. More than once, on the passage from the Sandwich Islands to Kodiak, we spared a thought for King Tomari, fearing that he must be conquered outright. Great was our pleasure, on learning at Canton the following year** that King Tomi-Omio's great army had indeed scattered in consequence of spreading disease, and that his project had come to nothing. The more surely to bring his plans against Tomari to fruition, we knew, Tomi-Omio had spent some time on Vagu making various military preparations, for example, collecting stones to fit his slings. A shortage of food for so many men, however, compounded by the time needed to transport extra foodstuffs to them, had led to the outbreak of the disease in question. It was like scurvy, and it forced Tomi-Omio to postpone the conquest of Atuvai Island.

The latest information we have suggests that King Tomi-Omio is now even stronger than before. Two of his vessels are commanded by Europeans. He has sent one of them to trade in Canton,⁺ while the other has gone to the Markizskie [Marquesas] Islands to look them over. It is the object of this new Nadir† to conquer a fifth of the world for himself. However, no new attempt against Tomari was made after 1805, though a friend who visited the Sandwich Islands much later than I has assured me that this was only because of Tomi-Omio's superstition. The king had taken numerous idols along on his expedition against Tomari, and had burned them all publicly, on his return, because they had given him no aid. This act was interpreted very unfavorably indeed for him by the priesthood, and his stomach for another attempt failed....

The natives of the Sandwich Islands are of medium height and graceful. Despite their dark skin, indeed, they are quite attractive, unlike the Kalmucks‡ and other savage peoples. The women are amiable, physically pleasing, agile, and remind one of the nymphs of Otageiti [Tahiti] so often described in accounts of voyages. They like Europeans moreover, and are seemingly the main inducement for the 150 Englishmen living on the Sandwich Islands to stay there. Having a good deal of common sense and the imitative instinct, they soon learn our European ways. One Sandwich Islands woman was on the celebrated Captain Mers' [Meares's] ship for two years, and grew so used to all the duties, pas-

* from Young at Kealakekua
** from an American shipmaster
⁺ *Lelia Byrd* (Canton voyage of 1812-13).[99] Writing in about August 1817, Berkh would not have known of Kamehameha's sending the *Kaahumanu* to Canton, under Alexander Adams.
† Nadir Shah (1688-1747), Persian monarch of notorious cruelty
‡ Central Asian people well known to the Russians

times, and fashions of European ladies that it was hard indeed to tell that she was not an Englishwoman. Even so, it must be said that the women of the Markizskie Islands are yet better looking and far more respectable and correct in their behavior too, since Europeans go to their islands less frequently.

Sandwich Islanders differ in many respects from the American savages. They are very energetic and capable of any work, but at the same time docile, obedient, and willing to work on any European vessel. I was told by one American captain of how he had put in at Ovagi Island in need of repairs which had obliged him to remain there more than four weeks. That was time enough for his men to make the close acquaintance of local women, who so enchanted them that, when it was time for him to put to sea again, less than half the original crew of eighteen were available. The captain was planning to spend the coming winter off the Northwest Coast of America, and did not dare continue his voyage with so few crew members; so he hired a dozen Sandwich Islanders. Within eight weeks, he told me, those young natives had turned into such proficient sailors that he could not have wanted better.[100]

Lying between 18° and 23°, the Sandwich Islands might be expected to be torrid, like all tropical lands, but in fact they have a delightful climate. This is because they are right in the middle of the Pacific Ocean, far away from the shores of America. Gentle sea breezes blow onshore from dawn to dusk, reducing the great heat of the sun and simultaneously purifying the land of noxious vapors. I was only there for six days, so I cannot discuss the Islands' weather from my own experience. I did hear from individuals who had been there three or four months, however, that there is poor weather and constant rain only during the equinoctial season.

There is a wealth of plant life on the Islands. (And Captain Dixon reports that the island of Atuvai is in numerous respects richer than Ovagi, which I myself saw. There are more hogs there, he tells us, the taro, bananas and sweet potatoes taste better, and it has more coconut trees than any other island in the group. Also, he says, the water on Atuvai is very pure and the salt so good that one could want no better for salting down provisions. Atuvai has sixty villages. Cook estimated its population at 30,000 and King at 50,000; but Dixon believes it has no more than 25,000 people: see Dixon's *Voyage,* page 265.)[101] The principal crops of Ovagi itself are sugar cane, sweet potatoes, yams, taro, and other roots. Some thirty years ago, there was rather a commotion in Europe about the breadfruit tree. In reality, the breadfruit is far less nourishing than yams or taro are and, besides, the tree does not always fruit, being easily damaged by cold air. The roots of yams and taro, on the other hand, may always be had in abundance, never spoil, and are so soft that the very biggest root can be made into small grains within five minutes. It is my own opinion that taro root is the most nourishing foodstuff on earth. The most important of the fruits that grow on the Sandwich Islands are bananas, coconuts, and watermelons.*

The Sandwich Islands support few quadrupeds. There are cattle, but they roam the woods. I saw a domesticated cow and calf only at the king's residence. However, there are many hogs--they thrive on the excellent climate and never-failing supply of food. They themselves, together with dogs, are favorite foods of the Sandwich Islanders, though it is the dog that is especially relished and considered a fine dish. There appear to be no domesticated birds on Ovagi apart from fowl.

Encircled by the ocean as they are, the Sandwich Islands must have an abundance of fish around them, and the lakes, too, contain plenty of fish. No minerals have been discovered as yet, I believe, but the pearl industry** promises very well.[102]

---

* Visiting *haole* indeed ate the introduced watermelon (see p. 98 here), but it was hardly as 'important' to them or to Hawaiians as Berkh suggests, even in 1816.
** The Russians' information about a 'pearl industry' is entirely erroneous, as such has never existed in the Hawaiian Islands.

E.E. Levenshtern (von Loewenstern)

June 7th   *Nadegda* [*Nadezhda*] came steadily toward the bay, covering two inches per hour.* Soon I shall have been serving one whole year aboard *Nadegda*. We could hardly have foreseen, at the time of our departure, that we should have more trouble from men than from the weather and the elements, with which indeed we are in perpetual conflict.

8th   The central mountain of Owachi, Mowna Roa [Mauna Loa], came in sight this morning, also Mowna Kaah [Mauna Kea]. The natives believe their heart and soul to be in the stomach and, as men in a natural state, are not altogether wrong.

Herr von Krusenstern does not want to anchor at Owachi, but rather to attempt to purchase hogs and fruits while sailing by and circling around. His reasons are that the natives are malicious and the anchorages very bad. It may be hoped that curiosity will drive Resanoff out here, as fear did when we were near the cliffs and coastal rocks in Taiohai [Taio-hae]. There, he looked pale and full of alarm. Here, he will put on his suffering face. The island of Owachi has a beautiful appearance and must be very fertile.

During the afternoon we were three English miles distant from the shore. Three craft came out to us, but only to satisfy curiosity, because the natives then went back without having boarded us. Through an error in tacking, Golovachev brought the ship even further away from land, but nevertheless ten more craft came out to us from the shore, bringing with them a piglet, half-a-dozen coconuts, and trinkets. The people here are of an ugly hue, of small stature, and are all lousy. Both front teeth are missing in each man. Many have old open sores. This spectacle so displeased our Jean** that he is not remaining here after all, but is coming along with us further.

The handicrafts of these islanders are finer than those of the Nukugivans [Nukuhivans]. The ropes they brought us were better than our own loglines, so soft were they; and the fiber,+ which is of mulberry tree [*wauke*]† bark, is strong, supple, and more brightly colored than on Nuku Giva. The natives also brought out a girl as a trading article. She had a most beautiful figure; indeed, not one of the Marquesas Island maidens could be compared with her. (I have taken the natives of Nuku Giva as my standard, in order to be able to compare the Sandwich Islanders with them.) At night, we remained under small sail, some way offshore.

9th   Herr von Krusenstern is not minded to remain on the eastern side of the island, so we have moved in toward the west side, but still, unfortunately, at too

---

* on the chart--probably Vancouver's
** le Cabri
+ fabric (barkcloth) or *kapa*
† *Broussonetia papyrifera*

great a distance from the shore. Last night I had an argument with Horner and Langsdorff about purchasing. Langsdorff spoke from self-interest, and reproached the captain without proper grounds for it. Horner and I, however, finally convinced him that trade is certainly not forbidden, the buying of hogs being the main object of our stay here, and so reduced Langsdorff to silence. To be honest, it is awkward for all of us that we are not anchoring here for a couple of days.

Around midday, we reached the southern point of Owachi, which is very heavily populated. The strong wind abated somewhat, but only two native craft came out to us, even so. One craft contained a small pig, which was purchased, the other a large hog. Its owner did not know what to ask in exchange for it, in his conceit, and--after long negotiations-- carried it off to the shore again, to our great regret.

Lisianskii had his last meal with us today. The sailors at the wheel brought us very near to *Neva* by their in attentiveness, steering to port when it should have been to starboard. For that, they earned a few light lashes. *Neva* sails from here to Kodiak, while we ourselves make for Kamtschatka [Kamchatka].

The native craft here are really remarkably well made. In the main, the natives themselves know a few words of English. With the large hog, there was brought out another girl who addressed us with the phrase, "How do you do?", etc. The natives here are courageous. The wind was extremely high, yet they came out to sea without fear. One man stretched himself out on the outrigger, in order to preserve the balance, and so returned to shore at an unheard of speed.

10th   Everyone is dissatisfied with Krusenstern. It is on his orders that we remain so far from land (and with too much [trading] stock on board). Soon it will be 10 a.m., and we are still 25 miles off. During the afternoon we shall approach the shores but before sunset we shall again be standing out to sea. There is simply not enough time to conduct trade with the natives while under sail. For the past two days, we have had a fresh wind which has hindered the natives from coming aboard; today the weather is calm and fine, but we remain too far out and even the better weather is impeding the ship's progress.

The sketching of this island is very difficult, it being so round. We have thought it necessary, in view of this, to calculate the height of Mowna Roa precisely.

Krusenstern has gone across to *Neva*, from which we separate here. He too is dissatisfied. We made a detour from the Marqueses [Marquesas] Islands to the Sandwitsch [Sandwich] Islands in order to buy hogs and fresh fruit here, but now that we are here at Owachi we are departing without so much as having approached its shores. Having expended so much time already, what difference would two more days have made?

Krusenstern returned from *Neva* at 7 p.m. and, with three cheers, we parted from our companion ship. God grant us health, for our diet will consist of salted viands, pease porridge, and *zwiebacken.* September alone* can excuse Krusenstern's conduct. As a consolation, we have just heard that our sugar is all gone. We do have a few tons of sugars in the hold, now unreachable to us; but fortunately the coarse sugar should hold out till we reach Kamchatka. All are most curious to see, on our unloading there, how many provisions of all kinds we really have....

11th   The Sandwich Islanders were tattooed, but very irregularly and for the most part with figures of lizards, goats, fish, etc....

---

* the pressure of Kruzenshtern's self-imposed timetable, designed to avoid monsoons

G.H. Langsdorf

We now set a course for the Sandwich Islands and Kamtschatka. The wind continued brisk and, after a few days only, specifically on 25 May in the afternoon, we crossed the Equator. We were now in longitude 146°31'W of Greenwich. During the day, the temperature was 22°[C], during the night--no less than 21°[C].... When in latitude 19°34'N, on 7 June, we came in sight of the eastern tip of the island of Owaichi [Hawai'i]. Our distance from it was thirty-six nautical miles. The largest of the group known as the Sandwich Islands, Owaichi is, of course, renowned as the place where the great mariner Cook so unhappily lost his life. Cook's worthy pupil, Vancouver, gave the world a complete map of the group not many years afterward.

Captain Krusenstern [Kruzenshtern] wished to reach Nangasaki [Nagasaki], the major commercial center of Japan, before the end of September. By thus speeding his voyage, he hoped to avoid the advent of the northeasterly monsoons, which often set in about the middle of that month. With a view to saving time, he now decided not to anchor in Karacacoa [Kealakekua] Bay but to barter straightaway with the Owaichi Islanders for such things as we required. Within a few days, he trusted, we might thus be well supplied with hogs and all sorts of provisions. So we cruised along the south coast of the island till the tenth of the month. To our very great concern, however, so few natives showed themselves during that period, and those who did demanded such a price for everything they brought, that Captain Krusenstern decided to be gone, and to proceed with all haste toward Kamtschatka. It was a decision made more possible by the good health of his entire crew.

The few natives we did have opportunity of studying were all unclothed and dirty in appearance, of middling height, not very solid in build. Their dull and dark brown skin was covered with sores and bruises, very likely the result of drinking kava or, perhaps, of a well-known disease which is rife amongst them.[103] Most of the men had lost front teeth. They said* they had been knocked out, in battle, by the use of slings. They were fine swimmers. Lizards, goats, muskets, and other things had been tattooed on their arms and bodies. The tattooing had, however, been less admirably done than on Nuku Giva. And no doubt the fact that we had only lately, on 17 May, left an island whose inhabitants must certainly be ranked among the very handsomest on earth, at least in point of stature and proportions, reinforced the bad impression that these natives of Owaichi had already made on us. For the rest, though, one must say that Sandwich Islanders have more affinity with Europeans than the Nukugivans do, no doubt because of far more frequent intercourse with European visitors. So little pleased was our Cabri[104] with the Owaichian natives, men or women, that he

---

* presumably with the aid of mime, which Langsdorf misunderstood

could not bring himself to live among them, and instead begged Captain Krusenstern (who had proposed to leave him there) to take him on to Kamtschatka. The Owaichian language appeared to differ quite significantly from the Nukugivan language; Cabri spoke the latter fluently,* but could not make himself understood to these new islanders. We did rather better by using some English.

The canoes of the Sandwich Islands are light and very neatly made and proved to us that the Owaichians had already made much greater strides in naval architecture than the Nukugivans had. They go out to sea many miles in them. The part of the coast that we cruised about was very pleasant and well-cultivated, too: we observed many groves of bananas and coconut palms. The majestic summit of Mouna Roa [Mauna Loa] naturally caught our gaze especially. According to observations made by others in the past, its peak should be 2,578 *toises*** above sea level. Dr Horner, our tireless astronomer, reckoned it, however, to be only 2,254 *toises*[+] above sea level. So gradually does that mighty mountain rise from seashore to peak, at all events, that it has a no less pleasing than arresting aspect. In reality,† it seems to be some 300 or 400 *toises* higher than the Peak of Teneriffe. Nowhere else can a man reach such a height with so little difficulty, even the warm climate assisting him. Despite the mountain's height, even its peak is only just above the snow line, the Equator being not far off. When we saw it, the peak was free of snow.... When we left Owaichi on 10 June it was regrettably, without having picked up any information whatsoever about the island's condition. As I passed the winter of 1805-06 on the Northwest Coast of America, however,‡ I then had opportunities of learning some particulars, which I may suitably set forth here, I think.

The Sandwich Islands are, as a group, extremely convenient for vessels making for the Northwest Coast of America, for the Aleutian Islands, or Kamtschatka. The islands have safe bays, and may well be visited. Here may be procured an abundance of swine, breadfruit, bananas, coconuts, taro, yams, *batates,* salt, wood, water, and other things needed on ships. United States vessels now touch at the Sandwich Islands almost annually, as they ply toward the northwest coast of their continent to get sea otter[++] skins, so highly prized in China. The Americans carry the skins straight to Canton: it is the object of their enterprise. To get the necessary skins, they give the Indians cloth, ironware (knives, hatchets, kitchen tools), rice and molasses, hardtack, flints, and pow-

---

* Cabri had probably exaggerated his knowledge of Nukuhivan to enhance his value in the Russians' sight.
** 15,468 feet--1 *toise* = 6 feet
[+] 13,524 feet
† actual height is 13,677 feet ASL
‡Langsdorf accompanied Rezanov from Kamchatka to Sitka and thence to Spanish California and back again as his private surgeon.
[++] *Lutra marina*

der.... If they do not manage to obtain a good cargo of otter skins to take off to Canton, they go in October or November to the River Colombo [Columbia] or, far more often, to the Sandwich Islands, where they may winter....

The way of life of those islands has, predictably, been much affected by the number of vessels visiting Karakakoa Bay and the consequent dealings between their crews and the natives. Such is the extent of this influence, indeed, that the islands might be said to be advancing in giant strides.* This nation itself seems likely to take the lead among all the South Sea Islands in becoming a civilized and ordered land.

From his constant dealings with sea captains from the United States of America, and particularly with Mr Young and Mr Davie [Davis]** who have both now lived with him for years, King Tomoomah [Kamehameha] has been induced to introduce numerous European customs. The two persons mentioned serve the king, as it were, as his ministers. So far has the king brought English into general use among his people, moreover, that few natives of Owaichi of any rank and distinction do not speak the language now.+ The king, who has recently succeeded in bringing all the Sandwich Islands under his sovereignty and is now their sole monarch, was soon enough brought to understand the value of a silver piece, and to prefer selling the products of his country to visiting ships for Spanish dollars or piastres. Once he had collected a tolerable sum, he purchased a vessel† from an American trader and manned it partly with his own subjects, partly with foreign seamen, of whom not a few now live in Owaichi. Sailors of the United States like so well to revel in a superfluity of natural products without much labor, and to have handsome young girls at their disposal, that a vessel almost never puts in at the islands without losing one or more seamen. However, the king allows no one to stay who has not a good recommendation from his captain. Taught by these foreign guests, the natives have grown yet more fond of the seafaring life; and excellent sailors they make. I spoke to several Owaichi Islanders serving on Boston vessels‡ while I myself was on the Northwest Coast. They were getting ten or twelve piastres a month as pay. They have so perfected the manufacture of all sorts of cordage and fishing nets in Owaichi, probably from *Phormium tenax* fibers,++ that ships are supplied with them. The Owaichian products are considered more durable, if used as tackle, than European cordage...

Tomoom-o evinces strength and activity of intellect in all he does. So greatly has his naval power grown within a little time that, even in 1805, he had fifteen vessels under his orders, including cutters, brigs, and even three-masters.[106] It

---

* this in 1809
** Young and Davis were English.
+ a doubtful assertion
† *Lelia Byrd*
‡ Jonathan Winship's *O'Cain*: see p. 116 here
++ a bad guess: *olonâ*, see p. 103[105]

was also in 1806 that he made known to Mr Baranov [A.A. Baranov], representative of the Russian-American Company at Neu-Archangel [Novo-Arkhangel'sk] in Norfolk Sound, that he had been told, by persons trading on the Northwest Coast, how greatly the Russian settlement had sometimes suffered in winter from a shortage of provisions. He himself, he gave Baranov to understand,* would be glad to send a vessel annually to that settlement, with hogs, salt, sweet potatoes, and other foodstuffs too, if he were given in exchange sea otter skins at a reasonable price. The latter he proposed to send on speculation to Canton. As I have learned since my return to St Petersburg, this trade in fact began in earnest, and the Russian company not only sent a vessel to Owaihi from Norfolk Sound for victuals, but even bought a cutter from the king.

What holds the king's attention more than any other subject, though, is shipbuilding. Already, it is said, he can accurately and with true discernment spot the strengths and weaknesses in any ship's construction. All equipment and tools relating to shipbuilding he regards as particularly valuable. One cannot do better, therefore, than to use such tools as articles of trade, when going to Owaihi.** Any sailor who is at the same time a ship's carpenter is particularly welcome there, and is straightaway presented with a piece of land and almost anything else that he may want.

Not many years ago, an unusual and very valuable discovery was made on Owaihi: an indigenous tree,+ the wood of which is said to be proof against the worms that do such damage, in those waters, by boring into ships.[108] Such timber must surely (if this is true) make it unnecessary to sheath vessels in copper--an absolutely essential precaution, as things stand. And yet another valuable product of Owaihi is sugar cane which, if cultivated to the proper point, could easily enough supply Kamtschatka, indeed, the whole of Siberia. So thoroughly has the attention of all ranks and sorts of people been absorbed by wars and political developments in Europe, of recent years, that even the trader's speculative eye has been averted. If ever freedom of the seas be re-established, though, and ships of every nation be at liberty to range at large, as earlier, then we may trust that the advantages which Cook and La Pérouse, Meares and Portlock, Le Marchand, Vancouver, and the Russian Krusenstern, to name but some, have pointed out as easily to be obtained by trading with the Sandwich Islanders, will not be quite dismissed.

It was at six o'clock on the evening of 10 June that we took leave of our companion, *Neva*, with reciprocal exchanges of three cheers. Our ways were now to part. Captain Lisiansky [Lisianskii] was to take his ship to the Northwest Coast

---

* through a Russian-American Company servant, Sysoi Slobodchikov, who called at the Islands in the little trader *Nikolai* in 1807
** What was true in 1809-10 was yet more so by 1815-16.[107]
+ sandalwood

of America. Not being as pressed for time as us, he resolved to anchor in Karacacoa Bay for a few days, to allow his crew some rest. Captain Krusenstern, on the other hand, judged it necessary... to proceed without delay toward Kamtschatka.

N.P. Rezanov (1806)

The King of the Sandwich Islands, Toome-Ome-o, has offered Mr [A.A.] Baranov his friendship. This will seem rather strange to Your Excellency, so I will first say something about the tsar of those natives, then explain how it came about. It was Captain Venchip [Winship] who told us* that Toome-Ome-o was attracting Europeans from all parts by his kind policies, and that those Europeans were starting to settle everywhere on his islands. Agriculture and cattle-breeding (said Venchip) are undertaken with great success, and the king gives the settlers liberty to leave their estates when they wish. At the same time, he lets his subjects go in foreign vessels without pay, requiring only that they return as experienced sailors; has bought as many as 15 one-masted vessels; has sent to Boston for a shipwright; has established an Admiralty; and has lately purchased a three-masted vessel from the Americans. Aboard Venchip's vessel [on her arrival at Novo-Arkhangel'sk] was a mate called Clark, who had been two years in the Sandwich Islands and had a wife and even children there, as well as various business interests.** This Clark had been several times in these parts and been very kindly received by Aleksandr Andreevich [Baranov]. Knowing the needs of this country, he told his king so much that he was sent to negotiate a commercial treaty; and, assuming that it is permitted (the crossing in question not being a very long one), the king himself wishes to come to Novo-Arkhangel'sk and lay the foundation for trade. Toome-Ome-o undertakes to send us foodstuffs such as breadfruit, coconuts, yams, taro, and hogs when he has a sufficiency, as well as bast cordage, taking ticking material, linen cloths, iron, and lumber for shipbuilding in return.[+] This unusual trade is to be started this next year....

---

* Jonathan Winship reached Novo-Arkhangel'sk in the *O'Cain* on 1 April 1806.
** The sum of the evidence suggests that Clark had reached the Islands in the *O'Cain* in 1803, when she had been under Captain O'Cain himself.
[+] In Langsdorf's comparable list (p. 112 here), sea otter skins loom large. They are oddly missing here.

PART THREE

Ethnographic Evidence

Barter

The Coastal Encounters (7-11 June 1804)

As they coasted hopefully along the shores of Puna, Ka'ū and South Kona, on the south side of Hawai'i Island, *Nadezhda* and *Neva* had four separate encounters with Hawaiian parties in canoes. The Russians, sorely in need of fresh provisions, expected and welcomed these visits, but the natives disappointed them as seaborne victualers and purveyors of essential foodstuffs. The significance of these preliminary and friendly offshore encounters, however, lies not so much in that disappointment (though indeed this prompted Kruzenshtern's hasty departure from the scene) as in the way that they foreshadowed and, to some extent, readied the Russians for the real form and currencies of barter in the area by 1804. Kamehameha's more or less enforceable monopoly of the important local hog trade with Europeans; the development of prostitution proper (see below, 'Disease and the Drinking of *'Awa*'); the devaluation of iron; the political significance of English residents and the Hawaiians' own acceptance of them and acquaintance with their ways and language; the importance of cloth in barter for provisions that the islanders now grew, or were required by their chiefs to grow, expressly for the purpose: all these themes were adumbrated in encounters miles out from the Hawaiian coast. If for that reason only, such encounters would merit attention; their additional historical significance (the first Hawaiian-Russian contacts ever) and the clarity with which the Russians have recorded them for us, make that attention vital.

Hawai'i's easternmost point, Cape Kumukahi, became visible from *Nadezhda*'s deck at approximately 8:30 a.m. on the morning of 7 June. *Nadezhda* and *Neva* had left the lee of Nuku Hiva Island together on 18 May and, after some cruising in search of non-existent islands had, by the 20th, been en route to the Hawaiian Archipelago in company. A strong wind and her better speed, however, had enabled Kruzenshtern to cross the Equator some eighteen hours sooner than Lisianskii; and the gap between the two vessels continued to widen, at a slower rate, till 6 June.[1] Thus, it was coincidence that *Neva* too saw Cape Kumukahi early on the morning of the first approach (approximately 9 a.m.), and in latitude 19°10' north. *Neva*'s approach was on the same northerly course but 24 hours later than *Nadezhda*'s, give or take 45 minutes.

At the moment of initial sighting, in her captain's and in others' estimation, *Nadezhda* stood some 36 nautical miles from the coast. By noon however, still in estimated latitude 19°10' north, she was due south of Cape Kumukahi. Simple calculations reveal her distance from the cape at that juncture as 24 miles, and her rate as about five knots. *Neva* was almost certainly invisible from the precipitous and rugged Puna shore.

Kruzenshtern "stood in for the southeast coast of Ovagi", presumably bearing northwestward, and approached the shore "to within six miles". At noon, *Nadezhda* stood 18 miles from the nearest point of the Puna coast--Hokuma Point--if she was truly "due south" of Hawai'i's "eastern extremity". No reefs were taken in aboard *Nadezhda,* and the wind continued brisk, so her rate may be supposed to have remained five knots or so. Hence it was about 2:30 p.m. when, six miles off shore, *Nadezhda* "went about and kept on a course parallel to it under nothing but topsails." Kruzenshtern was in urgent need of fresh provisions. Several hours of daylight remained for potential bartering. It is thus implausible that he had *not*, at noon, steered toward the closest stretch of shoreline between Hokuma and Waipuku Points. (Even had he sailed north or west of the potentially most fruitful course, *i.e.*, northwest toward Hokuma Point, however, he could not by 3 p.m. have reached a spot further than seven miles from that Point.) In sum, *Nadezhda* may be thought to have approached Hokuma Point, reefed in, then coasted gently west-southwestward along the Puna coastline., Shortly, "a few native craft" came out to the expectant Russians.

There is one major discrepancy between the Kruzenshtern and the Shemelin versions of the meeting that ensued. Shemelin, almost certainly confusing meetings with Hawaiians on the first and later days of *Nadezhda*'s stay, would have us think that *Neva* was present also and indeed, that the Hawaiians visited Lisianskii first--before, at last, paddling over to *Nadezhda* with their artifacts, foodstuffs, and human goods--"a young girl of 13 or 14, whom a native... wished to offer to the ship". Deplorable though such an error is, Shemelin's text in other ways usefully complements the shorter, drier Kruzenshtern account of Meeting 'A' (see map). The following emerges from collation of the two.

Three canoes, each containing four Hawaiians (Shemelin), came out from a settlement west of Hokuma Point but probably east of Ka'ena Point. The Hawaiians were friendly and ready to trade. An elderly native (Kruzenshtern) in the first canoe to reach *Nadezhda* offered the Russians a "quite young girl", and Kruzenshtern supposed that he wished to sell her 'services' and that, frustrated in his venal scheme, he had "left highly vexed that he had brought his goods in vain". In the second canoe was a "little suckling pig". It was purchased, together with six coconuts and twelve sweet potatoes, for "three *arshin* [seven feet] of red material" (Shemelin). From that same canoe, or from the third, the Russians also purchased a skein of fine rope. The same red material was used as currency. Kruzenshtern was disappointed by these results, the more so as the coast he was moving past, under small canvas, "seemed quite heavily populated and looked well cultivated too." The weather, meanwhile, was deteriorating fast. Rain developed into a summer squall soon after the Hawaiians had returned to shore, and the prudent Kruzenshtern, rightly convinced that trade was over for a time, moved off to the southeast. The night was passed some way off shore.

The lookout on *Neva* spotted Cape Kumukahi at 9 a.m. the next morning. By noon, says Lisianskii, that cape "bore N 3° W of us at a distance of some twenty miles." Some 18 miles had thus been covered in a little over three hours. Under strong and steady winds (from ENE), *Neva*'s rate was no slower than *Nadezhda*'s, in the same waters, the day before.

At noon, *Neva* lay in latitude 19° 10'N. The Puna coast ahead sloped on its northeast-southwest axis. Had Lisianskii made directly for it, he would first have weighed the risk of losing the prevailing wind, and secondly have needed to adjust his sails. In the texts, there is no mention of a lightening of sails; furthermore, it was understood that *Nadezhda* and *Neva* would rendezvous in Cook's Kealakekua Bay if anywhere around Hawai'i. All these factors lead us to suppose that *Neva* steered northwest or west a little after midday on 8 June. "By 2 p.m.," records Lisianskii, he was "close enough in shore to be able to make out with ease the native dwellings...." Assuming a rate of five to six knots, and a basically westerly course from noon coordinates, *Neva* would by then have been in longitude 155 plus or minus 5'--within five miles of the spot where Meeting 'A' occurred. There is further circumstantial evidence of this. "There are," says Lisianskii justly, "quite a number" of "native dwellings" on "the eastern end of Ovaigi". *Neva* had passed south of Cape Kumukahi itself, with its adjacent villages, at a distance of at least thirty-two miles. Lisianskii had the best of telescopes, indeed; but winds were high and, at that distance, the Hawaiians' structures built at or near sea level would have been invisible to him. Immediately to the east of Lae'apuki, on the other hand, there was a series of adjacent settlements with or without *heiau*. There are, then, reasons for believing that the "six craft, each holding two or three men" (Lisianskii), which came out to *Neva* between 2 p.m. and 2:30 p.m. between Lae'apuki and modern Kehena, had come from the same part of the Puna coast as those which had met *Nadezhda*. They were possibly from the same spot: the number of Hawaiians was again twelve.

Certain differences between this meeting, 'B', and that of the preceding afternoon, merit attention. For *Neva*, there was no suckling pig; no offer of a girl; and no welcome by an old or older man. As will be seen ('Hawaiian Attitudes to Trade') the natives' willingness to trade in hogs, of which Kamehameha claimed an absolute monopoly, was more or less dependent on the presence of their local chiefs. Lisianskii's disappointment of 8 June, like Kruzenshtern's unrecognized good fortune of the 7th, stemmed directly from the working of traditional authority ashore. That authority, of which the Russians still knew very little, was dependent on and mirrored Kamehameha's autocracy, whose evolution they themselves were to record from day to day.

Nadezhda, meanwhile, had rounded Ka Lae, Hawai'i's southernmost point, and stood off "that large village from which an abundance of provisions had been brought" to Captain Cook.[2] She was rejoined by *Neva* toward noon on 9 June off the southern coast of Ka'û. Meeting 'C', for which we have the fullest documentation, took place near Ka Lae that afternoon, involved both ships' companies, and lasted less than one hour.

The Hawaiians, all sources agree, came out to the Russians in three canoes at brief intervals. *Nadezhda* and *Neva* had brought to, no more than two miles out, but had been obliged to wait "two hours or even longer" (Kruzenshtern) before they were visited. In one of the canoes, which Shemelin alone identifies as the first to arrive, sat "three men and a young woman or girl of about 18". The woman was first aboard *Nadezhda*, it seems, and knew sufficient English "to be able to assist her fellow islanders in their trade with us" (Shemelin). In the canoe that had brought her, however, there were "no foodstuffs...nor anything else save...threads, cords, mussel shells and other trifles at which no one even wanted to look" (Shemelin). Very soon, the Russians were therefore glad to note, two other canoes arrived with more promising wares. At first, they headed for *Neva* but then "both made for *Nadezhda*" (Lisianskii). In one of these canoes "was a large hog weighing some two and a half *pood*" (Kruzenshtern). All were "cheered considerably" by such a "large fat pig" (Shemelin).

The Russian texts themselves contain reflections on the Russian failure to secure the wanted hog. The vendor, all agree, wanted only broadcloth, and preferably in pieces "large enough to envelop him, like a mantle, from head to toe" (Kruzenshtern). In view of Shemélin's basic lack of sympathy with Kruzenshtern and his officers, it is not surprising to find him charging that "the Captain did not see fit to satisfy him in that way" despite the "store of broadcloths" aboard with which, in fact, he "could have bought a half-dozen pigs, no matter how expensive." Kruzenshtern himself states that he was "not in a position to give" such pieces of broadcloth, possibly implying that the stuffs were in *Nadezhda*'s hold and could not readily or speedily have been produced. Shemélin makes the point in cutting terms. What is significant about the incident, at all events, is that the Russians were again confronted by, and in the case of Kruzenshtern much influenced by, the difficulty of purchasing viands. A further two-hour wait brought no other traders out. A single suckling pig lay on *Nadezhda*'s quarterdeck at 5 p.m. An hour later, the ship was moving south for safety overnight. *Neva* remained in company. The "very smartly got up and shameless" woman, Kruzenshtern observes with satisfaction, had enjoyed a "fate no different from that of her sister the previous day."

Nadezhda and *Neva* parted company, after another luckless trading morning, on 10 June off Kauna Point. On the 11th, the wind having obligingly swung round from north to west, Lisianskii coasted up past Kauna Point and Kamoi Point. At about 8 a.m., "a craft came out... from a little place called Peri-Rua." This may be connected with Na Pu'u a Pele--'r' and 'l' are commonly interchanged in the Russians', as in other Europeans', accounts (as, indeed, they may have been by the Hawaiians themselves). Aboard the solitary craft were two figures: an Englishman and an English-speaking native boy. It was apparently their purpose to meet and even to examine *Neva,* but not to trade with her. The fact suggests that they were acting on behalf of, or at least in consciousness of, regional authority. "This first craft was followed out by three more, one of which brought two small hogs" (Lisianskii). Meeting 'D' concluded well for all concerned. Perhaps with "Lewis Johnson's" consent, the hogs were bartered for thick cloth, and *Neva* was welcomed to South Kona. Twelve hours' delay would almost certainly have persuaded Kruzenshtern to remain another day or two himself, to the advantage of ethnographers today.

Neva cleared Palemano Point, on the south of Kealakekua Bay, at 5 p.m. on 11 June, dropping anchor toward dusk.[3]

Observations on the Market

In the course of their stay at Hawai'i and Kaua'i in June 1804 the Russians made purchases reflected by these (overlapping) data:

Article	(Page Reference)	Price
"two small hogs"	30	"nine *arshin* of cloth"
"native barkcloth"	30	"a piece of material"
"twenty arshin of their own best material"	31	"a single 4 1/2 *arshin* length"
"three large hogs"	32, 58	"one and a half iron bars
"two large hogs"	34	"two pieces of clothing"
"eight hogs"	36	"two bales of sailcloth"
"three large hogs"	46	"1 1/2 iron-bars"
"1 medium-sized hog"	46	"2 axes"
"1 small pig"	46, 70	"1 axe"
"1 suckling-pig"	46	"1 piece of printed linen, 4 1/2 *arshin* in length"
"6 to 8 bunches of sweet potato"	46, 70	"the same, cut in strips
"1 hen"	46, 70	"1 penknife or pair of scissors"
"two middling-size hogs and a considerable quantity of vegetables"	57	"three bottles of rum, two axes, and an adz"

"four large hogs"	151	"a piece of thin canvas"
"a large fan" [*kāhili*] (off Kaua'i)	80	"a small knife"
"eleven hogs"	176	"two *pood* and 20 pounds of bar-iron and sail-cloth more than 40 *arshin* in length"
"one suckling pig, 6 coconuts, 12 sweet potatoes"	182, 186	"three *arshin* of red material"
"one skein of fine...rope"	197	"1 1/2 *arshin* of red cloth"

Like other eyewitness accounts of the Hawaiian scene of the same period, for instance those of John Turnbull of 1802 and Samuel J. Patterson of 1805,[4] the Russian texts throw light on the spread of *haole* culture through the Islands as revealed by the natives' changing wants. The Russians arrived ready to barter, notwithstanding their failure to secure the desirable, two-and-a-half *pood* "piggy" off Ka Lae ("the Company had stowed...large axes, ... as much as 6,000 *pood* of bar iron, not a little sailcloth, ... and a sufficient store of broadcloths, of various prices and qualities", as well as scissors, knives, and mirrors).[5] They were struck by the sharp devaluation of both iron artifacts and, more annoyingly, of iron bits with which their ships were too abundantly supplied. "For the pieces of iron hoop that secured us six or ten coconuts... on Nuku Hiva, we could get only the most insignificant objects" (Lisianskii). "Today, though, the Hawaiians almost despise iron, nor have they much time even for the most necessary objects made from it" (Kruzenshtern). It was, above all, cloth that Hawaiians sought by 1804, a fact suggestive of a widespread recognition in the Islands that Kamehameha ruled and that, in view of the disaster at O'ahu, war was over for a time.

Insofar as the Hawaiians would accept iron at all, in exchange for food or artifacts, they wanted iron bars. Kamehameha's hand was visible: he had instructed his subordinates and representatives to view bar iron, like hogs, as currency for commerce of a military nature (see 'Kamehameha and Trade' below). Significantly, it was the chief of Kealakekua, not the numerous *maka'āinana* or commoners who had already been aboard *Neva*, who first agreed to take bar iron in exchange for foodstuffs. For the commoner, bar iron was of little worth. Shaped into knives, penknives, or mirror frames, and prettified, the metal had modest value to them; but it was "printed cloth" or "striped ticking" or other fabric suitable for use in *pā'ū* and in *malo* "that they really prized". "Nothing would satisfy them...that did not serve to gratify their vanity" (Kruzenshtern).

On approaching the Russian vessels, the Hawaiians more often than not offered cloth of their own manufacture which, on reflection, their visitors thought excellently made. They were invariably willing to accept, in return, "worn shirts, jerseys or jackets" (Lisianskii), indeed, any cast-off Russian clothing. If material were offered, however, the Hawaiians had a preference, so widespread and traditional in Polynesia, for red. The color was, perhaps, less powerfully linked with *kapu* and the sacred in Hawaiian minds, by 1804, than in Marquesan minds; nevertheless, it had a good deal of meaning. Red was certainly among the colors in the Russians' "striped ticking", which the natives found especially desirable; and, as was seen, it was for "three *arshin* of red material" (Shemelin) that, in the course of meeting 'A', they parted with a piglet, rope, and foodstuffs that the Russians needed urgently. Shemelin's comments on Hawaiian tastes in cloth suggest how swiftly contact with American and European mariners was weakening the ancient veneration for the color red: "the islanders will purchase broadcloth whether it be heavy or fine, just so long as it is dense and closely woven; nor do they prefer one shade to another...."

Hawaiian Attitudes to Trade

The Russian evidence suggests that all Hawaiians who were favorably placed to trade with visitors, did trade with them, persistently, for personal advantage, and with gusto. Certain coastal villages, the Russians rightly thought, were heavily dependent upon trade with *haole*: "shores...are populated solely with a view to fishing and trade with ships that may arrive, [and] the interior...is peopled with farmers who provision foreign ships with the surplus of their labors" (Lisianskii). Even villages and individuals far less dependent on these international contacts, Russian texts make plain however, took great pleasure in, and warmly welcomed, barter. By and large, the Russians found the islanders hard bargainers and shrewder traders than the Nuku Hiva islanders, with whom they constantly compared them. "The Hawaiians seemed...superior to their southern neighbors in point of intellectual capability" (Kruzenshtern). They were, predictably, familiar with European trading practices as the Marquesas Islanders were not--a fact to which both Kruzenshtern and Langsdorf give a faintly racist gloss, equating mental capability with recognition and a practical adoption of marketplace procedures. (In his defense, however, one must say that many other visitors confirm Langsdorf's remark that the Hawaiians showed a "much greater affinity" with "European nations" than did other Polynesian peoples of the period.) Not only did the Russians find their hosts hard bargainers; they also found them honest. Little or nothing was stolen from *Neva*, though "they could no doubt have stolen something or other. Every day [in Kealakekua Bay] as many as a thousand individuals came to trade with us, but we experienced nothing but honesty" (Lisianskii). The Russians were surprised by this, for which their predecessors' tart accounts of thievery had not prepared them.

"It must be said, however, that the absence of one vice was compensated for by another: the natives were the worst of profiteers" (Lisianskii). Profiteering, it emerges, was no more than the maintenance of price levels by general agreement. In reality, the Russians had no cause to criticize the practice. They themselves had, after all, failed to monitor successfully the current buying prices of specific items, or indeed to hide their need to buy in quantity. As for the way in which the prices sought by *maka'âinana* vendors tended suddenly to rise or fall, depending on the presence or absence amidst them of their local chief ("...barter went on advantageously for us... till the local chief's arrival on the scene, whereupon the prices of foodstuffs promptly rose"), it was a function of political and social structures which, as seen, the Russians did not fully understand.

Without exception, it appears, the Hawaiians went out to the Russian ships in hopes of getting broadcloth or, failing that, some other good material for use as clothing. Meeting 'A' brought home to Kruzenshtern the pointlessness of offering them bits of broken iron hoop: "the islanders would take nothing for their wares but broadcloth." For their own part, they were almost always ready to use "native cloth" as currency. Once settled in at Kealakekua Bay, the Russians began to trade in cast-off clothes. (The subject will be separately treated: see 'Clothing and Body Ornamentation' below.) Suffice it here to observe that, by supplying the Hawaiians of that region liberally with their worn-out shoes, caftans, jackets, and shirts, the Russians soon further depressed a market that American free traders had already overburdened. Even men of modest substance, it appears, were by 1804 unwilling to accept even new axes for their goods if there were striped ticking or broadcloth to be had; and one man, at least, "refused...complete suits of clothes, demanding only a piece of broadcloth large enough to envelop him, like a mantle" (Kruzenshtern). For all the pleasure that Hawaiians might derive from cast-off European clothing, one deduces, there was still, in 1804, more lasting satisfaction to be had from the traditional *malo* made of a European cloth--a fact suggestive of the coming, uncertain synthesis of *haole* technology and Polynesian culture of which later Russian visitors would write.

In general, *ali'i* seem to have been quite as anxious as the common people to secure "dense and closely-woven" (Shemelin) cloths from *Nadezhda* and *Neva*. Perhaps their dignity required that their visits to the ships be briefer than the lengthy stays enjoyed by *maka'âinana* ("every islander who came to barter...might tend to remain from sunrise to sunset, but all was quietly and peacefully done": Lisianskii), but they did not hide their readiness to trade. The chief of Kealakekua traded several times with Lisianskii; "the young chief with whom Johnson lived...had intended to visit the ship but was prevented from doing so by the death of his wife" (Lisianskii). As representatives of the royal authority, such chiefs were obliged to respect royal monopolies. The chief of Kealakekua did so, as also did John Young, to a noteworthy extent. When either traded with the Russians of *Neva*, it was in full consciousness of the need to take things useful to the kingdom as well as to the region--and especially themselves. Both traded, moreover, on a broader scale than the commoners around them, and accepted iron bars in payment for their hogs and other wares, on the tacit understanding that both cloth and alcoholic spirits, amongst other things, would also be forthcoming from the ship.

The very fact of being in authority placed Young and the *ali'i* in possession of a ware or commodity much valued by their visitors: goodwill, which might translate into a steady flow of foodstuffs for *Neva*. Lisianskii and his officers immediately strove subtly to buy it. So we are brought against the vexed question of gifts.

From the outset, gifts played an essential part in barter between Young and the Kealakekua chief, on the one hand, and Lisianskii on the other. On his very first appearance aboard *Neva*, the chief brought out as gifts (but expecting recompense) "two hogs and a fair quantity of tubers". He was gratified to be received "with great attention", and content with the *de facto* price paid for his tardy offerings--three iron tools and three bottles of rum. And there and then, he "undertook to continue to supply" the ship with "fresh provisions". Recognizing that the rum had made a deep impression on his host, Lisianskii then invited him to dine aboard, and gave him liquid hospitality till he was "quite drunk". It was regarded as, and was indeed, a good investment. Shortly afterward, the chief's goodwill toward Lisianskii cleared all Hawaiians from *Neva*'s decks at a moment of Lisianskii's choosing; and the gesture was repeated daily. Young, too, visited *Neva* bearing, as evidence of readiness to deal sensibly and promptly with her captain, six grown hogs. With his appearance, moreover, the significance of gifts was clarified yet further: "Young himself had brought six hogs, two of which he gave me as presents. For the other four he wanted one and a half pieces of fine canvas. The hogs, he assured me, belonged to the king." Convinced now, after four days in the bay, that he could victual without Young's active aid, Lisianskii entertained John Young politely as the situation certainly demanded but would give no more than a single roll of canvas for the hogs. The offer was rejected and, politely, Young went off with all four hogs. Next day, the deal was concluded, for a single bale and, persuaded that the Russians would not raise their final offer, the local chief at once agreed to let them have four more hogs, for another single roll of canvas. Goodwill, like other wares, had its upper market price.

Hawaiian attitudes toward trade, as reflected in the '1804' Russian accounts, were thoroughly pragmatic, notwithstanding Captain Kruzenshtern's remarks about the gratifying of vanity. Kamehameha had collected a considerable arsenal of weapons with a view to domination of the Islands. Small arms, falconets, and ammunition had begun to fall in price even by 1802 within his territory. With the return of peace, in 1804, Hawaiian chiefs had lost more interest than ever in materials of war. (On Kaua'i, by comparison, the Russians' iron bars and other stores of military significance were valued. Kaumuali'i, says Lisianskii, "asked persistently for bar-iron and paint, observing to us that he was building a large vessel.") Now, chiefs were looking out for cloth but still employing foodstuffs, grown by *maka'ainana* labor, as their currency of preference. Kamehameha's lengthy absence from the island of his birth, it may be said in this connection, was believed by certain influential islanders who stood to lose from it themselves to have reduced the surplus crops, that is, potential revenue for use in barter. "Left without supervision in the absence of their king and all his principal chiefs," Lisianskii was assured by an interested party, "the people had become so idle that the land was producing nothing like what it previously had." On Ni'ihau, ruled by Kaumuali'i, as in Kamehameha's domains, local authority saw to it that "various rootcrops...grow in intentional abundance," so that European and American free traders might "provision more than adequately"--at an ever-rising price. Lisianskii found cloth almost essential in his purchasing of foodstuffs; and the day was fast approaching when, contemptuous of ironware and surfeited with cast-off clothes, Hawaiians would demand cash on delivery. Why should they not? In Langsdorf's words, they had "abundance of swine, breadfruit, bananas, cocoa-nuts, taro, yams, batates, salt, wood, water, and other things particularly desirable for ship stores", and "the ships of the United States" were coming to the Islands in their dozens. As the Russian texts suggest so eloquently, the Hawai'i that *Nadezhda* and *Neva* called at in 1804 stood on the threshold of discovering its strength as an important food-source, *vis-à-vis* the *haole* and, by extention, its essential weakness, which Kamehameha's policies already recognized.

Kamehameha and Trade

Lisianskii understood Kamehameha's basic problem and approved of his solution: the establishment of good relations with the captains of foreign vessels to avert armed incidents in which Hawaiians would be gravely disadvantaged and to purchase weapons needed both to conquer the entire archipelago and to offer some protection from the foreigners themselves. The Russians reached Hawai'i when the royal policy of good relations with those foreigners, especially Americans, had almost reached fruition. Foreigners felt absolutely safe in his possessions and, by Polynesian standards, he himself was invincible. No less than eighteen ships from the United States, the Russians learned, called at Kamehameha's islands in a single year. Kaumuali'i, on the other hand, had made an unsuccessful effort to secure "the trust and affection of the Europeans", and complained that "no one visited him" (Lisianskii). Kamehameha's overall success rested on trade--on terms that he himself, to some extent, dictated.

For a quarter century, by 1804, Kamehameha had been bartering for military power. The Americans alone, the Russians saw, had supplied him liberally both with "cannon, falconets, and other sorts of weaponry" and, no less vitally, with expertise that made his ultimate success in any interisland warfare almost certain. As the Russians also noted, though, the king had wider aims than growing autocratic might. Like an improbable Peter the Great of the Pacific (and the Russians more than once praise his readiness to learn new skills and trades, as had their own great tsar a century before), Kamehameha was intent upon adapting to the changes in his world. "His conduct," as Lisianskii puts it, had resulted in "great benefit..., for arriving European ships furnish him with many things, some useful, others essential for his society." The Russians felt obliged to give their blessing to the king's attempt to borrow and adapt *haole* ways, at least to the extent that this meant sloughing off "their natural propensities, coarseness and sloth" and working "for the common good, tilling the land, raising domestic livestock, birds, etc" (Shemelin). Understandably, they also deprecated the increasing influence of the Americans and British in the Islands, not, indeed, out of concern for the protection of Hawaiian independence, but for fear that the Russians would be cut out by their European rivals from an *entrepot* and market of importance. (The Americans they found it harder to envisage in a colonizing role or thwarting Russian national interests successfully.)

Considered as a whole, the Russian texts reflect Kamehameha's personal achievement of developing Hawaiian-*haole* barter, and of turning it to maximum account, in an immediate and useful way. They show Kamehameha's readiness to treat security itself as a commodity, and the Americans' and others' readiness to pay for it ("ships call," as Lisianskii records, "...not only without the least danger but in full expectation of being kindly received"). They show his politic encouragement of trade by all his subjects, just so long as he himself and the autocracy were benefitted by it. Most persuasively of all, they leave a record of a royal interference in the free exchange of food for foreign goods. The Russians felt the (modified) effects of Kamehameha's personal monopoly of trade in hogs and cattle. Had they come some five years later, Shemélin tells us on the basis of the information that he gained from L.A. Gagemeister who had visited the Islands with *Neva* in 1809,[6] they would have felt its spread to trade in other foodstuffs, including coconuts and ti-based rum, as well as in sandalwood and other raw supplies.

Kamehameha's absence from Hawai'i and the epidemic on O'ahu that induced Lisianskii not to visit him there, were unfortunate both from the ethnographic standpoint (almost certainly the king would have presented gifts which would today be on display in Leningrad: see Part 5, 'The Collecting of Hawaiian Artifacts') and for Rezanov and the Russian-American Company. Relations between Russians and the king were promising in 1804; not until 1809 and Gagemeister's rapidly aborted effort to establish a proprietary foothold on the Islands for the Company, as represented by Chief Manager A.A. Baranov, were they soured.[7] Conscious of the strength of US merchants in his own domains, Kamehameha was already giving thought to the development of independent trade along the Northwest Coast of North America and in Canton.[8] By 1806, he would be writing to Baranov with proposals that the Russians and Hawaiians trade both regularly and in volume: food for cloth, iron, and furs.[9] There are good reasons for believing that such trade would have *begun* by 1806-07, had *Nadezhda* and *Neva* managed to meet him in that June of 1804.

Clothing and Body Ornamentation

Traditional Clothing

The Russians at Hawai'i and Kaua'i in June 1804 saw the traditional male loincloth or *malo*, female wraparound skirt or *pā'ū*, and raincape or *kihei*, in general use but threatened, at least in coastal settlements, by more fashionable European attire. They also saw new material (European cloth) being worked by certain islanders into garments of traditional style.[10] They heard described, but did not see, the full ceremonial attire of Hawaiian chiefs, including feather cloak [*'ahu'ahu*] and feather helmet [*mahiole*]. Kaumuali'i appears to have been simply dressed when he visited *Neva* off Waimea, though attended by a traditional retainer.[11]

Chiefs and commoners alike, the Russian evidence suggests, wore the *malo* most of the time. They wore it from a sense of modesty. On certain occasions and on certain *kapu* spots, however, social convention required them to show respect by wearing nothing more. "No islander may enter the chambers of the ruler of the Sandwich Islands with outer clothing on. He must wear the girdle or *malo* alone, with which these people cover their private parts for the sake of decency" (Lisianskii). In general, clothing other than the simple *malo* or *pā'ū* was associated with rank, as were highly decorated or especially well made *malo* and *pā'ū*. Cold weather alone might induce *maka'āinana* to cover themselves with 'thick cloth'. In general, records Lisianskii, Hawaiians were well content with "a piece of material some 4 1/2 *arshin* [10'6"] long and half an *arshin* [14"] wide or a little more.[12] Men use it as a girdle, while women wrap themselves in it or, in cold weather, put a rectangular piece of thick cloth, folded several times, round their shoulders.... In normal times the rich and the poor dress alike" (Lisianskii). A woman might wear a piece of bark cloth [*kapa*] or European material either from the waist down or, more usually, from just below the breast. "The women wrap a piece of cloth round themselves then fix it just beneath the breast, so covering themselves down to the knee. The cloth thus makes a sort of attractive skirt" (Shemelin). On occasion, as when swimming at sea, young women wore a smaller piece of material. The beauty who boarded *Nadezhda* off Ka Lae, says Shemelin, wore "nothing but an end of *khiabu* [*he pā'ū*], that is, a sash covering her in front." Korobitsyn alone of the Russians supposed that the Hawaiian people, like the Marquesans, went "always naked". He was mistaken, but may well have seen men naked on occasion.

At the time of the Russians' visit, the Hawaiians were still making *kapa* in quantity, partly with an eye to trade. "Cloth of their own manufacture they offered us in quantity" (Kruzenshtern). Lisianskii left a fairly full description of the manufacturing technique, quite likely on the basis of what he or his subordinates had seen ashore. If the Russians did not actually see the "bast...[being] soaked in water until [it] starts to rot" or "beaten on a rectangular board", they most certainly and often saw the finished product, which they thought superb. On first observing native cloth, indeed, Lisianskii "could not believe that savages could be possessed of such elegant taste. The color combinations and artistry of design...would bring fame to a maker even in Europe."

Some Hawaiian *kapa* was thick and dense, yet very flexible. It was precisely such qualities that the Hawaiians looked for in the Russians' own material, even if they meant to make no more than a narrow *malo* from it. Shemelin offers these particulars: "The islanders will purchase broadcloth whether it be heavy or fine, just so long as it is dense and closely woven:...they do not cut the cloth out, do not sew it, and make no [European-style] clothing from it: the men wear it in their *malo* sashes, but for that they need no more than a quarter-*arshin* length...."

The Russians saw and admired much decorated *kapa*. Their impression was that *kapa* was almost always dyed, yellow and red being the commonest and brightest hues, but that the maker was unhampered by tradition in producing his designs--or that traditional designs could be interpreted. In the vicinity of Napo'opo'o, on the eastern edge of Kealakekua Bay, the visitors were struck by the lack of breadfruit trees. "The plant used here to dye material red, conversely, was growing in relative abundance" (Lisianskii). The plant in question was a fern, probably *pala'ā* or *'āma'uma'u*, which still grow on the Kona Coast.[13] Its commonness may partially explain the local people's coolness toward the color red, a sacred hue in many parts of the Pacific, which had much excited the Marquesas Islanders a month before. Shemelin, ever sensitive to details, observed Hawaiians' readiness to cultivate "Indian saffron [tumeric, *'ōlena*], with its yellow root," at least on a modest scale, not for any marginal medicinal or economic benefits, but with a view to decoration. "They use it only to color their *maro-pau* [*malo* and *pā'ū*] a bright yellow hue," i.e., brighter than that given by the bark of *holei* (*Ochrosia sandwichensis*). Fine *kapa*, says Lisianskii, might also be dyed "with coloring substances obtained from roots and berries". The people of the Kona Coast used *'uki'uki* berries and the roots and nut coats of *kukui* [candlenut], to obtain pale blue and black coloring substances respectively. Gum from *kukui* bark was also used in the manufacture of *kapa* paint.

Kapa was being made at Kealakekua in the ancient way and in some quantity in 1804, with implements of traditional style but modified design: such was the influence of frequent contact with Americans and other *haole* and the introduction of iron. The Russians noted and collected several such implements: the calabash in which the bast was soaked; the *kapa* beater [*i'e kuku*]; the grooved 'rectangular board' [*papa hole*] for making ribbed *kapa* (illus. p. A-10, 'Lisianskii's Plates'); the 'narrow bamboo stick, one end of which has been split', for the painting of 'stripes and other patterns'; and the bamboo block or stamp (*'ohe kāpala*) with which to stamp designs. "Each face," Lisianskii writes in reference to second stage beaters or *i'e kuku* of the sort now in the Peter-the-Great Museum, Leningrad,[14] would be carved "in a particular way. For example, there might be narrow stripes on one side, thicker stripes on another, a third might show checks, a fourth snaking lines...." The making of *kapa*, he adds, was woman's work.

Hawaiians and European Clothing

On first visiting *Neva,* the chief responsible to Kamehameha at Kealakekua wore, not traditional attire, but canvas trousers and a satin waistcoat over an otherwise bare torso.[15] It was the attire of which he was proudest. Korobitsyn adds that "among those who boarded the ship, not a few were attired...in frockcoat or caftan or seaman's jacket, with hats on their heads. Such dress struck us as particularly extraordinary at the very start of our visit only." "An odd picture!" confirms the Archpriest Gedeon, also aboard *Neva.* "One walks out in a caftan alone without a shirt and trousers on, another in a camisole or waistcoat, a third in ordinary or sailor's trousers alone...."[16] "All such clothing, of course," Korobitsyn writes, had been "picked up from the English and the Americans."

The Russians mildly deplored the spectacle of handsome natives dressed in European rags and oddments. On the other hand, they willingly cast off their own unwanted clothes and reinforced a pattern that the earlier 'Bostonians' had set. "Worn shirts, jerseys or jackets," as Lisianskii frankly notes, "may very advantageously be bartered for their fresh provisions and other goods. We let them have clothing that was so threadbare as to be of no further use to us and they were delighted with it." Sensing that the local chief would find such gifts no less acceptable than did the commoners, Lisianskii gave him, amongst other things, a hat, caftan, and pair of shoes. The chief was wearing them as he escorted the Russians to the royal palace on the third day of the visit.

The Hawaiians had yet, in 1804, to associate individual European garments, or groups of garments, with particular occasions and/or social situations. The novelty of foreign dress had not yet palled for them, as had the ironware and trinkets of the previous decade. Nor, certainly, were they producing European-style clothing for themselves: to the extent that it was being used, wool cloth was forming *pā'ū* and *malo* in response to ancient tastes. In the opinion of Korobitsyn, whose information was not all firsthand, however, cast-off European clothing was the largest single item on the list of goods accepted by Hawaiians at the time of his own visit. Laborers who brought out water from the hills in calabashes, he asserted, received for all their trouble "mostly articles of clothing".

Body Ornamentation

Tattooing was less widespread at Hawai'i than at Nuku Hiva, and more superficially produced. "Their bodies lack the heavy tattooing and body ornamentation that covers so many of the Nukugivans" (Kruzenshtern). Nor, it seems, had the Hawaiians only recently been spurning extensive tattooing in the manner of the Marquesans and the Maori: even older people often went without tattoos.

Insofar as tattooing was practiced on Hawai'i Island, Shemélin and Langsdorf agree, it was crude and unsymmetrical. "Though a few patterns were in evidence on some individuals, they struck me as irregular and showing no symmetry" (Shemelin). Those patterns and motifs were of some interest, however, as reflecting major changes that had taken place within the past few years in the Islands, and which those who bore them permanently on their skins had witnessed for themselves. Sometimes seemingly traditional motifs like geometrical designs, lizards, and fish were to be seen tattooed on the same body as *haole* bayonets, muskets, and even goats. Tattooing was mostly or entirely executed on the upper body, it appears. "Their arms and sides were tattooed in figures of lizards, goats, muskets, and other things, but by no means so well executed as the figures we had seen at Nuku Hiva" (Langsdorf). Rezanov also saw[17] the signs of European-North American cultural influence engraved on the Hawaiians' very bodies, and not only in their attitudes and in a range of artifacts.

Contemporary evidence confirms that tattooing in Hawai'i was less skillfully and widely executed than at Nuku Hiva, and commanded less prestige among the people, who were used to seeing rich and influential *haole* with few or no tattoos. It may be ventured, even so, that the disease-induced "bruises and sores" (Langsdorf) on the natives' bodies, not a few of which "excreted pus" (Shemelin), predisposed the Russians to consider the Hawaiian Islanders, with or without tattoos, as physically unsavory compared with the Marquesans. Certainly, they dwelt on the alleged uncleanliness of the Hawaiians, young and old, male and female alike.

More pleasing in the Russians' sight, though also more bizarre, were Hawaiian hairstyles, which differed widely between men and women and between individuals. The men, Lisianskii writes, would cut their "black, coarse" hair "in various ways", but the commonest style was "that of the Roman helmet". Shemelin elaborates, describing Hawaiians' heads as shaved "from the brow to the occiput, leaving a band two or three inches wide untouched." This strip of hair, he gathered, was regularly cut, "being never more than one *vershok* [1.75 inches] in length, with the result that the native head looks strikingly like the helmet of the ancients, complete with plumage." This Roman style was apparently common at Kealakekua Bay, and was not confined to the chief and his family.

"Women, on the other hand, cut their hair quite close, leaving a ridge about an inch and a half long sticking up in front. They smear this ridge every day, after dinner, with a sort of lime obtained from coral: it produces a light yellow coloring" (Lisianskii). Men too smeared the crest of their hair with this natural substance, producing a dramatic two-toned effect, but in general paid less attention to their hair than did the women, who alone sometimes decorated their heads "with wreaths made of flowers or multicolored threads unraveled from the cloth that they get from Europeans" (Lisianskii). *Haole* cloth was thus employed, as *kapa* could not be, to satisfy aesthetic instincts in a way that took no reckoning of European use of those same materials, *i.e.*, of European culture. Many aspects of the ancient lifestyle of Hawai'i had survived at the Kealakekua of 1804; others, as in this case, had been modified in local ways and in response to local wants, creatively using new materials for the modification and extension of the traditional aesthetic.

In the person of the "very smartly got up and shameless young woman" (Kruzenshtern) who came out to *Nadezhda* off Ka Lae, the Russians saw-- and were somewhat shocked by--a coquette or girl of fashion. Shemélin describes her fully, paying due attention to her hair, which was not styled with frontal ridge. "Cropped around, her hair had been cut off in front in the old French *à la verger* [straight-fringed] style, and was a light yellow color." Intrigued by this coloration, he asked how it was produced and was told: "they make an ointment from a certain light white stone thrown up by the sea, then repeatedly smear their hair with it." The resultant shade, he records, was not so much yellow as auburn, or "the color of a light bay horse." The part of the hair to which this 'ointment' had been applied so often and generously was combed 'upward'. The rest of the hair was cropped, but then left 'in its natural state'. ("Unlike nearly all the other Islanders, the Sandwich Islanders did not smear anything onto their bodies": Lisianskii).

As might have been expected of a young woman alive to modern fashion, and with ample opportunity to meet *haole* seamen with a view to trade, "her ornaments were not products of the island itself, such as the Nukuhivans boasted, for on her arms, at her neck, and by her ankle-bones she wore beads of various hues, blue, green, red, white, and cherry, though only in single strings" (Shemelin). At Kealakekua, too, the Russians found evidence of changing tastes under the influence of frequent intercourse with foreigners. One should not, however, exaggerate the rate or the extent of change. It was precisely at Kealakekua, if anywhere on Hawai'i Island, that a visitor might have expected to encounter *haole* ornaments; and yet the watchful Russians saw no earrings and noted that Hawaiians did not (yet) pierce ears. There is no mention of rings, which they would certainly have noted had native fingers been flashing; conversely, they do specifically allude to ornaments of ancient origin still generally worn. "They do," records Lisianskii, "wear arm bracelets made from sea elephant or some other kind of bone." "From walrus-tusks," adds Shemelin," they make themselves an ornament like a hook, to be worn at the neck." These ornaments were, of course, the boar-tusk bracelet [*kûpe'e ho'okalakala*] and the whale tooth pendant [*lei palaoa*].[18]

The boar tusk bracelet, writes Buck in his Hawaiian *magnum opus, Arts and Crafts of Hawaii*,[19] was traditionally "of 19 to 24 tusks, matched as to length and with the hollow root ends in the same direction. Two holes were drilled...and a long *olona* cord was threaded through the upper set." It was evidently in common use at Kealakekua, though not, perhaps, by the common people,[20] and remained in high esteem.[21] To match this indication of the widespread popularity of ancient ornaments, however, is the Russian information that the no less venerable *lei palaoa* was, in general at least, of walrus tusk. A quarter-century before, as King makes plain,[22] such hook-shaped pendants had been made of whale ivory, or stone or even wood. The presence of *haole* at Hawai'i had not only made the ornament more common (if not commonplace), but had also hastened the demise of the wooden *lei palaoa*. The use of walrus tusk neck pendants of the sort seen by the Russians, Buck observes in that connection, "was common enough for Andrews, in his Hawaiian dictionary [1865], to give one of the meanings of *palaoa* as sea elephant, which meaning was later changed in Parkin's revised edition of the dictionary [1922] to walrus, an animal unknown to the Hawaiians except through its introduced tusks." *Palaoa* actually means sperm whale.

As is evident from the inclusion of a dog tooth leg ornament [*kūpe'e niho 'īlio*] in Lisianskii's invaluable *Sobranie kart i risunkov*, such ornaments were in use at Kealakekua--or at any rate had lately been in use--in 1804. The fact that the ornament drawn by Lisianskii and engraved in St Petersburg is not that now in the Peter-the-Great Museum of the N.N. Miklukho-Maklay Institute of Anthropology and Ethnography (see Part 4 below: 'The 1804 Hawaiian Artifacts in Leningrad', No. 6) may be taken as an indication that such ornaments were not (yet) rarities. The leg ornament drawn by Lisianskii will be considered briefly in Part 4, 'Lisianskii's Plates'.

Russian evidence of necklaces in use in Kona and Ka'ū at the turn of the century is tantalizingly slim. It is evident, however, that the women of the coastal villages wore necklaces of shells and beads and that at least one simple form of feather necklace [*lei hulu*] was in use. The "shameless young woman" from Ka Lae had already modeled "beads...in single strings" (Shemelin). Among the objects spotted by Shemelin in a native craft that same day, one recalls, were "threads, cords, mussel shells and other trifles...." Shemélin was not from a coastal town and was unfamiliar with shells, as this and other passages make plain. His "mussel shells" were very probably *Nerita* shells made into simple necklaces or bracelets. Such necklaces, of which the Bishop Museum has good specimens, are known to have been very popular in the Hawai'i of the early contact period. The shells in question had been brought out to the Russians, with "threads" and "cords", with trade in view. Nor is it plausible that, in the circumstances of a rapid trade session at sea, the natives had been eating 'mussels' in their craft. Time was too short. Because the feather necklace illustrated in Lisianskii's work is not described in his or any other Russian's narrative, it will be touched on in 'Lisianskii's Plates' (Part 4 below). So too, for the same reason, will the (partly ornamental) fan given as 'I' in Plate II of *Sobranie kart i risunkov*.[23]

Agriculture, Husbandry and Diet

Agriculture: General Observations

From diaries and logs kept by the members of Cook's final expedition whilst at Kealakekua Bay in 1779, it is apparent that the villages of Kealakekua and Ka'awaloa were then supported by extensive inland agricultural systems.[24] Recent aerial photography has substantiated the written evidence of Cook's own people that the aboriginal strip field system stretched at least three miles inland from the area of Ka'awaloa flats north some ten miles to Kailua.[25] Cook himself was favorably impressed by local agricultural techniques and, more especially, by the abundance of the produce from the *ahupua'a* [land divisions] in question.[26] Insofar as agricultural and allied matters are concerned, much of the interest and value of the Russian evidence of 1804 lies in its function as objective confirmation of at least three-quarters of the evidence of 1779. In short, the Russians found that ancient agricultural techniques--and attitudes--survived despite the recent and successful introduction of *haole* crops, and that the ancient field systems were intact and just as fruitful as the lesser chiefs and landowners could make them at the time.

It is a paradox that the 'plantations' and/or coastal field systems that the Russians gazed at longest, on the shore of Puna, they observed to least advantage--at a distance; nor, despite those slopes' "well cultivated look" and the significant "plantations of various kinds" (Kruzenshtern), "well situated" with regard to sun and the dependent settlements (Korobitsyn), were the Russians able to obtain from them even a portion of the crops that they so urgently required. For the people of *Nadezhda* in particular, we may suppose, it was frustrating to observe the "many groves" along a "pleasant and well-cultivated" stretch of coast (Langsdorf); but it is Russian evidence of agricultural development, conservatism, change in the Kealakekua-Ka'awaloa area that we must welcome most, because that evidence can be compared and collated with the Russians' predecessors' evidence of the previous twenty-five years.

Almost certainly, Lisianskii and his officers were never more than a mile from the ocean when ashore in South Kona. Their first landing and walk, northward from Waipunaula (by the Ka'awaloa flats) toward Kealakekua, set the pattern. Spurning the (in fact inevitable) foot trail above along the high sea cliffs,[27] they struck out up the surf-sprayed beach. What lay inland, east of the cliffs, was of less interest to them than what was on, or near, the water. Nonetheless their narratives are full of evidence of what *did* lie inland, beyond the lava-strewn and marginally cultivable strip behind the beach; and, on the basis of Shemélin's text at least, it may be argued that Lisianskii's men not only saw the walled and irrigated field system that extended to the east,[28] but also carefully examined taro beds and sweet potato plots. For good measure, they also offer insights into land ownership problems, the increasing spread of various imported crops, such as cabbages, onions and watermelons and, despite the swift expansion of a lucrative and well taxed food trade, the continuing importance to the islanders themselves of traditional Hawaiian crops and methods.

By and large, the Russian evidence for agriculture on Hawai'i was obtained at first hand. Some, however, was obtained at second hand, from John Young, whom all the Russians called the 'viceroy' of the island, or from the chief responsible for Kamehameha's estate at Kealakekua. Some additional data were gathered from mariners on the Northwest Coast of North America in 1805-1806. It is important to recall that Young, and not a commoner or petty tenant, gave the visitors to understand that, "left without supervision in the absence of their king and all his principal chiefs, the people had become so idle that the land was producing nothing like what it previously had" (Lisianskii). Perhaps the population in the region of Kealakekua had decreased, of recent years, as a consequence of famine, war, or royal policy. Perhaps Kamehameha's absence had in fact produced some lessening of effort on the part of some, as well as other forms of tax-evasion than had earlier been practiced on the island.[29] All in all, as will be seen, the Russian evidence is that the productivity of the Kealakekua region's *kula* land had risen, in proportion to the number of the *maka'âinana* working it, since 1789-1793.[30]

The Russian Evidence of Traditional Agriculture

While in Hawai'i, the Russians saw bananas [*mai'a*], breadfruit [*'ulu*], sweet potato [*'uala*], yams [*uhi*], taro [*kalo*], and coconuts [*niu*] under efficient cultivation. They also saw sugar cane [*kô*] growing wild in the hills and, almost certainly, the ti [*kî*] plant (*Cordyline terminalis*). They were offered sweet potato and coconuts, which were both to be had in abundance, in several trade encounters, but not, it seems, taro or yams. Bananas and coconuts they saw in numerous groves all along the shores of Puna and Ka'û; sweet potato, which was obviously an essential part of the Hawaiian diet at the time, they were given both off the south coast of the island and at Kealakekua Bay. June 1804 was not a time of shortage and want on the island, and famine foods, including the *hâpu'u* and *'ama'u* ferns and the *pâpapa*, are conspicuously absent from the Russian texts. Berries, too, are mentioned only casually in connection with the dying of *kapa*.

The fullest and most detailed information about Hawaiian traditional agriculture--that offered by the Company clerk Shemélin--derived less from his own stay in Hawai'i than from the 1809 reports on the archipelago by Captain-Lieutenant L.A. Gagemeister of the Russian Imperial Navy.[31] Langsdorf and Rezanov too, it should be noted here, offer pertinent and sound but also secondhand information about Hawaiian agricultural production. "The point," as Daniel D. Tumarkin writes, "is that following the visit to [Hawai'i and] Japan, Rezanov and Langsdorf left the *Nadezhda* and proceeded to Russian America. During their several months' stay in Novo-Arkhangel'sk...in 1805-06, they met American sailors who had visited Hawai'i... Among their informers were John

D'Wolf of Bristol, Rhode Island, who had sold his ship the *Juno* to the Russian-American Company in October 1805...and Captain Jonathan Winship of Brighton, Massachusetts."[32] Certainly, the state of agriculture on Hawai'i had not changed a lot during the one- or five-year intervals in question. Nonetheless, it was not static, and the sources of Rezanov's, Langsdorf's, and Shemélin's information must be borne in mind. All this, of course, will necessarily apply the more to Berkh's remarks, which were not published until May 1818.[33]

Even the slighter Russian evidence of 1804, however, makes a welcome contribution to our knowledge of the "farming situation" in Hawai'i at a time of rapid change and some political uncertainty. Unconsciously as well as consciously, Lisianskii mirrors that uncertainty itself in his peculiarly subtle and perceptive narrative. ("While we were at Ovaigi, many of the islanders were of the opinion that ... Kamehameha would soon be returning to Ovaigi, where his presence was seriously needed.") Although generally brief, the Russian evidence of 1804 supports and complements the data of Malo, I'I, and Kamakau. Two examples of that function may suffice. "The *uala*", Malo tells us, "grows abundantly on the kula lands, or dry plains... Kona was the part of Hawai'i most exposed to the sun, because of the prolonged dryness of the weather."[34] The Russians found *'uala* in plenty at Kealakekua: "6 to 8 bunches" were offered at a time for one piece of "printed linen" (Lisianskii). In a single day, *'uala* traded incidentally--the Russians were chiefly interested in viands--filled a small barrel aboard *Neva*. Again, remarks Malo, the people of Ni'ihau "were energetic farmers. They would clear the land and mulch it for many months..., after which they planted such crops as sweet potatoes, yams, or sugar cane."[35] Lisianskii amplifies Malo's remarks, as follows: "Various rootcrops, sweet potatoes and other sorts of vegetation grow there in intentional abundance: European ships may provision there more than adequately."

Taro [kalo]

"Despite Young's ban," records Lisianskii with a certain satisfaction, the Russians ended their second day on the Kona Coast, 12 June, with four hogs aboard "as well as a cask-full of sweet potato and a good number of...taro roots...." It is the only occasion on which taro is specifically mentioned as an article of barter at Kealakekua in June 1804. Taken together with the dryness of the area, the rockiness of the coastal strip itself at Ka'awaloa ("nowhere, from the seashore right up to the hills, did we see any vegetation, the whole area being covered with lava": Lisianskii), and the lack of reference to irrigation in the Russian narratives, the omission inclines one to believe that relatively little taro was available for barter, at that time at least, or usually, in the Bay. The local people would have given of their best for Russian cloth. It is conceivable, of course, that the Russians did not *like* taro and discouraged the Hawaiians from producing it for exchange. Even allowing for such factors, though, the Russians' silence on the matter is suggestive. Such taro as was cultivated was likely growing quite some distance from

Neva, on higher ground. This had traditionally been the situation. Moving inland from Nâpô'opo'o in January 1779, Samwell had "ascended the Hills" and, in due course, arrived in the "Plantations... Here we found breadfruit trees...Taroo root...and Sugar Canes."[36] Taro may take a year to mature. The offering of *some* taro, however, leads logically to the assumption that considerably more was no less ripe--had the Hawaiians been *disposed* to bring it out to *Neva*. It may be added that the presence of abundant sweet potato was itself an indication that the land around the Bay was not too suitable for taro cultivation. As Buck has said, "the sweet potato was the principal crop on dry or *kula* lands unsuitable for taro."[37] Russian evidence of 1804 supports the supposition that *'uala* was the main root crop at Kealakekua-Ka'awaloa, taro and other crops being grown further inland, probably without the aid of irrigation.[38]

Shemélin's description of taro cultivation in banked and irrigated pools would seem to rest on what Gagemeister saw on O'ahu in 1809.[39] It has several points of interest, and contains a blunder (taro does not mature, like *'uala*, "in six months"). Of interest, first, is the assertion that the taro pools may, initially, be as much as "six feet deep". This depth seems quite excessive; the modern pit is much shallower. It would, however, have allowed for silting up and a resultant lessening of depth, once water was "introduced by way of narrow ditches". Also noteworthy is the statement that, after flooding, the pools are stamped in to "soften" their bottoms, in order to make them "the more suitable for planting". It has been asserted, on traditional authority (by John Papa I'î), that "the trampling was to make the ground water-proof so that the water would not soak entirely away." Lastly, it is useful to read that the taro shoots or tops [*huli*] were planted out one foot apart, the pools being often surrounded by banana plants.

Sweet potato ['uala]

The people of Puna, Ka'û, and Kona all traded in sweet potato [*'uala*]. Off Hokuma Point, Kruzenshtern picked up a dozen "batates" (Shemelin), although "not without paying a high price" (Kruzenshtern). At Kealakekua Bay, "the local chief himself came out to us, bringing with him...a fair quantity of tubers" (Lisianskii). As Langsdorf broadly states, the island, like others in the archipelago, could provide visiting mariners with "abundance" of "batates", as well as other foodstuffs.

The Russians visited the Kona Coast in mid-summer. Mauna Loa and Mauna Kea were even then, as Korobitsyn writes, "usually lost in clouds because of the thickness of the atmosphere"; and several of the Russian texts confirm that much of Hawai'i's upper country was lush and misty. The Kona Coast, on the other hand, was dry. In the not so distant past, the Russians were informed, there had been periods of drought and famine, which had thinned the population. Lava flows were obvious enough when viewed from *Neva*, and even more so when the Russians took a walk. Returning to Waipunaula from "Karekekua" village, the path proved "so thickly strewn with stones that...we pretty nearly broke our legs".

There were no more than "three or four of the so-called bread trees" to be seen along the way,"and even they were in poor condition" (Lisianskii). Nothing much flourished, in fact, larger than *pala'â* ferns which had, presumably, found small pockets of shade. ("The plant used here to dye material red was growing in relative abundance...": Lisianskii.) On the south shore of Hawai'i, bananas might be prolific; here, not even sweet potatoes did well. The Russians traversed the very area to be described in 1925, by the Land Study Bureau, Honolulu, as "very poor" for husbandry.[40] It was an area that Cook's subordinates, including King, had wandered through in 1779. "For the first 2 1/2 miles," wrote King, "it is composed of burnt loose stones, & yet almost the whole surface beginning a little at the back of the town [Nâpô'opo'o], is made to yield Sweet potatoes."[41]

Judging by the Russian evidence, *'uala* were the mainstay of the local agriculture in the early nineteenth century, as in the day of Cook and King. The *maka'âinana*, says Shemélin, paid their taxes to the king and *ali'i* in such things as sweet potato, taro, fish, and animals. In consequence, numerous tenants would "deliberately cultivate" taro and sweet potatoes "on various small plots, so that the king will take produce from one or two of them, but not all." (Under Kamehameha's overall control, observes Shemelin, "the lesser chiefs permitted the commoners to live upon the land, taking in exchange a substantial portion of the crops raised."[42]

According to a 1968 report by archaeologists Soehren and Newman,"The Kona agricultural system of which Kealakekua is a part" (and which so readily supplied the Russians with *'uala* from the first day of their sojourn to the last) is, with the West Kohala system, the "only non-valley aboriginal agricultural system left in the state. All others have been destroyed by modern agriculture or construction."[43] However, it is only one of several physical features seen, and in some cases described, by Lisianskii and his men, which are visible today from the air, (see 'Religion' and 'Following Cook up to Hikiau *Heiau*' below).

Sugar Cane [ko]

Like taro, sugar cane was little used in barter with the Russians of *Neva* by the Hawaiians at Kealakekua Bay and, almost certainly, was not available in any quantity. The Russians, for their part, were struck by the availability of any quantity of it, however small, and were impressed by its quality. Reflection on the subject, and discussion with Americans then wintering at Novo-Arkhangelsk on Sitka Island, in 1805-1806 brought home to Berkh and Langsdorf the significance in international commerce of Hawaiian sugar cane. "If this were cultivated to any degree of perfection," Langsdorf thought, "in time Kamchatka and indeed all Siberia might be supplied with sugar thence."[44] Lisianskii had not needed time more fully to appreciate its economic meaning: "Sugar cane alone, which grows in great abundance and without the slightest supervision, might give [the Hawaiians] huge wealth if they saw fit to turn it into sugar or rum. Both products, after all, are now sold on the coasts of America in great quantity."

Bananas [mai'a]

The Russians found that bananas, too, were growing wild on Hawai'i and were flourishing without human assistance. Recognizing the improvement to their quality that tending gave, however, the Hawaiians had bestirred themselves, at least in southern regions of the island, and had planted out bananas in (to Kruzenshtern's and Langsdorf's eyes) attractive little groves. On O'ahu and no doubt elsewhere in the Islands, so Shemélin was informed by Gagemeister, young banana plants were placed around irrigated taro pools. The natives put them deep into the soil (...burying the young stems in the ground up to half their height": Shemélin). There, too, they grew wild in the "woods and hills". Plantains--large varieties of bananas which are usually cooked--were also much in evidence at Kealakekua and Ka'awaloa in 1804, as in 1779.[45] A common food, these, too, were used to deck the altars of *heiau,* but were not offered to the Russians, it appears. We may note, in this connection, that the individuals who came to trade aboard *Neva* as she stood anchored in Kealakekua Bay, and as commonly as not remained all day to add to, and enjoy, the market atmosphere on her lower deck, could not very well have been the 'farmers' who had long been growing dozens of species of bananas, amongst other things, with large-scale barter with the *haole* specifically in mind. For all the confidence of his description of these (mainly inland) well established tenant farmers of Hawai'i known as *'ili pilo*[46] ("the interior is...peopled with farmers who provision foreign ships with the surplus of their labors"), Lisianskii never met them. As for those with whom his dealings were most intimate and regular, their very lives were geared to a mutually profitable contact with such captains as himself, who neither warned Hawaiians of their coming nor remained too long ashore.

Breadfruit ['ulu]

As seen, Lisianskii and his men were unimpressed by the few struggling breadfruit trees at Ka'awaloa; before arriving there, they had not been offered breadfruit anywhere. On O'ahu, says Shemelin, breadfruit was sometimes put in a pit "for two months when not quite ripe". Mountain apples ['ôhia 'ai] were similarly treated.

Coconuts [niu]

To judge by Russian evidence, coconuts were plentiful in most parts of Hawai'i, much eaten by men (only), much used in trade with foreigners, yet little prized by the Hawaiians. The Russians saw "groves" of coconut trees on the south coast of Hawai'i and even on the burnt and rocky land of Waipunaula. They bought and stowed considerable numbers of coconuts, and noted the other local uses to which these were put. On the principal altar of the 'royal temple' at Kealakekua, for example, they "noted a quantity of scattered coconuts, plantain, and a small roast pig..." (Lisianskii). When persons of high birth were to be sacrificed there, so local informants told them, the "special altar" was invariably "covered with coconuts, plantain, and roots".

Little prized though coconuts might be, compared with other foodstuffs, they were readily available and sold to *haole,* in coastal barter, by the hundred every year. *Nadezhda* picked up "a few dozen" off Hokuma Point. Moreover, coconut fiber could be plaited into twine ['*aha*]. Such cordage, though weaker and less durable indeed than that made from *olonâ* fiber, had long been used throughout the archipelago for sewing up canoe parts and in rigging.[47] Coconuts, in brief, had some significance in trade with foreigners. The fact is unexpectedly substantiated by a comment in Shemélin's text. On O'ahu, writes Shemelin, there were many coconut palms, from which rope was made, "albeit in small quantity. The king, who has taken possession of all coconut palms [circa 1809?], gives the islanders one kernel apiece with which to make some." This was conceivably a regularly repeated allowance, but more likely a temporary restriction, perhaps related to the planned invasion of Kaua'i. "The organization of Hawaiian politics," remarks Malo, "and the traditional docility with which...commoners yielded to the wishes of their rulers, allowed Kamehameha to monopolize the principal sources of revenue within his kingdom."[48]

Yams [uhi]

Shemélin comments that these "roots" were "by no means despised by the islanders as a food." The yams were "prepared for consumption by cooking" in an earth oven. It was apparently on Niihau, however, that *uhi* was most intensively and extensively grown.[49]

Gourds and Arrowroot (pia)

Taken together, the Russian narratives make it apparent that a variety of gourds [*ipu, hokeo, hue,* amongst many other names] was cultivated, for a range of purposes, in quantity. The Russians' silence on the subject of arrowroot use is explained by the climate and conditions at Kealakekua-Ka'awaloa: *pia* was cultivated on the banks of wet taro patches or in swampy places of a sort not to be found where the Russians were.

Introduced Crops

The Russian accounts of barter at or near Hawai'i Island are curiously silent on the subject of imported vegetables. Lisianskii writes that Hawai'i produced "onions, cabbages, radishes, melons, watermelons, pumpkins, and other things besides", and he certainly knew that Vancouver (the Hawaiians' Kankono) and other captains had introduced seeds in order to foster, as Shemélin puts it, "the spread of kitchen vegetables."[50] And yet few if any such vegetables seem to have been available to the Russians in 1804: one may reasonably assume that, if they *had* obtained some, they would have mentioned it. The apparent unavailability of European greenstuffs grows more interesting in the light of comments by Shemélin in connection with the fact that, when 'Kankono' had himself laid out large seedbeds ten years previously, he had done so with the future welfare of mariners and of the native populace alike in mind.[51] "Now," writes Shemelin, "certain diligent proprietors can provide, at any time of the year, such greenstuffs as watermelons, melons, cucumbers, cabbage, potatoes, and turnips...."

The Russian Evidence of Animal Husbandry

At Hawaii in 1804, the Russians saw hogs, dogs, goats, and chickens being raised domestically for food and barter. They were told of, but apparently did not see, sheep. Only at Kealakekua, on Kamehameha's estate, did they see "a tame cow with a calf" (Berkh). Korobitsyn and Shemélin both, nevertheless, make interesting comments on the subject of the king's herd of feral cattle, which Vancouver had released in 1794. In general, the Russians' evidence of local stockraising and bartering in viands is extremely factual and plain. It was a subject, after all, close to their hearts.

Pig [pua'a]

Pigs were apparently abundant at Kealakekua Bay and not scarce in Puna. It was almost certainly the operation of royal fiat, not a lack of animals, that resulted in the Russians' disappointment on the south coast of Hawai'i, where purchases of pigs were concerned. At Kealakekua, Lisianskii saw pigs in or near many native dwellings and was disgusted by a general "dirtiness and slovenliness" which he partly attributed to that very fact. The pigs, he says, as "more or less inseparable companions of these islanders," were even fed in their huts and slept amongst their owners. In his view, pigs were plentiful in other parts of the island, too. ("Many swine are raised on Ovaigi.") Valuing the animals, the natives disregarded damage caused by them to the "low palisades" around their dwellings: "the latter have usually been broken in many places by swine or dogs" (Lisianskii). All in all, the Russian evidence supports Malo's contention that pigs "were in great demand as food both for chiefs and common people",[52] and suggests that the additional incentive of possible barter with *haole* in the area had further stimulated pig breeding at Kealakekua itself. The animals bartered for cloth, sail canvas, bar iron or axes were, it seems, mostly large hogs.

Shemélin throws a shaft of light onto the ease with which, as his compatriots confirm, Hawaiians reared pigs. "Quite an amount of sugar cane is cultivated," he records, "though it serves mainly as pig food. Moreover, much sugar cane grows wild in the hills, especially on the island of Atuai; and though the cane is fairly thick and tall, it seems juicy in comparison with West Indian sugar cane." In 1779, too, much sugar cane had been growing on the hills behind Kealakekua Bay.[53] Langsdorf's comments on that topic echo those of Peter Puget in 1793:

"the large and luxurious Growth of cane would abundantly repay in Quantity any Labour bestowed on it...."[54] By 1806, Langsdorf adds, Kamehameha was confident enough of a large scale annual pig production to propose to Chief Manager Baranov at Sitka that, since "the Russian establishment had sometimes suffered in winter from a scarcity of provisions..., he...would be glad to send a vessel annually...with hogs...and other foodstuffs, too, if he were given in exchange sea otter skins at a reasonable price." In this connection of the royal interest in the important pig trade with *haole*, it may be noted that it sometimes worked to the advantage of the latter. By the fourth day of *Neva's* stay in Kealakekua Bay, says Lisianskii, barter was continuing as before, "with the difference that everything but livestock had become more expensive." Kamehameha and John Young, his Hawaiian representative, had fixed the exchange rate for the pig and, by and large, it was adhered to.

The Russians saw evidence of pig sacrifice in the main *heiau* at Kealakekua, and were given further information about it by Young. "In the course of our inspection of the place," writes Lisianskii, "we noted...a small roast pig which had evidently been brought only recently." The pig lay on a *kuahu* or rustic altar made from a frame of poles. Whether it had been decapitated, as one might expect, the Russians do not say; but the animal had obviously not been eaten and was destined, it seems, to remain and rot.

Lisianskii and Shemélin give a full and detailed description of the method of preparing food for general consumption in the traditional earth oven [*imu*]. They had evidently seen an oven being used, and very likely seen it in the open air: in July, a dry time on the Kona Coast, no oven shelter [*hale imu*] would have been required. A considerable pit several feet in depth, the two agree, was dug, and "rows of stones" were placed over the bottom. Three rows were not unknown. John Wise adds that "the stones, about the size of a closed fist, were selected from the kind which would not burst when they were heated.")[55] The kindling was laid directly on the stones, the fire, as Lisianskii says, being "obtained by friction". *Olomea* or, more often, *hau* firesticks were in service on the Kona Coast. The Russians doubtless saw some. *Honohono* ("damp grasses" according to Shemelin) or "a thin layer of leaves or reeds" (Lisianskii) were next spread on the stones, which had themselves, the Russians state, been spread out evenly across the pit bottom with some implement unknown to them (probably a thick, heavy piece of midrib from a banana leaf or palm frond, trimmed and bent double to make a very effective pair of tongs). The pig which had been stifled for the feast "by tying a rope around the snout" (Lisianskii), was then placed carefully onto the leaves or reeds "and turned over until all the bristles disappeared." Any stubborn bristles left after a few minutes would be "scraped off with a knife or shell." Apparently, the iron tool was starting to replace the ancient pig-scraper consisting of a flat, rough piece of lava, two or three inches across. (The Bishop Museum has a specimen, B 1856, obtained at Honaunau.) Oven attendants would now "open up the belly and remove the viscera", while the fire was relaid. When the stones were once again red hot, some would be taken from the pit and placed, well wrapped in ti leaves, in the pig's abdominal and main thoracic cavities. The animal was then returned to the oven, this time resting on a single layer of stones and on some leaves. More specially selected ti leaves would be placed over the beast, making a *laulau* [wrapper], and the pit "filled in with earth and sand" (Shemelin). (Here, the Russians cast some doubt on Buck's assertions that "a final cover of earth...was apparently not used in Hawai'i."[56] The final cover process may, in fact, have been dropped in Hawai'i after the Russians' visit. This has been the case in some areas of southern Polynesia where the introduced wet burlap bag is substituted for the final earth cover, used to hold in the heat.) The cooking process [*kalua*] would continue for a full 24 hours.

In conclusion, Russian evidence confirms that hogs were bred in great numbers and for many purposes, including trade, in the Hawai'i of the early 1800s. Tenant farmers paid their land taxes in swine (and other animals), and as Shemélin emphasizes, the industry enriched the nobles and the king as much as, if not more than, themselves.

Dog ['ilio]

Dogs too were regarded as a source of food and wealth on the Hawai'i that Lisianskii visited. They were numerous and, to a point, destructive. In several respects, the Russians write, the dog was treated like the pig by the Hawaiians. It too was raised as food, lived in the dwelling house, was used to pay regular taxes, and was sacrificed on some occasions. Unlike the pig however the dog was associated with women: "nor," said John Young, were they sacrificed "except when the prayers being offered to the idols concerned women: for in the Sandwich Islands, dogs belong rather to members of the female sex than to men" (Lisianskii).

Among the artifacts acquired by Lisianskii at Kealakekua Bay was a dog tooth leg ornament [*kûpe'e niho 'îlio*] of precisely the sort seen there, and described, by King.[57] The ornament, now item 750-5 in the Museum of Anthropology and Ethnography of the Academy of Sciences of the USSR in Leningrad (see Part 4 and p. A-10 below), has a height from upper to lower border of no less than 30cm [almost a foot], and some 25 rows of canine teeth. It would have taken at least 200 dogs, by the present writer's reckoning, to supply the teeth on item 750-5. For all the size and social significance of this object, however, it was apparently not worn by a dancer in the Russians' presence; nor indeed does a single Russian narrative allude to dog-tooth ornaments or baked dog feasts.

Domestic Fowl [moa]

Possibly because the Russians themselves were more anxious to obtain large hogs by barter than domestic fowl, the Hawaiians appear to have supplied *Neva* with surprisingly few of the latter. On 12 June, the Russians acquired, among other foodstuffs, "ten fowl"; on the 13th, "about a dozen fowl" (Lisianskii). Such supplies would have been speedily exhausted in a single meal for the men of the lower deck. Lisianskii amplifies: "as for birds, there are few species on Ovaigi. The fowl is the only domestic one, and even the fowl is not numerous." Is this Russian emphasis on shortage a reflection, possibly, of earlier (and disappointed) hopes? Kruzenshtern, certainly, had reached Hawai'i in the pleasant expectation "that the islanders...would at once bring poultry and fruit out" (Shemelin). All in all, one tends to think that, though the Russians' hopes of getting poultry had indeed been far too high, domestic birds *were* relatively scarce as a trade commodity at Kealakekua Bay in 1804. As a daily sale to the Russians of a dozen birds would have reduced the local stock by 72, it was perhaps as well that larger creatures were preferred. Lisianskii's price list clearly reveals ("1 hen--1 penknife or pair of scissors") that fowl were the small change of Hawaiian-Russian barter, and that both parties were happier with larger trading units.

Goats and Sheep [kao, hipa]

At Kealakekua Bay, the people of *Neva* were not displeased to find, "nanny goats" had "been bred in great numbers." Two could be bought "for a trifle, and their meat was tasty" (Lisianskii). Many of these creatures, it appears, were domestic in the strict sense: as Shemélin writes, Vancouver "brought the Hawaiians billy goats and rams which today comprise their domestic livestock." Many more, however, were feral and had long been living in the hills. That very fact, as Lisianskii realized, was "the true explanation of their propagation, for nature herself looks after such animals far better here than do the islanders...." Thus, the Hawaiians had a permanent, though none too convenient, source of kids, should they wish to increase their village stock for trade or other purposes. As yet, they themselves ate little goatflesh. Goats were thus enabled to establish themselves across Hawai'i in numbers that, within one human generation, were to lead to large scale export of goatskins from the island.[58]

Sheep were apparently rarer on the Kona Coast in 1804 and, though Lisianskii observed that "arriving Europeans" would "soon be able to eat both beef and mutton", he saw none at Kealakekua.

Cattle [pipi, bipi]

In an effort to secure the safety of the cattle that he meant to leave on Hawaii in 1794, Vancouver had obtained from the council of chiefs, which Kamehameha headed, a ten-year *kapu* on the beasts.[59] He saw no reason why they should be slaughtered, on his leaving, as livestock left by Cook on New Zealand had been slaughtered by the Maori. The *kapu* had been duly placed on the animals, which had accordingly remained untouched by the Hawaiian people for ten years when *Neva* arrived. The Russian visit thus preceded by only a few weeks the expiry of the *kapu* which had not only left Vancouver's stock at liberty to multiply up-country, but had also largely formed Hawaiians' attitude toward the animals: that they were to be left alone.

Of Vancouver's stock, a few head had been kept on the wide Kamehameha lands on Hawai'i as domestic animals; but even these grew wild, so that ten years later the Russians saw, "on the king's property" at Kealakekua, "a cow and calf which were to be domesticated" (Lisianskii).[60] The other "horned cattle", as Shemélin puts it, had been left to their own devices from the start: "the natives left the animals in complete independence and they, to find food for themselves, went off into the woods and hills where they bred." (They also did such damage to the tender bark of *koa* trees [*Acacia koa*] that they left whole forests of that precious and once plentiful wood standing dead. They are, indeed, considered primarily responsible for the demise of this species.) Shemélin's native inform-ant was mistaken in believing that his people had acted in this way because they had not realized "how this livestock could be useful to them"; in reality, they had been following a royal order. It is true, nevertheless, that the *kapu had* effective-ly prevented the Hawaiians from appreciating the potential value to themselves of a creature with which they had not previously been acquainted.

Without natural enemies and with an ample food supply if they would forage for it, wandering from hill to hill, the cattle quickly multiplied. The people neither killed them nor consumed them. "Only foreigners, with the king's con-sent, sometimes kill a few head for their own requirements" (Shemelin). Grow-ing wild, and able to find food less easily as their numbers increased, descendants of Vancouver's stock were, by 1800, moving down into the popu-lated valleys of Hawai'i, trampling plantations, and disturbing all and sundry. Bulls, predictably, gave the most trouble. "Not long ago," Lisianskii was told, "a herd of bulls came down into a valley and damaged numerous small plantations. The king ordered that the beasts should be caught, and a thousand men were detailed for the operation; but the wild bulls...killed four men before losing them-selves in the hills again."

Lisianskii foresaw the day when Hawai'i would be "full of wild stock". He could not envisage the Hawaiians themselves tending large herds of cattle, or even Kamehameha's two new horses.

Fishing

Ocean fishing around Hawai'i was controlled by custom, and exploited by the chiefs. Land taxes, and other taxes, too, were often paid in fish. "The land, and the surrounding sea for fishing purposes," moreover, had "been divided up among the native court grandees and other deserving persons" (Shemelin). Even so, the ocean was the most reliable and largest source of food, regardless of the level of taxation in a given place and year. The Russians saw a good deal of shallow water fishing, drawing benefit from it themselves at mealtimes.

As *Nadezhda* coasted westward off Hokuma Point, (see 'The Coastal Encounters', p. 118), she was approached by three canoes, each containing four natives. Many such craft, writes Kruzenshtern, were visible along the shore. Together with the Russians' total silence on the subjects of canoe ornamentation, figureheads, and stern-pieces, and King Kamehameha's requisition of Hawai'i's war canoes for use against his rival, Kaumuali'i of Kaua'i, the remark allows us to assume that, like the other "native craft" that met *Nadezhda* and *Neva*, these three were modest multi-purpose *kaukâhi* [single canoes] of the sort that trader-fishermen might use, week in and week out.[61]

As a makeweight in a larger trade deal (cloth for food) or, conceivably, in an incidental, subsequent exchange, one native gave the Russians of *Nadezhda* "a skein of fine and skillfully twined cord, which could serve to replace our best log-line" (Shemelin). Such a cord could obviously have been used in fishing if not traded; and its presence in the craft might be regarded as suggestive of its owner's readiness to trade or fish, as circumstances might dictate. Perhaps that cord is not the line now held in Leningrad as item 750-6 (see Part 4); perhaps it is. In either case, the Russians did obtain a 22-foot length of cord of vegetable fiber, at the end of which was tied a handsome *aku* lure [*pâ hî aku*], with a *paua* shank and well ground dog-bone hook. The shank of *paua* shell is 6.5cm [2 5/8"] long, the hook 3.5cm [1 13/32]. As traditionally done, in chiefly fishing for the tasty and nutritious *aku* [bonito] of Hawaiian waters, white pig's bristles were attached to, and disguised by, the point where shank and hook were brought together by the snood. "The bristles," Kamakau tells us, "ruffled the water be-hind the lure...and the *aku* mistook the lure for an *'iao* [silversides] or other small fish and crowded around to seize the *pa hi aku*."[62] Much enjoyed though *aku* fishing was by chiefs and even kings, it was of far greater importance to the *maka'âinana*, all *kapu* that were connected with the fish apart;[63] and certainly the men who used Shemelin's "skein of cord" and item 750-6 were commoners. *'Opelu* [mackerel scad] being under strict *kapu* in June or *Ka'aôna*, and *aku* being caught instead,[64] the owner of the line and lure was no doubt less willing to exchange them for the Russians' goods than he would (sensibly) have been, if the *Neva* had reached Hawai'i four weeks later.

The Leningrad Museum offers further evidence of the pursuit of *aku* in Hawaiian coastal waters when the Russians visited. Item 750-8 is a complex *uhi* [mother-of-pearl bivalve] lure, comprised of four iridescent, nacred 'fingers', minus hooks, tied to a vegetable fiber twine. Such fine fishing-line twine [*aho*], made of *olonâ* or *hôpue* bark and braided into four-strand *lino*,[65] was also used in the manufacture of nets and bag-nets [*'eke*], some of which the Russians saw and admired. "They have so perfected the manufacture of all sorts of cordage and fishing nets in Owaichi," Langsdorf told his readers,"that ships are supplied with them. The products of Owaichi are considered more durable, if used as tackle, than European cordage." Shemélin disagreed, but still gave testimony of

Hawaiian cord's considerable durability: "it is not as good as hempen cord, perhaps, but it can still be used in case of need, when hempen cord is wanting."

To Hawaiians, Kruzenshtern observed, the ocean seemed a natural and proper element as it did not to the Marquesas Islanders, who viewed it apprehensively. Among the creatures that Hawaiians from the shores of Ka'û had tattooed across their arms and upper bodies, as Rezanov says, were fish. The Russians had been hoping to be met fifteen or eighteen miles out to sea by native craft, as European vessels had in other times; they had been disappointed. Of the "native craft" themselves, however, and Hawaiian expertise in using them, they had no criticism. In the words of Langsdorf, the canoes observed about *Nadezhda* and *Neva* were "light and very neatly made, and proved that the Owaichians had already made much greater strides in naval architecture than the Nukahivans had." Unwittingly, Lisianskii saw the evidence of recent fishing trips in just such *wa'a* [canoes] many miles out to sea: a quantity of freshly salted *loloa'u mâlolo* [gunard, a type of flying fish]. As Kamakau stresses, *mâlolo* [flying fish] were caught in special bag nets "in the deep sea almost out of sight of land."[66]

The Hawaiian Diet: General Remarks

Six days in Kealakekua Bay sufficed for Lisianskii and his men to form a clear impression of their hosts' regular diet. It was traditional and, for the *maka'â inana* at least, unaltered by a quarter-century of dealings with commercial travelers from the United States and Europe. Though even the chief at Kealakekua might eat willingly enough "everything brought to the table" in *Neva*'s wardroom on 12 June, he was plainly not accustomed to *haole* fare.[67]

The Hawaiian diet, Lisianskii writes authoritatively, "consists of swine and dog meat, fish, fowl, coconuts, sweet potato, bananas, taro, and yams. Sometimes they eat fish raw, but everything else they bake. The women are forbidden pork, coconuts, and bananas." (He might have added shark, whale, porpoise, and several fishes to the list in effect on Hawai'i Island at that time.) At Kealakekua, the Russians saw 'multi-unit dwellings', including men's eating houses [*mua*], *kapu* to women, and women's eating houses [*hale 'aina*]. "All...had been constructed in the same fashion from poles enclosed and covered by leaves" (Lisianskii).

Russian evidence suggests that the extensive use of local salt at Kealakekua Bay, observed by King in 1779,[68] was traditional and harmless. The Hawaiians in the area, observed Lisianskii, were "very fond of salted fish and meat." The salt was obtained from the ocean, of course, sea water being channeled into clay-lined, earth-banked pans along the shore[69] and the concentrated brine removed by local women using calabashes [*pôhue*] of the sort observed by Korobitsyn in ordinary huts, ("...a bit like pumpkins to look at"). Those actual water containers [*hue wai*], each of which would--according to the Rev. William Ellis--hold "from two to three bucketfuls of water...from the hills", would not, of course, have been contaminated by such contact with brine. In sort and size, though, salt- and freshwater containers were the same. The Russians were particularly interested in the excellent white salt of Kealakekua Bay, and spoke of it later that year to Chief Manager Baranov on the Northwest Coast. With or without the use of shallow ponds [kâheka] for quick evaporation, as Langsdorf in particular appreciated (though, unlike Lisianskii and Berkh, he had not been on the Kona Coast himself), the salt could "be procured in abundance" and had relevance to Russia's long-term interest in the Pacific. In 1809, Gagemeister took a cargo of Hawaiian salt to Sitka from O'ahu, and by 1821, Hawaiians were themselves exporting salt to Petropavlovsk-in-Kamchatka, with the help of Captain Sumner of the trader *Thaddeus*.[70]

When not eaten raw, fish were preserved with salt by the Hawaiians, most of whom, it seems, had known the misery of famine in their lifetimes. Russians saw the islanders "with various sorts of salted fish, including flying fish about a foot long" (Lisianskii). These flying fish [mâlolo] would have been salted down some weeks before *Neva*'s arrival: they were seldom caught in any number after April.[71]

On the Kona coast, the Russians saw, Hawaiians also used much salt as they themselves would do, as a spice, with the secondary object of preserving food briefly. 'Taro root flour' was so treated once the pounding on the *papa la'au* [board] was over: "they also prepare little balls of taro root flour, for consumption on long journeys. By soaking these in fresh or salt water, they produce something rather like meal dough" (Lisianskii). Judging by the tone and context of this reference to *pa'i 'ai* [or 'ai pa'a--hard, pounded but undiluted taro], it was widely known and used in 1804.[72] Lisianskii's evidence that many natives made considerable journeys around the island in the early 1800s is confirmed by that of Shaler (1808).[73] As Shemélin comments, "dried and pounded taro" was hardly worse than European flour, from the standpoint of nutrition, and was certainly "important in itself" in the Hawaiian diet.

By and large, the Russians found the natives of Hawai'i Island physically unimpressive: they were "of medium height" (Lisianskii); "shorter than the Nukuhivans, of anything but stately build" (Kruzenshtern); "lean" (Rezanov);"not of large stature, lean, not especially well knit in the body" (Shemelin). The Russians were most likely affected in their efforts to describe proportion (height and 'leanness') by the ugly scabs and sores which, they write unanimously, covered all too many natives' skins. Nevertheless, it is significant that several observant and objective visitors should have described the "average Hawaiian" met as *khudoshchavyi* [lean or spare]. Yet more striking is the readiness of both Company clerks to state, emphatically and unambiguously, that the populace at large did not eat adequately. Korobitsyn concerns himself with women on the island: "Women are not adequately nourished, because of this local custom of imposing tapus on certain kinds of food." Shemélin touches on the vexed subject of land taxes and produce confiscation thus: "In truth, the position of the ordinary farmer on the island is a wretched and onerous one, for the king will sometimes...take as much as two-thirds of the taro and potatoes he has grown... There are also many who, though they possess a sufficiency of their own swine and dogs, have never had the opportunity to eat their meat...." "Shemélin should have added," writes the Soviet historian of Polynesia, Daniel Tumarkin, "that this was paralleled by more harsh oppression meted out to the commoners by the local nobility for, with the development of trade with foreigners, the *ali'i* were enabled to exchange the surplus product of the labor of the *makaainana*...for foreign goods."[74] Thus, foreigners and the *ali'i* were colluding, in the interests of trade or self-enrichment, in the worsening and widespread exploitation of the laborers whose representatives the Russian party met. Moreover, adds Tumarkin, the Shemélin narrative reveals that New England missionaries like Dibble, Chamberlain, and Richards were mistaken in believing that the *maka'âinana* had received more than a third of all their produce in the days before the *haole* had come. "More probably," asserts Tumarkin on the basis of Shemélin's comments, produce confiscation of the truly harmful sort alleged (in those same comments) had begun of recent years only, when the "changes touched off" by the *haole's* activities "had set in on the Islands". In the present writer's view, Tumarkin overstates his case, resting too heavily on information gathered, not in 1804 but five or ten years later,[75] at second hand; but he is correct to view the Russian texts in question as indicative of an exploitative and mercenary attitude toward the 'workers' on the part of the *ali'i* and the king. As William Shaler saw in 1808, that attitude could well be "avaricious, cruel, and inhuman" if material rewards were large enough.[76]

Disease and the Drinking of 'Awa and 'Okolehao

Because almost certainly the greatest *'awa* [kava] addicts of the Ka'awaloa area were with Kamehameha on his military campaign, the Russians saw fewer symptoms of extreme addiction than had Cook in 1779. Conversely, *some* degree of scaliness appears to have been more evident among the commoners, *i.e.*, the populace at large, by 1804. The problem with the Russian evidence lies in a tendency to mix the symptoms of venereal diseases, syphilis especially, with kavahin-associated eye- and skin conditions, such as 'rheuminess' and interlocking scabs or scales. Sometimes, to their credit, Russians recognize their ignorance, declining to attribute a condition to persistent *'awa* drinking or to syphilis. "Of the Hawaiians that we saw..., there was hardly a single one whose body was not marked by *piaten* [patches] caused either by the disease of lasciviousness or by immoderate drinking of kava" (Kruzenshtern). "Many bear scars on their body that result from some venereal or scorbutic disease or other" (Korobitsyn).

It is difficult, upon consideration of the Russian evidence,[77] not to conclude that both syphilis and yaws were widespread in the Ka Lae and Ka'awaloa areas in 1804. Kruzenshtern himself ascribed the 'patches' that he saw to syphilis, mistakenly supposing that the *maka'âinana* had no access to the beverage produced from 'awa roots. Korobitsyn enquired how the natives tried to cure themselves of the affliction, and was given information (use of sea water and a specific root) which led him to the same conclusion, ("incontinence...infect one another..."). Certainly, the Russians witnessed prostitution, women offering themselves as 'gifts' ("from her words and motions...it was obvious that she had come to us with quite another sort of commerce in mind": Shemelin), and being offered by their menfolk ("one elderly native had brought a quite young girl out...and...was offering her to us as a victim to lust": Kruzenshtern). Lisianskii, too, who doubtless knew the symptoms of venereal disease, connected it with the Hawaiian girls and women who, as soon as *Neva* dropped anchor, swarmed around "exhibiting... most unequivocal tokens of pleasure, not doubting of admittance." It is only right to add here, to Kruzenshtern's, Lisianskii's, and their numerous successors' credit, that the Russian record with regard to passing sexual relations with, and consequent infection of, Pacific Island women, *is* incomparably better than the record of the British, French, Americans, or Spanish. As to physical liaisons between Russian seamen, who were usually under close surveillance by their officers whether ashore or not, and 'nymphs' whose very fathers were allegedly prepared to sell their favors to the highest bidder, it would seem that few young Russians fell from grace.[78] So all the Russian texts excepting Levenshtern's that touch upon the point assert, and one believes them: in the reign of George III, as in more recent years, Russians took 'Victorian' and somewhat prudish moral attitudes toward the relative sexual freedom found in parts of Polynesia.

Cook, too, had at times confused conditions caused by long-term use of 'awa with those resulting from venereal disease, and added salt to the confusion: "that [venereal disease] should rage more violently...here than at the Friendly [Tonga] or Society [Tahiti] Isles, I suppose may be attributed in a great measure to the quantity of Salt these people make use of...."[79] These uncertainties are echoed in the Korobitsyn account: "Their bodies were covered with some kind of sore which excreted morbid matter of a reddish-white color. There were few parts of the bodies not covered in these sores, indeed; and where there were not, weals and cicatrices took their place." This seems a good description of the working of what Cook described as the "venereal Distemper" or "the Clap", one might conclude: for Cook, too, "morbid matter issued out" from sores.[80] However, the Russian then says: "the islanders' bodies looked as though they had had poured over them a whitish liquid of some sort, which had dried to their backs." What at first glance seems an obvious description of venereal disease becomes, on closer scrutiny, a picture of the scabs and sores linked with 'awa, very possibly compounded by the signs of venereal disease [*kaokao*]--and made the more unsightly by salinity. 'Sores' and 'patches', after all, will not do service for the rash and spots of common syphilis; nor do those spots envelop the entire torso, as the Russians' 'patches' do. Again, a skin "almost encrusted" and (in the words of Cook) "pealing off in Scabs", like that of Kalani'opu'u in December 1778, and

Kao shortly afterward,[81] might well have struck the visitors as "covered with some kind of sore", to quote Korobitsyn, and as excreting a pinkish matter if the skin was also bleeding from assorted cuts and weals. The Russians saw much 'scaliness' and many 'marks' of *'awa* drinking,[82] but, because those marks were commonly *compounded* by the symptoms of venereal disease, they tended to attribute them to syphilis ("licentiousness": Korobitsyn). To judge by Russian evidence, which their informants were themselves, perhaps, inclined to misinterpret, *'awa* drinking--and the use of 'ti rum' and other intoxicating drinks as well--was fairly widespread and increasing on the Big Island in 1804. The use of those intoxicants, some introduced by *haole* (but very likely not including ti 'rum' [*'ôkolehao*] and alcoholic brews from 'ohi'a or potatoes in 1804),[83] would certainly have tended to accentuate the 'leanness' of the drinkers' bodies, on which virtually all the Russians comment. So too, of course, would the drinking of non-alcoholic but narcotic *'awa*, which had always been regarded as medicinally sound for the obese.[84]

Shemélin, who describes the Hawaiian method of distilling *'okolehao* from the cooked, chopped, and fermented roots, was in *Nadezhda,* not *Neva,* and so cannot have seen the process. Since a good part of his information was obtained from other men, moreover, after his return to Russia, one may think that ti rum making was an infant art in the Hawai'i of the early 1800s. As he comments, only natives with access to a boiler-*cum*-still could have indulged. As a result, it was the *haole*, a handful of important chiefs, and King Kamehameha who produced the rum in quantity.[85]

Religion

General Comments

Although, or possibly because, he was the son of a provincial priest, Lisianskii had a poor opinion of organized religion. When *Neva* had fitted out, in 1803, he had opposed the appointment to her of a chaplain. Overruled, he had proceeded to ignore the man appointed, Archpriest Gedeon of the Aleksandr-Nevskii Monastery in St Petersburg. The archpriest's subsequent complaints of shabby treatment in *Neva*, for example in letters to the Metropolitan Amvrosii of Moscow, have a ring of truth about them: ("...various sneering remarks made about religion...addressing me with the words, 'Father! To the health of the Mother of God!'...much offense...When we called at the Sandwich Islands I did not even go ashore...").[86] Such antipathy as he unquestionably felt toward some aspects of Hawaiian paganism--for example, human sacrifice--perhaps induced Lisianskii to insist upon them in his narrative at the expense of other aspects. Many of his predecessors in the Islands, one may say in his defense, had also done so. The important point, however, is that from the first day of *Neva*'s stay in Hawai'i to the last, Lisianskii felt obliged to take good note of the Hawaiians' attitude toward, and practice of, religion. As a serious observer and recorder of the local situation, as a scientific officer at anchor in a given bay for days and nights on end, he had no choice.[87] Religion was a vital and integral part of local life. He duly visited *heiau* in the bay, notably Hikiau, and discussed religious practice and belief with John Young and the chief priest then at Hikiau whom, regrettably, he does not name. The visits and discussions leave their mark on the Lisianskii narrative, as on the Berkh and, especially, Korobitsyn accounts.

The Russians were more favorably placed than they themselves appreciated as observers of religious practice and routines in Kealakekua Bay. Ethnographers and others have some reason to lament Kamehameha's absence from that bay during the Russians' presence. He and the *ali'i* of Hawai'i would undoubtedly have given information to their visitors, and acted themselves in manners likely to enrich the Russian narratives. Where religion is concerned, however, one cannot regret Kamehameha's absence from the scene. Lisianskii and his people saw the regular religious practices of the Hawaiians and their priests in, so to speak, non-festive season. The royal presence would, in itself, have modified that regular, routine observance. In conjunction with the known fact that Kamehameha and the great chiefs of Hawai'i had been absent from the island for a period of years, the Russian evidence lends powerful support to Malo's statement that, in other times, "great was the earnestness and sincerity [*ho'omapopo maoli ana*] with which the ancients conducted their worship of false gods."[88]

Local religious custom and observance touched the Russians' own lives in the very hour of *Neva*'s arrival, though at first they did not recognize this. As Lisianskii puts it: "I had feared that we should be met by a large number of little craft, and that these might hamper us in our operations. In the event, we did not see a single one--a result, as I discovered, of a tapu that had been placed...." *Neva* had entered Kealakekua Bay on 11 June. By the Hawaiian calendar, based on the synodic month of 29 1/2 days,[89] it was the twelfth or possibly thirteenth day [*Môhalu, Hua*] of the seventh month [*Ka'aôna*].[90] It was consequently the time of the *kapu Hua*, of two days and nights.[91] By weighing anchor on 16 June, Lisianskii unwittingly avoided the inconveniences to himself that would assuredly have arrived within three days due to *kapu Kanaloa*.[92] Unconstrained by any ban, the Hawaiians came out to *Neva* to trade at sunrise on 12 June.

Of the many signs of regular religious practice that the Russian shore parties noted, suffice to mention four. "The chief, not being one of the noble grandees of the place, could not walk up close to this principal temple [Hikiau *heiau*].... In the course of our inspection of the place, we noted...a small roast pig which had evidently been brought only recently" (Lisianskii).[93] The 'chief priest' of Hikiau *heiau*, and other 'priests' presumably, lived by it, as they had in 1779.[94] And Ka'awaloa, which the Russians examined on the afternoon of 15 June, "boasted nine small temples" (Lisianskii) and at least one resident 'priest'. (He was out fishing.) Ever anxious to be accurate, Lisianskii questioned both John Young and the 'chief priest' at Hikiau about Hawaiian polytheism, sacrifice, burial procedure. The information that the priest could give was limited by the linguistic skills of the interpreter, named Johns or Johnson; that which Young could offer was restricted by his ignorance of lore. Nevertheless, Lisianskii pieced a good deal together, both about his hosts' beliefs as such ("They recognize the existence of good and evil. They believe that after death they will have a better life") and, more importantly today, about the temple images that he deplored (see below) and the distinctions between 'temple priests' [*kâhuna pule heiau*] and 'sorcerers' [*kâhuna 'anâ'âna*]. In the main, the value of Lisianskii's and his people's evidence of the religion of Hawaiians at Kealakekua Bay resides in details of number, size, and function--that is, concrete fact--not in general deduction or reflection. Its value is significantly heightened by the fact that it so admirably complements the evidence of Cook and his subordinates, particularly in regard to Hikiau, of a quarter-century before. By literally walking in the footsteps of *Discovery*'s and *Resolution*'s men of 1779, the Russians were enabled to present us with a valuable cameo of an important temple as it was between the time of Cook and that of Freycinet. It is a cameo brought fully into focus by collation with the 'Hikiau drawings' of Surgeon William Ellis of *Discovery* (1782) and Arago of *L'Uranie* (1827-1839).[95]

Following Cook up to Hikiau heiau

Lisianskii and Korobitsyn left *Neva* in an armed launch "toward evening" on 13 June, intending to land by Kealakekua village, but in fact landing a little south of Waipunaula, where the surf was less ferocious. "The chief duly met us and informed us that he had placed a tapu on all the inhabitants. Sure enough, not a single person followed us on our stroll" (Lisianskii). As the Russians recognized, the institution of *kapu* had social and political significance, as well as wide religious connotations.[96] The Russians turned north, and almost at once passed "a number of poor huts" (Lisianskii). These were Cook's "Village to the S [of Hikiau *heiau*], or rather a continued range of Stragling houses in that direction."[97] As David Samwell justly observes, "Oipoona-oura [Waipunaula] lay partly at the back of Ohekeaw [Hikiau],"[98] partly along and above the sandy beach. A few minutes more, and the Russians "came into an alley of coconut trees", the trunks of which had "many slits and holes...produced by cannon balls at the time of Captain Cook's death" (Lisianskii). Samwell and King both describe the circumstances in a way that points up the chief's assertion that "many people had been killed by the English on that occasion."[99] Their curiosity satisfied, the Russians continued up the beach alone. "The chief had excused himself from accompanying us, as a temple lay on the way and he could not pass by it" (Lisianskii: 1812); "alleging, that he could not with propriety pass in front of a temple, which we should see on our way" (Lisianskii: 1814). This was, of course, the Hikiau *heiau*, of which the local people, sub-chiefs included, had all stood in awe in 1779. "No Canoe," records King, "ever presumed to land" before it, "apparently...thro a religious awe and respect... Not all our endeavors could prevail on the Women to approach us."[100] If a man would not land his craft in front of the *heiau*, he would be even less disposed to stroll before it. Evidently, the local chief held the place in as much "awe & respect" as the Hawaiians had in 1779.[101] By keeping to the beach, meanwhile, Lisianskii and his men were getting wet. The surf was very great. This would have been the point where the beach was narrowed by the ocean on the west side and a large pond on the east. Not far from Kealakekua, as Korobitsyn puts it, was "a small lake or pond with a few coconut trees and banana trees planted about it." North of this waist of sand stretched out the level area on which, in turn, Cook and Vancouver had been entertained by mock battles and martial exhibitions.[102] To the right lay Kealakekua village, which the Russian party entered (see 'Hawaiian-*Haole* Relations' below).

Korobitsyn and Lisianskii kept together on this little expedition, which cannot have lasted less than two or three hours; their interests, however, now diverged. Lisianskii, not surprisingly, paid much attention to the boatsheds, one of which had housed the thirty-six-foot schooner *Britannia* that Vancouver had had built ten years previously for Kamehameha's use and pleasure,[103] and to the king's own 'palace'. For the energetic clerk, such sheds held far less interest than did the small temples and structures that he saw beside, or not far from, the pond or little lake already passed.

Neither from Cook's and his subordinates' accounts of their transactions in the area in 1779, nor from the Russian texts, is it quite clear where these small *heiau* and associated structures stood in relation to Kamehameha's 'palace' and the village proper. From Lisianskii's 1814 text, one might suppose that they were all around the lake: "This palace...consisted of six distinct huts, erected near a tolerably large pond of stagnant water." Korobitsyn places the royal dwelling complex "not far away" from the lake. One thing, however, is apparent: there were many structures with religious and ecclesiastical associations, so to speak, beside this lake. Whether or not one of the little "heathen temples" (Korobitsyn) was "the royal temple" that Lisianskii saw, but could not enter, is debatable. The evidence of emphasis and order in the Russian texts is inconclusive, but inclines one to imagine that it was. The cluster of *heiau* and associated structures, notably, priests' dwellings, had also been noted by Cook. Kao and Keliʻikea, "head" and "2nd" priests of Hikiau *heiau* at the time, Samwell tells us, had in 1779 shared a house "in a low retired Ground among some Trees close to a large pool, amid some Temples or Houses consecrated to Orono [Lono]... These people have selected this Spot in a Grove & on the banks of a large pond for the Residence of the Priesthood & for the Situation of their sacred Buildings."[104] Time would have accounted for the shrinkage of a "Grove" to Korobitsyn's "few coconut trees and banana trees" (unless, as is conceivable, the clerk's descriptive terms were influenced by his memories of Nuku Hiva's verdant woods and hills). It is significant, however that may be, that Samwell should describe the *heiau* in question here as "some Temples or Houses". As Korobitsyn confirmed, "they are not large structures and are not distinguished in any way from the native houses or yurts." By definition, yurts are roofed. The fact heightens the probability that what Lisianskii terms "the royal temple" was among or near them: it was, he says, only "a small hut, fenced around with paling,...in which, we were told, his majesty takes his meals during the *tapu* days." As N.B. Emerson remarks,[105] "there seems to be no doubt that the *mua* and *heiau* were integrally one."

Kamehameha's *mau-heiau*, if we may so describe the 'royal temple' that the Russians visited, was evidently like the nearby 'heathen temples' by the pond in being an enclosed or fenced-in hut. By its entrance stood "a statue of middling size", "representing a deity worshipped by the islanders" (Lisianskii: 1814, 1812). Within the enclosure, "right by the entrance to the structure itself, stood six other large idols" (Lisianskii: 1812). In the phrasing of his English version only, Lisianskii seems to say that the image by the *mau-heiau*'s outer entrance was smaller than the six inside. Though prevented from entering the king's *mua* itself, the Russians plainly saw that it was empty. It was long since Kamehameha had himself been in the structure, to partake of food on *kapu* days or to pray.[106] "Near" or "in front of" the enclosure was "another enclosed spot", also containing images [*akua kiʻi*].

Here, for contrast, is Korobitsyn's description of the small *heiau* which, apparently without Lisianskii, he examined by the pond: "On its banks stand two heathen temples, called Ogio and Kaira, where sacrifices are offered and which contain respectively three and nine wooden images resembling neither man nor beast. In front of them are strewn great quantities of coconuts and other produce, which the natives bring as offerings. Entrance to these temples is forbidden to the common people, only the king and his officials and the priests having that privilege." The structures, as was seen, looked to the Russian very much like native dwellings in the area. Such structures, comments Kamakau, were in general associated not with kings or even chiefs of lofty rank, but with the lesser chiefs or commoners of substance. They were commonly "surrounded by wooden tabu enclosures, *paehumu la'au*,...with a single house within."[107] By "neither man nor beast", Korobitsyn presumably refers to 'crudely' carved *akua ki'i* of the sort that Cook had seen, and which the Russians saw themselves at Hikiau on a grander scale: "the most frightful Images of the human Countenance, the Head only... formed after the human figure."[108] Small though both the temples might have seemed to any stranger in comparison with Hikiau, they cannot in fact have been so very small. "Entrance" was "forbidden to the common people" (Korobitsyn), and one was large enough to hold nine images and "quantities of coconuts" (Korobitsyn), as well as worshippers.

What is of greatest value in the Russian word-picture is the passing comment that these two *heiau* were "called Ogio and Kaira". Russian has no aspirates; the letter 'h' in other languages is commonly replaced by the Cyrillic 'g'. As for the unstressed 'o' in medial or final position, it is commonly pronounced as 'a' or something rather closer to the schwa sound. Thus, 'Ogio' is 'Ohia' in Slavic dress. Why would a *heiau* be known by, or associated with, *'ôhi'a* wood (*'ôhia lehua*)? Images were often made of heavy, dark *ôhi'a* timber, certainly, as were enclosures and, especially, oracle towers [*lananu'u mamao*]; and the high country of Kona had *'ôhi'a* in abundance.[109] But the Russian's guide, presumably a local individual, would hardly have insisted on the name of the material of which the little temples' idols and enclosures had been made, and left him with that one word in his memory (assuming that the visitor *has* handed down approximately accurately what he heard), unless that word was of particular significance. Malo provides a clue in his discussion of Hawaiian plants and trees. "The *ohia*, a large tree,... was much used for making idols..., and from it were also made the sticks to couple together the double canoes."[110] Again, notes Malo, if a *heiau*--a *luakini* [large *heiau* for the use of ruling chiefs and where human sacrifices were offered] especially--were to be for worship "after the rite of Ku,...the fence about the place would be of *ohia* with the bark peeled off."[111] What link, one next asks, was there between Kû and the construction of canoes, double especially? Samwell provides an answer while describing Cook's induction as a god in Hikiau on 17 January 1779: "The Priest performed various Ceremonies..., then went round & touched the Images one by one & kissed that in the middle which is the smallest and they call it Coo-coi-araka."[112] Kû-'ôhi'a-Laka (Samwell might have caught the suggestion of his captain's name in the Hawaiians' brisk pronunciation of the 'Kû' and elision of the hard glottal stop sound ['], producing Kuk-ohia-Raka) was a deity essentially connected with trees for canoe-building. A *koa* tree quite suitable for hewing out into a craft having been found up in the mountains, says Malo, "the *kahuna* took the ax of stone and called upon the gods: "O Ku-pulupulu,... Ku-ka-ohio-laka!"[113] In Kealakekua Bay, English and Russian evidence confirms, both king and chiefs as well as (certain) common people worshipped him. Elsewhere on Hawai'i, very probably, the situation was as stated by Malo, that is, Kū-'ôhi'a-laka was not worshipped by *ali'i*, but by people largely occupied with the construction of traditional canoes ("those who went up into the mountains to hew out canoes").[114] As Kamakau puts it, he was an important "*'aumakua* of canoe-making".[115] Not far away, as seen, stood the structure where skilled local men had worked, during Vancouver's final visit, with Boid and other carpenters of *Discovery* on the first Hawaiian schooner in the European manner. Next to it, in 1804, a large double canoe was being built for the local chief himself ("on the stocks, but not yet finished": Lisianskii, 1814). Boatbuilding was a major and esteemed activity at Kealakekua, in the early nineteenth century as in the past. Kô-'ôhi'a-Laka held his own.

But who was 'Kaira'? Some tentative suggestions may be made. First, it will be noted that Korobitsyn understood that an entire temple was "called", that was, named for, 'Ogio', whereas in fact, an image or several images were so termed by his guide. In other words, the name picked up was one the god Kū had acknowledged while the wood from which the images were carved was still a tree, and was applied now, rather loosely, to the carved *akua ki'i* that were being pointed out to visitors. Secondly, Samwell elaborates on names applied to images in Hikiau, thus: "The small Image which is placed in the middle of the rest is the chief...; the four next to it are called Cahai, and the others Macaiva..."[116] These would have been (*akua*) *kâ'ai*, or images carved on a tall spearlike staff,[117] and *makaîwa* [mysterious eye]. Korobitsyn, the passing stranger, was shown *kâ'ai ra* [*la*] ('the *kâ'ai* gods over there'), just as he was shown 'Ogio'; and, on both occasions the physical representations of the deities were simultaneously pointed out *and named for him*.

Korobitsyn and Lisianskii walked together from the pond and little temples up to Hikiau. "The chief refused to follow us... This was rather mortifying to us, as we might stand in need of his assistance: he was not, however, to be persuaded, and we were obliged to proceed alone" (Lisianskii). As the Russians' own later accounts reveal, they could not have moved to Hikiau, on its "stone elevation" (Korobitsyn), without passing directly by the priests' houses below. ("About the pond," writes King in this connection, "were a few huts...perceiv'd to be inhabit'd entirely by Priests or People who had the Care of the O'heekeeow.")[118] There was no doubt, in short, that the *kâhuna* knew the foreigners were going up to Hikiau, and did not discourage or prevent them. Not long afterward, in fact, "the chief priest of the place came up to us" (Lisianskii), just as other priests had wandered up to Cook's men in another generation. The Russians found the *heiau* deserted, as one might expect.

To judge by Russian evidence, the *paehumu* [taboo enclosure] of Hikiau was in tolerably good repair. "The temple...is surrounded by a palisade of poles";

"the temple of the Sandwich Islanders is nothing more than an open rectangular space fenced in by paling or stakes", writes Lisianskii. Surgeon Ellis's drawing shows such stakes, replete with skulls (the conscientious Samwell counted twenty),[119] of which neither Russian makes a single mention. Evidently, the Hawaiians had replaced the palings bought by Cook as firewood on 1 February 1779[120] and, if the new enclosure had been similarly carried off (as Beaglehole so rightly comments in defense of Cook, such fencing was in no way sacred),[121] had again repeated the performance. Arago, it may be noted in passing, shows a palisade unlike that in the Ellis drawing: neater and made of thinner pickets, which are slightly separate from one another. Judging by Lisianskii's choice of nouns (*iz zherdei, kol'iami*), the fencing that replaced that bought by Cook was very much like that drawn by the Frenchman.

Inside Hikiau Heiau

The value of the Russian evidence where Hikiau is concerned lies in suggestions of the deep conservatism of religious practice in Hawai'i of the early contact period. Perhaps the gods were under pressure from the inferences to be drawn from the political and technological aspects of *haole* culture, if not yet from Christianity. If so, the fact was far from clear to Lisianskii and his people. By and large, the Russians found the great *heiau* as the English had described it. Differences will be noted below.

Images

Korobitsyn and Lisianskii agree that Hikiau contained, at the minimum, fifteen images in June 1804. Korobitsyn speaks of fifteen in all, Lisianskii of fifteen "on the side nearer the hill adjacent" and eight more, beside or facing them. Korobitsyn apparently regarded only the 'inner', more easterly of Hikiau's two *kahua* [courts] as the temple proper, and counts only the images within it. Samwell, too, had been conscious of the further, smaller "Area", which he inclined to look on as "the Sanctum Sanctorum".[122] Since Hikiau lay on an east-west axis, with the entrance to the west toward the bay, this 'inner court' would have been nearer "the hill adjacent" (and behind) than would the other *kahua*. Surgeon Ellis's depiction of twelve images, ranged in a curve inside that "inner court" facing a raised *kuahu* [altar] platform (Samwell's "seat called Coo-a-oo"), thus complements Lisianskii's observations. Since Cook's time, it appears, three more images had been erected in the temple's 'inner court'.

"To the right of the altar" before this large group of images "were two more small statues, and not far off--another small altar for another three idols" (Korobitsyn). Opposite these three, on the north side of the first *kahua* (?), stood yet another trio, one propped up by a pole because it was decayed. Lisianskii uses several terms to mean 'image', including *statuia, idol, istukan,* and *bozhestvo*, but does not use them so methodically or systematically as to enable us to make a judgment on the relative dimensions of the images in question. Even so, it is apparent that the fifteen images beyond the raised *kuahu* were, so to speak, differently treated and separately worshipped from the smaller images within the first *kahua*. Ellis's drawing and Lisianskii's verbal picture indicate that all fifteen were representative of Kû, the god of war. Korobitsyn confirms this: "the idols...are regarded as the gods of war and vengeance...." There are solid grounds for thinking that the images that Ellis saw and drew were those seen by the Russians, too: "a head three times as big as the torso", "carved blocks on their heads", all can be seen in Ellis's invaluable drawing. Temple images with high carved wooden blocks over the head were once found on Hawai'i and O'ahu, if not other islands of the chain, as Buck has shown.[123]

Lisianskii writes of eight images associated with the seasons, growth, or 'joy'. In what sense these last (three) were connected, as they no doubt were, with *makahiki* rites, we cannot know; but obviously all the others represented Lono, in one guise or another. 'Kaira' is thus less pertinent than Samwell's "Macaiva" [*makaîwa*]. East of the raised stone altar, Samwell tells us, he saw a little image [Kû-'ôhi'a-Laka]; four *akua ka'ai* staves; and several *makaîwa* images, all smaller than the images of Kû beyond. It is not hard to bring his total (1 + 4 + 3?) and Lisianskii's into harmony, or to appreciate the theological significance of "guardians of the maturing crops" (Lisianskii) and *makaîwa* images of Lono. Hikiau was a multi-purpose temple, in the courts of which the rites of Lono and of Kû had been observed.[124]

During the Russians' visit, as in 1779, the images of Kû were girded [*hume*] in *malo* ("wrapped in material from the waist down": Lisianskii). Services performed before these images, the Russians learned, were "performed only by the king, his officials, and the priests. The rest of the people have no knowledge of ritual..." (Korobitsyn).

Kuahu and Lele

The "semicircle of statues by a little raised platform" (Lisianskii, 1812) was precisely as Samwell had seen it. The Welshman's "seat" was Wendell Bennett's "stone-paved platform".[125] Right before this platform-altar [*kuahu*], as in 1779, there stood an offering-platform [*lele*]: "a platform made of poles is erected, called the place of sacrifice, on which we saw a roasted pig, and some plantains and cocoa-nuts" (Lisianskii, 1814). Korobitsyn and Samwell complement each other in their terse, but just, descriptions of this "Pile": "four posts running through Gourd Shells, on which and round the offerings are laid..." (Samwell); "a sacrificial altar, built on four stakes, man-high..." (Korobitsyn). The stakes, Lisianskii adds, were "unfinished" and "uncommonly like a drying-rack for fish". Ellis draws the *lele*, with its rat guards. All the offerings [*môhai*] seen in Hikiau by the Russians were the sorts that had been noted there in 1779.

Other Features

Samwell and Ellis saw the *lananu'u mamao* or oracle tower of Hikiau in a state of almost total collapse. It was no more than "a small pile of Stones abt. 2 yards high" from which protruded vertically "a number of poles", some nine or even ten yards high. The Russians make no mention of a pile. One deduces that by 1804 the tower had completely disappeared.

By the eastern palisade of Hikiau, near the entrance but not beside it, stood "a small cottage,...also in a ruinous state" (Lisianskii). This was the *hale pahu* [drum house]; the ruined *mana* (Samwell's "large House") of 1779, which stood across the "outer court", had evidently not (yet) been replaced.

The Priesthood

The Russians found Hawaiian 'temple priests' [*kâhuna pule heiau*] and 'sorcerers' [*kâhuna 'anâ'anâ*] exercising full authority over the lives of commoners, at least, and very likely all in the Kealakekua-Ka'awaloa area. They were impressed by the extent of that authority, which intermittent contact with *haole* had apparently not lessened in the ordinary people's sight, and noted how religious and political controls tended to overlap, if not quite fuse. Being quite genuinely interested in such matters, they pressed John Young and the *kâhuna pule* ("chief priest": Lisianskii) whom they met in Hikiau for particulars about, for instance, human sacrifice and proclamations of *kapu*. The message was the same: *kapu*, Lisianskii learned, "might be considered as religious", and in some cases "the king himself" was "absolutely bound" by them. But often a *kapu* was "civil or temporal, depending on the king's own will." In that event, significantly, priests announced the king's will to the people. Power thus remained with the *kâhuna*. As for human sacrifice, it was in general reserved for "prisoners or disturbers of the common peace and opponents of the government" and so had "more of a political than a religious nature" (Lisianskii), notwithstanding the involved and lengthy ceremonies in *heiau*-of-human-heads [*heiau po'o kanaka*] on those terrible occasions.[126] Not surprisingly, under the circumstances, the *kâhuna pule heiau* and Lisianskii's foreign-born interpreter conveyed only the essence of the matter to the Russians, disregarding problems and exceptions to the rules.[127] Both found it difficult and tiring to express religious concepts and abstractions to the visitors. ("I put many questions to the chief priest through my interpreter, but he by no means satisfied by curiosity": Lisianskii.)

For their information about spiritual and religious things, the Russians more or less depended on their two major informants, Young and the *kâhuna pule*. The informants often disagreed; and what they told the Russians often tells us more about their own outlooks and attitudes than points under discussion. True to form, the Russians faithfully report the disagreements, thus allowing us to estimate, for instance, the extent of Young's true understanding of the principles and practice of religion in the area where he had lived for many years. On the whole, Lisianskii tended to believe Young's versions of events--for example, procedures for the burial of kings and human sacrifices--rather than the priest's, as rendered by an English castaway. ("One would suppose that Young, having lived a long time amongst the islanders, would be able to get a clear idea of their procedures....")

One point on which Young and the *kâhuna pule heiau* agreed was that "the local priests are prepared for their calling right from infancy and, in times of tapu, give directions to the people" (Korobitsyn). That the priests' directions were involved and complex, and the various *kapu* demanding of punctilious and steady observation, there could be no doubt. On leaving Hikiau, Lisianskii and his party "climbed over a low stone wall. The priest...squeezed himself through its...loop-hole, assuring me that if he dared to follow our example...he would lose his life unfailingly. In these islands, there are a great many such injunctions" (Lisianskii). Hawaiian priests, Lisianskii was told, had "the same right with regard to wives" as "other islanders," *i.e.*, could have as many as they could maintain, but seldom had more than one or two.

At Ka'awaloa two days later, Lisianskii counted nine small "enclosures full of idols", but could not--or, rather, chose not to--enter them: "the priest appointed to look after them happened to be out fishing." *Kapu Hua* being over, the priest was at liberty to fish once more for untouched food.

It was presumably John Young who gave Lisianskii information about *kâhuna 'anâ'anâ*, "a special sect whose adherents claim that, through prayer, they can obtain from the gods the power to kill whomsoever they please" (Lisianskii). The employment of such local "sorcerers", according to Korobitsyn, was generally linked to revenge. The "offended party" or his family would "pay priests to pray to the gods for the death of the offender, or for avengement of the offense". The original antagonist would then, more often than not, "become pained with anxiety and even lose his mind" (Korobitsyn). Relations of that victim might then, adds Lisianskii, "hire a member of the aforementioned fraternity." Neither Young nor the *kâhuna pule heiau* informed their visitors about the *kuni* ceremony [a ritual meant to cause the death of a 'sorcerer'].[128] On the other hand, they made no secret of the whereabouts of the Koaiku cave in the cliff at Ka'awaloa known as Pali Kapu o Keôua, where royal bones had been deposited for generations. ("I was shown a cave in a rockface where rested the bones of the local kings up to and including the late Tairebu" (Lisianskii). The very fact, however, further shrank the Russians' readiness to credit all the "chief priest" told them. King Kalani'opu'u [*i.e.*, Tarei'opu'u or Tairebu], they had been told at Hikiau, had "been left forever in a *heava* or other temple specially built for that purpose." The *kâhuna pule* had no doubt alluded to the royal mausolea of Hawai'i.[129] Nonetheless, Lisianskii saw "a certain inconsistency" in his account of "Tairebu's" great funeral.

Hawaiian-*Haole* Relations

In the broadest sense, Hawaiian-*haole* relations interested and at times preoccupied Lisianskii and his people more than any other aspect of Hawaiian life. It was a matter, after all, that could not fail to affect them personally. Not surprisingly, that being so, the Russian narratives are full of references to Hawaiian-European contacts and, especially, to the results of foreign influence on the political and cultural development, or 'progress', of Hawai'i. Such an emphasis does not detract from the significance, or scientific value, of the Russian ethnographic evidence.[130]   Among the topics touched on and illuminated by the Russian texts are the position and activities of Europeans on Hawai'i Island, as of 1804; Hawaiians' readiness to work on European ships and travel, to the Northwest Coast, Canton, and yet more distant places; European influence on various traditional Hawaiian customs, crafts, and attitudes; Kamehameha's borrowing and adaptation of a new technology and consequent success in warfare; and the possible and likely futures of a 'civilized', *i.e.*, *haole*-influenced and modified, Hawaiian archipelago.

European Residents

As though to symbolize Great Britain's special role in the Hawai'i of Kamehameha, "a craft came out" to *Neva* even as she was first approaching Kona, and was found to be conveying an (apparently astute and sharp-eyed) "Englishman named Lewis Johnson and a boy named George Kernick, a native of Ovigi, who had sailed with Captain Puget and lived seven years in England" (Lisianskii: 1812). The latter had presumably sailed to England in the *Chatham* in 1794 and, supposing that he *had* stayed seven years, returned in 1801-1802.[131]   The former, whom in 1814 Lisianskii calls not Johnson, but "Johns", typified the foreign castaway or settler who, having "acted with propriety" at least on most occasions since arriving,[132] lived in comfort, supported by a chief. He showed his liberty of action on the spot, accepting a proposal from Lisianskii that he stay aboard *Neva* and act as his interpreter. So much, at least, may be inferred from Lisianskii's sending him next morning from *Neva*, then anchored in Kealakekua Bay, to advise the local chief that if supplies were not forthcoming speedily, the vessel would be gone.

Lisianskii pumped Johnson for information from the first, correctly reckoning that any Englishman in his position must be well informed about "conditions generally on the island of Ovigi". He was told of Kamehameha's absence on O'ahu, but assured that his ship would be received at Kealakekua with civility by the Hawaiian commoners and Young, who would "no doubt come out" on learning of the coming of a Russian ship. Omitted from the 1814 (London) edition of Lisianskii's *Voyage* is an interesting passage, illustrative of the Russians' faint uneasiness about Kamehameha's absence from the island and the power exercised, it seemed, by Young: "notwithstanding this assurance, I gave orders for the ship to stand prepared against every eventuality." From the uncertain tone in which Lisianskii writes of Johnson, too, now casual if not dismissive, now polite, one senses difficulty in correctly *placing* him and knowing just how far to trust him. Johnson seems to have performed his duties as interpreter with competence except, perhaps, when dealing with the "chief priest" and religious notions and procedures. He may surely be excused for that.

From the very circumstances of Lisianskii's and Johnson's first encounter, off the southwest coast of Ka'ū, it is evident that Johnson, and others with him very probably, were on the lookout for a passing European ship. Johnson had no doubt interpreted for *haole* visitors before. The fact suggests a lengthy residence.[133] Johnson held an honored place, it seems, within the district and the village 'Peri-Rua'[134], whence he hastened to *Neva* in his canoe. He lived with an *ali'i* as a favorite or *punahele*, came and went at his discretion, and no doubt served as an intermediary between Europeans and his chief who, we are told, sent presents to Lisianskii. One surmises that return gifts were expected. They were duly sent: "I presented...a gift to the young chief with whom Johnson lived, since he himself had earlier sent us gifts", including a hog, "and had further intended me the honor of a visit, but had been prevented by the sudden death of his wife."

Of John Young's position of authority, the Russians were, by contrast, never in doubt. Brief though their dealings with him were (two days at most), they were sufficient to allow Lisianskii's men to form a good impression of his use of that authority. Nor did Young prove inhospitable, presenting the Russians with two large hogs as gifts, escorting them to Ka'awaloa, introducing them to the local chief's extremely aged sister, and discussing many aspects of Hawaiian life with them at length. Lisianskii's short account of the Hawaiian wars of 1791-1804 rests more or less on Young's own *précis* of them; and, as seen, Young even rectified remarks made by the priest at Hikiau, on Lisianskii's pressing him and out of courtesy. The easy courtesy was afterward returned, Lisianskii speaking publicly of Young as one "entitled to credit" by himself and other strangers who might put in at Hawai'i. He was echoing the words of other visitors, from Puget's day to that of William Shaler, all of whom had found the 'viceroy' similarly civil.[135]

Even by 1804, the Russians knew, dozens of *haole* were living on Hawai'i, or on other islands, with the king's consent. By Young's account, no less than fifty were, or had been, actively engaged in military campaigns. Others were steadily engaged in shipbuilding, others again in husbandry and cattle-raising,[136] both of which, as Captain Winship of the trading ship *O'Cain* was soon to emphasize to Russians on the Northwest Coast of North America, were undertaken with success. ("The king gives the settlers liberty to leave their estates when they wish": Rezanov). As *Neva*'s chaplain, the Archpriest Gedeon observes, it was a royal policy to give not only land but also native labor to the useful foreigner.[137] But who, specifically, was useful to Kamehameha? Langsdorf gives the answer baldly: "Any sailor who is at the same time a ship-carpenter is particularly welcome; he is immediately presented with lands, and almost anything that he wants... The seamen of the United States like so well to revel in a superfluity of the productions of nature without much labor, and to have handsome young girls at their disposal, that...the king will not permit any one to stay who has not a good recommendation from his captain."

The Russians encountered two such seamen in Kealakekua Bay, on the fifth day of their stay. Presumably, the two Americans had just then reached it-- from another district of Hawai'i or from another island. At all events, they sought Lisianskii out. "One of the two had been on the Northwest Coast of America the previous year [1803] and told of the destruction of our settlement situated in...Sitka Bay...." The settlement in question had in fact been razed by Tlingit Indians on 26 June 1802; however, the American informant had not needed to be on the Northwest Coast in 1802 and 1803 in order to hear details of the event. The man cannot (yet) be positively identified, but he had likely sailed in Ebbets's ship *Alert* or in *O'Cain* (voyage of 1803-1805).[138]

In summary, the Russians found some foreigners in positions of authority on Hawai'i, but most were of importance only in their given district. Few were not employed to the immediate advantage of the kingdom--and the king. Kamehameha's ever more selective approach to would-be *haole* residents was bearing fruit by 1804. Lisianskii's text reflects the first phase of the subsequent, and logical, development of that approach: the gradual reduction of effective power, but retention of the privileges earlier obtained and exercised by all the island's foreigners, with the exception of Young and Davis. Later Russian visitors, notably V.M. Golovnin (1818) and M.N. Vasil'ev (1821), were to record the king's success in that regard.[139]

Hawaiians as Seamen and Abroad

As off the south coast of the Big Island, so also on the Kona Coast, the Russians were impressed by the considerable number of canoes, or 'native craft', in evidence. ("Even the number of craft plainly visible...left us in no doubt about the size of the local population": Kruzenshtern). They saw no war canoes. Kamehameha had Hawai'i's war canoes under his orders, with the *peleleu* [large type of canoe] fleet, on O'ahu. Neither threats of war nor even war, however, stopped the *po'e lawai'a* or full-time fisherman from fishing, especially if he were working on a small scale [*lawai'a li'ili'i*] like so many on the stony shores of West Puna and Ka'ū, which *Nadezhda* and *Neva* were coasting past. As for the would-be international trader, he was always at the ready with his small single canoe, in case such vessels did appear. By and large, the Russian evidence is clearly suggestive of repeated, largely speculative, offshore visits to *Nadezhda* and *Neva* by two- or three-man craft. In one instance, the evidence is more than suggestive: "a native craft overturned. The two paddlers responsible for it showed such agility that it was immediately righted" (Lisianskii). Such swift and manageable *ko'olua* would have lent themselves to in-shore fishing or to barter, as the situation might require, and were doubtless used for both those purposes by natives who, (the Russians rightly guessed), lived partly from the sea, partly by barter with *haole*.[140] To judge by Russian comments on the subject, and statistics in the Kruzenshtern appendices, the coastal traders of Hawai'i were prepared to go five miles out from shore. There is a single reference, Rezanov's, to a vessel with a plaited-leaf, traditional, Hawaiian sail [*lâ*]. It was off Ka Lae, in Ka'û. There is likewise one allusion to a large double canoe [*wa'a kaulua*]. It was, Lisianskii tells us, "on the stocks" and being built, not for the king, but for the chief who was the Russians' host. Such mentions are of interest, indeed; but they do not affect the overall impression, left by the Russian narratives, of numerous, unostentatious, small single canoes. How numerous they were at times around *Neva* may be inferred from, if not actually calculated on the basis of, Lisianskii's own remarks such as: "Surrounded by hundreds every day, we never experienced the smallest injustice..."; "every day, as many as a thousand individuals came to trade with us [in Kealakekua Bay]." There can hardly have been less than 300 canoes within a square mile.[141]

As Hawaiians were attracted to the cloth brought by the *haole*, however, so too were they drawn to foreign vessels *in themselves*: for whereas Kamehameha viewed Vancouver's schooner, *Britannia*, and other schooners modeled on her, through the eyes of naval war and strategy, his people--so the Russians thought at least, and with some reason--saw them largely as a means of ocean voyaging, of visiting the foreigners' own countries and, conceivably, of gaining wealth. (Already, some Hawaiians had returned from working visits to the Northwest Coast with property enough to keep themselves in greater comfort than before.)[142] Regrettably, the king was not yet sending any ships, in Langsdorf's words, "on speculation to Canton" or Sitka.[143] Would-be emulators of Kaiana with ambitions to see foreign countries had, accordingly, already come to terms with the commanders of such vessels as *Neva*. Lisianskii was approached by them, as European and American commanders and their mates had been approached since Colnett's stay of June 1791,[144] with eager honesty. "Many asked me to take them with me, and not only demanded no pay but would have surrendered all their movable property. Young assured me that United States vessels quite frequently carry islanders away, and that the latter in time become good sailors" (Lisianskii). Far from making difficulties for such islanders, Rezanov adds, Kamehameha let them go "requiring only that they return experienced sailors", fully capable of managing his own schooners and other foreign-style craft.

However, numerous Hawaiians never did return. Shemélin makes the point emphatically: "Hawaiians are to be found in Canton and in Boston itself. Though some return home when opportunity arises, not all do so...." Some Hawaiians are disposed of, on the Northwest Coast, to Tlingit Indians or other tribes, "as sacrifices for the deity" there worshiped. Some New Englanders, in short, traded in human flesh. It was a charge to be repeated by later Russian visitors to Novo-Arkhangel'sk, including Mikhail Vasil'ev in 1821.[145] While at Novo-Arkhangel'sk themselves, in 1805-1806, Rezanov and his private surgeon Langsdorf met a half-dozen natives of Hawai'i in the merchantman *Juno* (*Iunona,* after purchase by Baranov).[146] The Rhode Islander John D'Wolf, her captain, had apparently no qualms about abandoning the Polynesians to Baranov's mercy in the presence of such gentlemen as Langsdorf and Rezanov.

Among the six Hawaiians "was a youth of perhaps sixteen whose native name was Kenokhoia [Kanehoa?], and who, at the invitation of *Kammerherr* and *Chevalier* Rezanov..., agreed to travel to Russia with him. The youth had already been in both Canton and Boston" (Shemelin). In the event, Kanehoa did not go to St Petersburg with Rezanov: his patron and protector died at Krasnoiarsk early in 1807.[147] For a short time, the Hawaiian's situation was accordingly precarious. He did, however, travel to St Petersburg, where he gained another patron and a godfather in Vasilii Fedorovich Moller.[148] Christian baptism was followed by traditional Hawaiian name-exchange, at least as far as Kanehoa was concerned; and the Hawaiian subsequently answered to the name, Vasilii Moller. He was taught Russian and many other subjects in St Petersburg. including "ship-building..., law, sacred history, arithmetic, geography, history, English, marine draftsmanship, civil architecture, and sketching" (Shemelin).

Haole Influences on Traditional Hawaiian Life

As the Russian evidence makes clear, European cloth, small iron artifacts, and certain foodstuffs were among the foreign imports that had altered, or were altering, the lifestyle of some Hawaiians--the *ali'i* and the people of Kealakekua Bay especially. The Russians, for their own part, neither deprecated the accelerating pace of foreign influence, nor hesitated for a moment to distribute Russian iron-ware and cloth and worn-out clothing on their own account: they had no doubts about what formed 'civilization', and were ready to assist the Sandwich Islanders and others on their march toward it. What is striking on a reading of the Russian texts today, however, is the evidence of limitations on *haole* influences even in the much-frequented bay where, if anywhere within Hawai'i in the early 1800s, they might justifiably have been expected to be powerful and widespread. After all, there had been *haole* at Ka'awaloa or the villages near it since at least 1790.[149]

Notwithstanding the assertions that the Russians heard to the effect that, in the absence of Kamehameha and the grandees of the island, the Hawaiians had grown idle and the land far less productive than in other times, the Russians saw no indications that traditional Hawaiian crafts and industries were in decline. They certainly perceived no link between a lessening of general activity in any given area or areas and growing foreign influence. In local agriculture, fishing, house construction, and a range of handicrafts including rope and *kapa*-making, all continued in the ancient pattern. Diligence, not sloth, prevailed in a country whose traditions had not yet been undermined by frequent contact with *haole* like those aboard *Neva*.[150] To emphasize the point (particularly significant in light of so many accusations of a later period that the Hawaiians were a slothful people),[151] we may survey the Russians' comments about ordinary dwellings [*hale*] and Hawaiian *kapa*-making, as observed after a quarter-century of *haole*-Hawaiian intercourse.

In general, the Russian texts agree, Hawaiian *hale* had the look of Russian peasant barns or sheds, only with higher roofs and lower sides. They were constructed of poles and coconut palm or "reed leaves" (Korobitsyn) and, with very few exceptions, were "built with a single door only, with a frame as round our dormer windows, through which one can barely crawl" (Lisianskii). In the absence of a raised floor, the ground was "strewn with dry grass", on which "bast matting [*kapa*]" (Lisianskii) or--more usually--"grass mats" (Korobitsyn) were then cast. "Rarely do they have windows, and if they do, they are tiny" (Lisianskii). The poor had one such structure, the rich had several together. All shared their dwelling with their swine, fowl, and dogs. Nothing had changed since 1779, when Cook had seen precisely such Hawaiian huts, complete with entrances 'no larger than an oven door', "matts", "leaves of the Sugar Cane", and "Calibashes" on the wall,[152] unless it was a slightly wider use of 'tiny windows' at their corner.

Hawaiian skill in *kapa*-making, writes Lisianskii, was extraordinary, ("...exceeds what may be readily imagined"). Elegance of taste, effective color combination, strength and suppleness all justified the European praise. And all was brought about by the use of ancient tools and methods, which Lisianskii took the trouble to describe. What is here to be emphasized, however, is the *quantity* of *kapa* being made, by the traditional techniques, by islanders who knew of, and perhaps even possessed, *haole* fabrics. "Cloth of their own manufacture they offered us in quantity" (Kruzenshtern). Again, the Russians indicate that *haole* influence was only just beginning to be felt among the coastal populace at large, and had perhaps impinged hardly at all on commoners inland.

Of other Russian evidence that foreign influence was limited, both geographically and socially--in the Hawai'i that Lisianskii saw-- suffice to mention evidence of eating, drinking and (particularly) barter. Willingly enough though some Hawaiians would apparently eat Russian food, when given opportunity to do so, they adhered to their ancient diet in 1804. Specifically, consumption of imported vegetables was very limited. The 'Russians' chief', it may be noted secondly, was unaccustomed to alcoholic drink: given access to such spirits in the wardroom of *Neva*, he soon got drunk. No native, lastly, wanted money for his wares. For the moment, only King Kamehameha and the European settlers and residents like Young sought specie. The king, says Langsdorf, had by 1804 completely understood the value of a silver piece, even preferring "selling the products of his country to the ships that visited for Spanish dollars or piastres".

As the Russian texts make evident, however, one species of European in-
fluence--the spread of new diseases--was well advanced by 1804. Specifically,
the Russians saw the signs of syphilis.[153] Like other foreign visitors before
them, they confused the later symptoms of venereal disease with those produced
by constant *'awa* drinking.[154] But that syphilis was on the island, and combatted
ineffectually by the chewing of a certain root (*aienia*, according to Korobitsyn
[perhaps *'aieana*?]) and by the swallowing of sea water, there is no doubt.

Kamehameha's Centralizing Policy and War

Contact with foreigners had led to changes in the power structure of Hawai'i
and its archipelago. The Russian texts reflect those changes, at the same time
pointing up the likelihood of their enduring at least until Kamehameha died. As
Vancouver's *Voyage* shows us the political developments that had transformed
the four small potestarian (pre-state) formations seen by Cook in 1779, so Russian narratives throw useful light on the political and military developments that
had reshaped the power structure of the Islands since Vancouver's day. Specifically, they illustrate the last phase of the process by which one great chief,
Kamehameha of Hawai'i, was developing *his* chiefdom or, more accurately,
chiefdoms, into kingdom, and his power into kingship of a sort the Russian
visitors could recognize and, by and large, commend. Russian approval of that
process colors Russian evidence and is a factor to be reckoned with in weighing
it for truth. The occasional distortion that results from the Russians' tendency to
see Kamehameha as a new Peter-the-Great of Polynesia--introducing and adapting new technology, acquiring fresh skills himself, and approving and encouraging shipbuilding and trade--is, however, largely compensated for by our
familiarity with the informants whom the Russians met and used.

To the Russians of *Neva,* it was apparent that Kamehameha was indeed, as
they had read and as John Young assured them, the autocratic ruler of Hawai'i.
All deferred to and respected, if they did not always love, the absent king, whose
writ ran strongly in the Ka'awaloa area though he had not been near it for years.
All were conscious of, and publicly accepted, his monopolies and edicts. All,
above all, praised him to the Russians. ("According to all the information that I
could gather, Gammamea is held to be a man of rare abilities and extremely
brave": Lisianskii; "It is Tomio-omio's concern that his subjects...should exercise
themselves for the common good...and the king himself is not ashamed to pursue
knowledge appropriate to his rank": (Shemelin). It was, moreover, obvious that,
since Vancouver's day, Kamehameha had effected a complete redistribution of
the lands in his domains, removing rivals and bestowing lands and some
authority on his dependent followers who, in their turn, allotted lands to lower
ranking chiefs. Thus, the ancient holdings-distribution system and resultant sets
of multistage dependence, known for centuries before the *haole's* arrival in
Hawai'i, had been brought to perfection. Gone, by 1804, was any possibility that
such a man as Young should be presented with estates by many chiefs, and gain

political authority. ("Each of the native noblemen, wishing to console him," Young himself informed Lisianskii, had about twelve years previously given him some land. "As a result, he was suddenly rich.") Now, wealth in land and power were dependent on the royal will.[155]

John Young's own rise to power on Hawai'i Island, on the other hand, was illustrative of the king's adaptability. The very rank and function of a royal representative ("He has been left on Ovigi and fulfills the duties of a viceroy," says Lisianskii simply), were unknown before the late 1790s but were hallmarks of the rapidly evolving, centralized Hawaiian state. As students of political and social science both by training and by instinct (they were, after all, the children of the post-Enlightenment, increasingly uneasy landed class, *dvoriane*), liberal young Russian naval officers like Berkh and Lisianskii and, a little later, Kotzebue witnessed and reported on that evolution with some fascination.[156] Their reports retain their value to historian and anthropologist alike, and are a far from worked-out mine for ethnohistory.

Important though the Russian cameo of 'Viceroy Young' remains today, however, it is Russian evidence of royal use of ancient ways of social regulation and political control that most impresses. Three examples may suffice: Kamehameha's gradual extension of *kapu* to cover trade monopoly; upholding of a native father's right of life and death over his son (despite Young's protests); and refusal to remove himself from danger in the *kāli'i* or 'spear hurling' ceremony that had always taken place at *makahiki*. Thus was the authority of men (over their wives and children), priests (over the commonalty) and, above all, of the king himself, confirmed with all the sanction of tradition. Useful though some innovative methods might have proved in the creation of a modern yet Hawaiian apparatus of coercion, ancient methods of insuring the status and authority of men, chiefs, priests and kings were more important, when adapted-- as the Russians saw them skillfully adapted--to a modern situation. Of Kamehameha's overall success in managing that situation, by establishing appropriate relations with the foreigners whose guns could help him gain, and keep, authority, Lisianskii has the following to say: "Ships call at his islands...in full expectation of being kindly received and supplied with all necessary things for seafaring. His conduct has brought great benefit to himself."

Chief of those benefits, the Russians recognized themselves, were an 'invincible' militia; an embryonic standing army also tolerably well equipped, and officered by Europeans; and a fleet including 21 new schooners, some displacing 25 or 30 tons. Kamehameha's very absence from Hawai'i when the Russians came, they knew, was the result of that same policy which made their sojourn profitable: with his schooners, war canoes, some 7,000 warriors and 50 Europeans (by the reckoning of Young), he was supposedly preparing to attack Kaua'i from O'ahu. (In reality, the pestilence known as *'ōku'u* had been thinning out his forces for at least a month before *Neva* dropped anchor by Hawai'i.) Sham fights, long descriptions of traditional Hawaiian weaponry, accounts of martial training--all detailed in the Cook, King, and Vancouver narratives--are all missing from the Russian narratives. In 1804, the Kona Coast was quiet.

It is possible, but hardly probable, that *Neva* first brought the news of the *'ōku'u* on O'ahu to King Kaumuali'i of Kaua'i. ("I saw plainly that my words occasioned great joy in Tamuri": Lisianskii). What seems more likely is that Russians brought reliable and welcome confirmation of the news, and added details. The meeting with Kaumuali'i in the Kaulakahi Channel to the southwest of his island, and the earlier encounter with canoes outside Waimea Bay, throw interesting light on the political and military position at the time (19 June 1804). Whether or not the king expressed a readiness to cede his islands to the Russian Crown and pledge his fealty to Alexander I (as Berkh and Korobitsyn both assert) if *Neva* would only anchor at Kaua'i and help defend it from Kamehameha's onslaught,[157] he was certainly alarmed and, by exaggerating both his armed strength (30,000, 40 falconets, three six-pounders) and his willingness to struggle to the death, revealed his feelings. Both in the Russian narratives and in the Leningrad collection of Hawaiian artifacts acquired by Lisianskii or his people, there are ample indications that his nervousness was fully justified by military inferiority. Kamehameha, we may think, would not have asked for common paint, "observing...that he was building a large vessel", had he chanced to meet Lisianskii; nor could he have complained that "no one visited" his country.[158] Of the short barbed spears [*ihe laumaki* or *laumeki*] and *pololū* [long spears] purchased at Waimea Bay and now in Leningrad,[159] suffice to say that, though of classical proportions and extremely sturdy make like most such weapons of the period,[160] they would no more have helped a warrior who was confronted by an enemy with guns than would the Russian service swords which, we are told by Berkh, he and Lieutenant P. Arbuzov gave to Kaumuali'i as *Neva* bore off to set a course for Sitka. All the '1804' Hawaiian spears now in Leningrad are described in Part 4.

Hawaiian Artifacts & Illustrations

From the 1804 Russian Voyage

The Inventory Book and a label from Collection No. 750, Peter the Great
Museum, Leningrad

Wooden image of a god (750-1)

Dog tooth leg ornament showing front and rear views (750-5)

Marquesan feather ornament

B

8

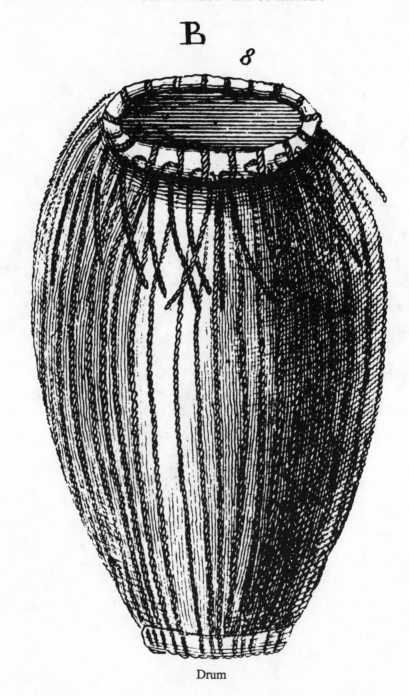

Drum

C

8

Basket of split *'ie'ie*

D 8

Feather God foundation

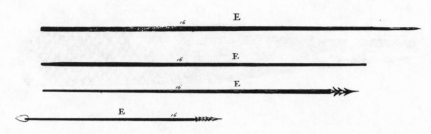

Illustrated spears

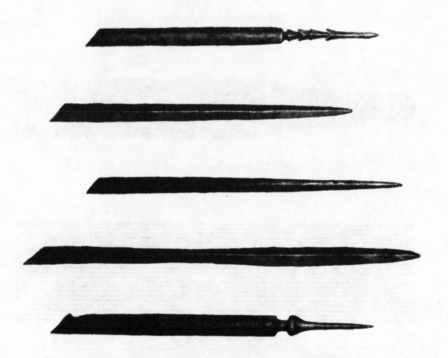

Collected spears (736-211, 212, 213, 215 and 217)

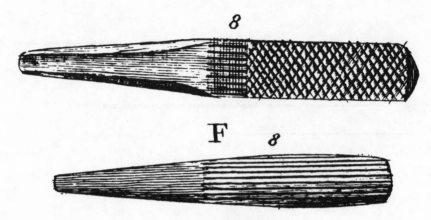

Illustrated *kapa* beaters

Collected *kapa* beater

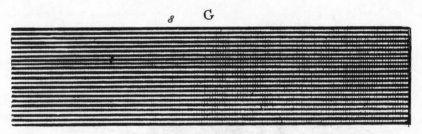

Grooved *kapa* board

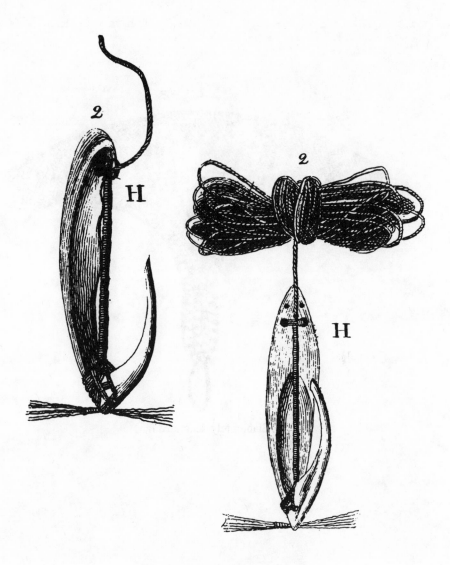

Bone and shell fish hooks

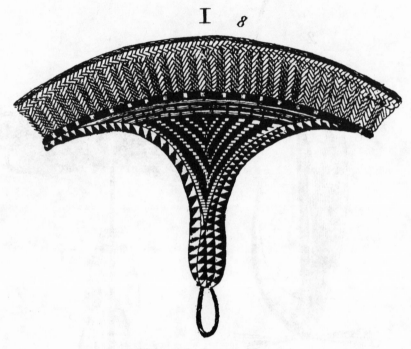

Elaborately decorated fan

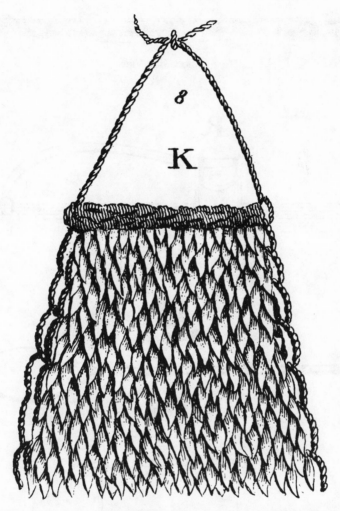

Dog tooth leg ornament

Canoe, Side View

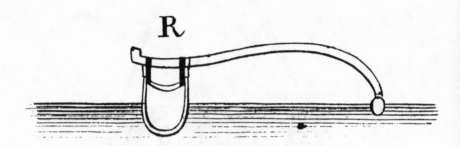

Canoe in cross-section, with outrigger

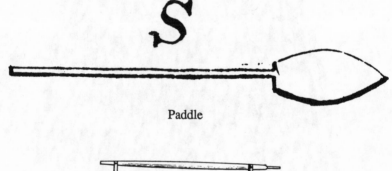

Paddle

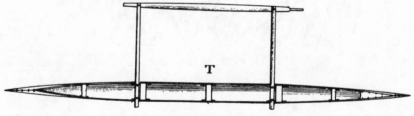

Canoe from above

U

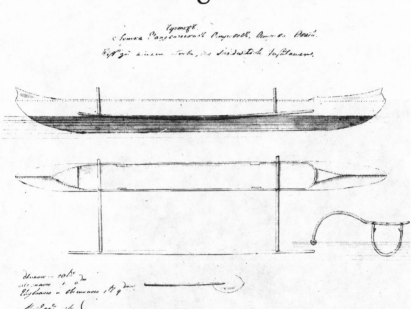

Sketch of a craft of the Sandwich Islands, side view, top view

V

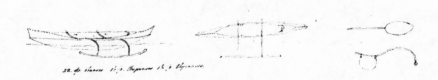

Sketches of a Hawaiian canoe with outrigger, cross-section and paddle
from the diary of Lieutenant E.E. Levenshtern: *TsGIAE, Tartu, Estonian SSR,
fond 1414, opis' 3, facing page 98*

Hawaiian god (750-1)

PART FOUR

The Evidence of Artifact and Illustration

The Collecting of Hawaiian Artifacts in 1804

Neither Kruzenshtern nor Lisianskii was especially encouraged by the Russian American Company, to which they were seconded on unusual and complicated terms,[1] to concern themselves with ethnography. They were loosely required to present the Company Main Office with "all that you learn and gain from observations on your voyage" [*vse, chto uznaete i priobretete vashimi nabliudeniiami v voiazhe vashem*] of significance "for natural history...or other sciences";[2] but no mention was made of artifacts in their instructions. 'Gain' could be interpreted to mean 'acquire', certainly, but objects could not be acquired by or from such 'observations' as the pair were enjoined to make, as could experience or knowledge. Thus, the actual collecting and eventual disposal of Pacific 'curiosities', which would in all events have negligible cash value at home, were both, in effect, left largely to the discretion of the captains of *Nadezhda* and *Neva*. As seen (in Part I) both men were strongly predisposed to read their orders in a way that favored study of the native peoples met in the Pacific and collecting of those peoples' artifacts, once all provisioning requirements and 'service duties' had been met.[3]

Lisianskii's interests in botany and in zoology dated from his childhood in the Ukraine. His ethnographic interests were of more recent origin: 1795-1797 and his sojourns in Antigua and Cape Colony. Whilst in South Africa, at least, and very likely in the West Indies as well, he had consciously and regularly complemented his botanical and zoological activity by learning what he could about the Negro and the bushman.[4] It was also in the late 1790s that he started the collections (mounted birds, birds' eggs, insects, Nautilus and other shells)[5] that afterward enriched both the Rumiantsev Museum and his own home.[6] Nuku Hiva saw the start of his collecting representative Pacific artifacts.[7]

Lisianskii's attitude toward the acquisition of such artifacts, as evidenced by orders issued to the clerk Korobitsyn within a day or two of the arrival of *Neva* in Taio-hae Bay, annoyed the clerk so much that, in his notes, he charged Lisianskii with collecting them--at the expense of others' effort--for his private use and pleasure.[8] The accusation was explicit ("...the islanders gave him various objects of the country which, in his greed, Lisianskii likewise appropriated as his own property") and has been refuted by Lisianskii's Soviet biographer, E. Shteinberg, on the basis of the artifacts' entire worthlessness to a commercial company, Lisianskii's right to order barter in a way most likely to ensure the initial purchase of sufficient quantities of foodstuffs for his people and, especially, his scientific motives in collecting them.[9] The truth would seem to lie somewhere between Shteinberg's contentions and the clerk's. What is significant within the context of this sketch is the inherent implication of the charge and the rebuttal, that Lisianskii was indeed in a position to embellish *his* collection--the more freely at Hawai'i having made his point in Taio-hae Bay. As his apologist himself remarks elsewhere, in connection with Kealakekua Bay, "not a few local rarities were collected besides provisions. The ethnographical collection started even during the... voyages of 1792-1795 was still further enriched."[10] The artifacts Lisianskii had collected as a Russian Volunteer with the British navy in the '90s were unquestionably his.

It is not known how many artifacts Lisianskii carried from Hawai'i and Kaua'i to the Northwest Coast in 1804, or to Kronstadt on 5 August 1806. A number were deliberately cast away during *Neva*'s stay on the Kona Coast or shortly afterward: "not only the officers, but also the men, were possessed of a variety of articles, many of which, though pleased with them for the moment, they afterwards threw away as useless and cumbersome" (see p. 57).[11] Others were doubtless lost elsewhere, as was usual on (and immediately after) distant voyages, by Russians as by others.[12] Certainly the number may be thought to have been greater than the sum of those in Soviet possession now. Perhaps not all the artifacts drawn by Lisianskii, printed in his 1812 *Sobranie...* (Plates II & III) and reproduced below, were taken back to Russia. Almost certainly, however, most were and their absence from the Leningrad and other sub-collections now associated with Hawai'i and the early nineteenth century is noteworthy and sad.

On 19 August 1806, two weeks after *Neva*'s arrival, *Nadezhda* dropped anchor at Kronstadt and provoked a ripple of public interest. Willing to draw maximum advantage and prestige from the expedition's (mixed) results, the Governing Board of the Russian-American Company had Chinese wares and Pacific Island artifacts placed on public display in a building rented by the Company on Gorokhovaia [Harrach] St, at the heart of the capital. The exhibition was well attended.[13] *Neva* presumably contributed Pacific artifacts to it. Lisianskii himself, however, not the Company, directed shortly afterward that artifacts collected at Hawai'i and at Kaua'i, amongst others, should pass into the keeping of three major institutions: the St Petersburg Imperial Public Library, the Admiralty

Department's own museum, and the *Kunstkammer* of the Academy of Sciences.[14]

How bulky the original collection of Hawaiiana must have been is evident from a description, written in Lisianskii's own hand, that has survived.[15] That description, of Hawaiian and Marquesan artifacts that entered the Academy in 1806-1807, lists more than a hundred objects: amongst other things, "a Sandwich idol", "Sandwich weapons, fans, utensils, dolls, and fishing nets." Another document extant in the Leningrad Division of the Archive of the Soviet Academy of Sciences (LOAAN) makes clear that Lieutenant Povalishin, late of the ship *Neva*, had also handed some Hawaiian artifacts to the museum of the Admiralty late in 1806.[16] With Lisianskii's own approval, and with better care and storage of Pacific artifacts in view, the Library was soon transferring "its" Hawaiian store to the Academy[17] and to the representatives of Count Rumiantsev, whose museum of ethnography could not--in view of his considerable power--be ignored. In due course (1826), the Rumiantsev *fond* was sent to Moscow, where Hawaiian artifacts brought in *Neva* in 1806 (and in the vessel *Riurik* twelve years later) remained on public view until the first years of this century. To the considerable loss of Polynesian studies, they fell victim to the general disturbances of World War II (the Soviets' Great Patriotic War). It was not long before the Navy, like the Library, had felt the pressure and indeed the inconvenience of housing growing numbers of Pacific 'curiosities". By 1828, the transfer of its Polynesian holdings to the *Kunstkammer* had started; it continued, intermittently, until 1830. Documents relating to the transfer have regrettably been lost, but certain artifacts remained firmly associated with Lisianskii and *Neva* and, on the *Kunstkammer*'s reorganizing and enlargement as the Museum of Anthropology and Ethnography (the Miklukho-Maklay Institute's Peter-the-Great Museum of today), they were listed together as *fond* 750. Comparison of numbers on surviving early nineteenth-century gummed labels (still attached to some Hawaiian artifacts in MAE's Collection 750) and of the numbering on an inventory drawn up in 1903 by the ethnographer Eduard Petri, shows very clearly that the Academy's collection was at one time twice or even three times larger than today. Those few Hawaiian artifacts that *Nadezhda* brought[18] had, meanwhile, similarly passed through the Admiralty Department Museum, but had ceased to be connected with her by the time they came (with other 'pre-1828' Hawaiian artifacts) to the Academy. It is consequently difficult, if not impossible, to identify *Nadezhda*'s purchases of 1804 among the 22 Hawaiian objects in the MAE collection No. 736.[19]

The '1804 Hawaiian' Artifacts in Leningrad

The following seven artifacts, from collection No. 750, were collected by *Neva*'s people in June 1804. A brief description is followed by comments. Numbers in parentheses refer to the artifacts' present enumeration within that MAE collection; thus the bonito hook is 750-6.

1. Bonito hook (composite), with line. The pearl-shell shank, 6.5cm long, is firmly attached by vegetable fiber lashing to a sharp bone hook, 3.5cm long. The base of the shell, which retains some luster, shows the thick hinge [*pu'u*] of the shell, *i.e.*, the segment was cut through it. A small bunch of white pig's bristles is fastened to the attachment point of shank and hook. The line is 660cm long. (6)

2. Composite lure, consisting of four elongated segments of shell, each attached at one end to a piece of vegetable fiber twine. The segments, which are potential shanks [*uhi*] for trolling hooks, are from 5.5 to 7.5cm long. (8)

3. Finely plaited, patterned mat [*moena*] 103cm by 51cm. The constituent fibers have been dyed brown, light yellow, and terracotta to form alternating wide and narrower stripes. (17)

4. Small plaited fan, considerably wider than deep (49cm from tip to tip across the curved top) and only 26cm from the handle base to the center of the top. The fan proper is a closely woven arc of split leaves, very likely pandanus [*hala*], attached to a lower arc, the borders of which are cylinders or bolsters of dark human hair. The surface of the lower part, likewise of tightly plaited human hair, has been embroidered in a zigzag pattern, with red, black, and dark blue woolen threads. At the handle, there is a small loop made of human hair twine. (4)

5. *Kapa* beater (*i'e kuku*), for the second stage of the beating process. Made of hard, dark wood, probably *koai'e*. The beating portion has four faces of approximately equal surface area, each differently cut to produce different patterns. One face or blade is *pepehi*, with 12 ridges, another has the more finely ridged *ho'opa'i* surface, with approximately 12 ridges per inch. All ridges are parallel. The handle, 10cm long, is roughly finished to give a good grip and narrows only gradually toward the end, which is 2.5cm in diameter. The length of the whole object is 37cm, the width of each blade, 4cm. (2) (illlus. p. A-10)

6. Dog tooth leg ornament [*kûpe'e niho 'îlio*], the rows of canine teeth being arranged in decreasing size from top to bottom row, and attached to a piece of woven *olonâ* fiber. Each tooth is attached through drilled holes to the *olonâ*-fiber backing by means of a two-ply cord of the same material. The backing forms an isosceles trapezoid, with parallel upper, longer border and lower, shorter border, and two converging sides of equal length. The upper border is 28cm wide, the lower border 18cm wide, and the ornament 30cm high. The dentine part of the roots of many of the teeth, which are in 25 rows, is now dark. (5) (illus. p. A-4)

7. Wooden image of a male god [*akua ka'i*], with prop remnant. Height, 38cm; width across shoulders, 7cm; length of head including a 1cm median crest, 9cm. The eyes and mouth are both well cut, the vacant sockets of the former

being intended for shell eyes. The half-open mouth shows the tip of the tongue. The abdomen is moderately curved. The left arm is broken off above the elbow, the right slightly bent forward, free of the body, as the missing arm clearly was also. The hand on the right shows only three fingers, and is roughly finished. The ears, too, are unfinished. The male genital organs are represented. The lower limbs are flexed, the thighs massive, and the calves disproportionately large. The feet are lost in the prop-top. Of the prop, only 6cm remains. (1) (illus. p. A-3 and A-16)

Comments on the Artifacts

1. This is a fine complete specimen of the Hawaiian *pâ hî aku*, complete with pig-bristle hackle [*hulu*] lashed crosswise to the iridescent shell shank, *i.e.*, not trailing behind in the traditional Hawaiian manner. The finger-length *uhi* segment itself, that is, the *pâ*, is of the sort described by Beckley (*Hawaiian Fisheries*, 1883, pp. 9-10) as *pâ ânuenue* or 'rainbow *pâ*'. There are indications that the outside scales on the back of the *uhi* segment were ground off, but that that process was not completed before the *pâ* was used. The bone point curves upward and forward from its fairly long (1.5cm) base in the usual manner of Hawaiian bonito hooks.

The Russians were at Hawai'i in *Ka'aôna*, the eighth month of the traditional Hawaiian year. Within three weeks, therefore (in *Hinaia'ele'ele*), *aku* were again to be *kapu* (Malo, *Hawaiian Antiquities*, ch. 40, sects 8-9). For that reason as well as because fishing for *aku* was so much enjoyed by Hawaiians of all ranks (see Kamakau, *The Works*, p. 75), *pâ hî aku* would have been out, in use, and consequently available for instant barter with the Russians.

The latter acquired a "skein of fine and skillfully twined and very strong cord" off the Puna coast on the afternoon of 7 June 1804 (see p. 92). That skein was 'for sale', indeed, but was evidently in use in a fishing craft, and was very likely an *olonâ* line [*aho*] like that still attached to the Leningrad bonito hook no. 750-6.

3. A fine *makaloa* sedge mat [*moena makali'i,*] of the sort once placed over others of coarser weave on the sleeping place or *ka'anu'a* of a dwelling. A rather small specimen.

4. This fan (*pe'ahi*) bears a striking resemblance to that held at the Bishop Museum and discussed by William T. Brigham in 1906 (*Mat and Basket Weaving of the Ancient Hawaiians*, BPBM Memoir, 2:11). Like the fan in the Bishop Museum (No. 7965), it has a "closely and neatly woven blade", a "spreading handle...carefully embroidered with human hair", and was less useful than ornamental even in the early 1800s. It, too, is now quite brittle and requires cautious handling. It is unquestionably a product of the post-contact period: the handle is embroidered, not with vegetable fibers, but with European wool. By 1804, as Lisianskii records, the Hawaiians were using wool for various local purposes, having first unraveled the imported material: "the women sometimes decorate their heads with...multicolored threads unraveled from the cloth that they get from Europeans." MAE has three similar fans, all dating from the period 1804-1828: 736-208, 736-209, and 4001-21.

5. *Kapa* making was in progress whilst *Neva* stood in Kealakekua Bay. Lisianskii himself drew a beater and wooden anvil [*kua kuku*], which appear in his *Sobranie kart i risunkov* (1812: plate II, figs F & G. See the following section here.) He took a second-stage beater aboard. The present writer has not managed to examine all four blade surfaces of that specimen. Two of them,

however, are of the parallel-ridged or fine-grooved types known as *pepehi* and *ho'opa'i* (see Buck, *Arts and Crafts of Hawaii*, 1957, V:171). The Leningrad specimen is well-worn. Even so, the ridges may have been cut with a *haole* knife and not a shark's tooth: the Russian evidence points to the rapid replacement of the traditional *niho 'ako lauoho* [single shark's tooth bound to a stick], for various functions, by the knife made of iron.

The second stage of *kapa* beating, known as *kuku*, often proceeded in a special building set aside for the purpose. The women often worked at the *kapa* in groups, and often dyed the finished cloth on the spot. In these circumstances, the special house could be large, and the adjacent drying-yard very large indeed. The Russians' failure to mention any such house or yard in Kealakekua Bay might be taken as indicative of small-scale *kapa* production. Seasonal factors apart, the area was not famed for its *kapa* as were other parts of the Hawaiian archipelago.

6. The dog tooth leg ornament collected by *Neva* in 1804 is of average horizontal border widths (upper: 28cm or 11"; lower: 18cm or 7"). It was clearly to be worn wider end uppermost--as drawn by Choris and not as by Webber (see Buck, *Arts and Crafts*, 1957, XII:554-55). In comparison with *kûpe'e niho 'îlio* specimens held in the Bishop Museum, the Leningrad specimen is remarkably deep, at 30cm or 12". The 25 rows of canine teeth have an average of approximately 40 teeth each, giving a total, for the ornament, of roughly one thousand teeth. As might be expected, in view of the increased area of "strong netting" (Cook, 1784, III:27) resulting from such depth, this total is higher than totals for most specimens to be seen in Honolulu. (The largest, No. 7763a in the Bishop Museum, has 1,242 teeth.) Successive rows of teeth on the Leningrad specimen overlap very slightly. If, as E. Arning suggested a century ago (*Ethnographische Notizen aus Hawaii*, Hamburg, 1883, p. 74), rows were added by successive generations of a family, this ornament would certainly have represented wealth and status.

It is improbable that the Russians witnessed dancing in the course of which this ornament was worn. Though Lisianskii drew a gourd drum, not one of the Russian texts makes even passing reference to music or dance.

7. An unusual feature of this wooden image is the free pendent position of the arms. Despite being attached to a pointed prop which could be stuck into the ground or into wall thatch, *i.e.*, an *akua ki'i*, the image has a right arm that could never have been attached to the thigh. The missing left arm would have been symmetrical. Such a position occurs rarely indeed in images with (surviving or truncated) pointed props. It is interesting that one exceptional image in this regard, Bishop Museum's L3438 (from Waimea Valley, O'ahu), has lower limbs and feet of exactly the same proportions and angle of flex as Lisianskii's image. The closest parallel, however, is between the Leningrad image and a free-standing image held by the National Museum in Dublin, Eire (fig. 299a in Buck, *Arts and Crafts*, 1957, XI:475). The Dublin image has abnormally protruding calves,

indeed, and stands in a more flexed position than does the Leningrad one; but the two share overall leg, torso, and head proportions, deep and vacant eye-sockets, flat ears, wide, well-formed nose, mouth showing tongue tip, short neck, free pendent arms and, of course (somewhat similarly damaged) median crest.

The right hand may well have had five fingers originally. As noted, the left arm and the crest have sustained damage since collection. A certain 'crudeness' in the carving of the abdomen and calves, however, as well as rudimentary ears, lead one to suspect that this image may never have been brought to its intended condition by the Hawaiian craftsman.

Lisianskii's Plates, 1806

As the Russian narratives enhance the ethnographic value of the '1804 Hawaiian' artifacts now held in Leningrad, providing circumstantial details of provenance and use, so are the ethnographic value and importance of the artifacts in Leningrad increased by the existence of Lisianskii's sketches of 17 more artifacts no longer with the Leningrad collection. That we have those sketches, which are reproduced below, is greatly to Lisianskii's credit. Recognizing that *Neva* was overladen and that space was lacking for the crowds whom both the Company Directors and the Crown proposed to place aboard her, he requested that half-a-dozen persons be excluded from the voyage. One of those accordingly excluded was the Ship's Artist, V. P. Prichotnikov, whom the Academy of Arts had only recently seconded to the venture.[20] Lisianskii himself assumed responsibility for seeing that the draftsman's duties were discharged during the voyage and, in fact, provided maps and illustrations for his own subsequent work. He was a first-rate draftsman.[21] Even so, the Admiralty took his fourteen sheets of maps and drawings coolly, in December 1806. Lisianskii's difficulties with the Admiralty, as a would-be published author, have been touched upon. Suffice to add here that, of the fourteen sheets, no more than nine were ever sent to the engravers of the Admiralty, and that pennypinching attitudes prevailed to the last.[22] The very publication of an 'atlas' to accompany his *Voyage* [*Puteshestvie*] of 1812 was an achievement, hardly recognized by a contemporary public caught up by the drama of Napoleonic War, that should make us yet more grateful for the drawings offered here.

Lisianskii's 'atlas' was published as *Sobranie kart i risunkov, prinadlezhashchikh k Puteshestviiu flota-kapitana 1-ogo ranga i Kavalera Iuriia Lisianskago, na korable Neve* [*A collection of Maps and Sketches Accompanying the Voyage of Fleet Captain of the 1st Rank and Chevalier Iurii Lisianskii, in the Ship "Neva"*]: StP, Morskaia Tipografiia, 1812. High production costs prevented the inclusion of his plates showing Hawaiian artifacts in the London edition of 1814. In the Russian edition, neither maps nor plates are correctly numbered, and there is no list of contents. However, the plates showing Hawaiian objects amongst others are headed II and III. Plate II offers 'Objects Proper to the Natives of the Sandwich Islands' [*Veshchi, prinadlezhashchie zhiteliam ostrovov Sandvichevykh*]:

A. Feather headdress [actually Marquesan] (illus. p. A-5)
B. Drum made from a calabash (illus. p. A-6)
C. Basket made of roots (illus. p. A-7)
D. Field Idol plaited from tree roots (illus. p. A-8)
E. Spears of various sorts (4) (illus. p. A-9)
F. Beaters by means of which material is stretched out (2) (illus. p. A-10)
G. Board on which material is stretched out (illus. p. A-10)

H. Mother-of-pearl fish hook with bone point (2) (illus. p. A-11)
I. Fan (illus. p. A-12)
K. Hog's teeth ornament, for the leg (illus. p. A-13)

On Plate III are:
Q. Craft of the Sandwich Islands (illus. p. A-14)
R. Its Cross-section (illus. p. A-14)
S. Its Paddle (illus. p. A-14)
T. Craft (from above) (illus. p. A-14)

Letters L to P inclusive indicate artifacts not from the Hawaiian Islands; letters A and K stand by a Marquesan feather necklace and a dog tooth ornament, respectively--the errors derive from Lisianskii himself. The frame of a feather god (*'aumakua hulumanu*), 'D', is described by Lisianskii as *pokhodnyi idol*. Russian *pokhod* signifies 'campaign' or 'marching'. It may be inferred that the Russians understood the god to have been carried to war.

Comments follow on items B-K. Lisianskii's illustrations of a canoe and paddle (Q-T) will be considered separately in conjunction with the complementary-- and rather more detailed--canoe illustrations in the diary kept by Lieutenant Levenshtern of *Nadezhda*.[23]

Comments on Lisianskii's Plates

B. This illustration is problematic. It may be a poorly drawn representation of a gourd or coconut knee drum [*pūniu*].

C. A closely-twined basked of split *ie'ie*, similar to the sort referred to in the Bishop Museum catalog as *hina'i poepoe*. This example is elongate, and very probably never contained a gourd or wooden bowl. The twining technique is twill (three-ply?). Both the shape of the basket and its flattish cover, with knotted *olonā* (?) cord, resemble those of B.6929 in the Bishop Museum.

D. Foundation of feather god, made of split *ie'ie* aerial rootlets woven into single-pair warp and one-pair interlocking weft, *i.e.*, as in *mahiole* of the close twined variety (see Buck, *Arts and Crafts*, 1957, 5:232, fig. 162a). The one-pair weft twines across and around each passive warp, producing a very uniform and neat appearance: the artifact was never completed and hence is quite unworn. The lips show two-pair weft work. The eye-sockets lack pearl shell eyes, and the mouth, dog teeth; the Russians presumably acquired the god from its maker before it was finished. Regrettably, all indications of size are lacking on Lisianskii's plates. In its proportion however this beautiful *'aumakua hulu manu*--to use the modern Hawaiian term--closely resembles Kūkā'ilimoku (BPBM, 7855), Kamehameha I's war god, which was found on the Kona Coast and had most likely been made there. Certainly, the art of *ie'ie* twining was highly developed there in the early nineteenth century.

E. Both long spears [*pololū*] on the top appear to be unfinished, and/or lack the usual butt enlargements. The spear second from the top seems to want even a point, unless it is spatulate. The longer barbed spear conforms to type, with three rows of barbs and stave gradually increasing in thickness from lower base to within a few centimeters of the point, where it tapers suddenly. The shorter *ihe laumake* has unusual features: relative shortness for six rows of barbs and, attached to the end of the stave opposite the barbs, what is probably a cord loop. The shape of Lisianskii's loop outline, faint though it is, also suggests the shape of a shark tooth dagger, possibly notched but unfinished, of the sort figured in Cook's *Voyage* (1784, Atlas, plate 67, 1). The weapon is a complex, hybrid one, at all events.

Mention may be made here of other spears also, almost certainly, collected by the Russians in 1804. "As for the Hawaiian objects that now form part of collection No. 736 [of the Peter-the-Great Museum, N.N. Miklukho-Maklay Institute of Anthropology and Ethnography in Leningrad], it is regrettably not possible precisely to determine by which of the earliest Russian circumnavigators they were gathered, since these objects went to the Museum from the Admiralty Museum only in 1830."[24] The problem, as implied here by Iu.M. Likhtenberg, is that several Russian captains had collected artifacts in the Hawaiian Islands by then: L.A. Gagemeister (1809), Otto von Kotzebue (1816, 1824-1825), V.M. Golovnin (1818), M.P. Lazarev, and others.[25] However, those captains who presented Hawaiian artifacts to the Museum of the Admiralty Department in the early nineteenth century, *i.e.*, presented artifacts to the authorities officially and in accordance with their orders, are identifiable. And of their number, none makes mention of Hawaiian spears. Bearing this in mind, let us recall that the Russians seemingly picked up eight spears in the course of an encounter with canoes off Kaua'i.[26]   Collection No. 736 in Leningrad contains eight spears, numbered consecutively (736-210-217).[27]   Five of them--736-211, 212, 213, 215, 217 (L to R)--are shown here in Plate Y. The evidence connecting them with the Lisianskii venture is indeed of inference and circumstance but, in the present writer's view, will justify these comments. All five weapons were in all events collected in the the first years of the century, and No. 217 is unusual enough to merit scrutiny.[28]

F. On the left, a preliminary stage *kapa* beater [*hohoa*], showing the traditional club shape. The beating part is grooved to form sharp parallel ridges [*nao*], unusually widely spaced in this specimen. On the right, a second stage beater (*i'e kuku*), also of hard wood, with quadrangular blade, four surfaces of equal area. The surface illustrated is cut in the 'net-mesh' [*maka 'upena*] pattern (lower three-quarters) and the vertical *pepehi* pattern (uppermost quarter). Another surface of this beater may well have been *ho'opa'i*, *i.e.*, cut with 12 or more vertical parallel ridges per inch, as shown on the plate (of item 5 in the '1804 Hawaiian' collection in Leningrad: see above here). This specimen is unusual in having two well-cut patterns on a single surface.

G. Grooved kapa board [*papa hole*] with *pepehi* surface, rectangular.

H. Composite bonito hooks very like No. 1 in the '1804 Hawaiian' collection in Leningrad (see 'Comments on the Artifacts' above for description and comments). In one, the thick hinge [*pu'u*] of the shell has been shaped to a point, in the other it has been left in a natural state. Both bone points have been drilled near the base in *two* places, and the resultant point lashings are not chevron-like. The transverse pig-bristle hackle [*hulu*] has been tied under the projecting chin of the point base, in local style. The skein of cord is of the type that favorably impressed the Russians off the Puna coast (see p. 92).

I. An elaborate fan, probably for chiefly use, of the sort illustrated by William T. Brigham in his *Mat and Basket Weaving* (1906, figs 9-11). The handle has *pua hala* and *hale* decorative motifs of the sort found on Kona *makaloa* mats of the same period.

K. A dog tooth leg ornament as drawn by Webber (Buck, *Arts and Crafts*, 1957, XII, fig. 341) and described by King (Cook, *Voyage*, 1784, III:27). Approximately 250 canine teeth are arranged in 15 or 16 rows. The 'lower' border is unbound, the 'upper' bound with remarkably thick braid.

Lisianskii's and Levenshtern's Canoe Sketches

Lisianskii's sketches of a canoe, from the side (Q), from above (T) and in cross-section (R), are complemented by similar ones drawn by Levenshtern (von Loewenstern) of *Nadezhda* as he coasted past Hawai'i. In view of his circumstances and the need to work rapidly, Levenshtern's efforts as a draftsman are highly commendable. Not only are his sketches clearly and precisely executed; they are supplemented--unlike Lisianskii's own--by data on size. One craft sketched was 20' long, 1' 6" in the beam, and 1' 9" deep. The outrigger, to judge by the proportions of the craft, was 13' in length, standing some 35" out from the canoe's side. The median bow and stern covers stretched back 30-33" from the craft's extremities. Levenshtern's second canoe is described as 22' long, 1' 6" broad and deep. The float [*ama*] has a pronounced convex curve, turning up at both ends, while that in Lisianskii's sketch 'T' has been cut away at the front to form a thin straight board of precisely the kind described by Hornell (*Canoes of Oceania,* Vol. 1, 1936, 23). Sketch 'R' clearly shows the outrigger boom's [*'iako*] inboard parts [*kua 'iako*] lashed to the U-shaped spreaders [*wae*] and gunwale [*mo'o*] strakes on either side. Levenshtern's longer craft is shown with two pairs of thwarts and one seat [*noho 'ana wa'a*] in position, whereas the shorter, 20' craft, has apparently only two pairs of thwarts. Lisianskii sketches in five seat-boards, each on comb cleats. Like Levenshtern's, his paddle 'S' is thick-shafted, with a wide ovate blade, but very much longer than broad in the blade and more sharply pointed.

Langsdorf also drew fine sketches of canoes and paddles during this visit.

PART FIVE

Reporters and Textual Sources

Observations follow in three sub-sections. The first concerns sources here translated and their authors: Lisianskii, Korobitsyn, Kruzenshtern, Rezanov, Shemelin, Langsdorf, Berkh, and Levenshtern. In the second, I discuss the Archpriest Gedeon and his narrative, from which I have quoted very briefly in this work, and touch on Dr Espenberg and his 'Remarks' and the diary and 'Memoirs' of Lieutenant Ratmanov. The third contains general remarks about the fate of accounts of their Hawaiian visit by members of the Kruzenshtern-Lisianskii expedition, and prospects of discovering new manuscripts in archives of the USSR. A biographical sketch of Iu.F. Lisianskii is offered as Appendix A below.

Iu. F.Lisianskii

As he had during the preparation of the expedition (1802-1803), so too, throughout the voyage of *Neva,* Lisianskii kept a detailed journal.[1] On the basis of it, he prepared the account of his voyage which, in mid-November 1806, he submitted to the Admiralty with a view to publication. The Admiralty Secretary, Apollon Nikol'skii, returned the manuscript with a note to the effect that "because of its numerous errors of language and style, it can certainly not be published in its present form to the credit of the Naval Department."[2] Other senior officials of the Admiralty questioned the need for an account by Lisianskii in view of the fact that Kruzenshtern was known to be writing one.[3] Believing himself to be the victim of political intrigue, Lisianskii declined to rewrite his manuscript. Having retired prematurely from the service, in 1809,[4] he set about publishing it at his own expense. A struggle ensued over possession of the nine plates of engravings which had then, by oversight, been ordered by the Admiralty and completed. (Lisianskii had submitted sketches and maps in 1806 sufficient to fill fourteen plates.) Finally, the Admiralty agreed to print 100 copies of the nine plates for itself, and 50 for Lisianskii. It had earlier been suggested that 1,200 copies be made.[5] Despite all such official opposition, Lisianskii pressed ahead with his plan to publish his *Voyage*, at his own expense. It was duly published, in March 1812, at a cost to him of 18,500 roubles.

Puteshestvie vokrug sveta v 1803, 4, 5 i 1806 godakh, po poveleniiu ego Imperatorskago Velichestva Aleksandra Pervago, na korable Neve, pod nachal'stvom...Iuriia Lisianskago appeared in two small and unillustrated volumes. The present translation is from pp. 164-236 of vol. 1, that is, from the texts of Lisianskii's seventh, eighth, and ninth chapters--VII: 'Plavanie korablia Nevy ot ostrovov Vashingtonovykh do ostrovov Sandvichevykh'; VIII: 'Opisanie ostrovov Sandvichevykh, a osoblivo ostrova Ovigi'; IX: 'Tsarstvovanie Gammamei'. The Hawaiian vocabulary on pp. 228-236 of the 1812 edition is translated and presented here separately from the preceding text. Also published in St Petersburg in 1812, the *Atlas* to accompany the *Puteshestvie* contained all fourteen of the earlier proposed plates. It was subtitled, and is commonly referred to as, *Sobranie kart i risunkov, prinadlezhashchikh k Puteshestvii flota-kapitana 1-ogo ranga i Kavalera Iuriia Lisianskago, na korable Neve*. Photographs used here are of artifacts on Plates II and III ('Veshchi, prinadlez-hashchie zhiteliam ostrovov Sandvichevykh') and of the 5th (un-numbered) map. Specifically, I discuss artifacts marked in Latin characters from A to I inclusive and K, on Lisianskii's Plate II, and Q to T on his Plate III.

Strained Anglo-Russian relations in 1807-1808 had adversely affected Lisianskii's naval career,[6] but he maintained his English links and, in 1813, returned to London with an English version of his *Voyage* (he was no mean linguist). Hoping to come to terms with an established, large publishing house over a new, English edition,[7] he contacted naval friends of 1794-1799, who soon put him in touch with John Booth & Company. Six months later, Booth took the lead in publishing 'Urey Lisyansky's' *Voyage Round the World in the Years 1803, 4, 5, & 6 in the ship "Neva"*,[8] which coincided with an upturn in the English public's interest in distant exploration-- particularly if the places under investigation had a trade potential-- and with growing British consciousness of Russia's own ambitions in the North Pacific. It sold extremely well.[9] The relevant part of the 1814 (Booth) edition, pp. 98-137, here presented, falls within Chapters VI: 'From the Washington to the Sandwich Islands' and VII: 'Account of the Sandwich Islands'. Two alterations have been made to the 1814 text, after some hesitation. Ship names are given in italics, as elsewhere in this study; and modern forms of transliterated words have been incorporated into the text in brackets.

High sales and favorable critical notices of the London edition of Lisianskii's work at length induced the Russian Admiralty to agree to defray the high cost of the 1812 (St Petersburg) edition. But again Lisianskii was thwarted by his nameless opposition. The 12,517 roubles eventually given left him almost 6,000 roubles out of pocket.[10]

N.I. Korobitsyn

Nikolai Ivanovich Korobitsyn, clerk [*prikazchik*] in the employ of the Russian-American Company, was required by the Company Main Office, at 7 Moika Quay, St Petersburg, to keep a journal from the first day of his voyage to the last.[11] He did so, making occasional retrospective changes to earlier entries and editing the whole in 1806. The resultant fair-copy found no publisher, for reasons to be seen, and disappeared into a file. It was found in a Leningrad second-hand bookshop in 1940. The finder, Dr E.I. Gleiber, then Director of the Archives Division of the All-Union Geographical Society of the USSR [Vsesoiuznoe Geograficheskoe Obshchestvo SSSR], deposited the manuscript in his own Archives under reference: *razriad* 99, *opis'* 1, no. 141. It remains there today.[12]

The original journal remained in Korobitsyn's keeping for some time. Even as early as April 1805, the Company Main Office had received an extract from it, of an interesting and politically delicate nature. The extract, 'Kratkii ekstrakt s zhurnala korablia Nevy prikazchika Korobitsyna s 26-ogo iiulia 1803 goda v prodolzhenie voiazha do ostrovov Sandvichevykh (Gavaiskikh) po 7e maia 1804, god' ['A Short Extract from the Journal of the ship *Neva*, kept by Clerk Korobitsyn throughout the Voyage from 26 July 1803 to 7 May 1804, to the Sandwich (Hawaiian) Islands"], made reference to Lisianskii's shortcomings as a commander. When preparing the fair-copy of his journal, in 1806, Korobitsyn removed such passages as portrayed his former captain in a less than favorable light or suggested tensions between the naval officers aboard *Neva* and the Company's own representatives, *i.e.*, Shemelin and himself. By then, however, the dramatic confrontations that had taken place (in 1803-1804) between Rezanov and 'his party', on the one hand, and *Nadezhda*'s officers, notably Kruzenshtern and Makar I. Ratmanov, on the other, were no secret to the government or public in St Petersburg. Rezanov's early death, in 1807, and Kruzenshtern's increasing social and political importance in the years that followed, proved sufficient to prevent the publication of a journal that had touched on, and could serve as a reminder of, Company-fostered criticism of the Navy that was (arguably) justified. Other contemporaneous accounts, such as Ratmanov's, of these clashes between Company and Navy, as embodied by Rezanov and an angry Kruzenshtern, also remained unpublished in the lifetimes of the various participants (see pp. 193-194).[13]

Gleiber also discovered the Company Head Office file that contained 'A Short Extract...'. We depend on it for such fragmentary data as we have on Korobitsyn's own life, and as a yardstick by which to judge the effort made by Korobitsyn in 1806 to improve his Russian grammar. Notwithstanding those efforts, as the Soviet historian A.I. Andreev justly notes, he wrote "a peculiar brand of Russian, often using a participle instead of the past indicative tense, for example, and so preferring a subordinate to a principal clause... It is the style of a man who confuses everyday colloquial speech and the literary language."[14]

The present translation is of the text of Korobitsyn's journal (1806 version) as given by A.I. Andreev in *Russkie otkrytiia v Tikhom okeane i Severnoi Amerike v XVIII-XIX vekakh: sbornik materialov [Russian Discoveries in the Pacific Ocean and North America in the 18th-19th Centuries]* (Moscow-Leningrad, ANSSSR, 1944), pp. 169-75. Andreev's text was kindly checked for me, by Dr A. Senchura, against the 'Zhurnal' still held at AGO (*razriad* 99, *opis'* 1, no. 141) and found to be accurate.

I.F. Kruzenshtern

Kruzenshtern spent the best part of three years preparing his account of his voyage on the basis of his own journals, those kept by his officers and scientists, and *Nadezhda*'s logs. *Puteshestvie vokrug sveta v 1803, 4, 5 i 1806 godakh...na korabliakh Nadezhde i Neve, pod nachal'stvom flota-kapitan-leitenanta, nyne kapitana vtorogo ranga, Kruzenshterna...* appeared in three volumes (1,310 pp.) from the Admiralty press (Morskaia Tipografiia) in St Petersburg; 1,200 copies were printed. Russian and German versions, the latter prepared by Kruzenshtern himself, were printed simultaneously. Volume 1 appeared in 1809. The text offered here is from pp. 231-41 of that volume, *i.e.*, the 'Hawaiian section' of Chapter X, headed 'Plavanie ot Nukugivy k ostrovam Sandvichevym, a ottuda v Kamchatku' ('The Voyage from Nuku Hiva to the Sandwich Islands, and Thence to Kamchatka').

The three volumes of Kruzenshtern's *Puteshestvie* contained offerings by a number of the participants in his expedition, including J.C. Horner, Tilesius von Tilenau, and Karl Espenberg, his old friend and *Nadezhda*'s surgeon in 1803-1806 (see p. 193), as well as by men who had not sailed with him (Lieutenant G. Davydov, D.I. Koshelev, Count N.P. Rumiantsev).[15] Only Espenberg's, regrettably, bore even briefly on *Nadezhda*'s visit to Hawai'i.

The *Puteshestvie*, with its Hawaiian passage, was translated into English by the traveler and linguist Robert Hoppner (*A Voyage Round the World...*, London, John Murray, 1813). It was also translated twice into Dutch (1811, 1815), and into French (1821), Swedish, Danish, and Italian. It was supplemented by an *Atlas* (StP, 1813) containing 15 maps and 105 plates.

N.P. Rezanov

Following his unsuccessful sojourn in Japan where, as would-be Russian Envoy, he felt unwelcome and uncomfortable,[16] Rezanov went with Langsdorf from Kamchatka to Novo-Arkhangel'sk. There, he met US sailors from the ships *O'Cain* and *Juno*, amongst others, Hawaiians whom the enterprising Captain Winship had brought up from the Islands,[17] and *promyshlenniki* whose deplorable condition made it obvious that there was something to be said for getting foodstuffs from Kamehameha. Rezanov's letter of 17 June 1806 to Count N.P. Rumiantsev, minister of commerce, was one of several that dealt with the provisionment and transport problems that had plagued Chief Manager A.A. Baranov for the past ten years or more.[18] That letter, translated here in extract, was printed by P. Tikhmenev in his *Istoricheskoe obozrenie obrazovaniia Rossiisko-Amerikanskoi Kompanii i deistvii eio do nastoiashchego vremeni* [*An Historical Survey of the Formation of the Russian-American Company, and of its Activities up to the Present Time*] (StP, E. Veimar, 1861-1863), pt II:278-81. The present extract is from pp. 279-80. The holograph used by Tikhmenev is now in TsGIAL, under archive reference: *fond* 13, *op.* 1, *delo* 687.

Rezanov's own journals of 1803-1805, which he had managed to rearrange and polish before his death *en route* to European Russia, formed the basis of his 'Pervoe puteshestvie Rossiian vokrug sveta, opisannoe N. Riazanovym, Polnomochnym Poslannikom ko Dvoru Iaponskomu, i proch' ('The First Voyage of Russians Round the World, Described by N. Riazanov, Envoy Plenipotentiary to the Court of Japan, etc.'). The work was published, in half-a-dozen installments, in the St Petersburg periodical, *Otechestvennye zapiski* [*Notes of the Fatherland*] in 1822-1825. The 'Hawaiian section' translated here is taken from pp. 246-53 of part XXIV of that periodical of 1825, *i.e.*, from Chapter VII of the manuscript as presented to its editor: 'Otbytie iz Nukagivy, ostrova Sandvichevy: Kamchatka' ['Departure from Nuku Hiva, the Sandwich Islands: Kamchatka').

F.I. Shemélin

Fedor Ivanovich Shemélin's original journal of 1803-1806 is preserved in the Saltykov-Shchedrin Public Library, Leningrad, under Manuscript Division (*Rukipisnyi otdel*) reference: F.IV.59. Although, unlike Korobitsyn, Shemélin did succeed in publishing an account of his travels, in 1816-1818, he too found himself under pressure to omit or alter certain passages composed in 1803-1804, and finally complied. In his case, the objections centered on specific references, in his manuscript journal, to the strained relations between Rezanov and Kruzenshtern. Shemélin was evidently asked to remove colorful episodes such as the Envoy's hiding in his quarters in *Nadezhda* from infuriated officers,[19] and all aspersions on Kruzenshtern himself, from the fair copy to be handed to the printers (in the event, the Government-financed Meditsinskaia Tipografiia). Hence, there are two or three major and numerous minor textual variations between the journal known as F.IV.59 and the published *Zhurnal pervogo puteshestviia Rossiian vokrug zemnago shara, sochinenyi pod vysochaishim Ego*

Imperatorskago Velichestva pokrovitel'stvom Rossiisko-Amerikanskoi Kompanii [*Journal of the First Voyage of Russians Round the World, Composed under the Imperial Patronage of the Russian-American Company*] (StP, 1816-18: 2 pts). No doubt because *Nadezhda*'s visit to Hawai'i coincided with a lull in the overt hostilities between her captain and Rezanov, the 'Hawaiian section' of Shemélin's journal did not 'need improvement'. Even so, I have preferred the 1816 to the 1806 (handwritten) text: as noted earlier, Shemélin made good use, after the expedition and his own return to European Russia, of data offered by Vasilii Moller, alias the Hawaiian Kanehoa, and by Captain-Lt L.A. Gagemeister of the Navy, who had visited the Sandwich Islands in Lisianskii's own old ship, *Neva*, in 1809.[20] If Moller-Kanehoa was a major source of data for the section of the 1816 text subtitled 'A Brief Description of the Inhabitants of Hawaii', Gagemeister was a yet more crucial source for observations offered in 'On Cattle-Breeding and the Cultivation of Vegetables on Hawai'i'. Specifically, the present translation is of pp. 140-161 of the 1816 text, covering these subsections: 'Pribytie k Sandvichevym ostrovam' ['Arrival at the Sandwich Islands']: pp. 140-148); 'Nebol'shoe opisanie o zhiteliakh ostrova Ovagii' ['A Brief Description']: pp. 149-152); 'O razvode skota i ogorodnykh ovoshchei na ostrove Ovagii' ['On Cattle-Breeding...']: pp. 152-158); and 'O sposobe, kakim obrazom na Sandvichevykh ostrovakh iz kornia Ti delaietsia napitok Ava ili rom' ['On the method by which the drink Ava or Rum is produced from the Ti root on the Sandwich Islands']: pp. 159-161).

Publication rights to Shemélin's *Zhurnal* were acquired in 1821-1822 by the owners of the periodical *Russkii invalid* [*The Russian Veteran*]. In somewhat modified form, Shemélin's account of his travels of 1803-1806 appeared in the literary supplements to that periodical [*Literaturnye pribavleniia k Russkomu invalidu*] in 1822 and 1823. The many installments[21] were generally headed, 'Otryvki iz zhurnala pervogo puteshestviia Rossiian vokrug zemnago shara', that is, 'Extracts from a Journal of the First Voyage of Russians Around the Terrestrial Sphere'.

G.H. Langsdorf

Like Kruzenshtern, Georg Heinrich Langsdorf took several years to prepare his account of his voyage round the world aboard *Nadezhda*. In part, it was success and honors that delayed him. Shortly after his return to St Petersburg, he was named an assistant [*ad'iunkt*] in the Botanical Section of the Academy of Sciences, then an Academician. But in part it was his wish to publish papers and deliver lectures on the rich botanical and zoological results of his experiences, on ethnology (tattooing in the area of Taio-hae Bay on Nuku Hiva), and on other sciences, that held him up.[22] *Bemerkungen auf einer Reise um die Welt in den Jahren 1803 bis 1807* was finished in 1810. Publication in France was considered, once the author had had word from the Academy of Sciences that it would meet the printing and engraving costs, whether or not the work came out in Russia; but the book in fact appeared in German (1812, Verlag Williams, Frankfurt-am-Main), in two volumes supplemented by two albums (43 plates).[23] The present translation rests on the chapter entitled 'Der Inseln Owaichi'. Something of that chapter's value is reflected in its author's introduction, as translated for the June 1813 London edition, *Voyages and Travels in Various Parts of the World during the Years 1803, 1804, 1805, 1806, and 1807*, by G. H. von Langsdorff (Henry Colburn), p. vi: "My endeavours have been directed to describing the objects which more particularly interested me, such as the manners and customs of the different nations we visited, their modes of living, and the productions of the countries...."

V.N. Berkh

Vasilii Nikolaevich Berkh, midshipman aboard *Neva* in 1803-1806, was much impressed--in retrospect at least--by the commercial prospects that the Sandwich Islands offered to Kamchatka and the Russian Northwest Coast. Though lacking seniority to further Russia's cause in the Pacific and America, on his return to Baltic duties, he maintained the interests with which he was associated still in 1830; Russia's North Pacific enterprise, hydrography, and seaborne exploration.[24] His interest in the Hawaiian archipelago as a supply base and, perhaps, imperial and naval *point d'appui* for Russia, was reactivated by the news of G.A. Sheffer's triumph of persuading Kaumuali'i, king of Kaua'i, to become a Russian subject.[25] More specifically, it was reactivated by the letter that contained that news, sent on 12 August 1816 by Baranov's second-in-command, Ivan Kuskov. Kuskov and Berkh had become acquainted whilst the *Neva* had been at Sitka in September and October 1804, and had met and talked again before the midshipman's return. "I think," wrote Kuskov, "you have not forgotten those pleasant moments when we conversed together in these distant parts... We spread the boundaries of our beloved fatherland from the Amur river to Matsmai [Hokkaido], from California to the Sandwich Islands... Ten years have passed since that happy time. Many new enterprises have occupied me and...we have sent several ships to the Sandwich Islands...."[26] Circumstances that had led the German surgeon in the Company's employ to try his hand on Kaua'i, wrote Kuskov, now made it possible for Russia to obtain a fruitful mid-Pacific base. The tsar had only to accept King Kaumuali'i's fealty.

Political events in Honolulu, London and St Petersburg soon overtook such schemes, and Dr Sheffer was officially discredited.[27] By then, however, Berkh had contributed to Company attempts to make the Government, and educated public, more aware of the potential of the Sandwich Islands and, in doing so, had drawn upon his memories of 1804-1806. In August 1817, at his home in Perm', he wrote a memorandum on the Islands, which he forwarded to I.I. Zelenskii, Chief Secretary at the Russian-American Company's Main Office in St Petersburg, together with a copy of Ivan Kuskov's letter to him of twelve months earlier.[28] The memorandum, short covering letter, and enclosure were received and circulated by the Company's Directors. Not long afterward, in 1818, there appeared in the journal *Syn otechestva* [*Son of the Fatherland*] (StP, pt 43), an article entitled 'Nechto o Sandvichevykh ostrovakh' ('Something About the Sandwich Islands'). As the Soviet historian D.D. Tumarkin writes, that article still "holds a somewhat special place" in the (expanding) literature on the Russian visit to Hawai'i of 1804. "Alongside recollections..., it contains some data obtained by the author in Canton in 1806 as well as those reported by a 'friend' (possibly Gagemeister), who later visited Hawai'i."[29]

E.E. Levenshtern

The travel diary of Emelian Levenshtern (von Loewenstern), *Nadezhda*'s Fourth Lieutenant and a youthful veteran of service under Admiral Ushakov off Corfu in the late 1790s,[30] returned with him in 1806-1807 to the Russian Baltic Province of Estonia (Estliandiia), where he was born and raised.[31] It has remained there, and is today held in the I.F. Kruzenshtern Archive (*fond* 1414) at TsGIAE in Tartu: *opis'* 3, *dela* 3-4. The diary is in two volumes of German copperplate, and contains a number of sketches made during *Nadezhda*'s voyage. The text here is translated from pp. 97-99 obv. of volume 1, entries under 27-30 May (Old Style), which contains brief references to the drift along the south coast of Hawai'i and to barter sessions. TsGIAE also holds Levenshtern's more official service journal of the voyage (*fond* 1414, *op.* 3, *delo* 5). It, too, has its 'Hawaiian section', but offers little of ethnographic significance. A copy of Levenshtern's diary was loaned to the State Historical Museum of the Estonian SSR (Eesti NSV Riiklik Ajaloomuuseum) in Tallin, some years ago, where it was typed out on a typewriter. The typed copy, which shows occasional variants from the manuscript, remains in the keeping of that Museum (17 Pikk, Tallin 200001) under reference: *fond* 225, *opis'* 1, *delo* 20. The 'Hawaiian section' is paginated 156-159 by the Museum staff.

Levenshtern's diary is of major ethnographic value, yet was apparently first used by a Soviet scholar in the early 1970s: in 1975, B.N. Komissarov used it as source material in his *Grigorii Ivanovich Langsdorf* (pp. 17-18, etc.). In the sixth number of *Sovetskaia etnografiia* of 1980, however, T. K. Shafranovskaia and Komissarov himself took a closer look at Levenshtern's diary as an ethnographic source in an article entitled, 'Materialy po etnografii Polinezii v dnevnike E.E. Levenshterna' ('Materials for the Ethnography of Polynesia in E.E. Levenshtern's Diary'). Further use will doubtless be made of that diary in the near future, in the USSR and in the West.

Archpriest Gedeon

Ieromonakh Gedeon, of the Aleksandr-Nevskii Monastery in St Petersburg, was a man of broad liberal interests, possessed of a working knowledge of several foreign languages, and was well acquainted with high dignitaries of the Church (Metropolitan Amvrosii) and State (N.P. Rezanov). These facts, as seen, did not improve his awkward situation in *Neva* where, for many months, Lisianskii treated him with scant respect. Gedeon reached Kodiak, his destination and the place where his (3-year) missionary work was to commend him to the Church authorities, with understandable relief. In private letters to Amvrosii and others, printed by the Valaam Monastery in 1894, *Ocherk iz istorii Amerikanskoi Pravoslavnoi dukhovnoi missii, Kadiakskoi missii, 1794-1837 [A Sketch from the History of the American Orthodox Church Mission, Kodiak Mission,1794-1837]* (StP), he touched on troubles borne at sea. "I was unfortunate enough to spend my time for almost a year...on the vessel *Neva*...people with unruly natures...the long prohibition on Sundays and the Lord's Holy Days to conduct God's services...sneering remarks."[32] At Hawai'i, adds Gedeon, he had not even gone ashore.

Gedeon's day-by-day account of his journey round the world formed, in due course, the first part of a manuscript, untitled but bound in red leather covers impressed (in gold), 'A Journey Round the World', which was long in the possession of the Valaam Monastery. The second part, that published in 1894, was a description of the Kodiak Mission itself, of Aleut attitudes, customs, and skills, and of relations between native people and employees of the Company--which were unsatisfactory, to say the least. Ethnography was a significant component of the first and second sections of the manuscript. The first, however, found no willing publisher: despite Lisianskii's own early retirement from service and political eclipse (only in 1814 did he briefly recapture status lost in 1808-1809, thereafter slipping into obscurity), the archpriest's criticisms of the Navy, as embodied in Lisianskii, Berkh, and Lieutenant Povalishin, only reinforced an unacceptability that was in any case inherent in his damning criticisms of the Company. As seen, even the second part was published only half-a-century after the deaths of most involved in scenes described.

Part 1 of the Valaam Monastery manuscript was based on, but was not identical with, Gedeon's original report of 1806 which had, in turn, been based on diaries that he had kept aboard *Neva*. That report, *Donesenie ieromonakha Aleksandro-Nevskoi Lavry Gedeona...o plavanii na korable "Neva" v 1803-1806 godakh [Report of the Archpriest Gedeon of Alexandr Nevskii Monastery...on his Voyage in the Ship* Neva, *1803-06]* is now, together with the diaries and brief biographical information about their author, in TsGIAL, under reference: *fond* 796 (1809), *opis'* 90; *delo* 273 holds several diaries, of 73 folios, fols 37-38 relating to *Neva*'s stay at Hawai'i. Related material by Gedeon, also written during the voyage or immediately before it, is held, in the same *fond* (1803), *opis'* 84, delo 408, fols 1-5. The report was addressed and sent, not to the Company Main Office, but to Metropolitan Amvrosii, Gedeon's 'professional superior'. It was discovered and first cited in print (in 1964) by the Soviet historian, D. D. Tumarkin.[33]

Though apparently confined by order to *Neva*, Gedeon made observations on the 'Viceroy' of Hawai'i, John Young, and on the many natives whom he also saw or met. Young's ownership of a stone house, large estates, and many workers impressed Gedeon no less than the Hawaiians' lack of interest in broken iron hoops and preference of sail cloth even to tools. "An odd picture!" he thought the natives swarming round *Neva* on the mornings of 12-15 June: "one walks out in a caftan alone without a shirt and trousers on, another in a camisole or waistcoat, a third in ordinary or sailor's trousers alone...."[34] Welcome though such cameos must be, however, Gedeon's remarks add nothing to the other Russian narratives, taken together.

K. Espenberg

Karl Espenberg, Surgeon in *Nadezhda,* was invited by his friend from Baltic days (both men were from Estonia, like Levenshtern) and former captain, to contribute a medical paper to the latter's *Puteshestvie.* The offering, 'Zamechaniia po vrachebnoi chasti, uchinennye vo vremia puteshestviia Kruzenshterna' ('Remarks Concerning Medicine, Composed during the Kruzenshtern Voyage'), was published in Vol. III of Kruzenshtern's work (StP, 1812: supplement). That section of it subtitled, 'Plavanie ot ostrova Nukagivy v Kamchatku' ('The Voyage from Nuku Hiva to Kamchatka'), pp. 295-96, contains remarks that bear on *Nadezhda*'s visit to Hawai'i. Among them are these:

"On the passage from Nuku Hiva we had prepared in the galley, for officers and men alike, an essence of yeast food... None of the healthy, not even the ambassador, *Kammerherr* Rezanov himself, ate fresh meat at this time. At the Sandwich Islands, though, we got only two small hogs and one dish of [sweet-] potato each.[35] Since the crew were healthy, as I testified at the Captain's request, and since I could not detect the slightest symptom of scurvy on any man, we did not stop at Karakakoa Bay in Ovagi but went on our way to Kamchatka. It soon became evident that I had been mistaken in my report. Seaman Egor Chernykh showed clear signs of the scurvy..."

M.I. Ratmanov

The original travel diary for 1803-1806 of Makar' Ivanovich Ratmanov, *Nadezhda*'s First Lieutenant, is now preserved at TsGAVMF under archive reference: *fond* 14, *opis'* 1, *delo* 149. A somewhat variant copy of that diary, apparently composed by Ratmanov while in Kamchatka in 1804-1805,is in the Manuscript Department of the Saltykov-Shchedrin Public Library in Leningrad, under reference: *fond* 1000, *opis'* 2, No. 1146. Because of their descriptions of angry scenes aboard *Nadezhda* and criticism of Rezanov and other dignitaries of the day, neither diary nor journal saw the light of day for many years.

'Zapiski kapitan-leitenanta Ratmanova' ['Memoirs of Captain-Lt Ratmanov'], published in several issues of the fortnightly journal *Iakhta* [*The Yacht*: StP] in 1876, (nos 16, 18, 24), were based on the original diary but were not completely faithful to its text. There are both omissions and editorial additions. The interest provoked, however, led to the publication of an article about Ratmanov and his voyage, 'Ratmanov, Makar' Ivanovich', in *Severnaia pchela* [*The Northern Bee*: StP, 1876], nos 74-76, 78.

One would-be editor of Ratmanov's 1803-1806 manuscripts, A. Bronshtein, wrote an introduction to them which remains of value, and is held in the Saltykov-Shchedrin Public Library (Manuscript Department): *fond* 791 (Titov Collection). However, the ethnographic value of Ratmanov's diary and journal themselves is slight, compared with that of Shemélin's, Korobitsyn's, or even Langsdorf's work.

Soviet Archival Sources and Hawaiian Ethnography

All 'men of science', officers, and midshipmen aboard the ships *Nadezhda* and *Neva* in 1803 were asked, officially, to keep journals and notes and, at the end of the Pacific expedition, to surrender them to Kruzenshtern.[36] He was in turn obliged to hand all written records kept during his voyage to the Company Main Office in St Petersburg, and to report to his professional superiors at its conclusion.[37] It was properly assumed that such materials as bore on service or on scientific matters would be copied out and sent on to the Admiralty, the Academy of Sciences, or both. Tilesius and Horner were submitting their reports to the Academy in any case.[38] All these procedures, whose complexity reflected that of an important, multi-purpose enterprise co-sponsored by the Crown and by a trading company and backed by two academies and half-a-dozen government departments, were apparently adhered to in 1806. *Nadezhda*'s and *Neva*'s two dozen officers and gentlemen[39] were not, of course, all *savants* in the Langsdorf mould, nor were their orders to concern themselves with native peoples, rather than with natural conditions met in the Pacific. Even so, their journals, diaries, notes, articles and (unofficial and official) letters offer valuable ethnographic data on the peoples they encountered on the voyage, in particular at the Marquesas and Hawaiian Islands, Kodiak, and Nagasaki in Japan. They were a hand picked company, well educated and astute, though--with exceptions--they were not imbued with anything of J.M. Degérando's ethnographic zeal ("careful gathering of means that might assist the truly philosophic traveller to penetrate the thought", etc.).[40]

Even the conscious use of expedition members' notes and journals and their subsequent appearance in an account composed by the leader of that expedition, to be sure, did not guarantee their publication. For the fate of source materials relating to Hawai'i or to any other distant place depended on the overall success of the whole venture, in the course of which the visit had occurred, as then perceived by the imperial authorities; and many factors might produce a 'failure verdict' on a naval enterprise. The Arctic and Pacific venture of *Otkrytie* (Captain-Lt Mikhail Vasil'ev) and *Blagonamerennyi* (Captain-Lt Gleb Shishmarev), for example, in the course of which two stops were made at Honolulu (March to April and November to December 1821),[41] was wholly overshadowed and outclassed by the contemporaneous Antarctic venture led by F F. Bellingshausen--at a time, moreover, (1822-1824) when much material relating to the post-contact Hawaiian Archipelago might otherwise well have been printed by the Russian Naval Ministry itself.[42] To glance over Vasil'ev's report on New South Wales, as presented by a Soviet historian in 1950,[43] is to recognize the almost certain interest of his 'Zapiski o prebyvanii na Gavaiskikh ostrovakh' ['Notes on a Sojourn in the Hawaiian Islands'], which remain today in manuscript in TsGAVMF (the Central State Naval Archive of the USSR, Leningrad).[44] In short, numerous records of revictualing stays at Polynesian or, particularly, Micronesian islands, by intelligent, objective individuals, were never published. It is fortunate for students of Hawai'i in the early 1800s that, for all its failure as a diplomatic venture and commercial enterprise, the Kruzenshtern-Lisianskii expedition *was* regarded as a triumph, by the Company, the Navy, and the Crown. But for the aura of success thrown over every part of it by scientific and political achievements, and by evidence that it had been a thoroughly successful naval exercise, that expedition's inner rifts and tensions would undoubtedly have been more keenly felt by Kruzenshtern himself, in 1806-1809, and would have hindered publication of his narrative.[45]

But what of all the other records of *Nadezhda*'s and *Neva*'s Hawaiian visit, *e.g.*, logs, journals and diaries by his people? The published narratives of Langsdorf, Kruzenshtern, Lisianskii, and Shemélin, after all, can hardly be supposed to have incorporated data gathered by a group of men six times more numerous (if we exclude those of the lower deck).[46] Some of those documents must be of interest to modern students of Hawaii: certain Soviet historians--for example, Ostrovskii, Lipshits, Kuznetsova, Shur, and Tumarkin--have implied or plainly said as much.[47]

With few exceptions, copies of the journals and reports in question were deposited in one or other section of that best-arranged of ministerial (State) archives of the nineteenth century, TsGAVMF (Tsentral'nyi Gosudarstvennyi Arkhiv Voenno-Morskogo Flota SSSR). That archive is officially a closed one to the Western visitor. Increasingly, however, its administration has been making small numbers of documents from earlier collections [*fondy*] available to Western scholars who have time enough, and excellent credentials from a country then in favor with the Soviet authorities. (In general, it may be said that scholars from the British Commonwealth or France fared better than Americans during the late 1970s.) Armed with a pass, the Western visitor will have his own archival worker or collaborator [*sotrudnik*] to assist him in the placing of specific orders for material. The problem is to know what one requires; and a major inconvenience to the American whose time and funds are limited is the annoying unavailability (to him) of detailed *opisi* [inventories] of various constituent collections now in TsGAVMF. A worse frustration is the absence of a modern, comprehensive guide to all its holdings, or a full card catalogue. But one can only take the secrecy surrounding the inventories with fatalism, having taken the precaution of examining before arrival in the archive block, *Arkhivy SSSR: Leningradskoe otdelenie Tsentral'nogo Istoricheskogo Arkhiva: putevoditel' po fondam* [*The Archives of the USSR: the Leningrad Division of the Central Historical Archive: a Guide to the Collections*] (Leningrad, 1933). Compiled by M. Akhun, V. Lukomskii, *et al.*, and edited by A. K. Drezen, this guide covered the archive in question as then constituted. Almost one fifth of its holdings were naval in content (described on pp. 197-248 of that reference work). Although shortly afterward transferred to TsGAVMF, those naval holdings were not redescribed or listed

elsewhere in published and accessible form. For this reason, and especially because internal ordering of *fondy* has been maintained over the years regardless of
the periodic renaming of the archive (or the building) that still houses them, the
1933 work has retained some usefulness. While waiting for results in
TsGAVMF, which may never be forthcoming, the Western scholar may inves-
tigate such holdings of the now enormous Central State Historical Archive in
Leningrad (TsGIAL) as seem to bear on Hawai'i.[48] Still useful, for want of a replacement, is S. Valk's and V. Bedin's *Tsentral' nyi Gosudarstvennyi Istoricheskii
Arkhiv SSSR v Leningrade: putevoditel'* [*The Central State Historical Archive of
the USSR in Leningrad: a Guide*] (Leningrad, 1956). Though quite selective, it
at least gives an idea of the archive's holdings.

Of particular significance and promise to the student of Hawai'i's history and
people, as reflected by the Russian evidence of 1804, are those of the 3,000 *fondy*
of TsGAVMF which contain the papers of and/or concerning officers aboard
Nadezhda and *Neva* who later reached the rank of Captain in the service. These
include the Kotzebues, Bellingshausen, Povalishin, Romberkh, Berkh, and Ratmanov.[49] Certain items bear directly on the artifacts collected on Hawai'i by
Lisianskii and his officers,[50] or on Lt V.N. Berkh's enthusiastic attitude toward
the prospect for continuing imperial-cum-economic growth by Russian interests
in the Pacific.[51]

The nearby but separate *Tsentral' nyi Voenno-Morskoi Muzei* [Central Naval
Museum], too, deserves attention by the student of the 1804 (and later) Russian
visits to Hawai'i. In its keeping are the ship's journal of *Neva* while she was at
Kealakekua Bay;[52] the original logbook, kept by *Neva*'s navigator, D.V. Kalinin,
with entries covering the thirteen-day 'Hawaiian' period, 8-20 June 1804;[53] and
drafts of many letters by Lisianskii to superiors and friends, some dating from
1803-1804.[54]

Baltic archives also merit notice. Kruzenshtern himself, as well as Romberkh
(or Romberg), Berkh (or Berg), Levenshtern (von Loewenstern), Karl Espenberg,
Otto and Moritz von Kotzebue (sons of the distinguished dramatist) and Fabian
von Bellingshausen, were of Baltic German origins. Specifically, all eight identified themselves with, and had parents or relations in, the Russian Baltic
Province of Estonia (Estliandiia).[55] Large *fondy* containing family and many
service papers of the Bellingshausens, Levenshterns, and Kruzenshterns are to be
found at TsGIAE *(Tsentral' nyi Gosudarstvennyi Istoricheskii Arkhiv Estonskoi
SSR)*, in Tartu. Papers in the I.F. Kruzenshtern collection *(fond* 1414) complement others in *fond* 14 at TsGAVMF, or illuminate the Baltic German officer's
approach to exploration--and encounters with astute Hawaiian traders. Lt E.E.
Levenshtern's journal and diary of 1804,[56] on which an article was published in
the periodical *Sovetskaia etnografiia* in 1980,[57] are among those documents.
Mention should be made, in this Estonian connection, of the State Historical
Museum *(Eesti NSV Riikliik Ajaloomuuseum)*, on the beautiful and cobbled Pik-
kstrasse in Tallin, only minutes from the Church-run school that Kruzenshtern at-

tended with his brothers in the mid-1780s.[58] Typically, the Levenshtern
materials in Tartu have their counterparts in the Museum's Manuscript Department (Levenshtern's personal diary of 1804 in typescript for example.)[59] Also
here are materials relating to the Berg (Berkh) and Bellingshausen families,
amongst which there are documents of a professional or service nature. Local
bibliographies and biographical materials may be consulted at the library of the
Academy of Sciences of the ESSR [*Teaduste Akadeemia Teaduslik
Raamatukogu*] The Berkh papers are perhaps especially deserving of attention,
since the former midshipman aboard *Neva*, and later Head of the Hydrography
Department of the Admiralty and historian of Russia's North Pacific venture, was
an able writer of reports and articles.[60] His 'Journal of a Voyage Round the
World, to Complement the Journal Published by the Captain of *Neva*', which was
presumably composed not long after the voyage, was intended for the printer but
was never published, and has since been lost to view.[61] It is, of course, the writings of Lisianskii's people, who were on the Kona Coast for days on end, that
promise most to the historians, ethnologists, and children of Hawai'i. In particular, the journals of the following may be supposed to offer useful data: Pavel
Arbuzov and Petr Povalishin, the lieutenants of *Neva* in 1804; midshipmen V.N.
Berkh and Fedor Kovediaev; Surgeon Moritz Laband; Navigator Danilo Kalinin
and Assistant Navigator F. Mal'tsev; and Under-Surgeon Aleksei Mutovkin.[62]
To examine the surviving diaries (of 1804) and private correspondence of
Nadezhda's people, for example, those of Romberkh and Tilesius von Tilenau,[63]
is to recognize how little they can offer the ethnographer and student of Hawai'i
in comparison with men who, like Lisianskii, Berkh, Korobitsyn, and Povalishin,
went ashore. It is encouraging that Soviet researchers are as confident today that
finds of documents relating to Hawai'i will be made, as were successful archive
hunters of the '60s and '70s, notably L.A. Shur and V.V. Kuznetsova.[64]

APPENDIX A

Iurii Fedorovich Lisianskii (1773-1837)

Lisianskii was by birth a Little Russian, a Ukrainian, though he was never to regard himself as anything but Russian and, perhaps significantly, chose not to retire in the South. On the maternal side, he was related to the powerful, land-owning families of Kiev Province, but his father, an enlightened man of priestly antecedents, was by no means well-to-do. It was in part because the training that it offered was so cheap, at least comparatively, that Lisianskii was enrolled at the cadet corps for future naval officers at Kronstadt at the age of only ten. Like many other boys, he suffered at the barrack-like, profoundly inhospitable, yet architecturally beautiful, *Morskoi Kadetskii Korpus,* ever afterward connected in his mind with idle bullying and sleepless, freezing nights. Like rather fewer, he evinced natural aptitude for sciences connected with his calling: trigonometry, geometry and algebra, hydrography, shipbuilding, navigation and marine astronomy. As in the classroom, so also at sea aboard a training ship (in June and July 1786), he won the overall approval of superiors without contracting special friendships with contemporaries. For the moment, three years' difference in ages barred familiarity with Kruzenshtern, with whom, however, he was well acquainted.

War, and the passing of another year, made such age-gaps--and much else--seem immaterial. Allowed to pass out from the Corps 'before his time' as midshipman, Lisianskii was in June 1788 appointed to a 38-gun frigate in the squadron then reforming under Samuel K. Greig, *Podrazhislav.* In her, he played an honorable part in at least three of the ensuing major actions of the Russo-Swedish War: those fought at Gotland, off the Aland Islands, and at Reval. From her captain, an unusually well-read officer named Grevens who had barely twelve months earlier been named to the (then imminent) Mulovskii expedition to the Northwest Cost of North America, he heard such things as made him anxious to improve on his acquaintance with Lieutenant Kruzenshtern. The latter was in daily contact now, aboard the sister-frigate *Mstislav,* with Mulovskii and, for good measure with Vitus Bering's grandson, Iakov.

Whether or not the young Lisianskii met Mulovskii or Trevenen, in the last weeks before they were killed in battle at sea, cannot be said with any certainty;

but probability and circumstantial evidence support the supposition that he did. He was unquestionably looking out for contact with, and knowledge of, the 'explorations section' of the naval service, which had fired his imagination, and is known to have had dealings with a half-dozen officers, some very senior, with interests or personal connections in the East or the Pacific. V.Ia. Chichagov and A.S. Greig (son of the Scottish-born Commander in the Baltic, S.K. Grieg) were among them.

For Lisianskii as for many others in the Baltic Fleet, peace came less as a respite and reward for service rendered than a positive impediment to pleasantly exciting action and continuing advancement. After gunfire and victory, a posting to a transport craft, *Emmanuil*, then on the Kronstadt-Reval-Riga run, depressed him. Matters brightened six months later. First, he was promoted lieutenant, then included in the list of those to be dispatched as Volunteers to Great Britain for a practical, three-year course in higher seamanship and, as events transpired, long-range cruising. Taking passage in a merchantman from Helsingfors in Finland, Lisianskii and his fifteen fellow-officers reached Hull in early January 1794. Some twelve weeks later, they were posted to their ships, Lisianskii to the frigate *L'Oiseau*, under Captain Robert Murray. Of his subsequent adventures as a Russian Volunteer, we may read in the arresting introduction to the 1814, English-language, version of his *Voyage Round the World*. An extract may suffice to give the flavor:

"Near the coast of the United States he was at the taking of a large fleet of American ships, which were bound for France with provisions under the convoy of the French frigate "La Concorde" and other armed vessels... By her superior sailing, the "L'Oiseau" captured, besides many merchant-vessels, an armed brig called "Chigamoga", on board of which was Monsieur Belgard, a black general, well known in the French West India islands. After this capture, the "L'Oiseau" repaired to Halifax to refit, and then sailed on a winter cruise. During this cruise she was blown off the coast of the Chesapeak[e], sprung a leak, and was carried to the West-Indies. There the writer of these memoirs was attacked by the yellow-fever... In the year 1795 he proceeded on a course of travels in America. He passed through the United States, from Boston to the Savanna; and, after spending the winter in Philadelphia, returned the following year to Halifax; where... he entered on board the frigate "La Topase", commanded by captain Church. In this frigate he was in a very smart engagement with "L'Elizabeth", a French frigate of equal force..."

It was, in sum, a happy and eventful period. It also reinforced Lisianskii's interest in distant parts and his earlier ambition to examine them himself. As seen, he did not hesitate, when opportunity arose, to join his comrades Kruzenshtern and Mikhail Baskakov on a pioneering mission of enquiry to Cape Town and, in due course, to Calcutta and Bombay. While in Bengal, it may be mentioned as suggestive of the veritable wanderlust that now held him in its grip, at the age of twenty-four, he was told of Matthew Flinders' survey work in *Norfolk*, then proceeding, and of plans to send another scientific and surveying expedition to New Holland, and was seized by the idea of himself assisting Flinders if permission could be won from the appropriate authorities. Having already rapidly examined British colonies in the West Indies, he welcomed any chance to see another one. He was acquainted with Vancouver's recent *Voyage of Discovery*, with its description of Van Diemen's Land and maps, and it was obvious that the work still to be done around the island-continent was that of the professional hydrographer. For all three reasons he was tempted by the thought of joining *Norfolk*, or another vessel like her. But he went no further east that season. He was ordered to return to active duty in the Baltic, and took passage on a homeward-bound Indiaman, taking his plans to visit China and New Holland back to Europe for a final eighteen months of incubation.

Kruzenshtern himself informs us that he chose Lisianskii as his second-in-command in 1802, for his experience at sea and proven 'zeal' for the service. If their subsequent relationship was less harmonious and smooth than later writers would have had their readers think, the fact remains that, all in all, Lisianskii proved a happy choice as second-in-command and--more significantly--as the captain of a ship that sailed independently for more than 700, or approximately two thirds, of the 1,095 days of the entire venture of *Nadezhda* and *Neva*.

Such strains as grew in 1806-1809 between the two old friends--and more significantly from the standpoint of Lisianskii's whole career, between *both* of them and agents of the Russian-American Company that they had served in the Pacific--were essentially the products of Lisianskii's feeling that his contribution to that venture, though officially acknowledged by promotion and the granting of a lump sum (almost 14,000 roubles) and a pension, yet deserved more recognition where it mattered: in commercial, Court, and Admiralty circles in St Petersburg. That feeling--doubtless sharpened by a consciousness of Kruzenshtern's celebrity in Baltic naval circles to which he himself, no scion of the Baltic, was as always the outsider, and enflamed by criticisms of his own role in a grand and costly venture that had failed on the economic front as on the diplomatic also--led to action when confirmed by the rejection by an official of the Admiralty, Apollon Nikol'skii, of his carefully redrafted journal of the voyage of *Neva* (see p. 182). It was (to him) apparent that his competence itself was being questioned, and on many levels. Forces were at work (it seemed to him), that made continuing advancement in the service problematical unless he met them with the politician's weapons, not the seaman's. Angry and depressed, he viewed his progress since returning to the Baltic in an altered light. Perhaps his posting as commander of the (Kronstadt-based) Imperial yacht squadron was indicative of a polite withdrawal from the mainstream of the service. He had 14,000 roubles, funds of unexpended energy, and a distaste for backroom politics. In February 1809, aged 36, he sought permission to retire. It was quickly granted, notwithstanding his distinguished record and his youthfulness.

Lisianskii spent the next six months arranging his affairs and the next six years adjusting to his altered situation. Though effectively discouraged by the Admiralty Board from doing so, he had his *Voyage* published at his own expense in 1812. The cost was high, the timing bad: the nation was preoccupied by war, and by the drama of Napoleon's invasion of the Western Provinces. Then Moscow burned. Lisianskii had no post or station to report to. He engrossed himself in local preparations to repulse the enemy, then in translating his unlucky *Voyage* into English. It appeared in London in the early weeks of 1814, and sold extremely well. Unable to dismiss the fact, the Russian Government at last agreed to meet the costs incurred in 1812, in publication of the first, Russian edition. Even so, Lisianskii found himself almost 6,000 roubles out of pocket. Vindicated, but disgusted, he resolved to have no other dealings with officialdom than were essential. He acquired an estate and left the capital, intent on managing his property efficiently and on a liberal, if not quite English, basis. He succeeded and, at last, his life unfolded to another, smoother rhythm. His five children (by Charlotte Gendre, *neé* de Brunoldt, whom he had married in 1807) were brought up in the country where the weight of the oppressively reactionary regime of Nicholas I (1825-1854) was less in evidence. One only, Platon, joined the Navy. He, however, reached flag-rank. Lisianskii died in February 1837. In St Petersburg, where the news of Pushkin's death had caused a shock only a fortnight earlier, his passing caused no ripple.

APPENDIX B

A Note on Hawaiian Artifacts Now in the MAE's 'James Cook' and 'Lisianskii' Collections (Nos 505 & 750)

Ten weeks after Cook's death in Kealakekua Bay, Hawai'i (14 February 1779), the new commander of the British expedition, Charles Clerke, brought *Discovery* and *Resolution* into Avacha Bay, Kamchatka. The weary British companies, who had sought an Arctic passage home to the Atlantic, were received kindly by Major Magnus von Behm, Governor of Kamchatka, and the Russians provided their unexpected visitors with ample provisions and a crucial opportunity to rest. In gratitude, Clerke presented Behm with a collection of Hawaiian, Tongan and Tahitian artifacts. It is not certain how many articles were included at the time of presentation (May 1779); nor was a specific figure given in the 1800 catalogue to the holdings of the St Petersburg Academy of Sciences' *Kunstkammer* (Orest Beliaev, *Kabinet Petra Velikogo*, 1800, Pt 2:229). Today, the '1779 Cook Collection', which is Collection No. 505 in the Peter-the-Great Museum of Ethnography, Academy of Sciences of the USSR, Leningrad, contains 32 objects. The majority (21?) of these are Hawaiian. Clerke's giving of the artifacts to Behm is adequately described by George Forster (see his *Geschichte der See-Reisen und Entdeckungen im Süd-Meer*, Berlin, 1778-88, Bd. VII:369). For data on the subsequent fate of Governor Behm, and on his friendly relations with the British in 1779 and later, see Beaglehole, III, Pt 1:clxiii-clxiv, 665-70. David Samwell, surgeon of *Discovery*, reports (*ibid.*, Pt 2:1248, journal for 26 May 1779) that the British gave the Governor, amongst other things, "several articles from the different islands we had visited in the South Seas", and that Behm always intended to present these Polynesian artifacts to the imperial authorities. In addition to Iuliia M. Likhtenberg's 1960 description of the Hawaiian collections now in Leningrad, 'Gavaiskie kollektsii v Sobraniiakh Muzeia Antropologii i Etnografii', SMAE, Vol. XIX:168-205, we have L.G. Rozina(-Bernstam)'s more specific treatment of the 'Cook Collection' entitled 'Kollektsiia Dzhemsa Kuka v Sobraniiakh Muzeia Antropologii i Etnografii' (*ibid.*, XXIII:234-253, 1966). Both articles are detailed, contain illustrations--unfortunately of a rather indifferent quality--and overlap helpfully. Regrettably, documentation of the 'Cook Collection' in the Peter-the-Great Museum is inadequate. In particular, the Soviet *opisi,* or holdings lists give no precise data on provenance; and this fact has resulted in much recent investigation of the matter by Adrienne Kaeppler of the Smithsonian Institution in Washington, DC and by other Hawai'i specialists in the West. There are, nonetheless, reasons to think that five objects (505-5,-6,-16,-19 and -28 by the Soviet enumeration) were indeed collected in the Hawaiian Islands in 1778-1779 and were in St Petersburg by 1780, *i.e.,* formed part of the earliest collection of Hawaiian artifacts ever to reach Europe.

(505-5) Dagger with sharks' teeth; loop cord attached through the center. Overall length 34cm, width 4cm; teeth, 2cm by 2cm. Several such items were acquired on 1-2 February 1778 ("weapons...made of a reddish dark coloured wood not unlike Mahogany": Beaglehole, III, Pt 1:282).

(505-6) Tabooing wand, of hardwood, sharpened; white dog's hair attached and, at place of attachment, there are the remains of *i'iwi* and *o'o* feathers stitched together with vegetable fibers, together with a small strip of *kapa.* Overall length, 63cm; length of handle, 19cm.

(505-16) Bracelet (*kûpe'e ho'okalakala*), consisting of 22 polished boar's tusks tied together by double rows of thread passed through apertures 0.5cm wide. Overall height, 8.5cm; circumference, 17cm.

(505-19) Feather cape (*ahu'ula*), yellow background with sickle designs of red and black feathers thereon; length of sides, 23cm; length of lower border, 174cm; breadth of cape across the center, 41cm.

(505-28) Stone adze; hardwood haft with coconut fiber cord binding; the stone is black, rectangular and well polished. Overall length, 57cm; haft length, 54cm; haft diameter, 3.4-2.4cm; stone part dimensions, 4.5 by 16cm.

The remaining Hawaiian artifacts in Collection No. 505 at the Peter-the-Great Museum in Leningrad are: feather capes [*ahu'ula*] (505-12,-17,-18), a feather cape largely of white *Phaeton lepturus* (White-tailed Tropic Bird) [*koa'e kea*] feathers, but with reddish-brown feather framing (505-9), *mahiole* (505-7,-11), *lei* (505-8, -13), a *kâhili* with black split feathers of *Fregata minor* (Frigate-bird) ['*iwa*] (505-2), a fan (505-4), material for use in feather ornamentation (505-3), a finely woven mat with eleven vertical brown stripes (505-30), a second-stage *kapa* beater (505-29), a large wooden fishhook with three-sided bone point (505-24), two polished shell fishhooks (505-25,-26),and a *pahoa* dagger of light brown hardwood (505-33). The Museum authorities consider items 505-25 and -26 to be certainly Polynesian and probably Hawaiian. Thus, the total number of articles in the collection that may be considered certainly Hawaiian and eighteenth-century is 21. L.G. Rozina-Bernstam provides details of them all in her 1966 article.

As observed, the great majority of the Hawaiian artifacts brought to St Petersburg by Russian naval officers (and their civilian passengers) were in the keeping of the Admiralty Department's own museum in the early 1800s. Some, as seen, were presented to Kruzenshtern's and Otto von Kotzebue's noble patron, the Chancellor of Russia, Count Nikolai P. Rumiantsev, and were later transferred, with the remaining 'curiosities' in that large natural historical, ethnographic, numismatic and printed collection, to Moscow. They there formed part of the Rumiantsev and Moscow Public Museum, the ethnographic section of which was taken over by Moscow State University, stored in various buildings and basements during the Great Patriotic War (World War II), and totally lost in 1943-1944. Others again were presented, by the Admiralty itself or even by individual naval officers with academic connections, to the *Kunstkammer* (Curiosities Cabinet) of the St Petersburg Academy of Sciences, from which developed the present Peter-the-Great Museum of the N.N. Miklukho-Maklai Institute of Anthropology and Ethnography in Leningrad. Instructions regarding the submission of (Polynesian and other foreign) artifacts to the Admiralty Department museum are preserved in the Leningrad Division of the Archive of the Academy of Sciences of the USSR (LOAAN), under archival reference: *fond* 2, *opis'* i (1897), No. 3:12-13. Also in that file are papers concerning the process of transferral of ethnographica to the Academy from naval keeping. At the Academy, all but a few of these 'pre-1828' Pacific artifacts were placed in two collections, Nos 736 and 750.

Hawaiian artifacts collected by the people of *Neva* appear, very soon after that expedition's end, to have been split into three groups (see p. 172). Most found their way to the *Kunstkammer* of the Academy. Lisianskii himself drew up a catalogue briefly describing them, 'Katalog iskusstvennym veshcham i odezhde raznykh Evropeiskikh, Asiatskikh i Amerikanskikh narodov' ('A Catalogue of Artifacts and Clothing of Various European, Asiatic and American Peoples'). This catalogue remains at LOAAN today under reference: *fond* 142, *opis'* 1, No. 108:1 (1719-1927). The terms 'American' and 'Asiatic' were loosely used; and among the peoples well represented in Lisianskii's (and Povalishin's) donation to the *Kunstkammer* were the Hawaiians. At about the same time, and again for the benefit of the *Kunstkammer*'s Director, Lisianskii drew up another short description of the 'foreign curiosities' brought back to Russia by *Neva*. This, too, survives in LOAAN (present address: 5 Universitetskaia Naberezhnaia, Leningrad 199164) under reference: *fond* 1, *opis'* 2:20 (1807), and clearly indicates that--at the least--a hundred Polynesian artifacts had been brought from Taio-hae Bay, the Kona coast of Hawai'i, and the south coast of Kaua'i--not to mention a good number of Tlingit and Aleut objects from the Northwest Coast of North America where *Neva* had wintered busily in 1804-1805.

Some Hawaiian artifacts collected by *Neva*'s people had, meanwhile, found their way to the Admiralty Department museum. (Others, one may reasonably think, trickled away from the imperial authorities and stayed in private hands.) Thus Hawaiian artifacts that had been brought back to St Petersburg together in 1806 were reunited (1828-1830) when the Academy assumed responsibility for Admiralty items. They were not then placed together in a single group, however. On the contrary, some went with the Hawaiian articles brought back to Russia in *Nadézhda* (Captain Kruzenshtern) and are, today, in Collection No. 736. Confusion was inherent in the fact that *these* Hawaiian artifacts, *i.e.*, not presented by Lisianskii to the *Kunstkammer* in 1807, did not appear on the 1807 list which was, in due course, used as a basis for a 'regular inventory' [*inventarnyi spisok*] of the artifacts collected from *Neva* in 1804-1806.

The ethnographic significance of these considerations is apparent from the facts that: *a*) barely a quarter of the Polynesian artifacts said by Lisianskii to have gone into the *Kunstkammer* by 1807 are today in the one collection, No. 750, officially known as 'Iu.F. Lisianskii's'; and *b*) that of that number--23--a mere 8 are Hawaiian. In themselves, these figures indicate that many of the articles collected by the people of *Neva* along Hawai'i's Kona coast in 1804 are now in Collection No. 736, and that many others very likely vanished in the shaken wartime Moscow of 1943-1944. (It is the view of Tat'iana V. Staniukovich, historian of the Soviet museums of ethnography and author of *Etnograficheskaia nauka i muzei*, Leningrad, ANSSSR, 1978, that many such Hawaiian artifacts were first mislaid as a result of institutional disruptions, storage movements and priority of war, then simply broken or destroyed. For safekeeping from shelling, they were kept in many buildings in the city and in one or two outside the city limits.) That Hawaiian artifacts brought back to Russia in *Neva* had *left* (the future) Collection No. 750 by 1828 is apparent. Is it possible, conversely, that not all of the eight definitely Hawaiian artifacts that form a part of it today were in fact brought in *Neva* in 1806? Describing the Leningrad Marquesas Islands collection, 'Kollektsiia MAE po Markiskim ostrovam', SMAE, XXI:110 1963, L.G. Rozina states baldly, "Collection No. 750 consists of things brought by Iu.F. Lisianskii in 1806", and observes that several Marquesan artifacts now in Leningrad "were sketched and appeared in the *Sobranie kart i risunkov, prinadlezhashchikh k puteshestviiu Iu. Lisianskago na korable 'Neva'* [*Collection of maps and Drawings relating to the Voyage of Iu. Lisianskii in the Ship 'Neva'*]." No documentary evidence, however, is adduced to support this claim that Collection No. 750's Polynesian holdings were all brought back to Europe by Lisianskii; nor are matters simplified by the fact that several Marquesan artifacts drawn by the multitalented Lisianskii and presented in his (1812) *Sobranie kart i risunkov*--for instance, the war club and fan that are respectively figures M & W on Plate I of that work--now form part of Collection 736 (-175,-184), not of No. 750.

Wishing to clarify this question, the present writer examined the official inventory or *opis'* to Collection No, 750 held at the Peter-the-Great Museum in

Leningrad. The *opis'* is kept in the Office of the Australia and Oceania Division (*Sektor Avstralii i Okeanii: komn.412*) in the original building of the second *Kunstkammer*, in the keeping (as of 1986) of Tamara K. Shafranovskaia. It is a brown folder and contains two distinct descriptions of the collection in question: a recent one (December 1964) by L.G. Rozina, and an older one (1903) by the then Director of the Muzei Antropologii i Etnografii, Dr E. Petri. The following is written, in Rozina's hand, on the first sheet of her own description: "Inventory to Coll. No. 750 Obtained from: Iu.F. Lisianskii. Time of acquisition: 1807? Collector: Iu.F. Lisianskii. Method of acquisition: gift. People: Polynesian. Composition of Collection: objects of daily and cult usage. Documentation: labels of the collector [*etiketki sobiratelia*], *taken from the objects of the collection. Number of articles: 23.*" Below is added the following remark: "The objects in this collection were gathered by Iu.F. Lisianskii and probably presented to the Kunstkammer of the Academy of Sciences in 1807. (On this, see 'Spisok veshchei, podarennykh Iu. Lisianskim v Kunstkameru Imp. Akad. Nauk v 1806 godu', in the Archive of the Academy of Sciences, *fond* 1, *op.* 2 No. 20, 1807; also see Iu.F. Lisianskii's *Sobranie kart i risunkov*, St P., 1812)."

The labels [*etiketki*] in question are, in fact, glued in the appropriate places on the pages of Petri's earlier inventory list to Collection No. 750. That list, headed 'Inventarnyi spisok kollektsii Muzeia Antropologii i Etnografii No. 750', is on worn folio paper. There are later nineteenth-century annotations here and there, between item entries. The labels, taken from Hawaiian artifacts and Nukuhivan artifacts alike, were evidently attached shortly after their arrival in St Petersburg. Delay would certainly have been unwise, since Polynesian artifacts collected in 1804 were among those put on public display, with the encouragement of the Directors of the Russian-American Company, on Gorokhovaia Street in St Petersburg, in September 1806 (see *Russkii invalid*, 1839, No. 31). Most labels refer to the original numbering of an article--*i.e.*, its numbering in the collection of about a hundred Polynesian items--and to a new numbering in No. 750. The articles themselves are described in the briefest way. Thus, a Hawaiian composite hook, item 750-6 today, is seen to have been No. 41 in the assemblage presented to the authorities in 1806-1807.

There are numerous extant specimens of Lisianskii's handwriting. In the Central Naval Museum (Tsentral'nyi Voenno-Morskoi Muzei) at the former stock exchange building in Leningrad, for example, are several journals kept by Lisianskii. One covers his period as a Russian Volunteer and passenger with the Royal Navy (1793-1800: reference 9170/1938) and has, appended, a number of personal letters from Lisianskii to his brother Ananii. Others, under references 9170/1938-3 and -8, contain his journal aboard *Neva* in 1803-1806 and holographs of private letters to various persons from 1803 to 1832. Comparison of labels stuck to Petri's 1903 inventory list and of MS9170/1938 at TsVMM makes clear that Lisianskii himself labeled his Hawaiian and Marquesan artifacts for the public benefit. Ink tests cannot, of course, determine the exact date of a handwritten label; and rough quality paper of the sort from which the labels are made was in use in Russia for two centuries at least. It is worth noting, however, that Lisianskii was on furlough (navy leave) until the spring of 1807, and so had time to be of service to Academy and public, firstly by labeling his 'curiosities', and secondly by assisting the Director of the *Kunstkammer* himself. Nor in the following two years did he have another base of operations than St Petersburg and the adjacent port of Kronstadt (see *Obshchii Morskoi Spisok*, IV:12 and the biographical essay in *Morskoi sbornik*, 1894, No. 1).

It was natural that Kruzenshtern should be in frequent contact with the Academy as well as with the Admiralty in the years 1806-1809. He had been made a corresponding member of the former body on 25 April 1803 (entry in *Protokol Konferentsii Akademii Nauk*, 13 April Old Style), and had academic friends of some distinction. Archive records indicate, though, that Lisianskii, too, had contact with the *Kunstkammer* during that period (papers in LOAAN, *fond* 142, *op.* 1, no. 108; TsVMM 9170-3/1938: *chernoviki pisem Lisianskogo...*, etc.), as well as with the influential Count Rumiantsev (and, by 1808, with Grand Dukes and Duchesses). It was because he was beholden to the Count, the main supporter of the venture in *Nadézhda* and *Neva* (and future patron of Lieutenant Kotzebue), that Lisianskii thought it proper to present him with Hawaiian and Marquesan artifacts. Soviet historian V.V. Nevskii writes, without exaggeration, that Lisianskii "left the richest collections of shells, corals, weaponry and clothing collected in various lands to the Rumiantsev Museum" (*Pervoe puteshestvie Rossian*, Leningrad, 1951, 193). These, as seen, were Polynesian artifacts that were to perish in Moscow in the early 1940s. What a loss was then sustained by Polynesian and especially Hawaiian studies may be gauged from the *otchoty* and reports of the Rumiantsev and Moscow Public Museum of the later nineteenth century. Suffice here to comment that when, in 1867, its previous 'Ethnographic Cabinet' was reformed as the basis of the Dashkov Ethnographical Museum, *that* was found to contain "about 400 objects, most used by Pacific islanders or the natives of Alaska and Japan..., all collected, on Count Rumiantsev's orders, during the round-the-world expedition of Kruzenshtern and Lisianskii" (*Piatidesiatiletie Rumiantsovskago Muzeia v Moskve, 1862-1912: istoricheskii ocherk*, Moscow, 1912, 164). The Hawaiian artifacts, amongst others, were briefly listed in several museum publications--such as *Sbornik materialov dlia istorii Rumiantsovskago Muzeia [A Collection of Materials for the History of the Rumiantsev Museum]*, Bk I:108-17, Moscow 1882--of which ethnologists and other Western students of Hawai'i have, as yet, made little use.

APPENDIX C

A Vocabulary of the Sandwich Islands, by Iu.F. Lisianskii

Lisianskii drew up a Hawaiian word list, on the basis of his own data of 1804, for inclusion in the first Russian edition of his *Puteshestvie vokrug sveta*. When that work finally appeared (St Petersburg, 1812), after many delays and difficulties that were touched on earlier (see p. 184), the word list--of 202 items--was on pages 228-36, and formed the conclusion of Chapter IX of the book's Part One. It was preceded and followed by these comments: "I think it necessary here to append a small collection of words of the Sandwich language which, for all its brevity, may yet be of great use to travellers who do not know the tongue of the natives of those isles." "N.B. The inhabitants of the Sandwich Islands generally lisp and speak softly. Some of them pronounce the letter 't' as a 'k'; the letter 'g' is muted or spoken very lightly." Lisianskii's 'g' is, of course, the Hawaiian aspirate 'h', and the Hawaiians did interchange 't' and 'k' (only with the advent of missionary printing presses was the 'k' taken as the standard and the 't' lost). Of the list itself, suffice to say that a motley assortment of words relating to food, the human body, time, structures and human relationships (body parts predominating), is followed by seven first person singular verb forms and by 24 numerals or terms of reckoning. Lisianskii himself prepared an overlapping but different Hawaiian word list--this time of 172 items only--for inclusion in his translation of his own *Voyage Round the World* (London, John Booth *et al.*, 1814): 326-28. That list is offered here.

The 1812 word list is, of course, arranged in accordance with the Russian alphabet (ABVGD, etc.). This fact, together with the inevitable replacement of Hawaiian 'h' by Cyrillic 'g' or 'kh', makes simple comparison of the 1812 and 1814 lists rather awkward. It seemed best, in the circumstances, not to collate the 1814 word list with a (reorganized and modified) English transliteration of the 1812 one. It may, however, interest the reader to know that words of many sorts that appear in the 1812 text are omitted from the London edition--for example, beard, shinbone, gimlet, (iron) nail, give me, pipe, angry, and neck. Also omitted are a number of question phrases such as "Is there water?" and "What is that called?" Some words are differently defined in the two lists--*Rio-hoolloo*, a sheep (1814) but *rio-gullu*, a ram (1812)--while some others are differently spelled, even taking into account Latin-Cyrillic alternates: *Taatee*, boy (1814) but *toaati*, boy (1812) [the Hawaiian word *keiki* actually means 'child', of either sex]. It is clear that Lisianskii or his London typesetters failed to render *pokaigiu* (the Russians attempt at Hawaiian for nostrils, *puka ihu*) as they should have; omission of the 'a' produced *Pokyhu*. Lisianskii's intentional omissions were perhaps influenced by his familiarity with later eighteeenth-century word lists and by a wish to avoid repetition for an English speaking readership.

A

Afterwards..........................Mamooree
Angry ....Hoohoo
Axe................................ Koeereepee

B

Bad, that is. .... Eyo ino
Belly...Opoo
Black ....Ereré
Boy...Taatee
Bread-fruit................................Ooloo
Bring hither ....Omy
Brother ....Tay tyina
Button.....................................Oppeehee
Buy, to. ....Tooay

C

Cabbage............... Tabetee *or* Kabekee
Cannon .... Kooniahi
Canoe, single...........................Hevaha
Ditto, double .... Mokorooa
Cat.. Popokee
Cloth of the country .... Tapa
Cloth which men tie round the waist
.... Maro
Ditto for women ....Paoo
Cock. ....Moakanee
Cocoa-nut.....................................Neoo
Come hither.....................Heré mayoé
Cry, to.. Avé

D

Dance, to .... Ahoora
Dart, a small................................ Ihee
Day.. Erapoo
Dead ....Makeroa
Do, how do you?........................ Aloha
Dog ....Rio
Door ....Pooka
Dry, I am ....Pimy vy

E

Ears .... Pepeiaoo
Earth.......................................Ehonooa
Eat, will you? .... E-ay-oé
Enemy .... Aoree maka maka
European .... Ehaouri
Evening.............................. Aheeahee
Eye ....Maka

F

Farewell .... Aloha
Father ....Makooakanee
Finger, fore............. ...Limameke poe
Ditto, middle ....Limoaina
Ditto, third....................... Limapeelee
Ditto, little..........................Leemyitee
Fingers .... Leema-leema
Fish .... Heyo
Friend............................... Makamaka

G

Girl .... Ty tamaheenee
Goat.. Riokao
Go away .... Herapera
Go with me, *or* Follow me
.....................................Mamooreeaio
God... Kooa
Good.. Myty
Grandfather ....Toopoonakanee
Grandmother .... Toopoonoaheenee
Grass .... Mou
Green................................... Omomao
Gun..Poo

H

Hair .... Lavohoo]
Hand....................................Leema
Handsome ....Nanee
Hat.................................. ..Papalé
He *or* she .... .Oera
Head ....Pou
Hen...............................Moa vaheenee
High.. Roeehee
Hog...Pooa
House .... Haree
Hungry, I am .... Pororeevou

I

I .... Vou
Island..................... Motoo, *or* Mokoo

K

Kill, to ....Papahee
Knee .... .Koolee
Knife .... Okeeokee

L

Lie ....Punee punee
Lips .... Elehelehé
Little...Poupou
Looking-glass...................... Aneeanee

M

Mad ....Hehena
Man ....Kanaka
Man, he is a good...... Ayakanaka.my.ty...
Mat (to sleep on) .... Moena
Mat (used for clothing} .... Ahoo
Melon ....Ipoopaeena
Melon, a water .... Ipoohoéoree
Moon..................................... Maheena
Morrow .... Abobo
Mother...........................Makuaheenee

N

Nails...Mayo
Night .... .Aoomoé
Noise, why do you
make a .... Kooreekoore
Nose..Ehu
Nostrils................................Pokyhu

O

Oar .... Ehoee

P

Pay you, I will .... Oreema reema
Plantains...................................... Myo
Plantation ....Ayna
Potatoes, sweet........................ Oovara
Priest ....Kahoona

Q

Quickly....................................... Veetee

R

Rat.. Ioré
Red ....Ooraoora

S

Salt ....Paky
Saw, a ....Paheeoroo
Scissars [sic] .... Oopa
Sea...Ty

Sheep....... Rio hoolloo, *or* Rio veoveo
Shew what
is that...................Nana meereemeeree
Sister ....Tay tooaheenee
Sit down .... Noho
Sky ....Heranee
Spear ....Pororoo
Stay a little ....Noohoo mareea
Step, a.......................................Vavy
Stone ....Poohakoo
Sun ....La
Swine, have you? .... Aori pooaoé
Swine, I have no........ Aoreepooa paha
Swine, I have.................. Pooano paha

T

Take that.................................. Erové
Teeth.. Neeho

Temple ....Heavoo
Thief......................................Ayhooé
Thigh.................................... Ooha
Thumb..................................Limanui
Tired, I am............................. Manaka
Tongue .... Alelu
Tongue,
hold your........ Hamaoo noohoo maria
Tree ....Laaoo

W

War.. Taooa
Water...Vy
Water, is your, good?............. Vymyty
Well, that is .... Eio myty
What is that? .... Ehara teyna
What, *or* where ....Eara
Where is he?.............................Ahvea
White......................................Keokeo
Who is that? .... Vaynoa eia kanaka
Woman .... Vahené
Work, to .... Hanahana
Wounded .... Tooitahee

Y

Yam, a root...............................Oohee
Year....................................Makaahity
Yellow .... Orena
Yes... Ay
You.. Oé

Numerals

1	Akahee	30	Kana koroo
2	Arooa	40	Kanaha
3	Akooroo	80	Arooa kanaha
4	Aha	120	Akoroo kanaha
5	Areema	160	Aha kanaha
6	Aono	200	Areema kanaha
7	Aheetoo	240	Aono kanaha
8	Avaroo	280	Avaroo kanaha
9	Yva	360	Yva kanaha
10	Aoomi	400	Aoomi kanaha
20	Iva koorooa	1000	Manoo

It may be mentioned in conclusion here that the Russian Navy continued to make contributions to Hawaiian language studies in the earlier 1800s. The work of Adelbert von Chamisso in particular, undertaken while in the Islands in the *Riurik* (1816-1817) and made public in the 1837 study *Uber die Hawaiische Sprache*, has long been recognized as precious. For that very reason, the linguist Samuel H. Elbert introduced a reprint edition (by Halcyon Antiquariaat of Amsterdam) in 1969. Another Hawaiian word list was drawn up in 1821 by Lieutenant Aleksei Petrovich Lazarev of the armed sloop *Blagonamerennyi* (Captain-Lt Gleb Shishmarev). That list remains in manuscript at TsGAVMF in Leningrad, under archival reference: *fond* 213, *op.* 1, *delo* 43), and is scheduled to appear in a Soviet compilation of Hawaiian-focused documents in 1989-1990.

Abbreviations

ACLS	American Council of Learned Societies
BCHQ	*British Columbia Historical Quarterly*
BPMB	Bernice Pauahi Bishop Museum
IVGO	*Izvestiia Vsesoiuznogo Geograficheskogo Obshchestva*
JRAHS	*Journal of the Royal Australian Historical Society*
MM	*Mariner's Mirror*
LOAAN	Leningradskii Otdel Arkhiva Akademii Nauk SSSR
OMS	*Obshchii Morskoi Spisok* (St.P., 1885-1907)
PRO	Public Record Office, London
PSZRI	*Polnoe sobranie zakonov Rossiiskoi Imperii*
SPB	*Sorevnovatel' prosveshcheniia i blagodeianiia*
SMAE	*Sbornik Muzeia Antropologii i Etnografii (L.)*
StP	St Petersburg
TsGADA	Central State Archive of Ancient Acts (Moscow)
TsGAVMF	Central State Archive of the Navy of the USSR (L.)
TsGIAE	Central State Historical Archive, Estonian SSR (Tartu)
TsGIAL	Central State Historical Archive of USSR (Leningrad)
TsVMM	Central State Naval Museum, Leningrad
ZGDMM	*Zapiski Gidrograficheskogo Departamenta Morskogo Ministerstva*

Notes

Part 1

1   For surveys and original materials, see A.I. Andreev, *Russkie otkrytiia v Tikhom okeane i Severnoi Amerike v XVIII-XIX vekakh* (Moscow-Leningrad, 1944); S.B.Okun', trans. C. Ginsburg, *The Russian-American Company* (Cambridge, Mass., 1951); G.R. Barratt, *Russia in PacificWaters, 1715-1825: a survey of the origins of Russia's naval presence in the North and South Pacific* (Vancouver, 1981).

2   Details in V.N. Berkh, *Khronologicheskaia istoriia otkrytiia Aleutskikh ostrovov* (StP, 1823): 70-72; see also S.R. Tompkins and M.L. Moorehead, 'Russia's Approach to America: from Spanish Sources, 1761-75', *BCHQ*, 13 (1949):235ff

3   These matters are treated by G. Williams, *The British Search for the Northwest Passage in the Eighteenth Century* (London, 1962), esp. pp. 169ff.; and W.L. Cook, *Flood Tide of Empire: Spain and the Pacific Northwest, 1543-1819* (London & New Haven, 1973):ch. 4.

4   Cook, *Flood Tide of Empire*, pp. 69-84; Tompkins and Moorehead, 'Russia's Approach', pp. 248-50

5   See J.C. Beaglehole, ed., *The Journals of Captain James Cook: the Voyage of the 'Resolution' and'Discovery', 1776-1780* (Cambridge, 1967), pt I:649-66; pt II:1240

6   See Beaglehole, *The Journals*, IV: Appendix,'Cook and the Russians'; Barratt, *Russia in Pacific Waters*, pp. 75-76.

7   Beaglehole, *The Journals*, III:pt 1:lxxxix

8   I touch on these issues in 'The Russian Navy and New Holland: Part 1', *JRAHS*, 64 (1979), pt 4:220-22. For a list of Russian versions of Cook's three *Voyages*, see T. Armstrong, 'Cook's Reputation in Russia', in R. Fisher, H. Johnston, eds., *Captain James Cook and his Times* (Vancouver, 1979), p. 128.

9   Beaglehole, *The Journals*, IV: Appendix, 'Cook and the Russians'; also S. Penfield Oliver, ed., *Memoirs and Travels of Mauritius Augustus, Count de Benyowsky* (London, 1904), intro. (on Benyowsky's escape from Kamchatka in 1771, official reactions, etc.); on the civilized von Behm, W. Lenz, ed., *Deutsch-Baltisches Biographisches Lexikon, 1710-1960* (Köln-Wien, 1970), p. 37

10 Cited by Beaglehole, *The Journals*, III:pt 2:1554

11 Published in 1780 as *Puteshestvie k iuzhnomu poliusu*. For details of availability to Russian readers of some other narratives by ex-participants in Cook's last voyage, all of which touch on Hawai'i, see G.N. Gennadi, *Spravochnyi slovar' o russkikh pisateliakh i spisok russkikh knig s 1725 po 1825 god* (Berlin, 1876-80).

12 Details in Beaglehole, *The Journals*, III:pt 2:1404. See also Barratt, *Russia in Pacific Waters*, pp. 75-78, and Williams, *The British Search*, pp. 210-11

13 See J.R. Gibson, *Feeding the Russian fur trade: provisionment of the Okhotsk seaboard..., 1639-1856* (Madison, Wisc., 1969), ch. 3-5; and Okun', *The Russian-American Company*

14 Beaglehole, *The Journals,* III:pt 1:714
15 It seems, however, to have been the publication of the Cook-King text (1784) that led to the dispatching of Hanna from Bengal to the Coast, and to the furthering of Dixon's and of Portlock's aims. Both had, of course, served under Cook: Beaglehole, *The Journals,* III: pt II:1473-75, and F.W. Howay, *A List of Trading Vessels in the Maritime Fur Trade, 1785-1825,* ed. R.A. Pierce (Kingston, Ont., 1973), pp. 3-5.
16 S.D. Watrous, ed. and intro., *John Ledyard's Journey Through Russia and Siberia, 1787-88* (Madison, Wisc., 1966), p. 10
17 Beaglehole, *The Journals,* III:pt 1:714
18 *Ibid.,* pt II:1474; Martin Sauer, *An Account of a Geographical and Astronomical Expedition...* (London, 1802), 1:5ff
19 C. Vinicombe Penrose, *A Memoir of James Trevenen, 1760-1790,* ed. R. C. Anderson and C. Lloyd (London, Navy Records Society, 1959), pp. 87ff
20 *Ibid.,* p. 90; Barratt, 'Russian Navy and New Holland', pp. 223-24
21 Okun', *The Russian-American Company,* pp. 16-17
22 The phrase indeed implies Japanese authority or ownership; but see G. Lensen, *The Russian Push Towards Japan,* ch. 4-5.
23 Vinicombe Penrose, *Memoir,* p. 96
24 *Ibid.,* pp. 91-94. The estimate of optimal ship sizes plainly reflects Trevenen's experience with *Resolution* and *Discovery.*
25 Barratt, *Russia in Pacific Waters,* pp.140-41
26 A. P. Sokolov, 'Prigotovlenie krugosvetnoi ekspeditsii 1787 goda pod nachal'stvom Mulovskogo', *ZGDMM,* 6 (StP, 1851), pp. 168-87
27 L. Golenishchev-Kutuzov, *Predpriiatiia Imperatritsy Ekateriny II dlia puteshestviia vokrug sveta v 1786 godu* (StP, 1840,) pp. 12ff,; Cook, *Flood Tide of Empire,* pp. 115-16
28 TsGAVMF,*fond* 172, *delo* 367, pp. 1-13
29 See note 2
30 See Okun', *The Russian-American Company,* pp. 16ff.; Andreev, *Russkie otkrytiia,* pp. 85ff
31 TsGAVMF,*fond* 172, *delo* 367, pp. 320-22
32 Sokolov, 'Prigotovlenie', pp. 173-78
33 PSZRI, vol. XXII: doc. 16530
34 Edict of 28 Oct. 1787
35 See M.S. Anderson, *Britain's Discovery of Russia, 1553-1815* (London, 1958), pp. 17ff; also, by the same writer, 'Great Britain and the Growth of the Russian Navy in the Eighteenth Century', *Mariner's Mirror,* 42 (1956), 1:132-46
36 *OMS,* IV:406-08; also A.G. Cross, *By the Banks of the Thames: Russians in Eighteenth-Century Britain* (Newtonville, Mass., 1980), pp. 159-60
37 TsGADA,*fond* Gosarkhiva, *razriad* X, *op.* 3, *delo* 16, pp. 132-33
38 Okun', *Russian-American Company,* p. 17; Gibson, *Feeding the Russian fur trade,* ch. 8-10
39 See A.G. Cross, *By the Banks of the Thames,* pp. 156-61, and 'Samuel Greig, Catherine the Great's Scottish Admiral', *Mariner's Mirror,* 60 (1974), 3:251-66. R.C. Anderson's list of 'British and American Officers in the Russian Navy', *Mariner's Mirror.,* 33 (1947) is incomplete and flawed, but suggestive in its very length.
40 Okun', *Russian-American Company,* p. 14; Barratt, 'The Russian Navy and New Holland', p. 228
41 See note 8
42 Armstrong, 'Cook's Reputation in Russia', p. 125
43 O. von Kozebue, *A New Voyage Round the World in the Years 1823, 1824, 1825, and 1826* (London, 1830), 2:173; but see also, for earlier criticism of Cook's treatment of certain native peoples, M.I. Ratmanov, 'Vyderzhki iz dnevnika krugosvetnogo puteshestviia na korable "Nadezhda"', *Iakhta* (StP, 1876), nos 16 & 18
44 A.J. von Krusenstern (Kruzenshtern), *Voyage round the World in the Years 1803, 1804, 1805,*

and 1806, trans. R. B. Hoppner (London, 1813), 1:90, 216; 2:203, 222; O. von Kotzebue, *A Voyage to the South Sea and to Beering's Strait...* (London, 1821), 1:6; see also my *Bellingshausen: a visit to New Zealand, 1820* (Palmerston North, NZ, 1979), pp. 1-9, 13

45 Also translations of nautical treatises: see Gennadi, *Spravochnyi slovar'*, 1:232

46 See my paper, 'Russian Verse Translation... A Note on Changing Conventions', *Canadian Contributions to the Seventh World Congress of Slavists* (The Hague, 1973), pp. 41-46

47 *Voyage dans l'hémisphère australe et autour du monde fait..en 1772, 1773, 1774 et 1775... traduit de l'Anglois par M. Suard* (Paris, Hôtel de Thou, 1778)

48 On Golenishchev-Kutuzov's versions of Cook, see V.I. Sopikov, *Opyt rossiiskoi bibliografii*, ed. Rogozhin (StP, 1813: reprinted by Holland House, London, 1961), nos. 9206-08; and Gennadi, *Spravochnyi slovar'*, 1:232-33. For interesting observations on his esteem for Cook, see also M.I. Belov, 'Shestaia chast' sveta otkryta russkimi moriakami', *Izvestiia Vsesoiuznogo Geograficheskogo Obshchestva*, 90 (Leningrad, 1961), pp. 107-08.

49 I.F. Kruzenshtern, *Puteshestvie vokrug sveta v 1803, 4, 5 i 1806 godakh na korabliakh Nadezhda i Neva* (StP, 1809-12), pt 1:12

50 K. Voenskii, 'Russkoe posol'stvo v Iaponiiu v nachale XIX veka', *Russkaia starina*, LXXXV (StP, July, Oct. 1895), and 'Posol'stvo Rezanova v Iaponiiu v 1803-1805 godakh', *Morskoi sbornik* (Leningrad, April 1919), no. 4:29-64. Also V.V. Nevskii, *Pervoe puteshestvie Rossiian vokrug sveta* (Moscow, 1951), pp. 195-211

51 See F.F. Veselago, *Admiral Ivan Fedorovich Kruzenshtern* (StP, 1869), pp. 5ff

52 Further on these contacts, see my study, *Russia in Pacific Waters*, pp. 107-110

53 PRO Adm. 1/498, cap. 370 (Murray to Stephen; 16 Aug 1794)

54 Barratt, *Russia in Pacific Waters*, pp. 109-10

55 On Lisianskii's actions at sea as a Volunteer, Shteinberg, *Zhizneopisanie*, pp. 74-76, 88-90; Urey Lisiansky, *A Voyage round the World, in the Years 1803, 4, 5, & 6: performed... in the ship Neva* (London, 1814), pp. xvii-xviii

56 Kruzenshtern and Penrose were nearly captured by a French ship off Ireland: AGO, *razriad* 119, *delo* 361, 'I.F. Kruzenshtern: O ekspeditsii frantsuzov v Irlandiiu v 1796 godu'

57 Notably Mikhail Baskakov: see Shteinberg, *Zhizneopisanie*, p.63n

58 *Materialy dlia istorii Russkogo flota*, XI (StP, 1886), pp. 40-43; *Arkhiv grafov Mordvinovykh*, 3 (StP, 1903), pp. 337ff

59 Barratt, *Russia in Pacific Waters*, pp. 108-09

60 Quoted by Shteinberg, *Zhizneopisanie*, p. 78

61 Lisianskii's manuscripts of this period are held by TsVMM ('Zhurnal leitenanta Iuriia Lisianskago s 1793 po 1800 god', no. 9170/1938) and TsGIAL ('Zapiski leitenanta Iuriia Fedorovicha Lisianskago, vedennye im vo vremia sluzhby ego volonterom...', *fond* XVIII veka, no. 5196, pp. 1-175).

62 Shteinberg, *Zhizneopisanie*, p. 79

63 *Ibid.*, pp. 99-100; also S. Ryden, *The Banks Collection: an episode in eighteenth-century Anglo-Swedish relations* (Stockholm, 1963), pp. 67-68

64 Shteinberg, *Zhizneopisanie*, p. 63

65 Lisianskii, *Voyage round the World*, p. xviii; J. Ralfe, *Naval Biography* (London, 1828), III:212 ;& IV:98-99; W. James, *Naval history of Great Britain from the Declaration of War by France* (London, 1822-26), I:495

66 PRO Adm. 1/1516, cap. 404 (Boyles to Nepean, 16 March 1797)

67 Martin Sauer, *An account of a Geographical and Astronomical Expedition to the Northern parts of Russia, performed in the Years 1785-1794* (London, 1802), 1287; Peter Dobell, *Travels in Kamtschatka and Siberia* (London, 1830), I:297-98

68 *Vneshniaia politika Rossii XIX i nachala XX veka* (Moscow, 1961-70), 2:297-98; L. Dermigny, *La Chine et l'Occident: le commerce à Canton au XVIIIe siècle* (Paris, 1964), 3:1240-42

69 This was *Caroline* (ex-*Dragon*: Captain Lay): see Howay, *List of Trading Vessels*, 33-35.

70 Kruzenshtern, *Puteshestvie*, 1:13

71 Nevskii, *Pervoe puteshestvie*, pp. 35-37; N.I.Turgenev, *Rossiia i russkie* (Moscow, 1915: 3rd ed.), pp. 90-92
72 Kruzenshtern, *Puteshestvie*, I:17; *Arkhiv grafov Mordvinovykh*, 3:312
73 See Gibson, *Imperial Russia in Frontier America* (NY, 1976), for details of this trade as it developed in the 1790s
74 Nevskii, *Pervoe puteshestvie*, p. 35, for detail
75 *Ibid.*, p. 37; F.I. Shemelin, 'Istoricheskoe izvestie o pervom puteshestvii Rossiian krugom sveta', *Russkii invalid* (StP, 1823), nos 23, 28, 31
76 K. Voenskii, 'Russkoe posol'stvo v Iaponiiu v nachale XIX veka', *Russkaia starina*, 84 (StP, 1895), no. 7:125-28; Shemelin, 'Istoricheskoe izvestie', no. 23
77 Nevskii, *op.cit.*, p. 37
78 Kruzenshtern, *Puteshestvie*, I:2-3; Barratt, *Russia in Pacific Waters*, p. 11
79 On Tilesius, see Nevskii, *Pervoe puteshestvie*, p. 57n
80 S. Novakovskii, *Iaponiia i Rossiia* (Tokyo, 1918), pp. 77ff
81 Voenskii, 'Russkoe posol'stvo', p. 126
82 Notably, V.M. Golovnin: see Barratt, *Russia in Pacific Waters*, p. 197
83 G. Lensen, *The Russian Push toward Japan* (Princeton, 1959), pp. 126-27; M.I. Ratmanov, 'Vyderzhki iz dnevnika krugosvetnogo puteshestviia na korable 'Nadezhda'', *Iakhta*, XXII (StP, 1876), pp. 30ff
84 Nevskii, *Pervoe puteshestvie*, p.54n.; Barratt, *Russia in Pacific Waters*, pp. 114-15
85 This emerges from the Levenshtern journal, part of which is translated here.
86 Novakovskii, *Iaponiia i Rossiia*, pp. 74-77; Lensen, *The Russian Push*, p. 145
87 Kruzenshtern, *Puteshestvie*, I:8
88 *Ibid.*, I:2
89 F.F. Veselago, *Kratkaia istoriia russkogo flota* (Moscow, 1939), pp. 178-90
90 Kruzenshtern, *Puteshestvie*, I:2-3
91 *Ibid.*, I:13
92 TsGIAL, *fond* 15, *op.*1, *delo* 1:fols 5ff
93 *Ibid.*, fols 7-8
94 Komissarov, *Grigorii Ivanovich Langsdorf*, pp. 15-16; Nevskii, *Pervoe puteshestvie Rossiian*, p. 57; also H. Plischke, *Johann Friedrich Blumenbachs Einfluss auf die Entdeckungsreisenden Seiner Zeit* (Göttingen, 1937), pp. 61-64
95 TsGADA, *fond* 183, *delo* 89: 'Ob otpravlenii iz St-Petersburg morem na Vostochnyi okean... Rezanova'. The Pacific writings of other graduates of that Institution, notably Aleksei Rossiiskii's 1814 sketch of New South Wales ('Zhurnal shturmana Alekseia Rossiiskago', published in *SPB*, 1820, no.11:125-46; no. 12:146-56,) give one cause to regret the 1803 exclusions.
96 Komissarov, *Grigorii Ivanovich Langsdorf*, p. 17; Kruzenshtern, *Puteshestvie*, 1:5
97 See T. Armstrong, 'Cook's Reputation in Russia', pp. 121-25
98 Kruzenshtern, trans. Hoppner, *Voyage*, 1:190, 216; 2:203, 222
99 Texts in Beaglehole, *The Journals*, 1:cclxxiii
100 L.G. Rozina, 'Kollektsiia Dzhemsa Kuka v sobraniiakh Muzeia Antropologii i Etnografii', *SMAE*, 23 (1966)
101 See S. Ryden, *The Banks Collection: an episode in 18th-century Anglo-Swedish relations* (Stockholm, 1963):68ff
102 *Protokoly zasedanii konferentsii Akademii Nauk s 1725 po 1803 god* (StP, 1911), 4 (Apr. 13 Old Style)
103 M.V. Severgin, 'Instruktsiia dlia puteshestviia okolo sveta...', *Severnyi vestnik* (StP, 1803), nos 2 & 3. Zoological instructions were written by Academician A.F. Sevastianov.
104 TsGIAL, *fond* 15, *op.* 1, *delo* 1: fol. 159
105 See my *Rebel on the Bridge: the life and times of Baron Andrey Rozen, 1800-1884* (London, 1975), pp. 17-32

106 Details in N.A. Ivashintsev, trans. G. Barratt, *Russian Round-the-World Voyages, 1803-1849* (Kingston, Ont., Limestone Press Materials for the Study of Alaska History, no. 14, 1980), pp. 136-37; also W. Lenz, ed., *Deutsch-Baltisches Biographisches Lexikon, 1710-1960* (Köln-Wien, 1970)

107 Kruzenshtern, *Puteshestvie*, 1:6; TsGIAE, *fond* 1414 (I.F. Kruzenshterna), *op.* 3, *delo* 3 ('Dnevnik flota-leitenanta E.E. Levenshterna...'), 8-10

108 Kruzenshtern, *Puteshestvie*, 1:5; LOAAN, *razriad* IV, *op.* 1, *delo* 800a (Tilesius von Tilenau's appointment); *Vestnik Evropy* (StP, June 1803), pp. 167-71 (contemporary responses to the expedition's aims).

109 'Izvestie o estestvennom i politicheskom sostoianii zhitelei ostrova Nukagiva', *Tekhnologicheskii zhurnal* (StP, 1806), pt 4

110 L.G. Rozina, 'Kollektsiia MAE po Markizskim ostrovam', *SMAE*, 21 (1963):110-19; Iu.F. Lisianskii, *Sobranie kart i risunkov...* (StP, 1812), plate I; Kruzenshtern, *Puteshestvie*, 1:110ff

111 B.N. Komissarov, *Grigorii Ivanovich Langsdorf* (Leningrad, 1975), pp. 8-15

112 Kruzenshtern, *Puteshestvie*, 1:35. Rezanov was similarly impressed: 'Pervoe puteshestvie Rossiian...', *Otechestvennye zapiski*, 12 (1822), no. 31:211

113 Plischke, *Johann Friedrich Blumenbachs Einfluss*, ch. 1; Komissarov, *op.cit.*, p. 19 (Banks's gift to Langsdorf, etc.)

114 TsGIAE, *fond* 1414, *op.* 3, *delo* 3; A.S. Sgibnev, 'Rezanov i Kruzenshtern', *Drevniaia i novaia Rossiia*, 1 (1877), no. 4; *Voenskii*, 'Russkoe posol'stvo', July 1895, pp. 126ff; Oct. 1895, pp. 211ff

115 Lisianskii, *Puteshestvie*, 1:91-93

116 See pp. 117, 127, 133

117 TsGIAL, *fond* 853, *op.* 1, *delo* 74: 'Zhurnal prikazov kapitana' (Apr. 1804)

118 F.I. Shemelin, *Zhurnal pervogo puteshestviia Rossiian vokrug zemnago shara* (StP, 1816), pt 1:121-22; A.I. Andreev, trans. K. Ginsburg, *Russian Discoveries in the Pacific Ocean and in North America...* (Ann Arbor, 1952), pp. 213-14 (notes by N. I. Korobitsyn)

119 Bibliographies in Nevskii, *Pervoe puteshestvie Rossiian*, pp. 267-71, and L.F. Rudovits, 'Pervoe russkoe krugosvetnoe plavanie, 1803-06; obzor nauchnykh rabot', *Trudy Gos.Okeanograficheskogo Instituta*, 27 (Leningrad, 1954), pp. 3-12; also note 109 above

120 See Tumarkin, 'A Russian View', pp. 128-29

121 See note 110

122 See note 113

123 Lisianskii, *Puteshestvie*, 1:128ff.; Shemelin, *Zhurnal*, pp. 129ff

124 Kruzenshtern, *Puteshestvie*, 1:233-34

125 Nevskii, *Pervoe puteshestvie Rossiian*, pp. 151-54 & notes

126 Kruzenshtern, *Puteshestvie*, 1:231

127 Further on this, see Part 4, 'The Collecting of Hawaiian Artifacts'.

Part 2

1 compare with p. 55
2 compare with pp. 55, 78
3 see Beaglehole, ed. , *The Journals*, III, pt 2: 1175, fig. 1
4 see Vancouver's *Voyage*, III:23
5 Lisianskii echoes Vancouver: see *Voyage*, II:130-31 ("stunned by the clamour and intolerable noise")
6 see Beaglehole, III, pt 1:607
7 *ibid*, III, pt 1:561-2; pt 2:1204
8 precisely where Cook and Vancouver had both seen mock battles: *ibid.*, pt 2:1174
9 *Britannia*: Vancouver, *Voyage*, III:18, 51-2
10 see Beaglehole, III, pt 2:1174
11 see Kamakau, *The Works*, p 146, note 9; Malo, *Hawaiian Antiquities*, ch. 37, sect. 70
12 see Malo, *Hawaiian Antiquities*, ch. 37, sect. 71
13 compare Beaglehole, III, pt 1:607
14 compare Beaglehole, III, pt 2:1176-77
15 see L.G. Rozina, 'Kollektsiia Dzhemsa Kuka v sobraniiakh Muzeia Antropologii i Etnografii', *SMAE*, 23 (1966):234-35,246-47
16 see Buck, *Arts and Crafts*, 1:53-54
17 contrast Cook's experiences: Beaglehole, III, pt 1:269n, 272n, 483, 501, 549 (honesty); pt 1:502, 515, 530-32 (thieving)
18 see Samwell's observations in Beaglehole, III, pt 2:1236-31
19 *ibid.*, pt 1:274-278
20 compare Samwell's *Eiree*: Beaglehole, III, pt 2:1160
21 Malo, *Hawaiian Antiquities*, ch. 28, sect. 85
22 Malo, *Hawaiian Antiquities*, ch. 12, note 5; ch. 36, note 1
23 Malo, *Hawaiian Antiquities*, ch. 36, sects 59-63 on this
24 pertinent comments by Malo, *Hawaiian Antiquities*, ch. 37, sects 36 & 72; Buck, *Arts and Crafts*, XI:527
25 Kamakau, *The Works*, p. 1430; Buck, *Arts and Crafts*, XI:518, 524
26 Buck, *op.cit.*, XI:495, 517
27 Kamakau, *op.cit.*, p. 136
28 Malo, *Hawaiian Antiquities*, ch. 36, sect. 118
29 see Ellis (1830), pp. 359-61; also Malo, *Hawaiian Antiquities*, ch. 27
30 see Buck, XIII:571 on the traditional raised pavement above an earth burial site
31 compare with pp. 133, 143, 152 below; also Buck, XIII:565
32 see Cook (1784), III:134
33 see Beaglehole, III, pt 1:503 & 620
34 *ibid.*, pt 1:264, 474, 497; pt.2:1151, 1154
35 details in Buck, *Arts and Crafts*, V:186-88
36 For a European summary of these military events, see Dibble, *History of the Sandwich Islands*, ch. 2.
37 Lisianskii's account broadly follows Vancouver's.
38 Vancouver, *Voyage*, III:52-53
39 Kruzenshtern, *Puteshestvie*, III:295
40 Beaglehole, III, pt 2:1177-78
41 Kamakau, *The Works*, p. 136
42 *ibid.*, pp. 129-30

43 For example, in no. 5 for 1802, p. 146
44 Bishop Museum has several such bowls: 4144, 9069, 9635 show teeth inlaid and cut flush. Kotzebue, *Voyage of Discovery* (1821), 1:313 saw a 'royal spittoon' which was also, in reality, an *ipu 'aina*.
45 These names reflect Captain Cook's usage: Atoui, Orrehua, Otaoora; see Beaglehole, III, pt 1:274-75.
46 compare this section with pp. 120, 148 here
47 Gabriel Franchere saw the next stage of this development: *Narrative of a Voyage* (1854), pp.67-68.
48 Malo, *Hawaiian Antiquities*, ch. 38 sects 9-10 illuminates this anecdote by reference to the role played by *kâhuna* in such affairs.
49 see note p. 41
50 on this see Beaglehole, III, pt 1:cvx, pt 2:1162-63. etc.
51 Kamakau, *The Works*, p. 130 confirms this assertion.
52 see note on p. 44
53 see p. 108
54 compare pp. 45, 96
55 but see Bernice Judd, *Voyages to Hawaii before 1860* (Honolulu, 1929) and Bradley, *The American Frontier*, p. 25
56 see note p. 48
57 on this fact, see Bradley, *The American Frontier*, pp. 27-28
58 details in Vancouver, *Voyage* (1798), 2:140
59 compare p. 113
60 R.J. Cleveland, *Voyages and Commercial Enterprises* (Boston, 1850), pp. 204-05, 210
61 see notes on p. 53
62 Lisiansky, *Voyage*, p. 251
63 Lisianskii, *Sobranie kart i risunkov...*
64 *op. cit.*, facing p. 256
65 Beaglehole, III, pt 1:283
66 compare with Lt King's description: *ibid.*, III, pt 1:598
67 see note p. 152; also Malo, *Hawaiian Antiquities*, ch. 16, sect. 14-15
68 Beaglehole, III, pt 2:1169; also pt 1:508 ("a small and dirty pond...")
69 for discussion of these names, see Part 3, 'Following Cook up to Hikiau Heiau'
70 see G. Dening, *The Marquesan Journal of Edward Roberts, 1797-1824* (Canberra, 1974), pp. 7-9
71 see Beaglehole, III, pt 1:605
72 see Kruzenshtern, *Puteshestvie* (1809), pt I, ch. XI:232
73 see Beaglehole, III, pt 1:263-64
74 see Beaglehole, III, pt 1: 503, 620n
75 Beaglehole, III, pt 1:264n
76 Beaglehole, III, pt 2:231-35
77 Beaglehole, III, pt 1:485-87
78 compare Beaglehole, III, pt 1:486 (Cook buying some hogs of over 60 lbs)--2 1/2 *pood* = 90lbs
79 see Lisianskii, *Puteshestvie*, 1949 ed., p. 113
80 Lisiansky, *Voyage*, (1814) p. 100-02
81 *ibid.*, pp. 108-09, 125
82 J. Meares, *Voyages made in the Years 1788, 1789, from China to the North West Coast of America* (London, 1790), p.7 (Kaiana and iron)
83 compare pp. 83, 87 on this (probable) prostitution
84 see note p. 39
85 see note p. 39

86 Beaglehole, III, pt 1:598, note 4
87 see Buck, *Arts and Crafts*, XII:545)
88 see Beaglehole, III, pt 2:1180 and Cook (1784), III:134
89 compare with Beaglehole, III, pt 1:499
90 *ibid.*, pt 1:629
91 compare Beaglehole, III, pt 1:629; pt 2:1171
92 see Buck, *Arts and Crafts*, 1:24
93 compare Beaglehole, III, pt 1:599; pt 2:1180
94 see Malo, *Hawaiian Antiquities*, ch. 22, sect. 9
95 Malo, *Hawaiian Antiquities*, ch. 36, sect. 16, suggests otherwise
96 see *ibid.*, ch. 38, sect. 74; also Dibble, *History of the Sandwich Islands* (Honolulu, 1909), p. 74 (forced labor)
97 see Kuykendall, *The Hawaiian Kingdom, 1778-1854* (Honolulu, 1938), 336
98 see Kamakau, *The Works*, p. 124, note 17
99 details in F.W. Howay, ed., *The Voyage of the New Hazard...* by Stephen Reynolds, (Salem, 1938), pp. 108-14
100 see pp. 113, 116
101 Berkh bases his comments on the 1789 (London) edition of George Dixon, *A Voyage Round the World... in 1785, 1786, 1787 and 1788...*
102 Berkh's source here, apart from Meares, *Voyages from China*, Appendix V and Turnbull, *Voyage Round the World*, II:79, was Kotzebue, whose reports and letters of December 1816 had just reached the Admiralty.
103 see Beaglehole, III, pt 1:266n, 498, 576
104 see p. 59
105 see p. 69; data in Buck, *Arts and Crafts*, VII:290
106 details in Bradley, *American Frontier*, pp. 30, 55-56
107 Langsdorf's remarks are echoed by Samuel Hill: see J.W. Snyder, ed., 'Voyage of the *Ophelia*', *New England Quarterly*, X (June 1947), p. 365
108 see Bradley, *op.cit.*, pp. 26-28, on true and false sandalwood

Part 3

1 Krusenstern, *Voyage*, 1:188-90; Lisyansky, *Voyage*, pp. 96-98
2 Beaglehole (ed.), *Journals of Captain Cook*, III, pt I:486
3 See map p. xviii
4 John Turnbull, *A Voyage Round the World, in the Years 1800, 1801, 1802, 1803, and 1804* (London, 1805); *Narrative of the Adventures and Sufferings of Samuel Patterson* (Palmer, Mass., 1817); pp. 12ff. and 65ff., respectively, for passages complementing the Russian texts
5 Krusenstern, *Voyage*, 1:119; Lisyansky, *Voyage*, p.75
6 Details in Pierce, *Russia's Hawaiian Adventure*, pp. 37-40
7 See Langsdorff, *Voyages and Travels*, pp. 187-88; also my *Russia in Pacific Waters*, ch. 7, and Bradley, *The American Frontier*, p. 47 and notes
8 Turnbull, *Voyage*, II:78-82; Langsdorff, *Voyages and Travels*, p. 187
9 Tikhmenev, *Istoricheskoe obozrenie*, II:280 (letter of N.P. Rezanov to Count Rumiantsev, 17 June 1806)
10 Gedeon, 'Donesenie', p. 38; Ratmanov, 'Zapiski', *Iakhta* (StP, 1876), No. 24:1332
11 See Malo, *Hawaiian Antiquities*, ch. 18, sects 47-51
12 10'6"x14"
13 See Brigham, W.T., *Ka Hana Kapa--The Making of Barkcloth in Hawaii* (Honolulu, BPBM Memoir No. 3, 1911), p. 138-48
14 See Iu.M. Likhtenberg, 'Gavaiskie kollektsii v sobraniiakh Muzeia antropologii i etnografii',*SMAE*, XIX (Leningrad, 1960), pp. 184-86; also Buck, *Arts and Crafts*, V:170-74, 191-202
15 Gedeon,'Donesenie', p. 37
16 *Ibid.*, p. 38
17 Rezanov, 'Pervoe puteshestvie', p. 250
18 See Buck, *Arts and Crafts of Hawaii*, XII:546-47
19 See Malo, *Hawaiian Antiquities*, ch. 22, sect. 5
20 See Vancouver, *Voyage*, III:16
21 Cook, *A Voyage to the Pacific Ocean*, 1784, III:134
22 Buck, *Arts and Crafts of Hawaii*, XII:535
23 Lisianskii, *Sobranie kart i risunkov* (StP, 1812), Plate II, K
24 See Buck, *Arts and Crafts of Hawaii*, XII:542-3
24 Beaglehole, ed., *Journals of Captain Cook*, I:521; II:1166
25 L. Soehren & T. Snell Newman, *Archaeology of Kealakekua Bay* (Honolulu, Special Report by the Departments of Anthropology, Bernice P. Bishop Museum and University of Hawai'i, 1968), pp. 3-6
26 Cook and King, *A Voyage to the Pacific Ocean*, II:244; among others similarly impressed were William Broughton, *A Voyage of Discovery to the North Pacific Ocean* (London, 1804), p. 37, and William Shaler, 'Journal of a Voyage between China and the North-Western Coast of America', *American Register*, III (1808), p. 166
27 See *The Diary of Andrew Bloxam* (Honolulu, BPBM Spec. Pub. No. 10, 1925), p. 72
28 See Beaglehole, ed., *Journals of Captain Cook*, II:1167. Behind Ka'awaloa itself, one thinks, there were no terraces [*lo'i*].
29 Malo, *Hawaiian Antiquities*, pp. 58, 142-43; Ellis, *Narrative of a Tour through Hawaii*, pp. 404-05; S. Dibble, *History of the Sandwich Islands* (Honolulu, 1909), pp. 74-75; Bradley, *The American Frontier*, pp. 5-6
30 As the Russians rightly supposed, Hawai'i's population had fallen appreciably since the 1770s. On cultivation of *kula* land, see Malo, *Hawaiian Antiquities*, ch. 39.

31 See note 6
32 'A Russian View of Hawaii in 1804', *Pacific Studies*, II (Honolulu, 1979), no. 2:1122, & note 17
33 See Part 2, above
34 Malo, *Hawaiian Antiquities*, ch. 14, sec. 4; ch. 39, sec. 14
35 This had been the case for many years: see Cook and King, *Voyage to the Pacific Ocean*, III:116; Malo, *Hawaiian Antiquities*, ch. 39, sect. 12.
36 Beaglehole, ed., *Journals of Captain Cook*, II:1166
37 Buck, *Arts and Crafts*, I:10
38 Had there been streams close by, the Russians and other *haole* would not have required Hawaiian assistance with watering; and the absence of streams at Ka'awaloa in turn precluded the making of irrigation terraces [*lo'i*] there.
39 Details on this subject in E.S. Craighill Handy, *The Hawaiian Planter: Volume 1* (Honolulu, BPBM Bull., No. 161, 1940), pp. 25ff
40 H.L. Baker, T. Sahara, *et al.*, *Detailed Land Classification: Island of Hawaii* (Honolulu, University of Hawai'i Land Study Bureau Bulletin No. 6, 1965),p. 33
41 Beaglehole, ed., *Journals of Captain Cook*, I:521
42 Bradley, *The American Frontier*, pp. 4-5; also Malo, *Hawaiian Antiquities*, index under *konohiki*
43 Soehren & Newman, *Archaeology of Kealakekua Bay*, p. 10
44 Langsdorf echoed Peter Puget: see PRO, Adm. 1: 'A Log of the Proceedings of His Majesty's Armed Tender *Chatham*', 2 February 1793
45 See note 16
46 Malo, *Hawaiian Antiquities*, ch. 39, sect. 15
47 Malo, *Hawaiian Antiquities*, ch. 22, sect. 9
48 Bradley, *The American Frontier*, p. 55
49 See Buck, *Arts and Crafts of Hawaii*, I:10
50 See Vancouver,*Voyage*, II; Tumarkin, 'Russian View', p. 112
51 Vancouver, *Voyage*, II
52 Malo, *Hawaiian Antiquities*, ch. 22, sect. 17; see also Buck, *Arts and Crafts*, 1:4
53 See note 16; also Handy, *The Hawaiian Planter*, pp. 183-4, and Buck, *op.cit.*, pp. 8-9
54 *Niles' Register*, 50 (27 Aug. 1836), p. 440; *The Polynesian* (12 Sept. 1840)
55 Wise, 'Food and its Preparation' in Handy (ed.), *Ancient Hawaiian Civilization* (1933), p. 93
56 Buck, *Arts and Crafts of Hawaii*, 1:19
57 Cook, *Voyage*, 1794, III:27
58 *Niles Register*,50 (27 Aug. 1836), p. 440; *The Polynesian*, 12 Sept. 1840
59 Vancouver, *Voyage*, III:53 (24 Feb. 1794)
60 Berkh, however, suggests that the cow was quite tame
61 Buck, *Arts and Crafts*, 7:227ff; Fornander, 'Hawaiian Antiquities and Folk-Lore', *BPBM Memoir*, vol. 5 (1919):630ff; Malo, *Hawaiian Antiquities*, ch. 34
62 Kamakau, *The Works*, p. 75; also, on bonito hooks, see Buck, *op.cit.*, 7:333
63 See Malo, *Hawaiian Antiquities*, ch. 4, sect. 23; ch. 36, sect. 75
64 *Ibid.*, ch. 40, sect. 9
65 *Ibid.*, ch. 9, sect. 16; ch. 22, sect. 9; Kamakau, *The Works*, p. 76; Buck, *Arts and Crafts*, 7:290
66 Kamakau, *The Works*, pp. 60, 75; also Buck, *op.cit.*, 7:311-12
67 See Vancouver, *Voyage*, III:61 (the chiefs' meat-tasting session)
68 Cook, *Voyage*, III:151
69 Ellis, *Polynesian Researches*, IV:397-98
70 Bradley, *The American Frontier*, p. 78; Malo, *Hawaiian Antiquities*, ch. 33, sect. 25
71 Malo, *Hawaiian Antiquities*, ch. 12, sect. 6
72 Buck, *Arts and Crafts*, 1:20
73 'Journal', *American Register*, 3 (1808):169; also Kotzebue, *Voyage of Discovery into the*

South Sea and Beering's Straits (London, 1821), 3: 246

74 Tumarkin, 'A Russian View', p. 128; Dibble, *History*, p. 74
75 See Part 2, 'Reporters and Textual Sources', on Shemelin's sources
76 See note 52
77 Including Ratmanov's 'Zapiski' (No. 24, p. 1333) and Romberkh's 'Pis'mo' (p. 37); particulars of both in Part 2 above
78 I discuss this in *Russia in Pacific Waters*, pp. 120-21 & notes.
79 Beaglehole, ed., *Journals*, III, pt 1:576 (3 March 1779)
80 *Ibid.*, pt 1:500 (1 Dec. 1778)
81 *Ibid.*, pt 1:499 & 504
82 *Ibid.*, pt 1:512 note; also 612, 629
83 Malo, *Hawaiian Antiquities*, ch. 14, sect. 16-17, note 7
84 Kamakau, *The Works*, p. 43; M. Titcomb, 'Kava in Hawaii', *JPS*, 57 (1948), pt 2:145ff
85 In 1809, if Gagemeister was Shemelin's informant, as is likely. It seems, however, that by then Kamehameha had four-year-old *'ōkolehao.*
86 Cited in *The Russian Orthodox Mission in America, 1794-1837, with Materials Concerning the Life and Works of the monk German, and Ethnographic Notes by the Hieromonk Gedeon*, trans. C. Bearne (Kingston, Ont., 1978), p. 151
87 Further on Kruzenshtern's and Lisianskii's sets of instructions of July-August 1803, see K. Voenskii, 'Russkoe posol'stvo v Iaponiiu v nachale XIX veka', *Russkaia starina* (StP, July 1895), pp. 124ff.; and Nevskii, *Pervoe puteshestvie*, p. 37
88 Malo, *Hawaiian Antiquities*, ch. 36, sect. 7
89 *Ibid.*, ch. 12, sect. 20 and notes by Emerson; Kamakau, *The Works*, p. 17
90 *Hawaiian Antiquities*, ch. 12, sect. 7 and notes; Kamakau, *op.cit.*, p. 16. Lisianskii writes of "Caona" correctly.
91 *Hawaiian Antiquities*, ch. 12, sect. 23; Kamakau, *op.cit.*, p. 18
92 Confirmation of the coincidence of *Neva*'s arrival at the end of *kapu Hua* lies in the fact that the Russians witnessed no other universal *kapu*, so to speak, though they remained six days. Nine days separated *kapu Hua* and *kapu Kanaloa* on Hawai'i, only two days separated *Kanaloa* and *Kâne* (Lisianskii's Ocané).
93 Presumably during *kapu Hua*, as a regular offering [*môhai*] to Kû
94 Beaglehole, ed., *Journals*, III, pt 1:508
95 Both are conveniently reproduced in Buck, *Arts and Crafts*, XI 488, 517.
96 *E.g.*, at the *kāli'i* [royal catching of spears] ceremony on the *makahiki* god's return from his circuit of the island (*Hawaiian Antiquities*, ch. 36,) which the Russians found intriguing. Tumarkin, in his paper 'A Russian View of Hawaii' (p. 119) asserts that by 1804 "taboos were primarily a tool of oppression by the nobility of the commoners." He does not substantiate the statement, but gives useful references to comments on the subject by Gedeon and A. Chamisso, who visited O'ahu with Kotzebue in 1816.
97 Beaglehole, ed., *Journals*, III, pt 1:607
98 *ibid.*, pt 2:1175. Vancouver's reference to "the two principal villages of Kakooa [Kealakekua] and Kowrowa [Ka'awaloa]" underlines the relative insignificance of Waipunaula and Samwell's other "Indian Towns" (Vancouver, *Voyage*, III:38). The Russian texts point to the continuing decline of Waipunaula and Kalama.
99 Beaglehole, ed., *Journals*, III, pt 1:539-40
100 *Ibid.*, pt 1:508
101 The chief was evidently a *konokihi*, and entrusted by Kamehameha I with the management of the royal estate at Kealakekua (see *Hawaiian Antiquities*, ch. 18, sect. 40,and Kamakau, *The Works*, p. 151), but not of the noblest descent.
102 Beaglehole, ed., *Journals*, III, pt 2:1172-74; Vancouver, *Voyage*, II:151-554 (the sham battle of 4 March 1793)
103 Vancouver, *Voyage*, III, 28 & 51-52. As Lisianskii learned, some ten other schooners had

been built locally since 1794 on the model of *Britannia*. "The very large shed or barn-like buildings" seen by the Russians at Kealakekua almost certainly resembled that seen by the English, four miles north, in 1793 (*ibid.*, II:164).

104 Beaglehole, ed., *Journals*, III, pt 2:1169

105 Malo, *Hawaiian Antiquities*, ch. 34, sect. 2, note

106 *Ibid.*, ch. 11

107 *The Works*, p. 132

108 Beaglehole, ed., *Journals*, III, pt 2:1178

109 See Kamakau, *The Works*, pp. 136-38,on *haku 'ōhi'a* rites

110 Malo, *Hawaiian Antiquities*, ch. 9, sect. 3

111 *ibid.*, ch. 37, sect. 4

112 Beaglehole, ed., *Journals*, III, pt 2:1159

113 Malo, *Hawaiian Antiquities*, ch. 34, sect. 7

114 See *ibid.*, ch. 23, sect. 8

115 Kamakau,*The Works*, p. 119. See also note 3 to Beaglehole, ed., *Journals*,III, pt 2:1159, where the links between Kū, *Metrosideros macropus*, and the Polynesian demigod Rata or Laka, as clarified to Emerson by S. Percy Smith in 1897 (Malo, *Hawaiian Antiquities*, ch. 23, sect. 8, note 5), are restated.

116 Beaglehole,ed., *Journals*, III, pt 2:1177

117 And so thrust easily into the ground

118 Beaglehole, ed., *Journals*, III, pt 1:508

119 *Ibid.*, pt 2:1177. Korobitsyn saw no sacrificial skulls [*po'o kea*] at Hikiau, but was told that they were impaled "side by side, as on a prison stockade". The subject had grisly fascination for *haole*.

120 Beaglehole, ed., *Journals*, III, pt 1:516

121 *Ibid.*, note 3; also pt 2:1174

122 *Ibid.*, pt 2:1177

123 Buck, *Arts and Crafts*, XI:494-95. The images with "mouths extended beyond the ears" (Lisianskii) were carved in traditional *'ōle'ōle* style (see Kamakau, *The Works*, p. 136).

124 Regrettably, the Russians were unaware of the differences between *kāhuna* of the orders of Kū and of Lono [*mo'o Lono*] and do not assist in the task of establishing to which the "chief priest" belonged. Circumstantial evidence suggests the order of Lono, despite the 15 images of Kū or Kū-variants.

125 Wendell C. Bennett, *Archaeology of Kauai* (Honolulu, BPBM Bull. no. 80, 1931),p. 44

126 See Malo, *Hawaiian Antiquities*, ch. 37, sect. 36, 72; Buck, *Arts and Crafts*, p. 527

127 Malo, *Hawaiian Antiquities*, ch. 37, sect. 72, note 34

128 *Ibid.*, ch. 28

129 Details in John F. Stokes, *Burial of King Keawe*, Hawaiian Historical Society Paper No. 17 (Honolulu, 1930), pp. 63-73

130 See G. Dening, 'Ethnohistory in Polynesia: the value of ethnohistorical evidence', *Journal of Pacific History*, 1 (1966):23-42

131 The boy was presumably named after George III and John Kendrick, whom other Russians refer to as Kernick and who visited the Islands three years before Puget and Vancouver, then again in October 1791

132 Archibald Campbell, *A Voyage Round the World, from 1806 to 1812* (Edinburgh, 1816),pp. 165-66

133 On the likelihood of this, see Bradley, *The American Frontier*, pp. 33-34.

134 Pele-lua(?)

135 Vancouver, *Voyage*, III:65-66; (Shaler), 'Journal', *American Register*, 3 (1808):162

136 But see Part 3, 'Hawaiian-*Haole* Relations'

137 Gedeon, 'Donesenie',p. 37

138 *Alert* was on the Northwest in 1802 and 1803; *O'Cain* moved several times between the Is-

lands and Novo-Arkhangel'sk in 1802-06: see Howay, *List of Trading Vessels*, pp. 48, 55-57, 70, and Rezanov's 1806 text.

139 V. M. Golovnin, *Puteshestvie vokrug sveta... v 1817-19 godakh* (StP, 1822), I:333, 343-44; Tumarkin, 'A Russian View of Hawaii', p. 124, note 92

140 See Malo, *Hawaiian Antiquities*, ch. 34, sects. 32-33; ch. 40, sects 16, 22

141 Compare Beaglehole, *Journals,* III pt 1:503, 620. The population of Kealakekua Bay had seemingly decreased greatly, in Kamehameha's absence from it.

142 Turnbull, *Voyage Round the World,* II:71; Choris, *Voyage pittoresque autour du monde* (Paris, 1822), 'Iles Sandwich', p. 15

143 This development, according to Langsdorf, occurred in 1806. N.P. Rezanov confirms the date. See, however, Turnbull, *op.cit.,* II:78.

144 F.W.Howay, ed., *The Journal of Captain James Colnett aboard the Argonaut from April 26, 1789 to November 3, 1791* (Toronto, 1940), p. 282; G. Franchère, *Narrative of a Voyage to the North West Coast of America* (NY, 1854), p. 85

145 Details in Tumarkin, 'A Russian View of Hawaii', p. 130

146 See my study, *Russia in Pacific Waters, 1715-1825* (Vancouver, 1981), pp. 130ff.; Howay, *List of Trading Vessels*, pp. 55, 64-65,70

147 See Part 5, 'Reporters and Textual Sources'

148 A high State functionary with naval connections and interests

149 *H.H.S. Twenty-Fifth Annual Report* (Honolulu, 1917), pp. 58-61

150 Archibald Campbell had the same impression: *op.cit.*, pp. 162-63

151 See H. T. Cheever, *The Island World of the Pacific* (NY, 1855), pp. 162-63; and E.S. Craighill Handy, *Cultural Revolution in Hawaii* (Honolulu, 1931), pp. 27-33

152 Beaglehole, ed., *Journals,* III, pt 2:1176

153 *Ibid.*, pt 1:266, 474-75; Ratmanov, 'Zapiski', No. 24:1333; F.I. Romberkh, 'Pis'mo', p. 37; also Korobitsyn and Shemelin texts here

154 See Tumarkin, 'A Russian View of Hawaii', pp. 129-30

155 Gedeon, 'Donesenie', p. 37

156 O. E. Kotzebue, *Puteshestvie v Iuzhnyi okean i v Beringov proliv v 1815-18 godakh* (StP, 1821-23), I:38-39; also V.M. Golovnin, *Puteshestvie vokrug sveta... v 1817-19 godakh* (StP, 1822), I:324, 334, 349-50

157 Berkh, 'Nechto o Sandvichevykh ostrovakh', p. 160; Korobitsyn, 'Zapiski', *Russkie otkrytiia v Tikhom okeane* (1944), p. 175

158 Further on this, John P. 'I'ī, *Fragments of Hawaiian History* (Honolulu, 1959), pp. 79ff

159 See Part 4, 'Comments on Lisianskii's Plates' (discussion of item 'E')

160 Buck, *Arts and Crafts,* X:418-421

Part 4

1   Barratt, *Russia in Pacific Waters*, p. 113
2   Cited by Nevskii, *Pervoe puteshestvie Rossiian*, p. 37
3   On this aspect of Cook's influence in Russia, see my study, *The Russians at Port Jackson, 1814-1822 (Canberra, 1981)*, pp. 5-6.
4   TsGALI, *fond* XVIII veka, *delo* 5196, pp. 40-41, 86-7
5   *Ibid.*, pp. 129-30; also 'Iurii Fedorovich Lisianskii', *Morskoi sbornik* (StP, 1894), No. 1 (Neofitsial'nyi otdel), p. 20
6   E.L. Shteinberg, *Zhizneopisanie russkogo moreplavatelia Iuriia Lisianskogo* (Moscow, 1948), p. 209
7   L.G. Rozina, 'Kollektsiia MAE po Markizskim ostrovam,, *SMAE*, XXI: 110
8   Korobitsyn, 'Zapiski', *Russkie otkrytiia v Tikhom okeane i Severnoi Amerike v XVIII-XIX vv.*, ed. A.I. Andreev (Moscow-Leningrad 1944), p. 168 & note 1
9   Shteinberg, *op.cit.*, p. 160
10 *Ibid.*, p. 166
11 As the lower deck indulged, barter for artifacts was certainly extensive.
12 Barratt, *Bellingshausen: a visit to New Zealand, 1820* (Palmerston North, Dunmore Press, 1979), pt 3
13 Nevskii, *Pervoe puteshestvie Rossiian*, p. 247
14 LOAAN, *fond* 2, *op.*1 (1827), No. 3:13
15 *Ibid.,fond* 1, *op.* 2 (1807), No. 20:1-2
16 LOAAN, *fond* 142, *op.* 1 (1719-1827), No. 108. For a basic list of 'Russian Voyages in the Pacific, 19th Century, *Russian Writings on the South Pacific* (Honolulu, University of Hawai'i Pacific Islands Program, 1974), p. 7; see also my work, *The Russians at Port Jackson*, pp. 82-3.
17 F. Russov, 'Beiträge zur Geschichte der etnographischen und antropologischen Sammlungen der Kaiserlichen Akademie der Wissenschaften zu St Petersburg," *SMAE*, 1 (StP, 1900); Staniukovich, *Etnograficheskaia Nauka*, p. 62
18 Described without specific attribution by Iu.M. Likhtenberg, in 'Gavaiskie kollektsii v sobraniiakh Muzeia Antropologii i Etnografii', *SMAE*, XIX:168-205
19 See comments in Part 4, 'The 1804 Hawaiian Artifacts'. Among the Hawaiian artifacts in Collection No. 736, and therefore taken to Russia *before 1828*, there are a stone axe and hammer (202-03), two bone fish hooks (220-21), five fans (208-09, 294a & b, 229), eight spears (210-17), a gourd whistle (219), and a beautiful *kahili* (207).
20 Krusenstern, *Voyage*, p. 5; Nevskii, *Pervoe puteshestvie Rossiian*, p. 56
21 Shteinberg, *Zhizneopisanie*, p. 203
22 'Russkaia morskaia biblioteka, period chervertyi', *ZGDMM*, VIII (1850), pp. 444-45
23 Plates U-V
24 Likhtenberg, 'Gavaiskie kollektsii', pp. 168-69
25 See note 16
26 Page 37 above
27 Description in Likhtenberg, *op.cit.*, p. 203
28 It is 259cm long, 2.9cm in diameter, the haft being quadrangular, the hardwood point toothed 16cm from the end, and the whole very heavy to feel.

Part 5

1 TsVMM, No. 9170-3 (1938), fols.1-93: 'Zhurnal flota kapitan-leitenanta Iuriia Lisianskago...
c 1802 po 1803 god: S-Petersburg', No. 9170-8 (1938); 'Zhurnal korablia "Neva" 1803-
1806 godov'; TsGIAL, *fond* 15, *op.* 1, *delo* 1: 'Instruktsiia Glavnago Pravleniia Rossiisko-
Amerikanskoi Kompanii Gospodinu flota kapitan-leitenantu Kruzenshternu, 29 maia 1803 g'

2 ZGDMM, pt 8 (StP, 1850), p. 444. This material was reprinted and well introduced by A.P.
Sokolov in a second edition of *Russkaia Morskaia Biblioteka: period chetvertyi* (StP, 1883),
pp. 137-38.

3 *Arkhiv kniazia Vorontsova* (Moscow, 1870-95), 19:114-15 (hostile letter by Vice Admiral P.V.
Chichagov (1767-1849) to A. R. Vorontsov

4 TsVMM, No. 9170-22zh (1938): 'Ukaz ob otstavke Iu.F. Lisianskago'; *Obschchii morskoi
spisok* (StP, 1885-1907), 4: 'Lisianskii, Iu.F'

5 Details in ZGDMM, pt 8:444-45

6 See the anonymous biographical article, 'Iu.F. Lisianskii' in *Morskoi sbornik* (StP, 1894), no. 1,
on the appointment as commander of the imperial yacht squadron, etc.

7 TsVMM, No. 9170-3 (1938), pt 2: 'Zhurnal...Iuriia Lisianskago s 1813 po 1814 god' (185 pp)

8 E.L. Shteinberg, *Zhizneopisanie russkogo moreplavatelia Iuriia Lisianskogo* (Moscow, 1948),
pp. 64-114, on Lisianskii's 'British period' and foreign contacts

9 V.G. Belinskii, 'Vzgliad na russkuiu literaturu 1847 goda', in *Sob. sochinenii v 3 tomakh* (Moscow, 1948), p. 112; also my *Russia in Pacific Waters*, ch. 7, on British awareness of Russian
progress in the Arctic and Pacific in the post-Napoleonic years

10 *ZGDMM*,, pt 8:444

11 TsGIAL, *fond 15, op.* 1, *delo* 1 (1802): 'O naznachenii pervoi krugo-svetnoi ekspeditsii..', and
related papers. Korobitsyn was formally attached to N.P. Rezanov's suite, and obliged to
report to him, and Company Main Office, not to the Naval Ministry.

12 As part of a *de facto* 'K.T.Khlebnikov and North Pacific trade' collection which includes *dela*
109-43

13 'A Short Extract' is now in TsGIAL, *fond* 15, *op.* 1, *delo* 1; pt 2:48-57

14 Andreev, *Russkie otkrytiia*, introduction, xii. Nevskii, in his *Pervoe puteshestvie Rossiian*, pp.
87-88, note 3, makes pointed criticisms of Andreev's editing of the Korobitsyn manuscripts.

15 Details in Nevskii, *op.cit.*, pp. 247-48. See also L.F. Rudovits, 'Pervoe russkoe krugosvetnoe
plavanie, 1803-1806: obzor nauchnykh rabot', *Trudy Gosudarstvennogo Okeanograficheskogo Instituta* (Leningrad, 1954), no. 27:3-12

16 K. Voenskii, 'Russkoe posol'stvo v Iaponiiu v nachale XIX veka', *Russkaia starina* (StP, July,
Oct.,1895), and 'Posol'stvo Rezanova v Iaponiiu v 1803-05 godakh na sudakh...
Kruzenshterna', *Morskoi sbornik*, Moscow, April 1919, no. 4: 29-64

17 Langsdorff, *Bemerkungen auf einer Reise*, 1:166; 2:83; Howay, *List of Trading Vessels*,
pp. 55,64-65, 70

18 See J.R. Gibson, *Imperial Russia in Frontier America* (NY, 1970), *passim*

19 Voenskii, 'Russkoe posol'stvo', pp. 212-13 (Oct., 1895)

20 Pierce, *Russia's Hawaiian Adventure*, pp. 37-40

21 Details in Polansky, *Russian Writings on the South Pacific*, pp. 18-19

22 'Opisanie uzorov, navodimykh zhiteliami ostrova Vashingtona na ikh tele', *Tekhnologicheskii
zhurnal* (StP, 1810), 7: pt 2: 'Observations météorologiques faites... dans la mer du Sud,
pour examiner les oscillations du barometre', *Mémoires de l'Académie Impériale de Sciences de St-Petersbourg*, 1809, 1: 450-86

23 Details in B.N. Komissarov, *Grigorii Ivanovich Langsdorf, 1774-1852* (Leningrad, 1975),
pp. 51-52

230   THE RUSSIAN DISCOVERY OF HAWAI'I

24 V. N. Berkh, trans. R. Pierce, *A Chronological History of the Discovery of the Aleutian Islands* (Kingston, Ont., 1974), Introduction
25 See Pierce, *Russia's Hawaiian Adventure*, pp. 121
26 *Ibid.*, p. 120
27 Bradley, *The American Frontier*, pp. 49-52 and notes, surveys this.
28 Pierce, *op.cit.*, pp. 113-21
29 'A Russian View', p.113
30 Barratt, *Russia in Pacific Waters*, p. 115
31 For biographical data on Baltic Germans with *Nadezhda* and *Neva*, see w.Lenz, *Deutsch-Baltisches Biographisches Lexikon, 1710-1960* (KÖln-Wien, 1970)
32 *Ocherk iz istorii... Kadiakskoi missii*, p. 140
33 Tumarkin, *Vtorzhenie kolonizatorov v 'krai vechnoi vesny'* (Moscow, 1964), pp. 74-73, 82, 180
34 'A Russian View', p. 116
35 See Beaglehole, *Journals of Captain Cook*, III, pt 1:479, note 2
36 Kruzenshtern's orders to his company of 15 July 1803 are in TsGIAL, *fond* 853 (M.M. Buldakova), no. 74; Lisianskii's of 1803, which similarly stress matters of hygiene at sea, in TsVMM, No. 9170-8.
37 TsGIAL, *fond* 15, *op. 1, delo* 1: fols. 159-60
38. TsGIAE, *fond* 1414 (I.F. Kruzenshterna), *op.* 3, *delo* 5:9-10
39 List given in N.A. Ivashintsov, trans. G.R. Barratt, *Russian Round the World Voyages, 1803-1849* (Kingston, Ont., 1980), pp. 136-37; see also note 34
40 J.-M. Degérando, 'Considerations on the Various Methods to Follow in the Observation of Savage Peoples', trans. by F.C.T. Moore in *The Observation of Savage Peoples* (London, 1969), pp. 64, 70
41 Ivashintsev, *Russian Voyages*, pp. 52-56 and map
42 E.E. Shvede touches on these questions in his introduction to the 1960 (Moscow) edition of Bellingshausen's *Dvukratnye izyskaniia v Iuzhnom ledovitom okeane i plavanie vokrug sveta;* see also my *Bellingshausen: a visit to New Zealand, 1820* (Palmerston N., NZ, 1979), pp. 17-18.
43 Lazarev, Aleksei Petrovich, *Zapiski o plavanii voennogo shliupa Blagonamerennogo v Beringov proliv i vokrug sveta dlia otkrytii v 1819, 1820,1821 i 1822 godakh* (Moscow, 1950), p. 154
44 TsGAVMF, *fond* 213, *op.* 1, *delo* 104: 34ff. Also in this *fond* are a descriptive memorandum by Aleksei P. Lazarev (*delo* 113: 'Zapiska o prirode, istorii, nravakh i obychaiakh zhitelei Sandvichevykh ostrovov') and a long letter by Midshipman N.D. Shishmarev, also of *Blagonamerennyi* (*delo* 730b, fol. 106,) bearing on the Hawaiian situation of 1820-21. Further on N.D. and G.S. Shishmarev's manuscripts, see B.G. Ostrovskii, 'O pozabytykh istochnikakh i uchastnikakh antarkticheskoi ekspeditsii Bellingsgauzena-Lazareva', *IVGO*, 81 (1949), pt 2, and V.V. Kuznetsova, 'Novyye dokumenty o russkoi ekspeditsii k severnomu poliusu' *ibid.*, (1968), pp. 237-45. As V.V. Kuznetsova observes, discoveries of new manuscripts relating to such an (Arctic-focused) expedition may well have significance for students of other parts of the Pacific basin, *e.g.*, Hawai'i.
45 Rezanov's sudden death in 1807 had significance, in this regard, though indeed Kruzenshtern's position as a corresponding member of the Academy of Sciences (*Protokol konferentsii Akademii Nauk, 13 aprelia 1803 goda*), and acquaintance with N.P. Rumiantsev and other grandees, made it likely that his observations on Hawai'i would be printed.
46 See note 39
47 B.A. Lipshits, 'Etnograficheskie issledovaniia v russkikh krugosvetnykh ekspeditsiiakh, *Ocherki istorii russkoi etnografii, fol'kloristiki i antropologii*, 1 (Moscow, 1956), pp. 320-21; L.A. Shur, 'Dnevniki i zapiski russkikh puteshestvennikov kak istochnik po istorii i etnografii stran Tikhogo okeana, (Pervaia polovina XIX veka)' in *Avstraliia i Okeaniia* (Moscow, 1970), pp. 201-12; Tumarkin, 'A Russian View', p. 111; also note 44 above

48 *E.g.*, the 794 folios of *dela* 1-2, *fond* 15, *op.* 1, relating to the Kruzenshtern-Lisianskii expedition, (materials spanning 1802-09), and *Ieromonakh* Gedeon's diary of 1804, in *fond* 796, (1809), op. 90, *delo* 273 (73 folios in a small hand)

49 Details from Lenz (see note 31), Ivashintsev (see note 39), and especially the *Obshchii morskoi spisok* (1885-1907)

50 For instance, *fond* 215, *op.* 1, *delo* 762: 'O postupivshikh v Museum redkostiakh ot kapitanov Povalishina i Lisianskogo' ('On Rarities Acquired by the Museum from Captains Povalishin and Lisianskii')

51 See note 24; also *Zapiski Uchonogo Komiteta Glavnago Morskago Shtaba*, 12 (StP, 1835), pp. 332ff

53 Log-books: op. 870 (1803), no. 2622

52 No. 9170-8 (1938)

54 No. 9170-3 (1938): 69 fols

55 On the naval and other implications of these regional associations, see J.G. Kohl, *Russia and the Russians* (London, 1843), 2:200-01; A. Haxthausen-Abbenburg, trans R. Farie, *The Russian Empire: its People, Resources...* London, 1856), pp. 344-46; and Barratt, *Bellingshausen: a visit to New Zealand*, pp. 3-4.

56 TsGIAE, *fond* 1414, *op.* 3, *dela* 3-4 (diary), 5 (journal). The diary was examined by A.S. Sgibnev in 1877 and cited by him in *Drevniaia i novaia Rossiia*, 1 (1877, Nov.), no. 4.

57 T.K. Shafranovskaia, B.N. Komissarov, 'Materialy po etnografii Polinezii v dnevnike E.E. Levenshterna', *Sovetskaia etnog.* (Moscow, 1980), no. 6

58 F.F. Vesalago, *Admiral Ivan Fedorovich Kruzenshtern* (StP, 1869), p. 2; Nevskii, *Pervoe puteshestvie Rossiian*, p. 21

59 *Fond* 225, *op.* 1, *delo* 20. Levenshtern's service record is also in that *fond* (in a duplicate copy): *op. 1, delo* 1.

60 Pierce, *Russia's Hawaiian Adventure*, p. 121 (Berkh's covering note of 12 August 1816), and notes 34 & 51 above

61 Tumarkin, 'A Russian View', p. 111, note 13

62 For the Hawaiian ethnographer, TsGAVMF holds most promise.

63 W.G. Tilesius von Tilenau's private journal, which contains material of interest for the student of the Marquesas Islands but virtually nothing on Hawai'i, is held at the Leningrad Division of the Archive of the Academy of Sciences of the USSR (LOAAN), *razriad* IV, *op.* 1, *delo* 800a. His beautiful album of sketches is in the Lenin State Library's *otdel rukopisei, fond* 178, M. 10693a. A letter from Lt F. Romberkh to friends dated Petropavlovsk, 16 August 1804, of slight interest or value from the Hawaiian viewpoint, is in the Saltykov-Shchedrin Public Library, Leningrad: *fond* 791 (sobr. Titova), no. 2272, fols. 35-38.

64 See notes 44 & 47

Selective Bibliography

Archival

Central State Archives of the USSR

Tsentral'nyi Gosudarstvennyi Arkhiv Drevnikh Aktov (TsGADA: Moscow)
fond 183, *op.* 1, *delo* 89: 'Ob otpravlenii iz Sankt-Peterburga morem na Vostochnyi okean deistvitel'nogo kamergera Rezanova na korabliakh Nadezhda...i Neva...' (Irkutsk merchant V.N. Bosnin's paper on the readying and objects of the *Nadezhda-Neva* expedition.)
fond Gosarkhiva, *razriad* 10, *op.* 3, *delo* 16 (membership of G.I. Mulovskii's proposed Pacific expedition; procedures and routes in the Pacific Ocean, use of serving men, etc.).

Tsentral'nyi Gosudarstvennyi Istoricheskii Arkhiv (TsGIA: Leningrad)
fond 853 (M.M. Buldakova), *delo* 74: 'Zhurnal prikazov kapitana Kruzenshterna komande sudov "Nadezhda" i "Neva"' (Kruzenshtern's orders to his people in the Pacific, 1804).
fond 15, *op.* 1, *delo* 1, pp. 150-51: 'Instruktsiia Glavnogo Pravleniia Rossiisko-Amerikanskoi Kompanii... 29 maia 1803 god' (Russian-American Company Main Office instruction to *Nadezhda* to visit Hawaiian Islands).
fond 796, *op.* 90 (1809), *delo* 273: 'Donesenie ieromonakha Aleksandro-Nevskoi lavry Gedeona... o plavanii na korable Neva v 1803-1806 godakh' (Archpriest Gedeon's report on his voyage of 1803-04, visit to Hawaii, and arrival in Kodiak, Alaska: fols 37--38 on Kealakekua-Ka'awaloa).
fond 13, *op.* 1, *delo* 687: N.P. Rezanov's letters to N.P. Rumiantsev *et al.*, 1806, touching on Hawaiian-Russian dealings, Kamehameha I.
fond 796, *op.* 84, (1803), *delo* 408, pp. 1-3: 'Po predlozhennomu... mitropolitom Novgorodskim pis'mu, poluchennomu im ot ministra kommertsii grafa Rumiantseva... o vozlozhenii v Amerikanskie zavedeniia ieromonakha Gedeona (service record and biographical details of Gedeon).

Tsentral'nyi Gosudarstvennyi Arkhiv Literatury i Iskusstv
fond XVIII veka, *op.*1, *delo* 5196: 'Zapiski leitenanta Iuriia Fedorovicha Lisianskago, vedennye im vo vremia sluzhby ego Volonterom na angliiskom

flote' (Lisianskii's notes kept while a Volunteer with the Royal Navy; ethnographic interests in West Indies, South Africa).

Tsentral'nyi Gosudarstvennyi Arkhiv Voenno-Morskogo Flota SSSR (TsGAVMF: Leningrad)
fond 14 (I.F.Kruzenshterna), *op.*l, *dela* 12-13 (Kruzenshtern's early service and interests); *delo* 149: 'Zhurnal leitenanta M.I. Ratmanova'.
 fond 213, *op.*l, *delo* 104: 'Zapiski kapitana-leitenanta M.N. Vasil'eva o prebyvanii na Gavaiskikh ostrovakh' (Vasil'ev's notes on his arrival at O'ahu in 1821; *delo* 113: his further observations on the Hawaiian situation).
 fond 215, *op.*l, *delo* 762: 'O postupivshikh v Muzeum redkostiakh ot kapitanov Povalishina i Lisianskogo' ('On the Rarities Received by the Museum from Capts. Povalishin and Lisianskii': Hawaiian objects).

Other manuscript Repositories in Leningrad and Moscow

Arkhiv Geograficheskogo Obshchestva SSR (AGO: Leningrad)
razriad 99, *op.*l, No.141: holograph of N.I. Korobitsyn's journal; (section on Hawai'i edited by A.I. Andreev in 1944; see below, Primary Printed Sources, Korobitsyn).

Saltykov-Shchedrin Public Library: Manuscripts Dept. (ROLGPB)
fond 1000, *op.* 2, No. 1146: 'Zhurnal M.I. Ratmanova'; 1947/88: Iu.E. Bronshtein, introduction of 1939-40 for a proposed edition of this Ratmanov journal. (On variants of that journal and derivative 'Zapiski,' see Secondary Material, under Shur, L.A. 'Braziliia').
 fond 791 (Sobranie Titova, A.A.), No. 2272. fols 37-38: 'Pis'mo F. Romberga k druziam' (Lt Romberkh on the voyage to Kamchatka, 1804) F.IV.59: 'Zhurnal Rossiisko-Amerikanskoi kompanii...prikazchika Fedora Ivanovicha Shemelina' (Shemelin's journal, covering 1804).

Leningradskoe Otdeleinie Arkhiva Akademii Nauk SSR (LOAAN)
razriad IV, *op.*l, *delo* 800a: the travel journal of W.G. Tilesius von Tilenau.

Tsentral'nyi Voenno-Morskoi Muzei SSR (Leningrad: TsVMM)
No. 9170-8/1938: 'Zhurnal korablia "Neva" 1803-06 gg': *Neva*'s log.
No. 9170-3/1938: 'Chernoviki pisem Lisiansogo k raznym litsam s 1803 po 1832 god' (originals of letters to various persons).

Archives in the Estonian SSR

Tsentral'nyi Gosudarstvennyi Istoricheskii Arkhiv Estonskoi SSR (Tartu)
fond 1414, *op.* 3, *dela* 3-4: private diary of Lt E.E. Levenshtern, kept during the voyage of *Nadezhda* (fols 97-99, observations on Hawai'i), *delo* 5: his official journal of the same period.

Eesti NSV Riikliik Ajaloomuuseum (Estonian State Museum of History, Tallin)
fond 225, *op*.11, *delo* 20: typescript copy of Levenshtern's diary of 1803-05: pp. 156-59 on Kealakekua-Ka'awaloa, Kona, June 1804.

Western Archives

Bibliothèque Nationale, Paris. Department des manuscripts, Slave.
NN. 103 (1), 104: copy of M.I. Ratmanov's journal of 1803-06: see note to Saltykov-Shchedrin Public Library, above.

Public Record Office, London
Adm. 1: Peter Puget, 'Log of the Proceedings of His Majesty's Armed Tender *Chatham*' (entries for 1793-94).

Primary Printed Material

Akademia Nauk *Protokoly zasedanii konferentsii Akademii Nauk s 1725 po 1803*

Bell, E. 'The Log of the *Chatham*,' *Honolulu Mercury*, I (1929), no. 4

Berkh, V.N. 'Nechto o Sandvichevykh ostrovakh', *Syn otechestva* (StP, 1818), pt 43: 158-63. For an English version of a variant text, see Pierce, *Russia's Hawaiian Adventure*, pp. 113-21; *Khronologicheskaia istoriia otkrytiia Aleutskikh ostrovov* (StP, 1823)

Bloxam, A. *Diary of Andrew Bloxam, naturalist of the "Blonde", on her way to the Hawaiian Islands, 1824-1825* Honolulu, BPBM Spec. Pub. 10, 1925

Broughton, W. *A Voyage of Discovery to the North Pacific Ocean...in the Years 1795-98* (London, 1804)

Campbell, A. *A Voyage Round the World from 1806 to 1812* (Edinburgh, 1816)

Chichagov, P.V. 'Zapiski admirala P.V. Chichagova', *Russkaia starina*, L-LIX (St.P., 1886-88) Letter to A.R. Vorontsov re Lisianskii in *Arkhiv kniazia Vorontsova*, ed. P. Bartenev (Moscow, 1870-95), 19: 114ff.

Choris, Louis *Voyage pittorésque autour du monde* (Paris, 1822)

Colnett, James *Journal of Captain James Colnett aboard the Argonaut from April 26 1789 to November 3 1791*, ed. F.W. Howay (Toronto, 1941)

Cook, James *A Voyage to the Pacific Ocean..for making discoveries in the Northern Hemisphere in..the "Resolution" and "Discovery"* (London, 1784: vol. 3 by James King) *The Journals of Captain James Cook...*, ed. J.C. Beaglehole, vol 3 (Cambridge, 1967): pts 1, 2

D'Wolf, John *A Voyage to the North Pacific and a Journey through Siberia* (Cambridge, Mass. 1861)

Ellis, William *Narrative of a Tour through Hawaii...* (London, 1827: 2nd ed.) *Polynesian Researches*, vol. IV (London, 1839)

Espenberg, Karl 'Zamechaniia po vrachebnoi chasti, uchinennye vo vremia puteshestviia Kruzenshterna', in I.F. Kruzenshtern, *Puteshestvie* (StP, 1812), III, suppl.

Franchère, Gabriel *Narrative of a Voyage to the Northwest Coast of America in the Years 1811-14*, trans. & ed. J.V. Huntington (NY, 1854)

Gedeon, Archpriest Letters to the Metropolitan Ambvrosii, in *Ocherk iz istorii Amerikanskoi pravoslavnoi dukhovnoi misii, Kadiakskoi misii, 1794-1837* (StP, 1894)

Golenishchev-Kutuzov, L. *Predpriiatiia Imperatritsy Ekateriny II dlia puteshestviia vokrug sveta v 1786 godu* (StP, 1840)

Golovnin, V.M. *Puteshestvie vokrug sveta... v 1817-19 godakh* (StP, 1822)

Kohl, J.G. *Russia and the Russians in 1842* (London, 1843)

Korobitsyn, N.I. 'Zapiski', ed. A.I. Andreev, *Russkie otkrytiia v Tikhom okeane i Severnoi Amerike v XVIII-XIX vekakh: sbornik materialov* (Moscow-Leningrad, 1944)

Kotzebue, Otto von *A voyage of discovery into the South Seas and Beering's Straits, undertaken in the Years 1815-1818* (London, 1821); English text of *Puteshestvie v Iuzhnvi okean i v Beringov proliv v 1815-18 godakh* (StP, 1823-26)

Kruzenshtern, I.F. *Puteshestvie vokrug sveta v 1803, 4, 5, i 1806 godakh na korabliakh Nadezhde i Neve* (StP, 1809-12): 3 vols *Atlas k puteshestviiu vokrug sveta* (StP, 1813) *Atlas Iuzhnogo moria* (StP, 1823-26)

Langsdorf, G.H. *Bemerkungen auf einer Reise um die Welt in den Jahren 1803 bis 1807* (Frankfurt, 1812)

Lazarev, Aleksei P. *Zapiski o plavanii voennogo shliupa Blagonamerennogo v Beringov proliv i vokrug sveta...v 1819-1822 godakh* (Moscow, 1950)

Ledyard, John *John Ledyard's Journal through Russia and Siberia, 1787-88*, ed. S.D. Watrous (Madison, Wisc., 1966)

Lisianskii, Iurii F. *Puteshestvie vokrug sveta v 1803, 1804, 1805, i 1806 godakh, na korable "Neva", pod nachal'stvom Iuriia Lisianskogo* (StP, 1812)
    Sobranie kart risunkov, prinadlezhashchikh k puteshestviiu Iuriia Lisianskogo na korable "Neva" (StP, 1812)

Maltebriun, A. 'O plavanii vokrug sveta korablei "Nadezhda" i "Neva" 1803-06 godov', *Vestnik Evropy*, pt 121 (StP, 1822), no. 1

Mordvinov, N.S. *Arkhiv grafov Mordvinovykh*, ed. V.A. Bilbasov, vol. 3 (StP, 1902)

Niles Weekly Register Entries for 1822-14, 1836

Penrose, Charles V. *A Memoir of James Trevenen, 1760-1790*, ed. R.C. Anderson, C. Lloyd (London, Navy Records Soc., 1959)

Puget, Peter See Bell, Edward

Patterson, S. *A Narrative of the Adventures and Sufferings of Samuel Patterson*... (Palmer, Mass., 1817)

Ratmanov, Makar' I. 'Vyderzhki iz dnevnika krugosvetnogo puteshestviia na korable "Nadezhda" ', *Iakhta* (StP, 1876),
    nos 16, 18, 24, etc.

Rezanov, Nikolai P. 'Pervoe puteshestvie Rossiian vokrug sveta opisannoe N. Riazanovym, Polnomochnym poslannikom ko Dvoru Iaponskomu, i proch.', *Otechestvennye zapiski*, XXIV (StP, 1825): 246-53

Severgin, M.V. 'Instruktsiia dlia puteshestviia okolo sveta', *Severnyi vestnik* (StP, 1804), nos 2-3

Shaler, William 'Journal', in *American Register*, 3 (1808): 167ff.

Shemelin, Fedor I. *Zhurnal pervogo puteshestviia Rossiian vokrug zemnogo shara* (StP, 1815-18)
    'Istoricheskoe izvestie o pervom puteshstvii Rossiian krugom sveta', *Russkii invalid: Literaturnye pribavleniia* (StP, 1823), nos. 247, 249, 250, 252, 256, 257, 259 etc.

Tilesius von Tilenau, W. 'Izvestie o estestvennom i politicheskom sostoianii zhitelei ostrova Nukagivy', *Tekhnologicheskii zhurnal*, 3 (StP, 1806), pt 4

Turnbull, John *A Voyage round the World in the Years 1800-1804* (London, 1805)

Vancouver, George *A Voyage of Discovery to the North Pacific Ocean and round the World* (London, 1798)

Secondary Printed Material

Akimov, A. 'Lisianskii, Iu.F.', in *Russkii biograficheskii slovar'*, ed. Polovtsov and Mod-
zalevskii (StP, 1896-1918), 10:122
A.L. 'Iurii Fedorovich Lisianskii', *Morskoi sbornik* (StP, 1894), Neofitsial'nyi otdel, no. 11: 1-24
Anon. 'O pervom puteshestvii Russkikh vokrug sveta', *Statisticheskii zhurnal*, 1 (StP, 1806),
sect. 1:281-89
Andreev, A.I. 'Ob arkhive Rossisko-Amerikanskoi kompanii', *IVGO*, 75 (1943), no. 3
Introduction, *Russkie otkrytiia v Tikhom okeane i Severnoi Amerike v XVIII-XIX vekakh*
(Moscow-Leningrad, 1944)
Armstrong, Terence 'Cook's Reputation in Russia', *Captain James Cook and his Times*, ed. R.
Fisher, H. Johnston (Vancouver, 1979)
Arning, E. *Ethnographische Notizen aus Hawaii* (Hamburg, 1883)
Baker, H.L., Sahara, T. *Detailed Land Classification: Island of Hawaii* (Honolulu, University of
Hawai'i Land Study Bureau Bull. No. 6, 1965)
Barratt, Glynn R. *Bellingshausen: a visit to New Zealand, 1820* (Palmerston N., NZ, Dunmore,
1979)
'The Russian Navy and New Holland', *JRAHS*, 64 (1979), pt 4:217-34
Rebel on the Bridge: the life and times of Baron Andrey Rozen, 1800-84 (London, 1975)
The Russians at Port Jackson, 1814-1822 (Canberra, 1981)
*Russia in Pacific Waters, 1715-1825: a survey of the Origins of Russia's naval presence in the
North and South Pacific* (Vancouver, 1981)
Beckley, Emma M. *Hawaiian Fisheries and Methods of Fishing* (Honolulu, 1883)
Belinskii, V.G. 'Vzgliad na russkuiu literaturu 1847 goda', in *Sobranie sochinenii v 3 tomakh*
(Moscow, 1948)
Belov, M.I. 'Shestaia chast' sveta otkryta russkimi moriakami', *IVGO*, 90 (1962)
Bennett, Wendell C. *Archaeology of Kauai* (Honolulu, BPBM Bull. No. 80, 1931)
Berg, L.S. *Pervye russkie krugosvetnye moreplavateli I.F. Kruzenshtern, Iu.F. Lisianskii:
ocherki po istorii russkikh geograficheskikh otkrytii* (Moscow-Leningrad, 1949)
Bradley, H.W. 'The Hawaiian Islands and the Pacific Fur Trade, 1785-1813', *Pacific Northwest
Quarterly*, 30 (1939):275-99
The American Frontier in Hawaii: the Pioneers, 1789-1843 (Gloucester, Mass., 1968)
Brigham, William T. *Hawaiian Feather Work* (Honolulu, BPBM memoir no. 1, 1899):1-81
Mat and Basket Weaving of the ancient Hawaiians (Honolulu, BPBM memoir, vol. 2, 1906) pt
1:1-105
Ka Hana Kapa--the making of bark-cloth in Hawaii (Honolulu, BPBM memoir, vol. 3, 1911)
Bishop Museum Handbook, Part 1: the Hawaiian Collections (Honolulu, BPBM special publ.
no. 5, 1915)
Buck, Peter H. *Arts and Crafts of Hawaii* (Honolulu, BPBM spec. publ. no. 45, 1957)
Cheever, H.T. *The Island World of the Pacific* (NY, 1855)
Cross, Anthony G. *By the Banks of the Thames: Russians in Eighteenth-Century Britain* (New-
tonville, Mass. 1980)
Dening, Gregory 'Ethnohistory in Polynesia: the value of ethno-historical evidence', *JPH*, 1
(1966): 23-42
Dibble, S. *History of the Sandwich Islands* (Honolulu, 1909)
Divin, V.A. *K beregam Ameriki* (Moscow, 1956)
Dobrovol'skii, A. Zubov, N. 'Ekspeditsiia I.F. Kruzenshterna vokrug sveta: vstupitel'naia
stat'ia', *I.F. Kruzenshtern: Puteshestvie vokrug sveta v 1803, 1804, 1805, i 1806 godakh*, ed.
N.N. Zubov (Moscow, 1950)

Dumitrashko, N.V. 'Iu.F. Lisianskii i russkie krugosvetnye plavaniia', in *Iu.F. Lisianskii: Puteshestvie vokrug sveta v 1803, 1804, 1805 i 1806 godakh, na korable "Neva"* (Moscow, 1947)

Edge-Partington, James, Heap, Charles *An Ethnographical Album of the Pacific Islands, Series 1-3* (Manchester, 1890-98)

Fornander, Abraham *Hawaiian Antiquities and Folklore* (Honolulu, BPBM memoir no. 5, 1919)

Gibson, James R. *Imperial Russia in Frontier America* (NY, 1976)

Golder Frank A. 'Proposals for Russian Occupation of the Hawaiian Islands', in *Hawaii: Early Relations with England-Russia-France*, ed. A.P. Taylor, R.J. Kuykendall (Honolulu, 1930)

Gvozdetskii, N.A. 'Pervoe morskoe puteshestvie Rossiian vokrug sveta', *Priroda* (Moscow, 1947), no. 1:85-88

Howay, F.W. 'An Outline Sketch of the Maritime Fur Trade', *Canadian Historical Association Annual Report* (Ottawa, 1932): 5-14

A List of Trading Vessels in the Maritime Fur Trade, 1785-1825, ed. & intro. R.A. Pierce (Kingston, Ont., 1973)

Haddon, A.C., Hornell, J. *Canoes of Oceania, Vol. 1* (BPBM spec. publ. no. 27, 1936)

Handy, E.S. Craighill *Ancient Hawaiian Civilization* (Honolulu, 1933)

The Hawaiian Planter: Volume 1 (Honolulu, BPBM Bull. no. 161, 1940)

Cultural Revolution in Hawaii (Honolulu, 1931)

I'ī, John P. *Fragments of Hawaiian History* (Honolulu, 1959)

Ivashintsev, N.A. *Russkie krugosvetnye puteshestviia s 1803 po 1849 god* (StP, 1872): trans. by G.R. Barratt as *Russian Round-the-World Voyages, 1803-1849* (Kingston, Ont., Limestone, 1980)

Jarves, James J. *History of the Hawaiian or Sandwich Islands* (Boston, 1844)

Kamakau, Samuel *Ka Po'e Kahiko (The People of Old)*, trans. M.K. Pukui from Honolulu newspaper articles published between 1866 and 1871 (Honolulu, BPBM spec. publ. no. 51, 1964)

Ruling Chiefs of Hawaii trans. from Honolulu newspaper articles published between 1866 and 1871 (Honolulu, Kamehameha Schools, 1961; index prepared by Elspeth P. Sterling and printed by BPBM Dept of Anthropology in 1974

Kelly, Marion 'Some Problems with Early Descriptions of Hawaiian Culture', in G.A. Highland, *et al.*, *Polynesian Culture History: Essays in Honor of Kenneth P. Emory* (Honolulu, 1967)

Komissarov, B.N. *Grigorii Ivanovich Langsdorf, 1774-1852* (Leningrad, 1975)

Kuykendall, R.S. *The Hawaiian Kingdom, 1778-1854: Foundation and Transformation* (Honolulu, 1948)

Kuznetsova, V.V. 'Novye dokumenty o russkoi ekspeditsii k Severnomu poliusu', *IVGO* (1968) no. 3:237-45

Lensen, George A. *Russian Push Toward Japan: Russo-Japanese Relations, 1697-1875* (Princeton, 1959)

Lenz, W. *Deutsche-Baltisches Biographisches Lexikon, 1710-1960* (Köln-Wien, 1970)

Liapunova, R.G. 'Zapiski ieromonakha Gedeona (1803-1807)--odin iz istochnikov po istorii i etnografii Russkoi Ameriki', in *Problemy istorii i etnografii Ameriki* (Moscow, 1979)

Likhtenberg, Iu.M. 'Gavaiskie kollektsii v sobraniiakh Muzeia Antropologii i Etnografii', *SMAE*, XIX (1960):168-205

Lipshits, B.A. 'Etnograficheskie issledovaniia v russkikh krugosvetnykh ekspeditsiiakh pervoi poloviny XIX veka', *Ocherki istorii russkoi etnografii, fol'kloristiki i antropologii* (Moscow, 1956

Lupach, V.S. ed. 'Ivan Fedorovich Kruzenshtern i Iurii Fedorovich Lisianskii', *Russkie moreplavateli* (Moscow, 1953):137-64

Malo, David *Hawaiian Antiquities (Moolelo Hawaii)*, trans. N.B. Emerson, 1898 (Honolulu, BPBM spec. publ. no. 2, 2nd ed., 1951)

Mehnert, C. *The Russians in Hawaii, 1804-1819* (Honolulu, 1939)

Nevskii, V.V. *Pervoe puteshestvie Rossiian vokrug sveta* (Moscow, 1951)

Nozikov, N.A. *Russkie krugosvetnye moreplavateli* (Moscow-Leningrad, 1941)

Okun', S.B. *Rossiisko-Amerikanskaia Kompaniia* (Moscow, 1939; trans. by C. Ginsburg as *The Russian-American Company*, Cambridge, Mass., 1951)

Orlov, Boris P. *Pervoe russkoe krugosvetnoe plavanie, 1803-06 godov* (Moscow, 1954)

Ostrovskii, B.G. 'O pozabytykh istochnikakh i uchastnikakh antarkticheskoi ekspeditsii Bellin-gauzena-Lazareva', *IVGO*, 81 (1949)

Petrov, P.N. ed. *Sbornik materialov dlia istorii Akademii Khudozhestv za sto let eio sush-chestvovaniia* (StP, 1864)

Pierce, Richard A. *Russia's Hawaiian Adventure, 1815-17* (Berkeley, UCLA, 1965; reprinted in Kingston, Ont., Limestone, 1976)

Plischke, H. *Johann Friedrich Blumenbachs Einfluss auf die Entdeckungsreisenden seiner Zeit* (Göttingen, 1937)

Pukui, M.K., Elbert, S.H., Mookini, E.T. *Place Names of Hawaii* (Honolulu, 1974: revised ed.)

Ratzel, F. 'Georg Heinrich Freiherr von Langsdorff', *Allgemeine Deutsche Biographie*, 17 (Leipzig, 1886):689

Rozina, L.G. 'Kollektsiia Muzeia Antropologii i Etnografii po Markizskim ostrovam', *SMAE*, XXI (1963):110-19

'Kollektsiia Dzhemsa Kuka v sobraniiakh Muzeia Antropologii i Etnografii', *SMAE*, XXIII (1966)

Russov, F. 'Beiträge zur Geschichte der etnographischen und antropologischen Sammlungen der Kaiserlichen Akademie der Wissenschaften zu St Petersburg', *SMAE*, 1 (1900)

Rudovits, L.F. 'Pervoe russkoe krugosvetnoe plavanie, 1803-06: obzor nauchnykh rabot', *Trudy Gosudarstvennogo Okeanograficheskogo Instituta*, Vyp. 27 (Leningrad, 1954):3-12

Ryden, Stig *The Banks Collection: an episode in eighteenth-century Anglo-Swedish Relations* (Götenburg, 1963)

Sgibnev, A.S. 'Rezanov i Kruzenshtern', *Drevniaia i novaia Rossiia*, 1 (StP, 1877), no. 4

Shafranovskaia, T.K., Komissarov, B.N. 'Materialy po etnografii Polinezii v dnevnike E.f. Levenshterna', *Sovetskaia etnografiia* (1980), no. 6

Shteinberg, E.L. *Zhizneopisanie russkogo moreplavatelia Iuriia Lisianskogo* (Moscow, 1948)

Shur, L.A. 'Brasiliia nachala XIX veka v neopublikovannom zhurnale krugosvetnogo plavaniia M.I. Ratmanova', *Latinskaia Amerika*, 3 (Moscow, 1969): 176-84

'Dnevniki i zapiski russikh puteshestvennikov kak istochnik po istorii i etnografii stran Tikhogo okeana (pervaia polovina XIX veka)', *Avstraliia i Okeaniia* (Moscow., 1970): 201-12

K beregam Novogo Sveta: iz neopublikovannykh zapisok russikh puteshestvennikov nachala XIX veka (Moscow, 1971)

Shvede, E.E. 'K 150-letiiu pervoi russkoi krugosvetnoi ekspeditsii Kruzenshterna i Lisianskogo', *Izvestiia Akademii Nauk SSR: Seriia geografii* (1953), no. 6: 57-66

Soehren, L., Newman, T.S. *Archaeology of Kealakekua Bay* (Honolulu: Special Report by Depts of Anthropology, BPBM and University of Hawai'i, 1968)

Sokolov, A.P. ed. *Russkaia morskaia biblioteka: period chetvertyi* (StP, 1883)

Stokes, John F. *Burial of King Keawe*: Hawaiian Historical Society Paper no. 17 (Honolulu, 1930)

Tikhmenev, P. *Istoricheskoe obozrenie obrazovaniia Rossiisko-Amerikanskoi Kompanii i deistvii eio do nastoiashchego vremeni* (StP, 1861-63: 2 pts)

Titcomb, Margaret 'Kava in Hawaii', *JPS*, 57 (1948), pt 2:105-71

Tumarkin, Daniel 'Iz istorii gavaitsev v kontse XVIII-nachale XIX veka', *Sovietskaia etnografiia* (1958), no. 6:38-53.

'Novye arkhivnye materialy o gavaitsakh', *ibid.*, (1960), no. 2: 158-60

Vtorzhenie kolonizatorov v "Krai vechnoi vesny": Gavaiskii narod v bor'be protiv chuzhezem-nykh zakhvatchikov v kontse XVIII-nachale XIX veka (Moscow, 1964)

'A Russian View of Hawaii in 1804', *Pacific Studies*, 2 (1979), no. 2:1009-31.

Veselago, F.F. *Admiral Ivan Fedorovich Kruzenshtern* (StP, 1869)

Voenskii, K. 'Russkoe posol'stvo v Iaponiiu v nachale XIX veka', *Russkaia starina*, LXXXIV (July 1895):123-41

Zubov, N.N. *Otechestvennye moreplavateli--issledovateli morei i okeanov* (Moscow, 1954)

Glossary

British Transliterations Of Hawaiian Words And Their Modern Equivalents

Acaw	Ka'û	Macahity	Makahiki
Apoona	Puna	Macaiva	Makaîwa
Atoui	Kaua'i	Macaree	Makali'i
Atowai	Kaua'i	Mahearona	Mahealani
Caero	Kâ'elo	Mooharoo	Môhalu
Caona	Ka'aôna	Morai	a Tahitian and Maori word

Morai — a Tahitian and Maori word (with cognates in other Polynesian groups) designating a place of community activity. In Hawai'i as in Tahiti, this place took on a more religious function than elsewhere in Polynesia.

Carocoocahe	Kâloakukâhi		
Carocoorooha	Kâloakulua		
Caropaoo	Kâloapau		
Cohola	Kohala		
Cona	Kona	Mové	Maui
Coo-a-oo	kuahu	Mowry	Mauli
Coohahi	Kukâhi	Namotahy	Namakeha
Coohana	kahuna	Noocahiva	Nuku Hiva, Marquesas
Coohana-anana	kahuna 'anâ'anâ	Nooy Nooy Eiry	nuinui ali'i
Coopaoo	Kupau	O'heekeeow	Hikiau
Eiree	ali'i	O'why'he	Hawai'i
Hamacooa	Hamakua	O-Wahoo	O'ahu
Hamamea	Kamehameha	Oatooa	Akua
Haykery	Kahekili	Ocane	Kâne
Heavoo	heiau	Ocaoorooa	Kaulua
Hidoos	Hilo	Ocona	Kona
Hoaca	Hoaka	Oero	Welo
Hooa	Hua	Oheero	Hilo
Hoona	Huna	Ohekeaw	Hikiau
Hopooas	ahupua'a	Oherenahoo	Hilinaehu
Hotoo	Hoku	Oherenima	Hilinama
Hoynere	Hinaia'el'ele	Ohiro	Hilo
Karakakooa	Kealakekua	Oipoona-oura	Waipunaula
Ka Mea Mea	Kamehameha	Omoocoo	Muku
Kiauva	Keawe	Onana	Nana

Onihoo	Ni'ihau	Poona	Puna
Orecoocahe	'Olekukâhi	Roacoocahe	Lâ'aukukâhi
Orecoorooha	'Olekulua	Roacoorooha	Lâ'aukulua
Orepaoo	'Olepau	Roaopaoo	Lâ'aupau
Oricoocahe	'Olekukâhi	Roi	Loa
Oricoocoroo	'Olekukolu	Ronoo	Lono
Oricoorooha	'Olekulua	Tagoora	Ka'ula
Origoa	Lehua	Tamoory	Kaumuali'i
Oripaoo	'Olepau	Tavaroa	Ka'awaloa
Orono	Lono	Tavoorapery	Ka'ula Pele
Orre'houa	Lehua	Toocoroo	Kukolu
Otaoora	Ka'ula	Tooroo	Kulua
Ottoway	Kaua'i	Toorooa	Kulua
Ou-why-hee	Hawai'i	Toovyhy	Kawaihae
Ouwai	Hawai'i	Towyhy	Kawaihae
Ouwaihee	Hawai'i	Tryshepoor	Kalanikupule
Owahoo	O'ahu	Tyana	Kaiana
Owyhee	Hawai'i	Tyreboo	Kalani'opu'u
Oykeekee	Ikiiki	Vainoonohala	Waipunaula
Oytooa	'Ikuwâ	Wahoo	O'ahu
Pekynery Eiry	pekepeke ali'i	Weymea	Waimea

Russian Transliterations Of Hawaiian Words
And Their Modern Equivalents

aienia	'aieana (?)	khiabu	he pâ'û
Akhu	aho	Kiauva	Keawe
Atuai	Kaua'i	Kohola	Kohala
Atuu	Kaua'i	Kuhahi	Kukâhi
Atuvai	Kaua'i	Kupau	Kupau
eiry	ali'i	Legua	Lehua
gaikanaka	haikanaka	Magearona	Mahealani
Gaikeri	Kahekili	makagiti	makahiki
Gamakua	Hamakua	Makagiti	Makali'i
Gammamea	Kamehameha	Makaura	Makahuna
Gavaii	Hawai'i	Markeskie	Marquesas, Marquesans*
geiava	heiau	Markeskikh	Marquesas*
Gidus	Hilo	Markezskikh	Marquesas*
Goaka	Hoaka	Markiziane	Marquesan*
Goineery	Hinaia'ele'ele	Marotogi	Molokini
Gopua	ahupua'a	Mauna-ro	Mauna Loa
Gotu	Hoku	Morekai	Moloka'i
Gua	Hua	Morotai	Moloka'i
Guna	Huna	Mouna-Kea	Mauna Kea
ipu-ara	ipu 'ai	Mouna-Roa	Mauna Loa
ipu-khave	ipu haole	Mounika	Mauna Kea
ipu-maia	ka'ukama	Mouru	Mauli
Kaero	Ka'elo	Move	Maui
Kagulave	Kaho'olawe	Mové	Maui
Kaira	kâ'ai la	Mowna Kaah	Mauna Kea
Kaona	Ka'aôna	Mowna Roa	Mauna Loa
Karakakoa	Kealakekua	Mugaru	Môhalu
Karakaroa	Kealakekua	Namatagi	Namakeha
Kararcacoa	Kealakekua	Nikhau	Ni'ihau
Karekekua	Kealakekua	nui-nui-eiry	nuinui ali'i
Karikakoe	Kealakekua	Oagu	O'ahu
Karikakopskaia	Kealakekua	Oakhu	O'ahu
Karo-kukage	Kâloakukâhi	Oatua	Akua
Karo-kuruga	Kâloakulua	Oero	Welo
Karo-pau	Kâloapau	Ogio	'ôhi'a
karra	kapa	Ogirinegu	Hilinaehu
Kau	Ka'û	Ogirinima	Hilinama
Kau	Kea	ogiro	Hilo
Kaula	Ka'ula	Oikiki	Ikiiki
Kenokhoia	Kanehoe (?)	oitua	'Ikuwâ

okane	Kâne	Tagura	Ka'ula
okané	Kâne	Taiana	Kaiana
Okaurua	Kaulua	Taiohai	Taio-hae*
Omuku	Muku	Tairebu	Kalani'opu'u
Onana	Nana	Tamaga-ma	Kamehameha
Onigio	Ni'ihau	Tamagama	Kamehameha
Onigu	Ni'ihau	Tamu-Aru	Kaumuali'i
Ore-kukahe	'Olekukâhi	Tamura	Kaumuali'i
orepau	'Olepau	Tamuri	Kaumuali'i
Origau	Lehua	Tamurii	Kaumuali'i
Origoa	Lehua	Tatio-Goe	Taio-hae*
Orikukage	'Olekukâhi	Taura-Peri	Ka'ula Pele (?)
Orikukoru	'Olekukolu	Tianna	Kaiana
Orikuruga	'Olekulua	Tomari	Kaumuali'i
Oripau	'Olepau	Tomi-Omi	Kamehameha
orona	olonâ	Tomi-Omio	Kamehameha
Otageiti	Tahiti*	Tomio-omio	Kamehameha
Otagiti	Tahiti*	Tomiomi	Kamehameha
Otavai	Kaua'i	Tomoom-o	Kamehameha
Ottu-Vai	Kaua'i	Toome-Ome-o	Kamehameha
Otuvai	Kaua'i	Towaiwai	Kawaihae
Ovagi	Hawai'i	Traitshepur	Kalanikupule
Ovagu	O'ahu	Tukoru	Kukolu
Ovaigi	Hawai'i	Turu	Kulua
Ovigi	Hawai'i	Turua	Kulua
Ovigii	Hawai'i	Tuvai-Gai	Kawaihae
Owachi	Hawai'i	Ukhi	uhi
Owaichi	Hawai'i	uvara	'uala
Owaihi	Hawai'i	uvara	'uala kahiki
Pekinery-Eiry	pekepeke ali'i	Vagu	O'ahu
Puna	Puna	Vainu-Nagala	Waipunaula
Raa-kuruha	Lâ'aukulua	Veimea	Waimea
Raa-opau	Lâ'aupau	Vororai	Hualalai
Rao-kukahe	Lâ'aukukâhi		
Renai	Lâna'i		
Roa	Loa	*non-Hawaiian Polynesian names	

Glossary Of Hawaiian Terms

'aha sennit; cord braided of coconut husk, human hair or other materials

'ahaniu a native sedge *Cladium meyenii*

anahulu ten-day period; for ten days

aho line, cord, lashing, fishing line

'ahu short for **'ahu'ula**

'ahu'ula feather cape or cloak formerly worn by kings and high chiefs, made from the feathers of **'ô'ô, 'i'iwi** and other birds, usually red or yellow trimmed with black or green

ahupua'a land division usually extending from the uplands to the sea, so called because its boundaries were marked by heaps (**ahu**) of stones surmounted by an image of a pig (**pua'a**) or because a pig or other tribute was laid on the altar as a tax to the chief or landowner

'aieana native shrub *Nothocestrum*, also **'aiea**

'ai pa'a cooked taro pounded into a hard mass not mixed with water, sometimes preserved in ti leaf bundles

aku bonito, *Katsuwonus pelamys*

akua god, goddess, spirit, ghost, idol; supernatural, godly

akua kâ'ai image wrapped in **kapa**; image consisting of a carved staff with a tuft of feathers at the top, bound to its bearer by a sash (**ka'ai**) and thus carried into battle

akua ki'i image representing a god

'alalâ Hawaiian crow *Corvus tropicus*

ali'i chief, chiefess, king, queen, noble

ama float for outrigger canoe; port hull of a double canoe, so called because it replaces the float; also **iama**

'ama'u ferns of the genus *Sadleria*. Formerly, in times of famine, the tasteless pith of the trunk was cooked and eaten; the fronds were used to mulch dry-taro land;the stems were plaited. Also **ma'uma'u**

'âma'uma'u plural of **'ama'u**, also **ma'uma'u**

'ao dried baked taro or sweet potato, in Ka'u made by hanging this food in baskets in the wind to dehydrate; used on voyages, probably related to ô, sea rations

'auku'u Black-crowned night heron *Nyctictorax n. hoactli*

'awa a narcotic drink made from the pounded roots of the **'awa** (pepper) plant *Piper methysticum,* mixed with water

bipi cattle (transliterated from the English word beef); also **pipi**

'eke bag shaped fish net, sack, pocket

ha'aheo proud, haughty; pride, haughtiness; to strut

hai offering, sacrifice

hai kanaka to offer human sacrifice

hala pandanus *Pandanus odoratissimus,* a native tree (**pû**) with many uses: leaves for mats and baskets, fruit sections (red to yellow) for **lei** and paintbrushes, male flowers (**hinano**) to scent **kapa** and to plait fine mats

hale house, building

hale 'aina women's eating houses

hale imu oven shelter

hale pahu drum house, especially in a **heiau** where prayers were uttered

hale poki shrine where bones of dead chiefs were kept, as Hale-o-Keawe at Kona, Hawai'i

hâpu'u giant tree fern *Cibotium splendens*

hau a lowland tree *Hibiscus tilaceus* with light, tough wood formerly used for canoe outriggers, bast for rope and firesticks; the sap and flowers were used medicinally

he a, an (the indefinite article)

heiau pre-Christian places of worship, ranging in construction from simple earth terraces to elaborate stone platforms

heiau po'o kanaka heiau where human sacrifices were offered

Hilinaehu ancient Hawaiian month, occurs* July-August; the name of a star; also **Hilinehu**

Hilinamâ ancient Hawaiian month, occurs* August-September

Hilo first night of the new moon, of the Hawaiian month and of the **Ku kapu**

hîna'i poepoe a round basket or container braided around a calabash

Hinaia'ele'ele ancient Hawaiian month, occurs* June-July; the name of a star

hipa sheep (transliterated from English). This word was obviously coined at a later time. According to Lisianskii's word list, *sheep* was, at the time of his visit, 'rio hoolloo' ['îlio hulu]--hairy dog--or 'rio veoveo' ['îlio weuweu]--fluffy or bushy dog.

ho'omapopo maoli ana genuine understanding

ho'opa'i to slap

Hoaka second night of the Hawaiian month and of the Ku kapu

hohoa a rounded **kapa** beater, also **hoahoa, pepehi**; a stick beater for washing clothes

hôkeo long gourd calabash used to hold food, clothing, fishing gear

Hoku night of the full moon

hôkû star

honohono short for **honhonokukui**, basket grass *Oplimenus hirtellus*, so called because it is often found under kukui trees

hôpue the orange finch *Psittirostra palmeri*, found only in the Kona and Ka'û districts of Hawai'i island

Hua the thirteenth night of the lunar month

hue a type of gourd, water calabash, any narrow-necked vessel for holding water

hue wai gourd calabash for carrying or storing water

hulu feather

Huna eleventh night of the Hawaiian month

hûnâkele hidden in secret, as a corpse in a secret cave

'iako outrigger boom

'iao silversides *Pranesus insularum*, used as bait for fish such as aku

i'e kuku second stage kapa beater

'i'iwi scarlet Hawaiian honeycreeper *Vestiaria coccinea*, the feathers of which were used extensively in featherwork

'ie'ie an endemic woody branching climber *Freycinetia arborea*, the aerial roots ('ie) of which were used for weaving and plaiting such items as baskets, hats and **mahiole**; one of five plants used on the **hula** altar

ihe spear

ihe laumaki barbed spear, also **ihe laumeki**

ihe laumeki barbed spear, also **ihe laumaki**

Ikiiki ancient Hawaiian month, occurs* April-May

'Ikuwâ ancient Hawaiian month, occurs* September-October

'ili pilo smelly skin, said of industrious farmers

'îlio dog

imu traditional earth oven, also **umu**

ipu general name for container such as cup, calabash; the bottle gourd *Lagenaria siceraria*

ipu 'aina scrap bowl

ipu'ai edible melon

ipuhaole watermelon (*lit.* foreign gourd)

ipu hula dance drum made of two gourds sewn together

ipu kuha spittoon

'iwa Frigate-bird *Fregata minor*; a native fern *Asplenium horridum*, also called 'alae

ka'anu'a sleeping place in a grass house

Ka'aôna ancient Hawaiian month, occurs* May-June

Kâ'elo ancient Hawaiian month, occurs* December-January; name of a star, possibly Betelgeuse

Ka'eokulani (often called Ka'eo) ruler of Kaua'i and Ni'ihau; father of Kaumuali'i; half-brother of Kahekili; after Kahekili's death fought his nephew

Kalanikupule for rule of Maui, Moloka'i, Lâna'i and O'ahu; killed in battle near 'Aiea in 1795

kâheka   pool, especially a rock basin where the sea washes in and salt forms

Kahekili   ruling chief of Maui, Moloka'i, Lâna'i and O'ahu (and, some say, indirectly of Kaua'i through Ka'eo); son of Kekaulike; father of Kalanikupule; half-brother of Ka'eo and Kaiana; rumored to be the real father of Kamehameha; successfully challenged by Kamehameha for rule of his islands, but regained them when Kamehameha was recalled to Hawai'i to defend his interests there; died at Waikîkî of natural causes in 1794

kâhili   feather standard, symbolic of royalty

kahua   platform, foundation, as of a house

kahuna   priest, sorcerer

kâhuna   plural of **kahuna**

kahuna 'anâ'anâ   a sorcerer, especially one who prays people to death

kahuna pule heiau   heiau priest (*lit*. prayer expert)

Kaiana   high-ranking chief of Kaua'i and Maui ; son of Ahu'ula and Kaupekamoku; brother of Namakeha; half-brother of Kahekili; first chief to travel to foreign lands (to Canton in 1787, returning in 1788); became close ally and trusted adviser to Kamehameha; rumored to have had an affair with Kamehameha's wife Ka'ahumanu; defected to fight alongside his cousin Kalanikupule against Kamehameha at O'ahu in 1795 and was there killed in battle

Kalani'opu'u   ruler of Hawai'i (island) at the time of Captain Cook's death; son of Kalaninuii'amamao, ruling chief of the Kâ'û district, and Kamakaimoku; father of Kiwala'o; uncle of Kamehameha; defeated rival chiefs to rule whole of Hawai'i (island); named Kiwala'o as his successor and Kamehameha as keeper of the war god Kukailimoku; died of natural causes at Ka'û in 1782

Kalanikupule   son and heir of Kahekili; became ruler of Maui, Moloka'i, Lâna'i and O'ahu at his father's death; defeated his uncle Ka'eo[kulani] of Kaua'i who disputed his rule; was defeated by Kamehameha in the 1795 battle of Nu'uanu on O'ahu, but escaped; was captured several months later and sacrificed to Kamehameha's patron god, Kukailimoku

kâli'i   the ritual of hurling a spear at a chief when he landed in a canoe so that he could demonstrate his dexterity and courage

kalo   taro *Colocasia esculenta*

Kâloakukâhi twenty-fourth day of the Hawaiian month (*lit*. Kâloa standing first); the second of the two nights of **Kapu kâloa**, sacred to the god Kanaloa (the first being the previous night, 'Olepau)

Kâloakulua   twenty-fifth night of the Hawaiian month (*lit*. Kâloa standing second)

Kâloapau   twenty sixth night of the Hawaiian month (*lit*. last Kâloa)

kâlua   baked in a ground oven

Kamehameha   son of Kekuiapoiwa, a niece of Kahekili, and Keouakalani of Kohala district, Hawai'i (though it was rumored that Kahekili was actually his father); nephew of Kalani'opu'u; became ruling chief of Hawai'i (island); eventually conquered all the major Hawaiian Islands and founded a dynasty that lasted for five successions, until 1872; encouraged trade with foreigners and introduction of Western tools, techniques and materials, and established trading village at Honolulu and died of natural causes at Kailua, Hawai'i, in 1819

Kâne   twenty-seventh night of the Hawaiian month; one of the four primary Hawaiian gods; a sacred star, interpreted by priests as portending great misfortune, such as the death of a chief

kâne   man

kânekupua   mock spear battle

kao   goat (transliterated from English)

kaokao   syphilis (from **hâkaokao**--decaying, as taro a few days after cooking)

kapa   tapa or barkcloth made by beating the inner bark of **wauke**, the paper mulberry *Broussonetia papyrifera*

kapu   taboo, prohibition; sacred, consecrated

kapu hua   ancient monthly **kapu**, occurs on the days called **Mohalu** and **Hua**

kapu kaloa   ancient monthly **kapu**, occurs on the days called **'Olepau** and **Kâloakukahi**

kapu kâne   ancient monthly **kapu**, occurs on the days called **Kâne** and **Lono**

kapu ku   ancient monthly **kapu**, occurs on the days called **Hilo**, **Hoaka** and **Kukâhi**

kaukâhi   single canoe

ka'ukama   cucumber *Cucumis sativus* (transliterated from English)

Kaulua   ancient Hawaiian month, occurs* January-February; a double canoe

Kaumuali'i   son of Ka'eokulani and Kamakahelei; half-brother of Keawe; ruling chief of Kaua'i and Ni'ihau in the absence of his father and after Ka'eo's death, though on a couple of occasions supplanted by Keawe (who died in 1796); remained unconquered by Kamehameha, but realized eventual conquest was inevitable and agreed in 1810 to cede rulership at his death; fell under the influence of Georg Anton Scheffer, who was employed by the Russian-American Company, allowing the Russian occupation of Kaua'i in 1816-1817; taken prisoner of state in 1821 at O'ahu by Kamehameha II (and so remained until his death); accepted marriage to Kamehameha's widow Ka'ahumanu, an 'honor' he shared with his son Keali'iahonui; died in Honolulu in May 1824 (some claimed by poison)

kea   white

Keuôa   son of Kanali'opu'u and half-brother of Kiwala'o; cousin of Kamehameha; continued to fight against Kamehameha's dominance following Kalani'opu'u's then Kiwala'o's deaths; was finally overcome by ruse and slain by Kamehameha's men at Pu'ukohala near Kawaihae in 1791

Kiwala'o   son and successor of Kalani'opu'u as ruler of Hawai'i (island); challenged by his cousin Kamehameha and killed in battle, the fight being continued for a decade by his half-brother Keuoa

kî   ti plant *Cordyline terminalis*

kîhei   cloak of **makaloa** matting; rectangular **kapa** garment worn over one shoulder and tied in a knot; shawl, cape; bed covering

kioea   Bristle-thighed curlew *Numenius tahitiensis*

kîpapa nu'u   high paved terrace

kô   sugar cane *Saccharum officinarum*

koa   the largest of native forest trees *Acacia koa*, prized for canoes and now also for furniture

ko'olua   two-person canoe

koa'e kea   the white-tailed tropic bird *Phaeton lepturus dorotheae*

koai'e   a small native tree *Acacia koaia*, closely related to koa, formerly used for spears, fancy paddles and **i'e kuku**

ko'ele   small land unit farmed by a tenant for the chief, also called **hakuone**; large, tough **'opihi**, the shells of which were used as scrapers and peelers; seaweeds, also **ko'ele'ele**; a small pond, reserved for a chief, where fish could be kept alive until required

konohiki   headman responsible for **ahupua'u** land division under the chief; land or fishing rights under the control of the **konohiki**

Kû   a major Hawaiian god, recognized in various forms but best known as a god of war

kua   kapa anvil, usually a plank

kuahu   altar

kua 'iako   inboard parts of boom lashed to the U-shaped spreaders and gunwale strakes on either side

kua'āina country (as opposed to town); rustic, person from the country (*lit.* back land)

Kukāhi third night of the Hawaiian month (*lit.* first Ku), last night of the Ku **kapu**

Kukolu fifth night of the Hawaiian month (*lit.* third Ku)

kukui native candlenut tree *Aleurites moluccana*, large oily kernels burned for light, polished nuts strung in **lei**, roots and nut coats used to make a black dye, bark gum used for painting **kapa**, soft wood used for canoes

kula plain, field, open country. An Act of 1884 distinguished dry or **kula** land from wet or taro land

Kulua fourth day of the Hawaiian month (*lit.* second Ku)

kuni a retaliatory magic ritual intended to result in the death of a sorcerer who has caused a death; involves the burning of an object taken from the corpse of the sorcerer's victim for whom revenge is sought

Kupau sixth night of the Hawaiian month (*lit.* last Ku)

kūpe'e ho'okalakala bracelet of boars tusks

kūpe'e niho 'īlio dog tooth leg ornament

la there, then, that

Lā'aupau twentieth night of the Hawaiian month

Lā'aukukāhi eighteenth night of the Hawaiian month

Lā'aukulua nineteenth night of the Hawaiian month

lananu'u mamao oracle tower at a **heiau**. The lowest level was the **lana** where offerings were placed; the second and more sacred level was the **nu'u**; the highest level, where the **kāhuna** stood to conduct ceremonies was the **mamao**.

laulau wrapper, wrapped package; originally of ti or banana leaves and usually containing food

lawai'a fisherman, to fish

li'ili'i piecemeal, here and there

leho general name for cowry shell

lei garland, wreath; necklace of flowers, leaves, shells, feather or other materials given as a symbol of affection; any ornament worn around the head or the neck

lei hulu feather necklace or garland

lei niho palaoa whale tooth pendant, also **lei palaoa**, rarely made of stone or wood, later made also from walrus tusk, now any pendant in the shape of the old whale tooth pendant; also a necklace of strung whale's teeth

lele sacrificial altar

lino to weave, twist, braid, tie

loa long

loloa'u mālolo gunard *Dactyloptena orientalis*, a type of flying fish

Lono twenty-eighth night of the Hawaiian month; one of the four major Hawaiian gods brought from Tahiti (**Kahiki**), god of the **makahiki** harvest festivities and of agriculture, medicine and weather; Captain Cook was mistaken for this god when he first arrived in Hawai'i

luakini large heiau where chiefs prayed and human sacrifices were offered

Māhealani sixteenth night of the Hawaiian month, night of the full moon

mahiole feather helmet

mai'a the general names for all bananas; about seventy varieties were known at the time of European contact, today half that

maka 'upena net mesh; 'net-mesh' pattern as carved on a **kapa** beater

maka'āinana commoner, people in general

makahiki ancient festival beginning about the middle of October and lasting about four months, with sporting and religious festivities and a taboo on war

makaîwa mother-of-pearl shell eyes as in images of the god Lono (*lit.* mysterious eye)

Makali'i ancient Hawaiian month, occurs* November-December; the six summer months collectively; tiny, very small, fine makaloa   a perrenial sedge *Cyperus laevigatus* with long slender unbranched stems formerly prized for weaving fine mats

makaula   a variety of dark lizard

malo   loincloth, the primary apparel of Hawaiian males prior to the introduction of European clothing

mâlolo   flying fishes in general

mâmaki   small native trees *Pipturus*, the bark of which was used to make a kind of **kapa** which was coarser than that made from **wauke**

mamao   uppermost level of oracle tower

mamo   Black Hawaiian honeycreeper *Drepanis pacifica*, endemic to the island of Hawai'i and not seen since the 1880s

mana   divine or supernatural force or power; a **kapu** house in a **heiau**

Mauli   twenty-ninth night of the Hawaiian month

mauna   mountain; mountainous

mo'o   gunwale strakes of an outrigger canoe

moa   chicken

moena   mat; to lie down; couch, bed

moena makali'i makaloa sedge sleeping mat

môhai kuni burnt offering

Môhalu   twelfth night of the Hawaiian month, and first of the Kâne taboo

mua   men's eating houses

Muku   thirtieth night of the Hawaiian month when the moon has entirely disappeared (**muku**)

Nâmâkeha   a chief of Maui and Kaua'i ; brother of Kaiana; defected with Kaiana to fight against Kamehameha in 1795 on O'ahu, where Kaiana was killed; led a 1796 rebellion on Hawai'i, forcing Kamehameha to direct his attention away from the conquest of Kaua'i yet again

Nana   ancient Hawaiian month, occurs* February-March

nao   ripple, ridge as on a **kapa** beater; streak on **kapa**

Nâpu'uapele the hills of Pele, Ho'opûloa, Hawai'i island

niho   tooth, teeth

niho 'ako lauoho   single shark's tooth bound to a stick

niu   coconuts *Cocos nucifera*

noho 'ana wa'a   canoe seats

nuinui ali'i   important chief

'ohe kâpala   a carved wooden implement with which to stamp designs

'ôhi'a 'ai   the mountain apple *Eugenia malaccensis*

'ôhi'a lehua a native tree *Metrosideros macropus*, valued for its wood

'Olekukâhi   seventh night of the Hawaiian month

'Olekukolu   ninth night of the Hawaiian month

'Olekulua   eighth night of the Hawaiian month

'Olekupau   tenth night of the Hawaiian month

'ôlena   tumeric *Curcuma domestica*

'olê'olê   wide-mouthed grin, as of an idol

'Olepau   tenth night of the Hawaiian month, last of the 'ole night (**pau**=over, ended, finished)

'ô'ô   a black honeyeater *Acrulocerus nobilis* with a tuft of yellow feathers under each wing which were used in feather work; endemic to Hawai'i island, now extinct

olomea   a native shrub or small tree *Perrottetia sandwichensis*, the hard wood of which was formerly used with soft **hau** wood to produce fire by rubbing

olonâ   a native shrub *Touchardia latifolia*, bark formerly prized for its strong fiber which was used to make cord for fishing nets, nets for carrying containers and as a base for ti leaf raincoats and feather capes

'ôpelu   mackerel scad *Decapterus pinnulatus*

pâ   fence, enclosure; mother-of-pearl shell lure

pâ ânuenue   rainbow lure

pa'a kâhili bearer of the royal (feather) standard

pa'i 'ai   hard, pounded but undiluted taro (*lit.* **pa'i**=package, bundle, esp. of food; **'ai**=eat)

paehumu   taboo enclosure around a **heiau** or a chief's house

pâhoa   short dagger; sharp stone, especially when used as a weapon; taboo sign

pala'â   the lace fern *Sphenomeris chusana*, formerly used to make a brownish-red dye

palaoa   whale; ivory

papa hole   grooved board for making ribbed kapa

papa kaua   group of men armed with **pololû** spears surrounding the king

papa kui 'ai   flat surface for pounding **poi**

papa lâ'au   board, plank

pâpapa   the hyacinth bean *Delicho lablab*, a long vine similar to that of the Lima bean, with edible pods; grows wild in Hawai'i

pâ'û   formerly a length of **kapa** or cloth worn by women by wrapping it around the body and tucking the end inside the wrap, usually worn beneath the breast and ending at the knees but occasionally worn at the waist; now most often tied above the breast and usually called by its Tahitian or Samoan name (pareu or lavalava); woman's skirt

paua   bivalve *Isognomon* with richly iridescent inner shell, also **pâpaua**

pâ hi aku   fishing lure for catching **aku**

pe'ahi   fan

pekepeke ali'i   lesser chief (*lit.* dwarf, midget, tiny); contrast with **nuinui ali'i**

peleleu   a very large type of canoe, sometimes a double canoe

pepehi   surface of a **kapa** beater formed by deep grooves with the wide ridges rounded off in the form of an inverted U

pia   Polynesian arrowroot *Tacca leontopetaloides*, used as food, medicine and talcum powder

pî'ao   to fold ti leaves into a cuplike package, as for dipping water or baking food in the oven

pipi   cattle (transliterated from the English word beef), also **bipi**

pipipi   general name for small molluscs

po'e   people, persons, assemblage, group

po'e lawai'a full-time fishermen

poi   pounded taro paste, diluted and often eaten sour; a popular staple food

pololû   long spear

po'o kea   ash colored, also **po'o hina**

pôhuli   sucker, shoot, sprout; to sprout, usually of bananas

pu'u   any kind of protuberance, from a pimple to a hill

pua   flower

pua'a   pig

puahala   a kapa design

punahele   a favorite

uhi   yams *Dioscorea alata*; mother-of-pearl bivalve

uki'uki   blue native lilies *Dianella*, the blue berries of which were formerly used to make pale blue dye for **kapa**

'uala   sweet potato*Ipomoea batatas*

'uala kahiki   white or Irish potato *Solanum tuberosum*, native to the Andes and introduced to Hawai'i in the early 1800s

'ulu   breadfruit *Artocarpus incisus*

umu   an older form of the modern word **imu**

wae   U-shaped canoe spreaders where the outrigger boom is lashed to the hull

wauke   the paper mulberry *Broussonetia papyrifera*, used to make strong **kapa** for clothing and bedcovering. It lasted longer that **mâmaki kapa**

Welehu   ancient Hawaiian month, occurring October-November

Welo   ancient Hawaiian month, occurs* March-April

* There was considerable diversity of opinion amongst people from the different islands about the order in which the month-names occurred and which of them marked the beginning of the yearly cycle.

Glossary Of Russian Terms

ad'iunkt   assistant, esp. assistant professor

arshin   Russian unit of measure (=28 inches)

batates   borrowed word for sweet potato, used by the Russians

bozhestvo   deity

dvoriane   nobles

etiketki   labels

etiketki sobiratelia   the collector's labels

fond   collection

fondy   collections

fufaiki   waistcoats, jackets

grobov nikakikh net   there are no tombs whatever

idol   idol

inventarnyi spisok   inventory

iskutan   idol or statue

iz zherdei   made of poles or stakes

kholst   broadcloth

khudoshchavyi   lean or spare

kol'iami   with stakes

kopek   1/100 of a rouble

koren'ev   tubers

Kunstkammer   cabinet of curiosities, for ethnographica (German word borrowed by Russians)

naboika   cloth--suggests a finer material than broadcloth

opisi   inventories

otchoty   reports

piaten   patches

pokhod   campaign or marching

pokhodnyi idol   camp or traveling idol

pood   Russian unit of measure (=36 pounds)

prikazchik   clerk , factor

promyshlennik   hunter-trader, esp. in eastern Siberia and the North Pacific basin

promyshlenniki   plural of promyshlennik

sazhen'   fathom [6 feet] (at sea); 7 feet (on land)

sotrudnik   assistant, esp. in Soviet archival or academic institutions

statuia   statue

toises   French unit of measure used by the Russians (=6 feet)

vershók   Russian unit of measure (=1.75 inches)

verstá   Russian unit of measure (=3,500 feet)

voisko   army

Place Index

Ship Index

Name Index

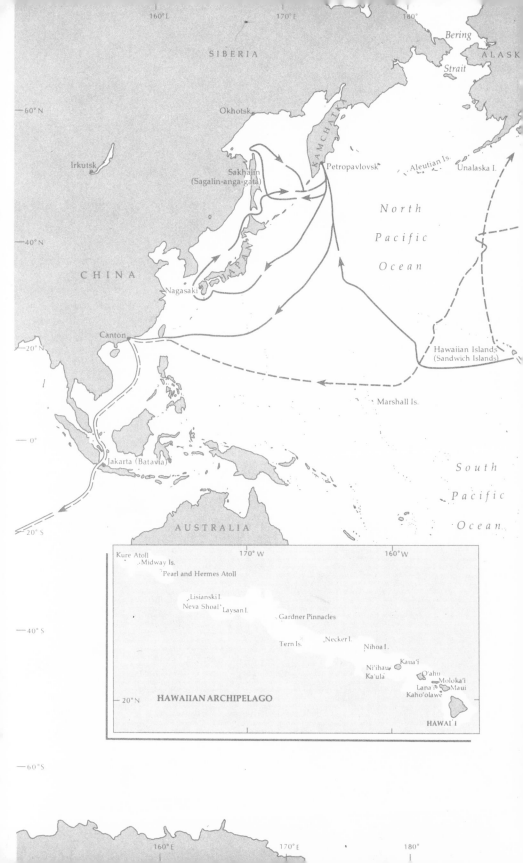

SIBERIA

Bering
Strait

ALASK

—60° N

Okhotsk

Irkutsk

Sakhalin
(Sagalin-anga-gata)

Petropavlovsk

Aleutian Is.

Unalaska I.

KAMCHATKA

North

Pacific

Ocean

—40° N

CHINA

Nagasaki

Canton

—20° N

Jakarta (Batavia)

—0°

Hawaiian Islands
(Sandwich Islands)

Marshall Is.

South

Pacific

Ocean

AUSTRALIA

—20° S

Kure Atoll
Midway Is.
Pearl and Hermes Atoll

170° W

160° W

Lisianski I.
Neva Shoal
Laysan I.

Gardner Pinnacles

—40° S

Tern Is.

Necker I.

Nihoa I.

Kaua'i
Ni'ihau
Ka'ula

O'ahu
Moloka'i
Lana'i
Maui
Kaho'olawe

—20° N

HAWAIIAN ARCHIPELAGO

HAWAI'I

—60° S

160° E

170° E

180°